The Enoch Train Pioneers

Trek of the First Two Handcart Companies - 1856

The Enoch Train Pioneers

Trek of the First Two Handcart Companies - 1856

Robert O. Day

illustrated by
Linda S. Day

Day to Day Enterprises   *Oviedo, Florida*

Books and Plays
By Robert O. Day

March of the Mormon Battalion: Called to Serve
Nine Blasts of the Cannon
Theres a Frog on a Log in the Bog (President's Book Award Winner)
Say Me A Say, Play Me A Play
Nursery Rhymes and Fairy Tales (Volumes 1-13)
F.B. and the Gang
Oral Language Arts for the Elementary Teacher
Two, Three, Four and More - Reading Together is Fun (Volumes 1-3)

Cover and Interior Design by MyLinda Butterworth
Illustrations by Linda S. Day © 2001, 2003, 2006

Copyright © 2003, 2006 by Day to Day Enterprises
All rights reserved.
Printed in the United States of America
08 07 06   10 9 8 7 6 5 4 3 2 1

Second Edition 2006

ISBN 10: 1-890905-21-6
ISBN 13: 978-1-890905-21-7
Previous ISBNs 1-890905-01   hardcover (limited edition); ISBN 1-890905-16-X softcover

Library of Congress Cataloguing-in-Publication Data on file

All rights reserved. No part of this publication may be reproduced or transmitted in any form or by any means without the prior written permission of the publisher, excepting brief quotations in connection with reviews written specifically for inclusion in magazines or newspapers, or single copies for strictly personal use.

Published by
Day to Day Enterprises Oviedo, Florida
http// www.daytodayenterprises.com

    This book is dedicated to my dear family, past, present and future, with my great hope that it may strengthen their faith in an all wise and loving God, and trust in their Savior to provide them with leadership in the Kingdom that will never lead them astray. The men and women who lived "this page in the Book of Eternity," have all now graduated from the cares of mortality, taking with them the lessons of this life as a guide for living in eternity. I can only hope that my posterity will be spiritual enough to faithfully follow those that God has chosen in this period of time to lead them, as the early pioneers followed Brothers Joseph and Brigham.

    I wish to thank the *Enoch Train* pioneers that carefully kept a record of their journey to Zion that provided information that allowed their story to be told; especially Archer Walters, Truman Leonard, Edmund Ellsworth, John D. McAllister, Daniel McArthur and Mary Powell Sabin.

    Special thanks is given to my sweet wife Linda Sue Weaver Day, who labored long and with great love to provide the art that illustrates the contents of this book. And to my dear daughter Mylinda Sue Day Butterworth for her technical assistance and arranging for its publication.

TABLE OF CONTENTS

INTRODUCTION x
PREFACE ix

CHAPTER I: WHY WOULD THEY RISK SUCH A LONG AND DANGEROUS JOURNEY? 1
    The Apostasy 1
    The Restoration 1
    The Gathering 2
    The Gathering In The Last Days 2
    The Perpetual Emigration Fund 3

PHASE ONE:
CHAPTER II: VOYAGE OF THE SAILING SHIP, *THE ENOCH TRAIN* 7
    Preparing To Sail 10
    Preparations For A Successful Journey 11
    The Time For Departure 13
    Life Below Deck During A Storm At Sea 17
    General Conference Observed 20
    A Tall Tale At Sea 22
    One of Many Healings 26
    Almost To America 28
    Waiting To Go Ashore 28

PHASE TWO:
CHAPTER III: JOURNEY BY OMNIBUS, STEAMSHIP AND TRAIN TO IOWA CITY 38
    By Omnibus To The Railroad Station 38
    Traveling Pioneer Passenger Class On Immigrant Train Cars 40
    Waiting To Cross The Mississippi River 42
    Loaded Onto Open Boxcars To Travel On To Trails End 44

CHAPTER IV: WAITING AND WORKING AT THE IMMIGRATION CAMP NEAR IOWA CITY 47
    From Rails End To The Iowa City Campground 48
    Life In And Around Tent City 48
    Sabbath In The Iowa City Camp 51
    Waiting To Cross The Prairie To Florence, Nebraska 52
    Preparing The Handcart Companies To Leave 58

PHASE THREE:
CHAPTER V: HANDCARTS WEST TO FLORENCE, NEBRASKA (WINTER QUARTERS): THE GREAT HANDCART EXPERIMENT BEGINS 61
    The First Handcart Company Leaves For Florence, Nebraska 61
    The Second Handcart Company Leaves For Florence, Nebraska 62
    Some Turned Back 63

Death And Burial On The Trail 64
Early Starts And Usually Short Days Of Travel Across Iowa 66
Discontent & Harrasment At Norton, Iowa 66
And The Handcarts Must Keep Moving 68
Little Arthur Parker Is Lost 73
Strangers In The Camp 76

PHASE FOUR:
CHAPTER VI: TRAVELING FROM FLORENCE TO THE SALT LAKE VALLEY 79
The Final Push Toward The Mountains Of The Lord 81
Struck By Lightening 84
The Trial Of Faith And Enduring To The End 87
The Handcart Song 91
Buffalo 93
Mother's Bathgate And Park 96
Another Sunday On The Trail 97
Deer Creek And Wagons Of Flour 100
McArthur's Company Finally Catches Up With The First Company 104
Escorted By President Young And Party Into Salt Lake City 110

APPENDIX A: A Brief Account of the Apostacy, Restoration and Gathering of Modern Day Israel & the Perpetual Emigration Fund 113
APPENDIX B: The *Millenial Star* on The Perpetual Emigration Fund 123
APPENDIX C: Composite Passenger List of the *Enoch Train* 129
APPENDIX D: Composite Passenger List of the *Samuel S. Curling* 143
APPENDIX E: Births and Deaths - Alphabetical & by Date 158
APPENDIX F: Days and Dates of Journey Breakdown by Travel Segments 160
APPENDIX G: *Clayton's, The Latter-day Saints Emigrant's Guide* 164
APPENDIX H: Handcart Logbook for 20 March – 6 June 1856 185
APPENDIX I: Handcart Logbook for 9 June - 8 July 1856 198
APPENDIX J: Handcart Logbook 17 July - 28 September 1856 214
END NOTES, By Chapter 242
BIBLIOGRAPHY 248
INDEX 251
About the Author 261

MAPS, PICTURES, LISTS & ILLUSTRATIONS

FIGURE		PAGE
1	Poem: *And The Ways Of God And The Ways Of Man*	1
2	Painting: *The Sailing Ship **Enoch Train***	6
3	Painting: *At the Docks*	10
4	Map: Route From Liverpool to Boston	14
5	Painting: *Life Below Decks*	18
6	Painting: *A Tall Tale At Sea*	24
7	Painting: *Funeral at Sea*	27
8	List: *Enoch Train* Passenger List	31
9	Painting: *Taking an Omnibus to the Train Station*	38
10	Painting: *Pioneer Passenger Train*	40
11	Map: ***Enoch Train*** Pioneer Railroad Route From Boston to Iowa City	42
12	Painting: *Waiting at the Train Station*	43
13	Painting: *Steamer Ferry on the Mississippi*	45
14	Painting: *Emigrant Camp at Iowa City*	46
15	Painting: *Two Types of Handcarts*	51
16	List: First Handcart Company – Edward Ellsworth, Captain	55
17	List: Second Handcart Company – Daniel D. McArthur, Captain	57
18	List: *Enoch Train* Passengers Not Listed As Being In The First Two Handcart Companies	59
19	Map: Iowa City, Iowa to Florence (Winter Quarters), Nebraska	61
20	Painting: *A Coffin For Little Emma*	71
21	Poem: *But Not Much Rest*	71
22	Poem: *Ever On To Zion*	72
23	Painting: *Little Arthur Parker Returned to His Mother*	75
24	Painting: Steam Ferry "Nebraska"	77
25	Painting: *Mother Bathgate leads pioneers towards Devil's Gate*	78
26	Map: From Florence, Nebraska to Fort Laramie, Wyoming	82
27	Painting: *Indian Chief Pulling A "Little Wagon"*	83
28	Painting: *Struck by Lightening on the Trail*	84
29	Painting: *Handcart Pioneers Heading To A Home In Zion*	87
30	Map: Handcart Trail – Fort Laramie To Jeffrey City, Wyoming	99
31	Map: Handcart Trail – Jeffery Wyoming To Salt Lake City, Utah	104
32	List: Section from the *Emigrant's Guide*	108
33	Poem: *Zion Gathered to This Place*	112

Introduction

When Robert first dreamed of writing a historical drama for the Church Museum of History and Art in Salt Lake City, his desire was for accuracy and drama. He spent great deals of time researching and documenting every piece of information he found about this courageous group of saints. Everything had to be perfectly accurate for it to be approved by the general authorities of the church before it could be presented in play format. Painstaking effort went into every aspect, from the script to the costumes to the artwork. The play "Journey to Zion: The Enoch Train Pioneers" was presented to standing room only audiences and received great reviews from those who saw the spectacle.

So massive was the research he compiled for the play that when we went to print his book the first time, **The Enoch Train Pioneers: The Trek of the First Two Handcart Companies-1856** we decided to leave out all the full journal entries he had intended for an additional three appendices. To celebrate the arrival of the saints into the valley 200 years ago this year, we have decided to add all three appendies to this new addition. The book you hold in your hand contains Robert's full research notes from those journal entries and just like the book the typos and incomplete sentences are left just the way they appeared in those journals. Each chapter deals with a particular time period during the trek and starting in chapter two when he started finding entries for each company we put them in side by side fashion so you could compare the entries.

Just as my father had intended, I hope you find joy in finding your ancestors and learning about your heritage.

MyLinda Day Butterworth
Editor and daughter

Preface

Much has happened since that spring morning in 1820, when in response to the fervent prayer of 14 year old Joseph Smith, Jr., God The Father and His Son Jesus Christ personally appeared in the Sacred Grove. Much has happened since the Priesthood was restored and Christ's Church was once again organized under divine direction; the promised gathering of the Saints from the world began, first to Kirtland, Ohio; then Jackson County, Missouri; Far West, Missouri; Nauvoo, Illinois; and finally to the Valley of the Great Salt Lake in Utah. Wherever the persecuted Saints were led, like Israel of old out of Egypt, they diligently moved toward the "Promised Land," being ever proved and purged along the way in preparation for Zion.

This book contains one small, but highly significant account, of a shipload of 534 gathering Saints from Liverpool, England. They were for the most part very ordinary people, poor in financial means, but burning with the hope that comes with finding the purpose of life, and having the faith to do whatever is asked to help build the restored Kingdom of God on the earth. They were unique as pioneers, as they had responded to the unusual directions of a prophet to be the first to gather by handcart across the frontiers of America to Zion in Utah Territory. The Saints that were passengers on the sailing ship *Enoch Train*, made up all of the first handcart company and most of the second. The balance of the later company being filled by some Saints from the sailing ship *Samuel S. Curling*.

Those that have come to be known as the "*Enoch Train* Pioneers":
- Began their pioneer trek with: 39 day sea journey to the new world.
- Followed by 11 days of travel to reach the Iowa City, Iowa campground.
    - Departing first by omnibus from Boston harbor to the local train station.
    - Making a short train trip, followed by a river crossing on a steamship ferry because there was as yet no bridge over the waterway.
        - Then by train again to Rock Island, where they left the train to take a steam ferry across the Mississippi River, because the railroad bridge had been damaged by a train wreck.
        - Leaving the ferry they again traveled by train until they reached Iowa City, Iowa.
- Then a 27 day wait at the Iowa City campground while their handcarts were completed, etc.
- Finally a 103 day trek by foot, with an 8 day layover at Florence, Nebraska, (Winter Quarters), for repairs and supplies.

Their journey lasted 188 days from Liverpool, England to Salt Lake City.

They gave everything they had then, as we of the Church should give our all now, to help the Lord God complete His Holy mission as the gathering of the elect goes on.

"For behold, this is my work and my glory—to bring to pass the immortality and eternal life of man." [Moses 1:39]

When we became the Lord's disciples and members of His Kingdom, we took upon us His name and holy cause. We no longer need to be handcarts pioneers, but we still have pioneering trails to follow and tasks to accomplish in helping to build the Kingdom as we enter the 21st century. Over 150 years of latter-day preparation stands completed, but the "immortality and eternal life of man" – living and dead – is still not finished, and will not be until the great Jehovah declares it so. There is as great a need as ever to put a shoulder to the wheel and do our part, and a source of great spiritual energy can be found in learning of the trials and triumphs of our ancestors, the early pioneers.

> "And the Lord called his people ZION, because they were of one heart and one mind, and dwelt in righteousness; and there was no poor among them." [Moses 7:18]

Every effort has been made to keep the people and the events of this book historically accurate, as well as inserting from time to time "probable dialogue", and an "empathetic stream of consciousness" to provide an insight into the possible feelings of the people, events and situations they dealt with on their long journey. To accomplish this task, great care has been exercised to make such inserts as historically and factually accurate as possible, while allowing these great pioneer's story to be experienced as faithful, dedicated Saints, not just historical data.

As a means of clearly indicating to the reader where these insertions have been made, the **type style** has purposely been **changed**. Please note that the quotes have remained true to the original text including typos and improper grammer.

And the ways of God and the ways of man were planned before the start,
And each knew the end from the beginning and had vowed to do his part.
By the Word was nothing left to chance, though agency reigned free,
Love, faith, repentance, covenants.......... obedience eternally.[1]

Figure 1: *And the Ways of God and The Ways of Man* by R.O. Day

CHAPTER I

WHY HANDCART PIONEERS WOULD RISK SUCH A LONG AND DANGEROUS JOURNEY

Between 1850 and 1878, during a time of a great religious awakening in the world, over 85,000 people joined The Church of Jesus Christ of Latter-day Saints. Willingly leaving their old lives behind them, they traveled to a place know to them as Zion, because God had called them to this holy task through His living prophet.

To understand why in 1856 men, women and children would be willing to cross the mighty Atlantic Ocean; travel hundreds of miles in crude and uncomfortable train cars; load and unload hundreds of pieces of luggage between a ship, trains and steamboat ferries; then push and pull handcarts with a 400-800 pound cargo 1300 miles; it is essential to understand the reality of "the gathering" as members of The Church of Jesus Christ of Latter-day Saints did in the 19th century. The gathering was, and still is, a holy responsibility for the faithful of Christ's restored Church to prepare all things for His Second Coming to the earth, in this the Dispensation of the Fullness of Times.

During the days of the Old Testament, wars in the Holy Land had caused the people of Israel to be scattered to the four quarters of the earth. The most notable scattering being the carrying away of the "lost ten tribes" into the north county, which mainly left the descendants of Judah and Levi. Of course there have been some of each of the tribes found in Israel and scattered throughout the world, but they all basically refer to themselves as Jews rather than descendants of a particular "tribe of Israel". By the time that Jesus was born in Bethlehem, the Holy Land was in bondage again, this time to Rome. The pure in heart accepted Him as the Messiah, but the powerful Jewish Sanhedrin pushed the people to reject Jesus, getting rid of him as they did anyone that stood in their way, and convinced the Jews that their Savior was yet to come.

THE APOSTASY (*See Appendix A for a more detailed account.)
The Holy Scriptures taught that there would be a falling away of the people of Christ's Church into apostasy in the "Meridian of Time" [when Jesus was on the earth]. Then a full restoration of all things as they were at first, in the "dispensation of the fullness of times [today]."[2] For seventeen centuries the world had waited and hoped for the promised restoration that would occur just before the great Millennium of Christ's personal reign upon the earth.

THE RESTORATION (*See Appendix A for a more detailed account.)
After centuries of Catholicism, many within the ranks of the clergy began to question what they saw as changes in the doctrines of their church. Added to this dissension came the period of the renaissance; the invention of the printing press; and for the first time people, other than the clergy and those selected from the ranks of nobility, began to master the ability to read and to think for themselves. This was followed by a great protest against practices, which were then understood to be contradictory to Scriptures:

> "Members of the various sects of that portion of Christendom which broke off from the Roman Catholic Church during the Reformation in the 16th century, as also the members of those sects which have since broken off from these original dissenting groups, are called Protestants. Martin Luther and others, for instance, first remonstrated and protested in the most solemn manner against the practices and doctrine of the Roman

Church, and then finally, in good conscience, had no choice but to sever their affiliation with this organization. **This Protestant revolution was inspired of God; it was one of the necessary occurrences which prepared the way for the restoration of the gospel."**[3] (Emphasis added.)

God sent forth great men like Martin Luther, John Wesley, Roger Williams and Thomas Jefferson to lead the Christian revolution to prepare the minds and hearts of men. Following the reformation that would lead eventually to the restoration of the fullness of the Gospel in "a land choice above all other lands" on the face of the earth.

The masses, having been made of aware of so many truths that they had not had known before, wanted to be the masters of their own spiritual and temporal lives, then and in the future. And, with the era of global exploration and colonization by the great powers of the Old World, many eventually found themselves in North America. After several years of submission to a tyrannical king and the government that supported him, they engaged in a revolutionary struggle that won 13 English colonies freedom from their mother country.

As a means of providing the people a guarantee of freedom that they had not enjoyed before, great leaders of the young United States of America, under divine inspiration, forged first the Articles of Confederation: later a Constitution for the nation was written, with a carefully thought out set of guarantees for freedoms they called the Bill of Rights. These Amendments added to the Constitution insured the fundamental freedoms that allowed the coming forth of a great religious awakening in the nation. Thus fulfilling ancient prophecy and setting the stage for the coming forth of the full restoration of the Gospel of Jesus Christ.

All things had been put in order to bring about the restoration, in this the dispensation of the "Fullness of Times." A restoration was necessary:

> "**Since** the **gospel** was **first given to Adam, each time** it was **thereafter lost by apostasy** and then **revealed to man again** has **been a restoration of the gospel**. Our **Lord** in his **personal ministry**, for instance, **restored the original gospel**, the same plan of salvation, which he had revealed to Adam in the beginning. But when men in this day speak of the restoration of the gospel, they mean the final great restoration, which has now taken place as part of the restoration of all things. This dispensation is the age of restoration to which all the ancient prophets look forward. In it all things are to be restored 'which God hath spoken by the mouth of all his holy prophets since the world began.'[4] **All things** are **being gathered together in one in Christ**."[5&6] (**Emphasis added.**)

THE GATHERING (*See Appendix A for a more detailed account.)

With the prayer of a fourteen year old boy, Joseph Smith, Jr., who was pure in heart and prepared from before the foundation of the world, the final Gospel dispensation was ushered in. One by one all things were put in order that would allow God's Saints to be gathered to a central location where they would be taught eternal truths; build a temple to receive God's endowments; learn what they would need for exaltation of themselves, their ancestors, and their progeny; and go forth to preach the Gospel to all nations. A place from which the Gospel could roll forth as "a rock cut out of the mountain that would roll forth and fill the whole earth." A place where the "pure in heart" would dwell, with "no poor among them", a land called Zion.

Peter taught anciently that the Second Coming of the Son of Man could not take place "until the times of restitution of all things, which God hath spoken by the mouth of all his holy prophets since the world began."[7] By the time Joseph Smith, Jr. was martyred at age 38, all things of the Kingdom of God necessary to the exaltation of mankind had been divinely restored and the final "Gathering of Zion" had begun. Brigham Young and every prophet of the Lord since Brother Joseph have been anxiously engaged in the continuation of the gathering.

THE GATHERING IN THE LAST DAYS (*See Appendix A, pp., 115-118 for a more detailed account.)

One of the great New Testament parables taught by the Lord had to do with the wheat and the tares. The ancient apostles understood what was meant by the parable, but not many others did. While most today would understand that it had to do with the last day judgment, the saving of the righteous and punishment of the wicked required to exist together until their final separation. Few understand that the gathering of the wheat is first and foremost the **gathering** of the righteous to Zion in the last days. It was a call to bring His people out of Babylon to Zion: Judah will gather to Jerusalem, but all other tribes will gather to the New Jerusalem, the Zion of America.[8]

The gathering of the last dispensation is unique; in as much as the Lord says He will gather together all things in heaven and earth.⁹ All gathered to Zion will live there in peace, having mutual protection, spiritual reinforcement, instruction, and equality.¹⁰

"And it shall be **called the New Jerusalem, a land of peace**, a city of **refuge**, a place of **safety** for the **saints** of the Most High God; And the **glory of the Lord shall be there**, and the terror of the Lord also shall be there, insomuch that the **wicked will not come** unto it, and it shall be **called Zion**. And it shall come to pass **among** the **wicked**, that **every man** that **will not** take his **sword against his neighbor** must **needs flee** unto **Zion for safety.**

"And there **shall be gathered** unto it **out of every nation under heaven**; and it shall **be** the **only people** that shall **not** be **at war** one with another. And it shall be **said among the wicked**: Let us **not** go up to **battle against Zion**, for the inhabitants of Zion are terrible; wherefore we cannot stand. And it shall come to pass that the **righteous** shall be gathered out from among all nations, and shall **come to Zion, singing** with **songs** of **everlasting joy**."¹¹ (**Emphasis added**.)

A primary responsibility of the gathered Saints is to build a temple where they can stand in holy places and the Lord can reveal unto His people the ordinances necessary for their exaltation. When first gathered to Kirtland, one of their first tasks was to build a temple. The first and foremost reason being that many aspects of the "restoration of all things in this dispensation could not take place until the Kirtland Temple was dedicated and those holding the keys of the various ordinances and dispensations of the earth delivered those keys to the prophet Joseph Smith.

After it was learned through revelation that Independence in Jackson County, Missouri was to be Zion, the New Jerusalem, the prophet Joseph marked the spot for the temple and plans were started for its construction. After being driven out by the mobs to northern Missouri, another site for a temple at Far West was designated. When they were driven from Missouri and settled in Illinois, again one of the first tasks was the designation of a spot for a temple at Nauvoo. That temple was barely completed, and used but a very short time, before the last of the Saints were driven out again, into the wilderness of Iowa. After Brigham Young was shown the place for the settlement of Zion in the valleys of the mountains of Utah, again one of the first items of business was to designate a site for the temple in Salt Lake City, a temple which took 40 years to complete. While the work went on there, an endowment house was established in Salt Lake City and other less elaborate temples in Utah were completed and used for providing temple ordinances.

"Verily this is the word of the Lord, that the city **New Jerusalem shall be built by the gathering of the saints, beginning** at **this place**, even the place of the **temple**, which temple **shall be reared in this generation**."¹²

"Behold, it is my will, that **all they** who **call** on **my name**, and **worship me according** to mine **everlasting gospel**, should **gather together**, and **stand in holy places**."¹³ (**Emphasis added**.)

It is absolutely essential that the Lord have a temple in which he can teach His people, bless them, and provide ordinances that form binding eternal covenants with Him that bring exaltation. There are certain holy forms of worship that can only rightly be performed in the House of the Lord.

When all things are taken into consideration regarding the Second Coming, there had to be a means for spreading Christ's Gospel for the last time to the four quarters of the earth. To accomplish this task the authority of God's priesthood and powers had to be restored to the earth, by calling the prophet Joseph Smith, Jr. Then a tool for restoring the fullness of the gospel had to be made available, in the *Book of Mormon*. Missionaries had to be sent forth to find the faithful and a place had to be established where converts could come to prepare more missionaries.

Then to be able to bless the lives of the converts and to fulfill prophecy, the Saints had to be gathered to one place where they could be spiritually and temporally strengthened and blessed. To provide them with the fullness of the Gospel and restoration of all blessings, a Temple would be needed to restore all keys, and a dedicated place separated from the ways of the world where the worthy could be trained and prepared for exaltation. Hence, the gathering prophesied in the *Old* and *New Testaments*, *The Book of Mormon*, and modern revelation was a necessity.

THE PERPETUAL EMIGRATING FUND (*See Appendix A for a more detailed account.)

By the middle of the nineteenth century, missionary work and the gathering to Zion were well underway. With very few exceptions, all of the newly converted Saints desired to gather to Utah, but there were many of the poor that could not. President Young and the Brethren spent much time agonizing over what could be done before a decision was reached in 1849:

"...'The Perpetual Emigration Fund" was **established**. It had for its **purpose, first**, the **removal** to the **mountains** of **all the worthy Latter-day Saints exiled from Illinois, who desired to gather** to the main body of the church, and after that to **extend aid to the worthy poor among the saints** throughout the **world**.

"The '**perpetual**' feature of the plan was to be **maintained by those** who **received aid** from this emigrating **fund returning "the same, in labor or otherwise, as soon** as their **circumstances will admit**," and "with interest if required," in order that the **means might be used again to aid others**..."[14]

"...We wish all to understand, that this **fund is perpetual**, and is **never to be diverted** from the object of **gathering the poor to Zion while** there are **saints** to **be gathered**, unless He whose right it is to rule shall otherwise command...."[15] (**Emphasis added**.)

On 12 October 1849, the First Presidency wrote of the general manner for the use of the funds in an epistle to the Church:

"... therefore, ye poor, and meek of the earth, lift up your heads and rejoice in the Holy One of Israel, for your redemption draweth nigh; but in your rejoicings be patient, for though your turn to emigrate may not be the first year, or even the second, it will come, and its tarryings will be short, if all the saints who have, [means] will be as liberal as those in the valley."[16]

"While the Church leadership had taken on the task of raising funds to start the PEF [Perpetual Emigrating Fund], it needed a means of impressing on those who were blessed by the fund, that they had an obligation to repay the fund as soon as possible. A written contract was signed by the recipients as a means of keeping the fund solvent, which included a payment of interest whenever possible. Of course the brethren responded to individual circumstances regarding the recovery of interest."[17] During the 1880 Year of Jubilee, many of the poor with pressing circumstances had half of their debt forgiven, others were totally forgiven at the direction of President John Taylor.

Of course the first use for the PEF was to gather the poor from Illinois, but by January of 1852 its scope was widened to actively assist the poor of Great Britain. Eventually it was expanded to assist the poor of the world. In an effort to give the fund greater stability, it was sanctioned by the Utah Territorial government.[18]

The first suggestion of using the Perpetual Emigration Fund to gather Saints to Zion using **handcarts**, was made by First Presidency in 1851:

"This method of emigrating the saints was first suggested by the **presidency** of the church in their **sixth general** epistle, addressed "to the saints scattered throughout the earth," and bearing date of September 22nd, 1851. In that epistle **great emphasis** was laid upon the subject of the **saints "gathering to Zion**," as may be judged by the following excerpt:

"O ye saints in the United States, will you listen to the voice of `the Good Shepherd'? **Will you gather?** Will you **be obedient** to the **heavenly commandments**? **Many** of you have been looking for, and **expecting too much**; you have been expecting the **time would come** when you could **journey across** the **mountains** in **your fine carriages**, your **good wagons**, and **have all the comforts** of life that heart could wish; but **your expectations are vain**, and if you wait for those things you will never come, * * * and your faith and hope will depart from you. How long shall it be said in truth `the children of this world are wiser in their generation than the children of light.' **Some** of the **children of the world** have **crossed the mountains** and **plains**, from Missouri to California, with a pack on their back to worship their god—gold! Some have performed the same **journey with a wheel-barrow**; some have accomplished the same with a **pack on a cow**. **Some** of the **saints**, now in our midst, **came** hither with **wagons or carts** made of **wood**, without a particle of iron, hooping their **wheels with hickory**, or **rawhide**, or **ropes**, and had as **good** and **safe** a **journey as any** in the camps, with their well **wrought iron wagons**; and **can you not do the same**? Yes, **if** you **have** the **same desire, the same faith**. Families might **start from** the **Missouri river, with cows, handcarts, wheel-barrows**, with **little flour**, and **no unnecessaries**, and **come** to this place **quicker**, and **with less fatigue, than** by following the **heavy trains**, with their cumbrous herds, which they are often obliged to drive miles to feed. **Do you not like this method** of traveling? Do you **think salvation costs too much**? If so, it is not worth having. **Sisters, fifty and sixty** years old, have **driven ox teams** to this **valley**, and **are alive and well** yet; true they **could have come easier by walking** alone, than by driving a team, but by driving the oxen, they helped others here; and **cannot you come the easier way?** There is **grain** and **provision enough** in the **valleys for you** to come to; and you **need not bring more** than enough to **sustain you one hundred days**, to insure you a supply for the future."[19] (**Emphasis added**.)

In 1855, PEF pioneers were informed that the following year their only means of gathering would be restricted to the use of handcarts, once they reached Iowa City, Iowa.

"We propose sending men of faith and experience, with suitable instructions, to some proper outfitting point to carry into effect the above suggestions; **let the saints**, therefore, who **intend** to **immigrate the ensuing year, understand** that they are **expected to walk and draw their luggage across the plains**, and that they **will be assisted by** the **fund in no other way**."[20] (**Emphasis added**.)

> "**...let them pursue the northern route from Boston, New York, or Philadelphia,** and **land at Iowa City** or the then terminus of the railroad; there let them **be provided with handcarts** on which to **draw their provisions and clothing, then walk and draw them**, thereby saving the immense expense every year for teams and outfit for crossing the plains."[21] (**Emphasis added.**)
>
> "**We are sanguine** that such a train will **out-travel any ox train** that can be started. They **should have a few good cows** to furnish **milk**, and a **few beef cattle** to drive and **butcher as** they may **need**. In this way the **expense, risk, loss and perplexity of teams will be obviated**, and the saints will more effectually **escape** the **scenes of distress, anguish** and **death** which have often **laid so many** of our brethren and sisters **in the dust**."[22] (**Emphasis added.**)

The *Millennial Star* reported that in 1856, a total of "4,326 souls" emigrated to Zion. The Perpetual Emigration Company funded 2,012 individuals.[23]

B. H. Roberts, in his *Comprehensive History of the Church*, reported PEF totals as:

1850—432	1856—1,273	1859—54
1852—298	1857—1	TOTAL—4,769
1853—400	1858—0 "(owing to Utah difficulties)"	

The cost was "about three hundred thousand dollars". It was "but a small portion of the yearly 'Mormon emigration' no record of which, so far as I am acquainted, has ever been [kept], not could there be, [kept such record], as persons emigrating on their own means have come and gone at pleasure."[24]

The Congress of the United States of America brought the Perpetual Emigration Fund to an end in 1887 in a bill known as the Edmunds-Tucker Act. As a means of forcing the Church to end its practice of Polygamy, the act dissolved the Perpetual Emigration Fund Company as well as The Church of Jesus Christ of Latter-day Saints and seized all assets. For the PEF, that amounted to over $800,000. Of course the matter was appealed to the Supreme Court of the United States, and in the meantime differences with the government were worked out to return Church assets with the guarantee that polygamy would no longer be practiced nor permitted.[25]

Between 1850 and 1887, over 85,000 Mormon emigrants made their way across an ocean and two-thirds of a continent to reach a valley in the high deserts of the Rocky Mountains. Because a prophet said it should be done, between 1856–1860, some 3,000 of the 30,000 men, women and children helped by the PEF, were willing to push and pull handcarts.[26]

Surely this was the literal fulfillment of Isaiah's prophecy centuries earlier:

> "And it shall come to pass in the last days, that the mountain of the Lord's house shall be established in the top of the mountains, and shall be exalted above the hills; and all nations shall flow unto it. And many people shall go and say, Come ye, and let us go up to the mountain of the Lord, to the house of the God of Jacob; and he will teach us of his ways, and we will walk in his paths: for out of Zion shall go forth the law, and the word of the Lord from Jerusalem."[27]

Figure 2: *The Sailing Ship Enoch Train*

Phase One:

CHAPTER II

THE VOYAGE OF THE SAILING SHIP THE ENOCH TRAIN

The year was 1856, and at eight a.m. on Sunday the 23rd of March, an American sailing ship *The Enoch Train*, had raised anchor at Liverpool dock and was being towed by the steamer tug *Independence* toward the Atlantic Ocean. For the crew it was just another cargo of immigrants being transported to the port of Boston. Just one more sailing by the vast number of ships constantly traveling back and forth from the old world to the new and the new world to the old. For these passengers, and the thousands of other converts being gathered from "Babylon," it was the next step in their journey of faith to reach a promised Zion.

As ships go, the *Enoch Train*, named after her owner, was of the packet type, built in East Boston, Massachusetts by Paul Curtis in 1854. She was 1618 tons, measuring 211 feet by 41 feet by 28 feet; with three masts; and cargo holds that were at present filled with newly constructed sleeping areas where huge stacks of bales and barrels would normally be lashed into place for a long sea journey. With the great demand for passenger space during this period of time, the usual practice was to have the carpenters rough in stacks of bunks for passenger use as they sailed west to America and on the return trip east to England, rip them out to make room for regular cargo. It might seem like a great deal of trouble to go through for each journey, but the money to be made more than compensated for the effort. They didn't have to worry about the bedding used on the bunks, as that was the responsibility of the passengers and varied according to what they could afford. The poor usually slept on quilts or ticking stuffed with straw or hay. There were however, some who could afford feathers in their mattress, pillows, and cushions. Passengers mainly used what they had to rest their heads on, be it clothing, blankets, or nothing at all. With the use of the Perpetual Emigration Fund to gather the poor and needy, most had the necessities to make their journey without unusual deprivation.[1]

To those gathering to this seaport, it seemed like they had been in preparation for ever. Once they had heard the Gospel message of the Mormon missionaries, understood the plan of salvation and been baptized and confirmed, they were anxious to be with the rest of the Saints in the gathering place. They worked hard, and carefully followed the council and direction of their church leaders, to qualify for passage to America. Most were too poor to be able to pay the costs of such a journey all at once, and they were overjoyed and grateful for the Perpetual Emigration Fund. In Zion an inspired prophet requested funds be raised from the Church membership to pay the costs of bringing converts to the Utah Valley, with the understanding that those using the funds would repay the amounts to provide the same opportunity for others. Said agreement being made in the form of a written covenant:

"PERPETUAL EMIGRATING FUND COMPANY
"Organized at Great Salt Lake City, Deseret, U.S.A., October 6th, 1849
"We, the undersigned, do hereby agree, and bind ourselves to the PERPETUAL EMIGRATING FUND COMPANY, in the following conditions, viz–

"That, in consideration of the aforesaid Company emigrating or transporting us, and our necessary luggage, from [Name of Country] to Utah, according to the Rules of the Company, and the general instructions of their authorized Agents;

"We do severally and jointly promise, and bind ourselves, to continue with, and obey the instructions of, the Agent appointed to superintend our passage thither, that we will receipt for our passages previous to arriving at the port of disembarkation in the United State, at the point of outfit on the Missouri river, prior to arriving in G.S.L. Valley, and at any intermediate stopping place the Agent in charge may think proper to require it;

"And that, on our arrival in Utah, we will hold ourselves, our time, and our labour, subject to the appropriation of the Perpetual Emigrating Fund Company, until the full cost of our emigration is paid, with interest if required."[2]

As a means of making sure there would be no misunderstanding regarding requirements for emigrants, the following instructions were printed in *The Latter-day Saints' Millennial Star*, No. 2, Vol. XVIII on Saturday, 12 January 1856, which sold for the cost of "One Penny":

The Latter-day Saint's Millennial Star*

SATURDAY, JANUARY 12, 1856

General Instructions.

In view of the approaching departure for America of many of the official members of the Church in the British Isles and Foreign Missions, and the general change that will shortly take place in appointments, we publish the following General Instructions for the benefit of the officers of the Church, and also the members, but especially newly-appointed officers, that they may enter upon the duties of their respective callings with an understanding of the way in which business is conducted by this Office with the Conferences and Missions.

EMIGRATION DEPARTMENT

"*Application for Passage.* — All applications for passage to America must be accompanied by the name, age, occupation, and name of native country, of every individual; and a deposit of £1 for each over ONE YEAR OLD, without which no berths can be secured. The time the applicants wish to embark should also be stated, and they will be accommodated as near that date as possible.

"When a vessel is engaged, we notify such applicants as wish to sail about the time she will be going, by printed circular, giving the date of embarkation, price of passage, and all particulars, to which we require an immediate answer, stating whether the parties notified will embark or not, that in case they are not ready we may have an opportunity to notify others. If we receive a reply that passengers will embark in a certain ship, we immediately secure berths for them; and if they do not embark in that ship their deposits are forfeited, unless they are prevented by sickness or death, when we require to be informed of the fact at the earliest moment, that substitutes may be procured to occupy the berths thus rendered vacant.

"No persons who have recently been exposed to small-pox or other contagious disorders should come forward for embarkation, nor children having them be brought, as the lives of such would thereby be jeopardized, and death probably be sown among all the ship's company. Furthermore, in all cases where it is apparent to the Government Medical Inspector that passengers are in such a situation, they are rejected by him, and cannot proceed on their voyage until free from contagious sickness.

"These regulations respecting passage are necessary to secure the Office from the loss that would accrue from a ship going to sea with a number of empty berths.

"*Provisions and Price of Passage.*—The recent British and American Passenger Acts have very largely increased the scale of provisions formerly allowed, and have made all persons 8 *years of age and upwards statute adults.* Two children over 1 year and under 8 years old count as one statute adult. This, of course, has correspondingly increased the price of passage, but as it necessarily varies more or less on each ship, we cannot here quote a fixed rate. The prices on the first ship sent out by us under the new Acts were £4 5s [4 pounds 5 shillings]. for adults, £3 5s [3 pounds 5 shillings]. for children, and 10s. for infants. We hope there will be no particular advance on these prices, but we can scarcely expect they will be much lower.

"THE SCALE OF PROVISIONS AS NOW FIXED BY LAW IS AS FOLLOWS—To each adult, or every two children, weekly—

3½	lbs Bread,	2	lbs Potatoes,	2	oz. Salt,
1	lb Flour,	1¼	lbs Beef,	½	oz. Mustard,
1½	lbs Oat Meal,	1	lb Pork,	¼	oz. Pepper,
1½	lbs Rice,	1	lb Sugar,	1	gill Vinegar,
1½	lbs Peas,	2	oz Tea,		

3 quarts of water daily, and 10 gallons daily to every 100 for cooking.

"Ships clearing out between the 16th of January and 14th of October are provided for 70 days, and those clearing out between the 15th of October and the 17th of January for 80 days.

"The new Acts also require each ship to be provided with *Medical Comforts*. The following scale has been fixed upon by the Government Emigration Commissioners for vessels sailing from this Port to North America.

"FOR TWO HUNDRED ADULTS AND UNDER—

14	lbs Arrowroot,	30	lbs Sugar,	½	gallon Brandy,
25	lbs Sago,	12	lbs Marine Soap,	2	doz. milk. in pints,
20	lbs Pearl Barley,	2	gallons Lime Juice,	1	doz. Beef Soup, in lbs,

3 doz. Preserved Mutton, in ½ lbs.

One half of the above scale to be added for every additional Hundred."

"Passengers furnish their own beds and bedding. A straw mattress will answer very well for sleeping upon when they do not bring feather or other beds with them. Each single passenger also requires a box or barrel to hold provisions; and the following articles for cooking, &c.—a boiler, saucepan, fryingpan, tin porringer, tin plate, tin dish, knife, fork, spoon, and a tin vessel to hold 3 quarts of water.

"Where families emigrate together, one boiler, one saucepan, one fryingpan, and one provision box, of suitable size, will be sufficient for all. The water bottles also may be made to convenience in size and number, but they must hold the number of quarts due the whole family per day.

"*Luggage*.—As much as possible of passengers' luggage should be marked "*To go below,*" that it may be put into the hold of the ship. Only that which is absolutely necessary during the voyage should be retained on deck.

"*Emigrants for the United States only*.—As we design to have the business of the present season's emigration concluded a month earlier in the year, if possible, than was last season's, we request that intending emigrants for the United States only will apply immediately, as we wish to ship them about the 1st of February, or as soon after as practicable. We cannot, as we did last season, ship this class of emigrants with those going through to Utah.

"*Through Emigrants*.—To such as purpose to go through to Utah on their own means, we have to say that teams can be ordered through us as heretofore, and will be supplied at the point of out-fit for the Plains by our agent. We think £55 will cover the cost of one wagon, with bows, yokes, and chains, four oxen, and one cow–perhaps two. All who wish us to order for them must inform us immediately, and send the needful, that we may transmit the same to our agent. The 1st of March will be as late as we can receive orders for this season, but it will be much to the advantage of purchasers and ourselves if we can know by the 15th of February what will be required.

"Tenting and wagon–cover material we also purpose to supply as heretofore. For a tent 44 yards are required, for a wagon–cover 26 yards. The material is a good British Twilled Nankeen, 27 inches wide, and will be 6 ½d per yard.

"*P. E. Fund Emigrants*.—Persons ordered out by the P. E. Fund Company are notified to that effect on our receiving the instructions from the President. The order holds good for *one season only*. Those persons unable to go are requested to state the reasons why, for transmission to the President, after which a new order from him will be required before such parties can be forwarded out.

"P. E. Fund Emigrants, whether ordered out or selected here, are forwarded entirely subject to the regulations of the Company which exist when their embarkation takes place. That portion of the journey between Great Britain and the United States is performed in accordance with the requirements of the Passenger Acts, as set forth at the commencement of this article.

"After landing in America they are forwarded in charge of Agents of the Church from place to place until they arrive in Utah. The mode in which the American part of the journey is conducted varies some little each year. For that which will be pursued the present year, we refer to the *Millennial Star*, No. 51, Vol. XVII, and to further instructions which will shortly be given through the same medium. [*This document in its entirety may be found in AppendixB pp. 122-127*]

PREPARING TO SAIL
For several days prior to sailing, the passengers of the **Enoch Train** arrived in Liverpool to take care of any final details and eventually be allowed to board the ship. It was an awesome time of anticipation by each individual, be it a lone soul or a family, each individual in their mind and heart felt great joy mixed with cautious fear. In the mind echoed the stern warnings of family and friends that they were being "lied to, led astray, entrapped by devils that would enslave them in gloom, doom and damnation." Some knew they would never again see their loved ones nor their native lands, some were disowned. All would be frightened and flee such possibilities, were it not for the testimonies they had gained of God and His loving intent for them, if they were but willing to exercise faith and pay the price. For many, this was their Gethsemane, their last pause before the final step that would forever close the doors of their life on one type of existence and open another of infinite possibility.

As each Saint arrived in the port area, they were drawn as a moth to a flame, to find their way to the dock and view the sea chariot that would transport them to Zion, a ship named the **Enoch Train**, if they still dared go. Upon arriving at the dock, each would stand looking up at this great ship. There, tied to the dock by huge ropes, a wooden ramp traversed the area from the dock to the ship's entry. What seemed to be endless lines of people were passing back and forth over the gangway, bustling with armloads of goods, baskets and bales of supplies, and by the use of ropes and pulleys, water and food barrels, cartons of all sizes and descriptions, were being pulled

Figure 3: *At the Dock*

high into the air, swung over the deck and lowered into appointed storage places. Men were everywhere working, calling out orders and warnings, making the ship fit for a long sea journey. Where in all this great organized confusion would the passenger go, where would he or she be stored? How could a single soul so lacking in anything but a knowledge of their own everyday life fit into something that seemed so foreign? Doubt upon doubt! And then a soft voice is heard and the touch of a hand on the shoulder:

> "Pardon me, but is that the Enoch Train? I'm on my way to America. I'm to sail on the Enoch Train and just wanted a look at the ship that will take me on my way to my family and a home in the mountains of Utah. It seems as if I have been waiting to leave forever."

There stood a woman of small frame, holding a boy by the hand, looking up at the ship with love and hope and wonder in her eyes. An average appearing woman dressed in clean homespun, with the glow of an angel about her face. Such obvious faith and joy removing all doubts from a troubled soul, as one spirit touched another in a shared moment of understanding. A nod of the head was all that was spoken, but both knew they were fellow citizens with the Saints.

It was finally Thursday, 20 March 1856, and the final preparations for the 534 church passengers were being completed. Many were already onboard the *Enoch Train* and trying to settle into the grand scheme of things. Some were still at the Emigrants Home completing final tasks, yet others were just arriving at the Conference departure office to book their passage.

John D. McAllister recorded in his journal for this date:

20 March 1856 - Thursday
"went to the Enoch Train and received a Berth. visited the Saints in the 'Emigrants Home' bought some things for the voyage. Visited Bro. Perks P.M. accompanied Bro. Ferguson to the Ship. E. Train. Spent the afternoon with him, we Took tea at Bro. Perks. Evening we visited at the Conference House, and finished Packing up. Met Bro. Joseph A. Young, Wm G. Young, Edwd Martin, Jesse Haven, F. O. Leonard, Wm C Dunbar, Johns Kay, Samuel A. Little and Daniel D. McArthur all from the baley. we Spent a good time together about 2 past 2 o'clock we retired to rest."[3]

Archer Walters wrote that he had "booked his families passage at the office, 36 Islington." Which was probably an act of finalization regarding his travel intentions. The usual practice, as found in the above *Millennial Star* instructions, was to have everything finished before arriving at Liverpool.

That evening, as everyone onboard ship was trying to settling into bed, the birth of a baby is recorded to Sister Mary and Elder Thomas Lyon:

"2 past 9 P.M. Sister Thomas Lyon delivered of a baby daughter on board ship named Christina Enoch, delivered by Sister Janett Hardie from Edinburgh."[4]

While there might be some curiosity about the middle name given this little girl, it was a rather common practice during this period of time, though not a requirement, for children born onboard a ship to be given some or all of the ship's name. The midwife, Janett Hardie, was a very busy woman during the trip from Liverpool to Salt Lake, as many good sisters required her assistance, and their children owe their survival, to her delicate skills and angelic dedication to service.

PREPARATIONS FOR A SUCCESSFUL JOURNEY

As with any successful accomplishment, effective planning and preparation were absolutely essential, and this was not an easy task. Over the several decades that passengers were shuttled to the new world, many different methods were employed to see to their feeding, health, leadership, etc. During that time there were many tragic results because things had not been adequately prepared for.

For example, some of the first groups had too many people and were overcrowded, resulting in lack of privacy, sanitation, water, food, etc. The wealthy passengers brought many more items of just about everything, which they really did not need, which left the less wealthy to do with what ever space was left. Some had an abundance of food and servants to prepare it, while others brought very little, soon being without food and usually having no way to store and/or cook what they did have, which often led to rotten food, malnutrition and disease. Of course this was a much greater problem among emigrants that were not Church members than those who were, as charity with a "brother/sister" was always easier than with a stranger.

Cooking facilities also varied from ship to ship, but in all cases were limited and difficult to work with. For individual and/or single families, cooking pans and pots, though limited in number, were their own responsibility. As large groups became the norm, like the divisions organized by the Saints sponsored under the Perpetual Emigration Fund, cooking assignments were made to a specific few and were prepared in large containers. On some ships the pots were so large that the cook could get inside them. Soup, stews and other large volume dishes in these cases were the result. Bread was not baked, instead biscuits were made, which quickly became hard and dry. Food could not always be properly cooked nor seasoned to make it acceptably healthy or appetizing, but they ate it and made the best of things to ensure their survival.[5]

Even the precious drinking water, that they absolutely could not do without, did not escape problems. Water, usually taken from local rivers, was placed into "leak proof" containers, usually wooden barrels, and stored aboard the ship before departure. The barrels had been burned black on the inside, which eventually turned the water black as well. Water placed into large, rusty iron barrels, changed to red. In all cases they never tasted fresh and clean, and many a soul was heard to remark how much they missed the water from their well.[6]

Sleeping quarters between the decks were of the rudest type, being usually overcrowded in these smaller ships, and primitive. It was not unusual to have people sleeping on bunks that were tiered along each side of the hold, roughed in so wide that three people could easily have room in one of them to lie side by side. Of course that did not mean only three adults would occupy the space, often it was more, depending on the individuals size, sometimes even being allocated to an entire family with several small children.[7]

A ladder or steep stairs between the "sleeping area" and the main deck provided the only way in or out, and during storms at sea the quarters were "hatched down" to keep water from flooding the hold. Light below decks was limited to a few lamps hung in strategic locations that projected only a dim yellow glow. Sanitary facilities consisted usually of buckets or chamber pots, which left an ever present odor in the air no matter how clean things were kept. Of course during the night, and storms, the contents could challenge even the strongest of stomachs. This, plus uncontrollable, crowded, and damp conditions, even with the best efforts, created an environment that would often spawn disease.[8]

Eventually shipping officials had to pass laws on minimum requirements for passengers, which helped some, but not all. Understanding these problems, the leadership of the Church became very careful to insure that they did everything within their ability and resources to see that every possible necessity was provided for before any ship sailed. First and foremost in their planning was to see that all were cared for and treated equally. One of the great goals of Zion being, that there would be no poor or uncared for, but all were fellow citizens and Saints.

The Brethren in every way possible wanted every emigrant to be as prepared as possible in advance for what they would need to face and endure on the sea. As a result:

> "The Saints knew what to expect when they boarded ship. They were told of the discomforts, sanitation problems, disease, storms, lustful sailors, poor food, and the sheer tedium of days at sea. Church leaders often gave detailed instruction on cleanliness, preparation of food, scheduled teaching and study, and the importance of discipline. Emigrant companies were organized into wards with presiding officers, and because of their discipline the Mormons usually fared better than other emigrants.[9]

Of the 534 Church member passengers of the *Enoch Train*, 431 were financed by the Perpetual Emigration Fund. This insured having adequate funds to see that there was enough food and supplies to bring everyone safely to America. Also, the rules that were established for all Church passengers to meet were strictly adhered to, and approved Church leadership on board ship ensured that every person was accounted and cared for as the Lord intended.

21 March 1856 - Friday

"went on board and assisted in serving out provisions. P. M. went to Bro. Perks along with Bro. McArthur Took tea. Evening attended meeting at 26 Idlington. Bro. Franklin Presided. present of brethren from Zion, James Ferguson, C ... Wheelock, W. C. Dunbar, Jim Haven, E. L. Ellsworth, L. D. Rudd, I. A. Hunt, J. O. Lenard, E. Martin Sfrien[?], W. Crandall, N. T. Posty[?].

"James Ferguson was unanimously chosen to Preside over the Saints on the Enoch Train. Edmund Ellsworth and Daniel D. McArthur his Counselors. The Brethren felt well and spoke their feelings which were good.

Bro. Franklin and Wheelock Blessed us in the name of the Lord....Seperated at Midnight. Bro. McArthur and I slept at Bro. Perks..."[10]

However, even the best of intentions and planning did not eliminate problems. For while it was very sensible to buy food and general supplies for everyone and have it already stored onboard ship, such efficiency didn't always account for differences in cultures and individual tastes. For example, for this trip the Church passenger population listed:

- 19 from Switzerland
- 2 from the Cape of Good Hope, South Africa
- 503 from the British Isles (England, Scotland, Ireland, Wales, etc.)
- 2 from the East India Missions
- 2 from Denmark
- 8 Returning American Missionaries
  [See different totals on p. 141]

One major item of food supplied was rice, highly filling and nutritious, but far from being a normal menu item in most of the passenger's homes. This was true of several foods, and the issue of even those items most liked were not always provided when passengers wanted or desired them. Then of course there was the problem of cooking. A limited amount of space and equipment to use for the preparation of meals necessitated specified groups were assigned to do their cooking and eating at specified times, but not every group always had someone skilled in cooking the foods provided, etc., etc., and so forth. So even something as simple as eating had to be dealt with using great patience and tolerance.

Of course salted and stored meat could, and often did go bad, as did flour and other food items. Fresh produce was not only difficult to keep eatable, but items like potatoes were absolutely essential to keep people from getting illnesses like scurvy. As a result, such foods were kept under very strict security and often in areas that were not all that good for their longevity, so they would go bad. To avoid any greater loss than necessary, it often made for unusual menus as they struggled to use food before it would go bad and save that which had longer storage life. People being human, did not always try to understand such peculiarities, nor were they usually happy about it, but they did "endure it as best they were able."

Then there was the water ration, which was very carefully monitored, as the ship could only carry so many barrels of water. There was a certain amount allowed each day for each person to drink, usually once in the morning, midday and late afternoon/early evening. Water for "bathing", washing, and general hygiene was greatly limited.

It would only take 39 days to cross the Atlantic, but under the varying sea conditions, every day brought both challenges and blessings.

THE TIME FOR DEPARTURE

By Thursday evening, 20 March 1856, most of the passengers reported onboard the *Enoch Train*, they were assigned their berths, etc. and tried to settle in as best they could under the circumstances. Some like young Mary Powell were overcome with excitement as they hurried up the "gang plank" and stepped onto the ship.

"Hello! My name is Mary Powell, we're Mormons going to Zion in America, so we can live there with the rest of the Saints the way the Lord wants us to. This is so exciting! I'm so happy that I just know I will burst! Oh! just look at that, and what can that be, and... and..., oh mother for some reason I suddenly do not feel so well!"

Mother Powell watched her daughter with great concern as she ran back and forth looking at things on the deck.

"Why you're as white as a sheet, Mary. What's wrong dear?... Mary, what's wrong?"

"I don't know," Mary mumbled, "I think I'm going to throw up or fall over, or something, Ohhhh, I'm...."

Suddenly there appeared behind the sinking girl, Captain Henry P. Rich, who took her into his arms and knelt down, easing her gently to the deck. Looking up at Mother Powell, he commented:

> "Excuse me, but you had better take your little girl down below and I will see that she is sent some medicine that should make her feel better."
>
> "But what will you give her Captain?" Mother Powell asked, "She has such a delicate constitution."
>
> "It's a medicine we use all the time, it's made of a mixture mainly of brandy and sea water. It will help her sleep."

Quickly Mary's father swept her into his arms and followed a seaman who had been directed by the Captain on what needed to be done. Down the steep stairs they went, to the space between decks where the passenger sleeping area was located. There Mary was given the medicine and quickly drifted off to sleep, no longer aware or concerned with the noise from the deck over her head or the terrible feeling in her head and stomach as she lay on her mattress in the sleeping section assigned to her family. Mary Powell later recorded in her journal:

> "At some time during mid-night, I awoke and felt the gentle sway of the ship as it rocked from side to side. A large light was shinning in the arch way and my two sisters were sleeping peacefully beside me in the berth. It wasn't long, however, before I too was again asleep. Oblivious to an area of the ship that would not always be remembered with happiness."[11]

On Friday, March 21st, at eight a.m., the gang plank was hauled up, the entry rail replaced, the ship was untied from the dock and towed out into the river where it was anchored for the night.

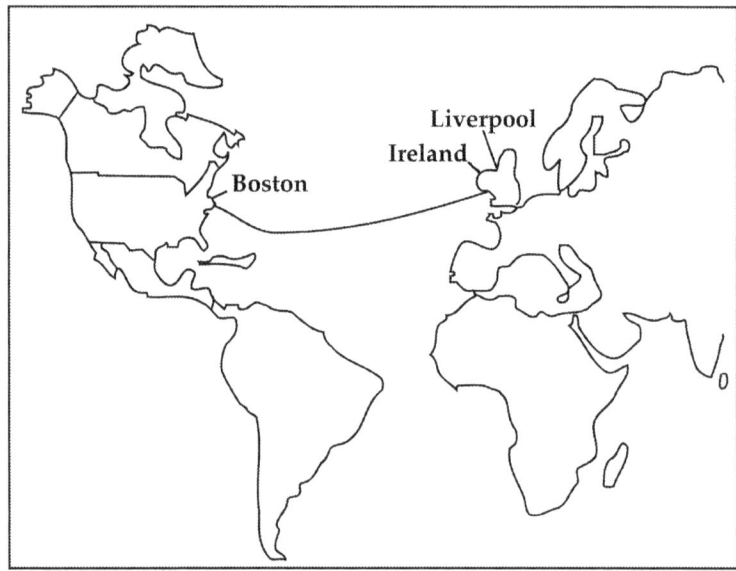

Figure 4: Route From Liverpool To Boston

22 March - Saturday
"A. M... At 10 o'clock went on board the ship with President Richards, Bro Wheelock, Ferguson, Ellsworth, McArthur, Hunts, Dunbar, Rudd, Porter and many others of the Brethren. The Ship's Company of Emigrating Saints was assembled on the quarter deck and received us with cheers, all passed the Doctor and Government officers, after which Bro. Franklin ... Ferguson and several other Brethren left the Ship while the band under Ellsworth direction played "Auld Langsyn" and we gave them ...three cheers at a quarter to 3 P. M. Bro. Ellsworth Called us together and after a short address I was Chosen Clerk of the Company. on motion of Elder E. Ellsworth, seconded by Elder D. D. McArthur that the Ships Company be divided into 5 wards and that Elder John A. Hunt Preside over No. 1 ward and that Elder N. L. Porter over No. 2. Elder A. Galloway over No. 3, Elder S. W. Crandall over no. 4 and Elder T. Leonard over no. 5 also was Chosen Captain of the Guard, the fore going motion was carried unamiously after a few remarks by Elder Ellsworth, we numbered off the wards prepared the guard List and posted the Guard at 8 o'clock. Prayers were attended to by the Presidents of the wards and all retired to rest. ...was called upon to accompany Bro. Wheelock and Ferguson ashore, returned between 9 and 10, and 1 I retired to Rest."[12]

23 March - Sunday
"A. M. at 6 o'clock the horn was blown. The Decks were Cleaned and at ½ past 7. the different wards assembled for prayers. about 8 we weighed anchor, wind N.N.E. weather fair, was towed down the river by the Steam tug "Independence" at ½ past 9 o'clock all the Comp. was mustered to see if there was any stoway's, found none, while the inspection was going on a Steamer came along side with a McHodgetts and Some additional officers to search the Ship for the former's family."[13]

An officer aboard the approaching tugboat stood at the captains rail, cupped his hands to his mouth and hollered loudly:

"Ahoy there **Enoch Train**, heave to and prepared to be boarded."

Captain Rich, who had been busy with the inspection for possible stowaways, turned, walked to the rail and shouted back.

"State your business! Why do you seek permission to come aboard? We've already had our departure clearance!"

"Aye, but we have a citizen who has sworn out a complaint that there are members of his family on board being held against their will, be'un spirited off with these Mormons to America. He has formally demanded a search and their return! His name is McHodgett."

The Captain scowled, his face reflecting controlled aggitation called back,"You have our permission to come aboard, but we'll not stop our tow. If ya' wish ta search, you'll have to do so while we're under way. Understood?"

"Aye, Cap'n. Stand by to receive Mr. McHodgett and our inspectors."

Quickly McHodgett and the inspectors came aboard, and after a short search, Mrs. McHodgett and the children made their presence known. It was quickly obvious that none of the family wished to leave the ship, except Mr. McHodgett. But finally after a serious discussion with Elder Wheelock, Ferguson and others, a compromise was reached. Mrs. McHodgett, standing with both feet planted firmly on the deck, her hands on her hips, and fire in her eyes, stared straight into her husbands face and demanded:

"Then it is clearly understood that you will allow our two eldest to continue the trip and I will return temporarily with the other three children?"

"Yes," he replied, with great conviction in his voice, "that is what we have agreed upon. After all, they are 15 and 17 years old, and we have the word of your leaders that they will be carefully looked after."

She responded, without hesitation, "But remember you promised to sell out your business and our house so that we can follow them with the next group of Saints sailing to Zion?"

"I have promised, and you know I always do my best to keep a promise."

"Mrs. McHodgett did not wish to go back ....[but] She consented to do so. Took three of her Children with her and left two behind... at midday water was served to all the Company about 5 P.M. Bro. Wheelock and Dunbar left us in the tug that had been towing all day. They gave us three Cheers, we all returned it and the Band played a lively air. at 8 o'clock the guard was posted. ½ past 8 prayers were attended to. all went to rest. a fresh Breeze filled our Sails and we glided ..."[14]

At about 5 p.m. the tug had hauled in her tow ropes and headed back up the river toward the port. The sails of the *Enoch Train* were now filled with a steady wind and our adventure across the Irish channel and eventually into the vast blue waters of the Atlantic Ocean had begun.

As if to celebrate, early Monday morning at 2 a.m., March 24th, Sister Agnes Hargraves delivered her husband Samuel, a son they named Enoch Train. Then, as if not wanting to be outdone, at 10 p.m. William and Elizabeth Johnston's son Hamilton was born. These were the 2nd and 3rd of four children Sister Janet Hardie would deliver on the journey to Boston.[15]

At first the ship seemed to be gliding across the water at the rate of about five knots, that is about 5.75 miles per hour. The measurement of a "knot" being one nautical mile per hour, which is approximately 1.85 Kilometers or 1.15 miles per hour. Such a rate of speed causes some motion of the ship, but nothing like it is when the speed increases, especially if the sea is in anyway "choppy". At about midnight between the 24th & 25th the ship began to roll heavily and the speed increased to 11 knots (just over 12 ½ miles an hour). Those who had not yet developed their so called "sea legs" quickly experienced what it meant to be "seasick".

> Oh God! who made these seas to roll
> To pitch and toss and squeeze my soul,
> I do not mind a test or two
> If in my heart I know that you
> Will safely hold me in your hand
> Until at last we find some land.
> Please calm my stomach, mind and bowels
> Please cause the winds to blow, not howl,
> And ease my tortured, frightened frame
> Adjust my balance and keep me sane,
> Until like seasoned sailors be
> Serenely calm while on the sea.
> Oh God! who hears my every prayer
> From here and there and everywhere,
> Bless me with calm and peace of mind
> That I may **survive** to serve mankind.......Amen.
>
> *("Oh God! who made these seas to roll" by Robert O. Day)*

25 March - Tuesday
"A. M. 6 o'clock the horn was sounded, a great many so sick they could not rise. at 7 prayers were called very few attended. Ship still sailing, going 10 Knots wind E.S.E. weather Cloudy. Ship making 10 Knots. 8 o'clock raining very fast and Squally .... I was very sick but kept about. Many of the sick were administered to by the Elders. Some of them got better ..... Posted the guard at 7. 1/4 past prayers were attended to. About this time we Cleared the Chanel and Sailed on the broad Atlantic."[16]

26 March - Wednesday
"Sickness not so bad. I am better and am thankful. My wife, Henry and Harriet and Lydia and Sarah still sick. Ship going at good speed; wind nearly south. Harriet very sick. Rained hard towards night. All went to bed. Could eat nothing for we had no salt nor vinegar and we could not eat pork. The ship rocked all night. Was very poorly; no appetite. Rough breakers; sea wind blowing southeast, east."[17]

On the 5th day of our journey we saw in the distance another ship, that was soon identified as the barque *Emily Flyn* out of Belfast. The crew of our ship lowered a boat over the side and manned it for the purpose of transferring our Channel pilot, who was still on board, to the *Flyn* to be returned to Liverpool. However it was soon discovered that she was bound for Hamburg, and the pilot had to be brought back aboard. It was interesting that the captain in referring to the event said they "**spoke** the barque *Emily Flyn* of Belfast." Evidently "spoke" meaning communicated with, or contacted, while passing at sea.[18]

27 March - Thursday
"All better except Harriet, for which I thank my Heavenly Father. Wind blowing briskly after a wet night. Now 12 o'clock and all well and merry. Most are getting over their sea sickness."[19]

"Nearly all the sick were on deck, chatting, singing, and running about. We had a splendid run for a few days, and expected to be in Boston in four weeks, but it was ordered otherwise by a kind Providence. The captain steered south to escape the ice."[20]

"A. M. Ship making 6 knots wind East weather fair at ½ past 5 o'clock the horn Sounded the rise. The Brethren turned out, and Scrubed decks. ...The day passed off very plesant. P. M. posted the guard at ½ past 7 o'clock, at ½ past 8 attended prayers...."[21]

With the Birmingham band on board, on good days there was music and frequent dances. Children, when they did not have chores to do, or they didn't suffer from seasickness, played their games and especially enjoyed the days when the weather was pleasant and allowed them to be on deck.

Families also had their times together, and the elderly enjoyed their opportunity in the sun with activities such as checkers and handicrafts. Church services were also held on deck, as weather permitted, as were work periods when tents were cut and sewn together to be used for the trek west across the plains.

As much as possible was done on deck, because as the days multiplied on the sea journey west, the region between decks became a place that was not always pleasant. No matter how great the effort to keep their sleeping, cooking and living areas clean and tidy, when the Saints couldn't be on the upper deck, it was not a very nice place to be. Of course these between deck experiences were not as bad or as hard on the Saints as they were on other emigrant passengers sailing the Atlantic. The Saints had an advantage, they had the trials they would probably face carefully explained to them by their leaders before they left England, as well as instructions on how to make the best of things.

They knew just how essential cleanliness and cooperation was going to be. They understood about the food they would receive, limited water supplies, lice, fleas, and disease that would be encountered and how to deal with it. They were counseled on what personal items to keep with them between the decks and how to store them. They understood there would be slop buckets for human waste and puke buckets to throw up in. Also how to deal with those unexpected accidents that always seem to happen. They were told about dim lights, limited sleeping space, and the foul odors that would occur, especially if they had to have the hatches battened down. They were counseled that during such times when they might feel trapped, they were to keep a prayer in their heart, patience in their minds, when possible a song on their lips, and to apply the "golden rule" with great love and energy.

And Christians they were, true and concerned Saints. With few exceptions, they made the very best they could of all situations. And the Lord was mindful of them and answered their prayers. For example, on one occasion when they were "becalmed" (the wind ceased to blow), and they were still on the waters:

> "Friday, March 28th, at ½ past 5 a.m., the horn was sounded. ....the wind was becalming, it was cloudy with rain. At ½ past 7 o'clock we attended prayers and the Brethren prayed for a favorable wind, which came immediately from the Northeast, causing the ship to sail at the rate of 8 Knots. The weather cleared and the Saints were able to go up on deck where they enjoyed themselves. [22]

Of course there were also days that were not so pleasant, and could easily drive a Saint to distraction.

> "All well. Some good boiled rice for breakfast, but the children cried for gruel. Mother didn't like it and Sarah grumbled, causing mother to scold. Henry's sick and mother and Harriet are crying because there's no sugar. They gave Henry some preserves, then he went to bed very sick. If they grumble now, what will they do before they get to the Valley?[23]

LIFE BELOW DECK DURING A STORM AT SEA

On Monday, March 31st, the night of the 9th day at sea, the first death in the company occurred. Sister Esther Devereux, an ancient lady of tender constitution, passed away at the side of her loving companion of many years, a victim of "consumption".[24]

Poor John had watched her slowly weaken and wilt away each day, much like a delicate flower left standing in a vase without water. Dear Esther did not wish to leave her John, but she was old and tired of fighting so hard each day to just "hang on" to life. It had finally become too much of a struggle. And John knew, down deep in his heart, that he needed to let her go. Each day she had spoken of her mother and father, her grandpa and aunt Louise, whom she missed and longed to see "if only one more time." John tried to gently remind her that they were already on the other side of the veil, but she paid no attention to his reminders. John loved her so much and didn't want her to go unless he could go as well. They had been together man and wife, without separation, since he untied her from her mother's apronstring. And all of her parents arguments and tears made no difference, she was his and would always be. Even now as she lay there with her soft white hair and wrinkled brow, he saw only the sweet young lass of their wedding day. He always saw her that way, her laughter always sang in his heart as did her hugs and kisses and the memories of a lifetime. Now she was at eternal rest and he was alone, so far from their native home of Dymock, Gloucestership, England.[25]

Almost as a tribute to her passing the sea became calm, but then gradually boiled up into an ugly gale, that blew the ship so violently it was forced off course by four degrees. The Captain and crew knew what was coming and began to make their preparations, but for the Saints below decks trying to gain a nights rest, they found themselves quickly drawn into an unforgettable experience – enduring a violent storm at sea.

As the storm builds, the ship begins to pitch back and forth and your stomach, that before had been relatively calm, begins now to "churn" and you become "lightheaded" with the side to side and up and down motion of the ship. The few lanterns that are lit are swinging back and forth, casting unusual shadows overhead, and bouncing off the dark shapes of things lashed to the sides of the hold. With the increased violent motion, a strain is put on anything that might move. Ropes spring with tension, unsecured items on tables and bed are tossed in which ever direction the ship leans. Frightened children are crying out for their parents, and those that had been sleeping are suddenly awake and momentarily frozen with a fear of an unknown threat. Some are rolled or tossed onto their neighbors, while others "fly" from their bunks onto the deck.

Overhead, water from the violent ocean is splashing in through the open cargo hatch, at first in little sprays like a gentle dew on morning grass, and then in a volume that could be measured in buckets and barrel loads. Water is now sloshing across the floor and wetting down tables, benches and bunks. The wind screams like a long lost child and the snap of canvas straining against the ship's masts crack like a thousand whips, sending shudders through every plank and board of the ship. The sound of pounding feet running back and forth across the deck is recognized and the muffled shouts and curses of voices fly through the air between the Captain and his crew, as they labor to control the ship in the storm. Then the command is heard to:

"Batten down the hatches!"

...and suddenly the only connection to the outside world disappears, as crewmen tightly cover the overhead exit to the main deck, to prevent the water washed over the sides of the ship from filling up the cargo hold and causing her to sink.

Like a bug in a bottle, you feel trapped and filled with panic, which like a fire is fed by the reactions in the

Figure 5: *Life Below Decks*

panic of your fellow passengers who are also in your bottle. Now the only air you have to breath is what is stored with you in the hold, and a great fear bubbles up that it will not be enough and you find yourself breathing short shallow breaths, hoping to save enough to make it last. Then, in the semi-dark, suddenly your other senses seem to sharpen. The normal odors of unwashed clothing, partially filled buckets and chamber pots begin to reek. Some have tipped over, scattering their contents anywhere the ship moves. Babies are crying with fear; and people of all ages are heard groaning with seasickness. It's dark, and damp, and the beating of the waves on the side of the ship and the noise of the busy crew overhead increases in volume, but the pounding of your heart is louder than all the rest...all this...all this and the great fear of what could happen in the great unknown is almost overwhelming....Then, like a soft, sweet kiss of an angel is heard one voice singing:

> "Come, come ye Saints, no toil nor labor fear, but with joy wend your way.
> Though hard to you this journey may appear, grace shall be as your day.
> Tis better far for us to strive our useless cares from us to drive;
> Do this, and joy your hears will swell— All is well! All is well!"[31]

Quickly another voice and then another joins the song, until all who are able, are singing with tears running down their cheeks and gratitude filling their hearts, ushering up from every fiber of their being the strength of their individual character, their love for their God and a great appreciation for every neighbor. Great faith is now exercised, that indeed all is and will be well. That this too shall pass. That the Eternal Father of all would not call his children to gather to a Zion on the other side of the world and not sustain them as they obey. Has He not always rescued His faithful Israel? Has He not always cared for His own no matter how great the peril or how mighty the demand might be. Isaac was saved from the awesome command given to Abraham; Moses parted the Red Sea; the Savior silenced the wind and the waves of Galilee. He who rules all, knows all, and brings all mankind to be tested, is in control, so what is there to fear? Peace, be still....be still....

With the eventual passing of the storm, the hatch is finally uncovered and all set about the task of putting things back into some order. By five o'clock they were even able to move Sister Devereux's body up onto the main deck to an area called the "hospital", where it will remain until the weather permits her funeral.[26]

2 April - Wednesday

"At six a.m., Sister Devereux was committed to the deep, in lat. 41" 32' N, long. 24" 42' W...."[27] "It was the first I ever saw buried in the sea and I never want to see another. A rough day all day."[28]

A burial at sea is a most unusual event. On land it is difficult enough with long ceremonies at a funeral followed by the long journey to the graveyard, words of parting, tears and the dropping of flowers and dirt upon a grave. Then departure from the scene while men with long ropes lower a casket into the ground and using long handled shovels cover it over with dirt and set in place the grave marker. The final right of passage into the ground not usually viewed by any but those doing the work.

At sea there is usually little or no time nor opportunity for any elaborate funeral or farewell. The usual practice is to wrap the body in a blanket, if one was available for such use, and then placed in a large piece of sailcloth that was wrapped about the body and stitched closed. A weight is attached to the bottom of the shroud, by either being sewn inside the sailcloth at the foot end, or a weight attached around the outside after it was closed to enable the body to sink into the sea without trouble or delay. In the case of Sister Devereux, with the weather being bad, they had to keep the body on board longer than usual, and since it was in no way preserved, was quickly moved to the upper deck to await burial.

When the time for services arrived, the passengers were called to come up on deck, where they gathered next to the rail on the side of the ship. Resting on the ship's rail was a bare wooden plank, with the wrapped body resting on top. The Captain and the Church leaders stood at the end of the plank away from the rail, behind the body, and a few comments of comfort were delivered, and words were read from the Scriptures that fit the occasion, especially the part about the resurrection "when the sea shall give up her dead." Then with little other ceremony than a nod from the captain, the crewmen lift the end of the board and the body slides off into the sea, where it sinks instantly below the waves.

The Captain and his crew move quietly and respectfully from the site, while good Brother Devereux stands with tears in his eyes, receives hugs from his fellow Saints, and numbly watches the waves cover his Eternal Love as the wake of the ship goes past. Soon...soon he will once again be with her in a better life. There where there will be no more sorrow, nor pain, nor care, all burdens will be laid down. Warm in the presence of the love of their family waiting in the Spirit World and the comforting arms of his Savior, hoping to hear the words, "Well done my good and faithful servant, enter now into thy rest."

3 April - Thursday

"A fine morning; almost all on deck. Some few below sick...The band from Birmingham is playing and merrily; the ship rocking now and then sends them sprawling and make them laugh if one fell on top of another or 4 or 5 together. 11 o'clock and then we are out of a day's water and no extra water for cooking at all but all night we are happy. Several songs during the afternoon by Messrs. McAllison, Frost, Walters, etc. Band playing and dancing until dark when all went below...Sister Leasly fell and hurt herself during the night but is better this morning." [29]

4 April - Friday

"All well.... Nearly 12 o'clock. The wind blowing nearly west and not going very fast. Waves kept splashing on deck. Wind blowing against us...All merry on board... Sons up and down stairs...We went to bed, committing our souls into the care of our Heavenly Father and bid each other good night."[30]

"A. M. the horn was Sounded at 5 o'Clock, Prayers at 7 ½. the day being fine the Saints got upon deck. two Ships passed us yesterday. Homeward Bound. P. M. potatoes was Served to the Company."[31]

5 April - Saturday

"All arose at 6 o'clock. A beautiful morning. Many on deck with cheerful countenances. Henry better. Some potatoes for breakfast and gruel. Double working, tomorrow being the 6th of April. Rations served out, both beef and pork. Henry well. Saw two ships sailing slowly. The finest we have had since we left Liverpool. All the sick on deck. Band playing, dancing and singing until a late hour. Cooking until 12 o'clock at night, tomorrow being the anniversary of the 6th of April."[32]

GENERAL CONFERENCE OBSERVED

The date was Sunday, 6 April 1856, it was the 15th day of travel and a special day to Latter-day Saints everywhere. On this date in 1830 the restored Church had been formally organized. This had also been revealed by the prophet to be the proper day of the birth of the Savior and the proper time for what was now known in Christianity as Easter. If they had already been in the Valley of the Great Salt Lake, on this day they would be gathered with all faithful Mormons in the annual General Conference of the Church where they would be instructed by the prophet, apostles and general leaders of the Kingdom.

Being hundreds of miles away at sea they could not attend the proper conference, but they could remember and celebrate the occasion by conducting a conference of their own. On this occasion Archer Walters observed:

6 April - Sunday

"A beautiful morning. No cooking, only tea kettles boiling. Most all up at 7 o'clock washing and preparing for a good time today. All my family are well and I do not know how to feel thankful enough to my Heavenly Father for it. If I was a Methodist, as I once was, I should shout glory and Hallelujah. Two porpoises were seen but they were thought to be whales. Soon a whale made its appearance and threw water into the air a great height. My children were astonished and asked a thousand and one questions, which I could not answer.[33]

With the sea smooth and calm under a clear sunny sky, at 2 p.m., according to appointment, the Saints assembled in a Conference capacity.

"... At two p.m., ... the company assembled ... Elder James Ferguson presided. The hymn commencing, 'O Lord, thy people bless' was sung. Prayer by Elder McAllister. 'Now let us rejoice in the day of salvation' was then sung. The blessing of the children who were born on board, and several others, was then attended to. The usual Conference business then commenced, by motions being made to sustain the general authorities of the Church in Zion, and also to sustain President F. D. Richards and his Counsellors, and the authorities of the company as it was then organized. These motions were adopted by a unanimous vote. Elder McArthur was then called upon to address the Conference.

"He spoke upon the first principles of the Gospel, and practical 'Mormonism,' and bore his testimony to the truth of the same. Elder Ferguson bore his testimony to what had been said, and spoke upon the principle of marriage; and advised the Saints, those that had come on board with the intention of getting married, to wait until they got home to Zion. He also made some remarks upon the death of sister Devereux, and her burial at sea, and gave instructions calculated to do good to the company. Elder Ellsworth gave some very good instructions, and bore his testimony to the truth of 'Mormonism.' A committee of cleanliness, and one to keep order around the galley, were then appointed.

"The Conference closed by Elder McAllister singing the 'Merry Mormons.' Benediction by Elder Spicer

W. Crandall. The Captain then presented Enoch Train Hargraves with a sovereign. The day was lovely, and the sperm whales played about us for some time. The weather was warm and everybody rejoiced exceedingly."[34]

The children that had been born on board were also named and blessed during the meeting. The first was named David; the second Enoch Train; and the third, Rebecca Enoch. With the Conference adjourned until it would next be convened with the rest of the Saints in Utah, the remainder of this beautiful Sabbath was left for all to spend as they felt most impressed to so do . At least until the trumpet would sound for prayers.[35]

As with many things in life, when one thing seems to improve, it seems to be quickly followed by another ... challenge? The whole of the next week, days 17-21, seemed to be mainly filled by a long list of complaints or dissatisfaction by many. But in spite of the many who went about with long faces and sullened brows, there were others that found happiness in little things, and others a great opportunity for working on tents and items to be used when the handcart companies would cross the great plains.

7 April - Monday

"Wind blowing contrary. Rather cold and windy. Saw no ships. Quite dull and wet at times. Much grumbling about cooking. One man said if he had his money and could get to Liverpool, he would go to Hell if he would not, but it takes very little to prove some; the spirits soon show what they are..."[36]

"A. M. the Horn was blown as usual prayers at 8 o'Clock. Served water to the Company. Wind W. Ship heading N. N.W. making 6 Knots. the Boxes ... were unlashed and Ship got a thorough Cleaning."[37]

8 April - Tuesday

"Rather wet morning; wind ahead and has been for a week past. Still some grumbling about cooking. 10 gallons of water for every 100 persons but none did we get. My children dissatisfied about the victuals; some could eat one thing and some another; could not please all but expect they will get better as they get used to it. But a biscuit and water with health is a blessing for which I feel thankful. Dancing at night on deck."[38]

"A. M. the rise was Sounded as usual Prayers at 7 ½ o'Clock not much wind Sea Smooth weather fine. water Served as usual. Bro. Ellsworth assisted me in drafting and Cutting Tents the Saints Commenced their tent making for the Plains. Evening all assembled at the main Hatch when Bro. Ferguson addressed us gave Some Council and instruction necessary for our Circumstances."[39]

9 April - Wednesday

"A. M. the usual duties of the Ship were attended to. water and Potatoes Served to the Company. wind unfavorable. Posted the guard at 7 ½ o'Clock, attended prayers at 9. administered to Several of the Sick who were relieved imeaditly."[40]

10 April - Thursday

"Windy and wind more favorable. Grumblers about cooking. Lost my Tomiliner hat. Henry very poorly and he says that he will never come on the sea again. Feel not very well myself but am thankful. All things will work right and will be for our good. The wind still in the west. Ship rolling and the sea rough; a deal of tacking about which makes plenty of work for the sailors." [41]

"A. M. wind more favorable Ship making 6 Knots. Squaly with rain the Saints arose and attended prayers as usual. Served water to the Company. felt unwell. P. M... Spent the Evening with Sister Hardies family her birthday was celebrated with wine and cake. Ferguson and several others present."[42]

11 April - Friday

...Henry sick all night...Ship rocked until morning..."[43]

"A. M. the Horn Sounded at 5 o'Clock prayers 7 ½. water Served to the Company. wind N.W. Ship making 6 Knots weather fine. P. M. the wind haul'd more favorable. Evening attended meeting and in connexion with others addressed the Saints."[44]

12 April - Saturday

"Provisions served out today. The change of diet is worse for all of us than the sickness of the sea. Henry almost sick if you mention rice. Little Lydia the best amongst us all. A calm day up to 3 o'clock. The children glad to have some sugar. No sooner than we got out pork than Harriet wanted the frying pan. Busy on deck making and sewing tents; dancing commenced at 6 o'clock, prayers at 8 o'clock and then, it being a moonlight night, another half hour was given on deck; drop hankerchiefs; songs; and went to bed. Ship sailed fast all night."[45]

"A. M. 5 o'Clock ... Ship becalmed, wind bafling weather cloudy. Served water and Provisions. P. M. assisted in cutting out some tents. the wind hauled[?] fair. towards evening the Ship made 9 Knots on her right course. the guard was Posted as usual Prayers at 9 o'Clock."[46]

Another Sabbath, our fourth aboard ship, the third on the great ocean that never seems to end nor to truly be at rest. On what God called the second day of creation in the Scriptures he divided the waters with some to be a covering atmosphere above the earth and the rest to lie over the earth. The third day he divided the waters together that rested on the earth and allowed the dry land to appear. One must wonder if from the second period of creation if this vast ocean ever stopped moving. Even on the days when the ship becomes becalmed, the water never seems to rest – always in motion – always anxious that some new thing will happen and it must be ready. How many souls have stood on such a deck as now and stared hard across the waters wondering if there were any other things left in creation but this ship, this people, awash in the midst of never ending motion, going what appears to be nowhere?

But then on the distant horizon a small speck. Is it a cloud, a bird, or an angel hovering there so long at that far point between two shades of bluegreen? Time passes and the sky begins to darken with a storm. A sailor calls out to Captain that our speed is now at 9 knots. The sails now greatly swollen with wind from the southwest strain to push us harder, and the dot on the horizon continues to grow until it is finally recognized as another ship. Soon identified as the English Barque **Architect of Windsor**, 21 days from Aberdeen and bound for Halifax.[47] As she passes it is interesting to see another soul standing on her deck looking out at sea, straining hard to absorb our passing as a reminder that they too are not alone on an endless waste. Does she too sigh with relief of a renewed knowledge that others share her restlessness and impatience for the journey's end?

14 April - Monday

"Ship run well all night and is going well this morning. Rather a dull day. We hope to be in Boston next Monday if all's well. The Bros. want me to shave. I do not know what to do my top lip is so tender and I have shaved myself for this 16 years passed, and I have determined in my own mind long since as soon as I got aboard a ship I never would shave again until I reached the Valley, and not then until I was told. Band played; trumpet for prayers. The moon shined and the lads and lasses were playing on deck until nearly 11 o'clock."[48]

A meeting was called below deck and some counsel and instructions were given by the Elders. They spoke about the grumbling that seemed to be too often given, and calmed the concerns of some that claimed to have seen the body of a man float past the ship. And there was some very good council about tobacco smoking, obedience and several other little things that needed to be dealt with before they became problems.[49] There was also concern and council about the number of the older Saints that seemed to be doing poorly. All were reminded of the need for the love and care for each soul, without being asked, reminded or admonished. And, oh yes, there were still many tents to be cut and sewn by those who were able.

The tents were of "good British twilled Nankeen", that was "27 inches wide and 6 ½d per yard". Each tent required 44 yards and each wagon top 26 yards.[50] Because this company was designated for handcarts, they spent their time only sewing tents.

16 April - Wednesday

"...the wind blew Strong and fair. Ship making 9 Knots ..."[51]

A TALL TALE AT SEA

One day Mary Powell's mother sent her on an errand to the upper deck. As she ran along hand in hand with Ann Jones, and John following close on their heels, they weren't paying much attention to the roughness of the sea and the rocking of the ship, and they bumped into an old sailor and knocked him down. There they lay all in a heap on the deck, staring with open mouths and wide eyes at one another, not being quite sure what they should do or say.

Suddenly the old sailor sat up, with his legs spread far apart, and his feet dangled to the side like maybe they would fall off any second.

"Well blow me down! I've hung frum the riggin' in a hurricane's blow, been knocked ta' th' deck by a typhoon, almost been thrown ov'r th' railun' mor' times th'n ah' kin' count, but Davy Jones take ma' sole, this iz' th' f'rst time 'un thirty years any chil' 'uv ev'r knock' me down!"

And with that he quickly hopped up, with a spring much like a frog, bent over with his hands pushing down on his legs, just above the knee, and looked down on the startled children. When he did, his stocking cap with the long tail fell over his head and down across his nose. Flipping his head to the side, the tail flew back over his head and he stood bent over squinting down with eyes that seemed to dance with mischief.

The children all started to talk at once, while trying to unwind themselves from their piled up condition. Each almost babbling in urgency to do something, and pained with the thought they may have committed a grave offense. They were all talking at once:

"Oh, no! We're so sorry!...
      We didn't mean to knock you down!...
                                     Are you all right?
Please let us help you up!
        Sorry!   Sorry!"

Scrambling to their feet, they surrounded the old man and began to pat, pick and pull at him in an effort to assure he was all right. On every face was the countenance of concern and urgency. The sailor, who was obviously delighted at all of the rapt attention being given him, backed away a bit and began to make huge gestures of brushing himself off.

"Uv' cors' I'm alright! Ev'rythin's ship shape now. Ya' can't 'urt 'un ole' seadog like me by a knock down."

Just then John looked down at the deck where the sailor had fallen and saw a 2-inch hole in the deck. Immediately his face clouded over with concern and a panic was heard in his voice.

"Oh-Oh! Look at that hole in the deck. Did we do that when we knocked ya' down?"

Immediately everyone gathered around the hole and bent down to examine it closely. Mary moved over to the sailors side and looked up at him, speaking slowly and hopefully:

"Are we in trouble?"

"Corse' not!" said the mate, "that 'oles bi'n ther' a 'long time, it 'as!"

Ann crossing over to the other side of the man and looked up at him intently. John went down on one knee in front of them, peered into the hole, and asked:

"Why would someone want a hole there for?

What's it used for?"

"So you wanta' know whut the 'ole's fer, do ye'? Well, it'll take a bit-o-time to explain Mate, 'er ya' shur ye have tha' time?" said the old man, and scratched his stubbled chin with a long weatherbeaten index finger.

"Of course we do, don't we?" Mary called out, "My friends and I wish to hear all about it. It's the only place on the whole upper deck that we've seen such a hole."

Figure 6: *A Tall Tale At Sea*

The sailor looked carefully around, front sides and rear, as if to see who might be listening. Acting if he was about to tell some great secret that should never be spoken, and checking to see that no one would be eavesdropping. Then he reached to the side of the deck and picked up a bucket, which he turned upside down and sat himself upon it, just above the hole, and looked long and careful down into the space intently with one eye closed and the other squinting. At this the children all quickly gather up in a circle around the hole, dropped down to their knees, closed one eye and squinted with the other into the hole as well. All fully expecting to see some great vision suddenly burst into focus. After a few prolonged moments of silence, where only measured breathing could be heard from the children, the sailor blurted out in a raspy whisper:

"Well, it's not a story that I'd be tellun' ever'budy, cuz' some might not be 'uv 'un understandun' h'art as ye' ar'."

And again he looked around as if he did not want to be heard by anyone but the children. Then he continued in a tone of voice that was molded to set a spell, and the look on his face and the tensions of his body caused the children to sit under that spell. They listened intently to every word, to every shade of vocal inflection, watching and responding to every look on his face and every gesture of his hands.

"It 'appened sev'ral years ago righ' af'er the ole **Enoch Train** f'rst wen' ta' sea. There wuz' a terr'ble storm commenced ta' blow un' the ship was a tossin' this way 'un that, 'un th' crew wuz' sent up on deck ta' make sur ever'thin' wuz' batten' down proper sos' nothin' would be lost inta' th' sea. Ye know whu't 'ah meanz'?"

And the children all nodded, with mouths partly open, and eye staring in anticipation. They listened so closely; one could almost see electricity sparking between the teller and the told. Finally, Mary forced out a whisper:

"Yes, please go on, the ship was tossing and you were..."

"We we'r makun' sur' all 'uz ship-shape, 'un tight. Then it happen', quicker'n skat!"

"What happened?" squeaked Ann.

"A pike the't 'ad been hung 'un th' upp'r deck came fly'un thru' th' air 'un planted itz'elf point-fu'rst inta' th' deck, why it just missed ole' stumpy by a cats whisker!" And the sailor flung his arm out and his finger down into the hole.

Mary screamed, "What almost hit ole' stumpy?"

"A pike young mistrus', thatsa' long pol' with a met'l point 'un it." said the sailor and he gestured with his arms and hands to outline the item.

"And it stuck deep inta' the deck?" whispered John.

"Aye' that it did, 'un if'un that wern't bad enuf', the ship suddenly 'it headon inta' a mountin' 'uv a wave that slapped th' ship up and down like that!" he sputtered, and slapped one hand forcefully down upon the other making a great smashing noise. "An that threw ole' stumpy back'erds again' that ther' pike's pole makin' it snap up outta' th' deck 'un bringun' with it a piece, leavin' th' 'ole thet' ye' see there infronta' ya'."

And again the old sailor bent down and squinted into the hole, as did all of the children. Then John looked up with great concern into the old man's face and asked, "Did Stumpy get hurt?"

Quickly sitting up straight, followed immediately by the children, the sailor scratched his stubbled chin again with his finger and chuckled: "Ole' stumpy git hurt, git on wit' ya', nothin' bothers 'un ole' seadog like him. By the by, did I tell ya' how he got th' name Stumpy?"

All the children shook their heads from side to side and leaned forward so as not to miss a word.

"I didn', well I'll be fish bait! It wuz' 'cuz he 'ad only one leg, a shark 'ad bit off th' bottom' part 'uv hiz' 'uther leg below the knee, soz' he hada' wear a peg leg."

Mary then rose straight up full length onto her knees and leaned in to look intently into the old man's eyes. "Really and true?" she said, as if somehow suddenly skeptical about a shark.

Without changing the expression on his face the sailor looked her right back in the eye and proclaimed seriously, "Aye, wel' ole' Stumpy found hiz'elf skooted all th' way down almos' ta' th' end of th' ship's railun', so'e picks hiz'self up offun' th' deck, an' no sooner iz' he standin' than a great wave slops o'er th' other end uv' th' ship and 'its 'im full in th' back. It wuz' gonna' send him down th' deck un' over the side withouta' doubt, un' the poor man wuz' skeared likun' unta' death. But then it happen'd!"

Immediately the children all drew straight up, almost like a nails being pulled by a magnet, and exclaimed together in an urgent voice: "What happened?"

Without hesitation he went right on, gesturing widely and speaking with a voice that pulled the children right along with the action. Causing great pictures to be painted in their minds and swelling emotions in their hearts.

"Well, az' that wave wuz' washun' and pushun' 'im 'long th' deck, 'iz peg leg caught inta' that 'ole right 'er 'un stuck fast, 'un th' wave washed right o'er th' top of 'em, but 'e wuz' held fast with iz' peg leg stuck fast in that 'ole. There 'e stayed th' 'ole nite' thru with giant waves washin' f'rst this way, un' then that, but 'iz leg ne'er moved, un' nether did he. Nex' mornin' they found 'em still stuck fast in th' 'ole."

John, no longer able to stand the suspense, leaps up on both feet yelling, "How did they ever get him out again?"

Leaning back on the bucket, the sailor calmly said with a straight face, and great calmness in his voice, "Oh, that wuz'nt 'ard, all the ships carpenter did wuz ta' go below deck, take a mallit 'un 'it 'til his peg leg finally popped out'ta th' 'ole. Frum' that time on, they nev'r bother'd ta' fill in that 'ole. They always said they never knew when Stumpy might need it agin' sometime!"

Mary then sat back on her bottom, braced the weight of her arm behind her on the deck, and with some bit of skepticism asked, "Is that really a true story?"

With that the old sailor stood up, picked up his bucket off the deck and asked, "Why Missy, do ya' think I'd try ta' spin a tall tale un' ya'? Why ole' Stumpy w'uld ne'er do a thing like that."

Then he tipped his fingers to the rim of his cap and strolled away down the deck calling over his shoulder, "Good'ay Missy, I hafta' git back ta' work now." and whistled a loud sea tune until he was out of sight.

The children looked at each other in silence for what seemed an eternity, then as if raised by an unseen hand, in unison they scrambled across the deck and ran laughing toward the stern of the ship. From that day on, every time any of the children passed that spot on the deck they always paused to squint with one eye down the hole in the deck.

ONE OF MANY HEALINGS
On Sunday evening, April 20th, Archer Walter's stood at the bow of the Enoch Train watching the last red rays of the setting sun dissolve among the fleecy golden clouds on the far horizon. The slight sea spray in his face was refreshing and brought him memories of walking through the glen in the sunset with the fog's mist all about him. The little shadows of his memory bringing back the silhouettes of untold things floating in the half darkness. He could even smell the meadow and hear the crack of dead tree stems underfoot and hear the old owl that lived in the dead tree.

The weather had stayed good and most everyone remained up on deck to sing until around eleven o'clock, Mrs. McAllison leading them, full of smiles and warm fellowship. Archer right now was not in the mood to sing, his mind kept wandering from one thing to another, and when that happened the best thing he could do was to go off on his own and think until "everything came once again into focus." Suddenly his mind was on earlier events of the day. They had held Church services on deck where Brother Leonard had given a short history of his mission; Brother Galaway had spoken on obedience and President Ferguson on cleanliness. Then, of all things, the last item of business before the closing song and prayer was the appointment of a "Louse Committee" which was instructed to meet and begin their labors the next day. What a way to end a meeting, but he guessed they must have just forgot to deal with it earlier.... or something.

All thorough the meeting he had noticed Sister Leasly of and on, and he had wondered at her state of health. So at the conclusion of the meeting he had crossed the deck to pay his respects.

"Beautiful morning, Sister Leasly, even though the ship does seem to be going a bit slowly right now."

"Good morning, Brother Walters," Sister Leasly replied, "I was just thinking what a wonderful day it is to be alive, and not only to be alive, but to feel so strong and healthy again."

"Yes, I had heard you were not well, and now there you stand. Could it be that our Lord had a hand in your recovery? "

Turning so that she could look directly into his eyes, she softly responded, "Oh yes, and it could have been no other way, for this is the full of it. I was feeling very sick, but somehow managed to bring myself up onto this upper deck. There, in my weakened condition I fell back, hit my head, and was carried below, back to my bed. The Elders were sent for, and after they laid their hands on me and blessed me, I recovered and became as you see me now. For which I most gratefully thank God!"[52]

That night the weather stayed good, and most everyone remained up on deck to sing until around eleven o'clock, Mrs. McAllison leading them, full of smiles and warm fellowship. Everyone was so happy, that when they finally lay down, sleep came quickly and peacefully.

21 April - Monday

"Cloudy morn...Some lice found on several.... 798 miles from Boston 12 o'clock."[53]

"Spoke to *Typhoon* (iron ship) bound for Liverpool. We wanted her captain to take our pilot, and some letters to England, but he would not."[54]

22 April - Tuesday

"Wet day. Sewing and making tents...Ship rocked. The sailors all cleaning the ship. Expect to be in on Saturday."[55]

"...Today noon 650 miles from Boston."[56]

23 April - Wednesday

"Wet morning. Ship sailing about 6 knots...Last night went on watch ½ past 7 o'clock. Very cold night and the coldest day that has been since on board the ship."[57]

"A. M.... at 8 o'clock. wind .... but very light. Ship nearly becalmed. Water and Potatoes Served to the Company. The Saints worked on the Tents. wind ahead all day."[58]

Again, without warning, on April 24th, between 2 and 3 a.m., another life expired. This time it was Hugh and Jane Clotworthy's little two year old Jane that died of "consumption of the bowels".[59] This poor little soul, who had been so tenderly, attentively and anxiously cared for by her parents and friends, slipped gently into the world of Spirits, where she would suffer no longer. There to be wrapped in God's loving arms and care until her parents would join her in the resurrection.

Such sorrow rained down from the eyes and hearts of her parents as they dressed her in her best clothes, wrapped her into a blanket, and gently tucked it beneath her tiny chin. One more time her mother picked her up and rocked her in her arms, humming gently the lullaby she always used to put her down to sleep. While her father laid out a large pink and green quilt that before had always covered her to keep her warm, that would now be sewn about her little body for her last mortal "sleep" in the wide arms of an oceans bed. Softly sobbing this

Figure 7: *Funeral At Sea*

good father turned his wife into his arms, while friends finished the job of weighting the gentle package and carried her to the upper deck, into the warm afternoon sun.

Laid gently upon the cold bare plank that rested against the ships rail, all gathered around the little bundle, and as many as could reach Jane and Hugh touched them gently or hugged them tightly, as a hymn was sung and Elders Ellsworth and Ferguson spoke of the great Plan of Salvation and the absolute assurance of little Jane's exaltation. Such a sadness hung on the gentle breeze, even the sailors looked on with tears in their eyes, yet they too somehow felt the assurance that this little one was now with the angels. Finally a scripture was read and a prayer concluded. The Captain nodded his head and the board was raised. Over the side and into eternity slipped this dear child. Silently she entered the water and quickly was gone from sight, but not from the hearts of all gathered there, or ever from the sight of her Heavenly Father.

Latitude 42.52, longitude 59.32, 33 days at sea and 513 miles from Boston. [60]

ALMOST TO AMERICA

A few more days and the sea journey of the *Enoch Train* will be at an end. Various journals indicate a variety of events taking place:

25 April - Friday
"Last night...the Saints assembled for meeting between decks. Elder Ferguson and Council addressed them. After the instruction, Hosannah was shouted three times. A heavenly time we had, and one never to be forgotten. The five Presidents were instructed to look after their wards while journeying to the frontiers, and to select two Counsellors each. The Saints were instructed to remain on the ship until all should leave it. If they needed anything from Boston they were counselled to inform their Presidents. All agreed to do so. By a unanimous vote ...a resolution was passed, instructing brother Ferguson to tender ...sincere thanks for the provisions and medical stores...kindly provided... We have just passed the doctor. The inspection - from the time he jumped on deck until he got on his own craft again - occupied about fifteen minutes."[61]

"...wind fair. Ship making 11 Knots weather Cold and rainy."[62]

26 April - Saturday
"A. M. at ½ past 4 o'clock we Struck a for and aft Schooner, her main Topmast caught in our crockir[?] yard, and was carried away...Distance from Boston today noon 185 miles. weather very cold, wind fair. Ship making about 5 Knots."[63]

27 April - Sunday
"Ship nearly becalmed, scarcely made any head way all night. weather fair... engaged most of the day with the Saints...for their passage to Boston...attended meeting between decks Elder Ferguson and Ellsworth, McArthur and Several others addressed us. A note of thanks was tendered to Capt. Rich through Ferguson."[64]

28 April - Monday
"Captain Rich is a man in every sense of the word, and has been very kind to us. At a previous meeting a vote of thanks was tendered to him through President Ferguson...When...present to the Captain, he presented ...letter for President Ferguson, written ten days previously...

"Gentlemen- Boston lights are now in view, and soon we must part, but may we hope, not for ever. But previous, allow us to tender to you our thanks for the spirit of kindness manifested by you all during the present voyage, tending to the health, and comfort of our passengers under your charge. If such rules and regulations could be followed by all emigrant ships, we should have less, far less of sickness and distress at sea. Cleanliness is part of your religion, and nobly you have carried it out. May your trip across our states be one of pleasure, and when this is passed, and you are encamped upon our western prairies, may your thoughts wander back with pleasure to your ocean voyage. Gentlemen, farewell, may health, peace, and prosperity go with you, and when your pilgrimage is accomplished on earth, may a bright immortality be yours, in the world which is to come. Most respectfully, Henry S. Rich, Master, *Enoch Train*."[65]

"We have no grumblers and no murmurers, everybody is contented and happy. Yesterday our pilot was received by three cheers from the company, and 'Yankee Doodle' by the band."[66]

WAITING TO GO ASHORE
29 April - Tuesday
"A very fine morning and the Captain and crew rather troubled about a buoy being in a place they never saw before and he hoists a flag for a pilot. Spoke to a fisherman and found plenty of water and only 15 miles from Boston. A pilot soon came on board. We soon anchored on Quarantine, 9 o'clock in the evening, 3 or 4

miles from Boston. A general meeting below deck and thanksgiving to our Heavenly Father for his protecting care over us while many perish on the sea at the same time."[67]

"... P. M. Spoke the Schooner *Flag of Truce* of Gloucester who informed us we were 24 miles from Opa[?] Ann and 12 from Boston. 4 o'clock the Pilot Boat "Jane" of Boston came along Side and put a Pilot on Board of us. The Band and all the Company of Saints were on deck and gave them hearty cheers. the Band played "Yanke Doodle. land in Sight water served to day as usual. Posted the guard at 7 ½ o'clock. at 9 ½ we cast anchor. The Company assembled between decks for Meeting Elder Ferguson and Council addressed us...."[68]

30 April - Wednesday

"A. M. was visited by the owners of the Ship. Quarantine, and other officers they considered us the best passengers that ever arrived in Boston. the Doctor passed us all in about 15 minutes. P. M. I accompanied Bro Ferguson ashore Met Elder N. H. Felt in Train ... office. He returned to the Ship with us in a Small boat, ...Spent the night on board."[69]

1 May - Thursday

"Landed at Boston Constitution Wharf. Ladies came to visit us and sent oranges for the children, New Testament to all heads of families and many little cards and books for children."[70]

With such a reception, and the quickness with which the passengers of the *Enoch Train* were cleared for entry into the country, it might be expected that their departure from the ship would be almost immediate. That, however, was not the way of it. With the exception of a few leaders, all remained on board the rest of Wednesday and all of Thursday, while arrangements were finalized to move them on to Iowa City.

It was now Friday, May 2nd, 41 days had passed since sailing from Liverpool and Judith Kettle, age 42, wife, mother and an impatient Saint, stands leaning over the ships rail, staring hard at the dock and muttering to herself.

"Every one on board was up early again and at prayers, just like yesterday. Once again we've gone through the motions of checking everything for departure, but still we wait."

Her little boy Samuel, age 5, standing at her side looking up at her feels her frustration and begins yanking impatiently at her dress, first with his right hand, then with both. "Mother, isn't it time yet? The sun's been up a long time, can't we go? I want to go to Zion!"

Mother Kettle mustering up a look of great self-control stared down at him, "Samuel," she said as calmly as she could, "that's the **tenth** time you've asked me that question since we gathered for prayers this morning. It will be time to leave, when the Brethren tell us it 's time to leave and not one moment before."

Mary Ann, age 18, suddenly appeared from behind a stack of boxes and "slithered" up to her mother's side to add her anxious opinion on the subject. "You really can't blame him for being impatient mother, anyone would think after being tied up to this dock for two days, someone would have worked it all out by now. Well... wouldn't you?"

"You too?" the poor embattled mother sighed, "Now my eldest is acting like my 5 year old?" Then, wrapping her arms over Samuel's shoulders, Mother Kettle pulled Samuel close to her and glared into her daughter's eyes beginning to boil up with frustration. "Mary Ann, why don't you.. go...go... " Then like a steam kettle taken off the fire, "go – get Hannah from your father. Then you'll be so busy you won't have time to think about the wait."

Shocked at her mother's reaction, Mary Ann put both hands on her hips and started to reply, but before she could get the words out was interrupted by her father John. "Good news Judith!" came a call from a tall man hurrying across the deck. As John Kettle approached Mary Ann, he placed a small girl in her arms and passed on by without slowing down.

"They've called off the rest of the journey and we're all going to be translated instead?" Judith Kettle replied a bit sarcastically.

"Not quite," he said, bending over to pat Samuel on the chin and then straightened up to kiss his wife on the cheek. "But Brother Ferguson sent word that we will be leaving the ship within the hour and heading for the railway station. I let need to let some of the others know, so I'll be back in a bit." Quickly he turned and started to leave, then after a few steps turned back, "Oh, and they are handing out a half ration of provisions for today. I sent Robert down to get in line. I'll help him with our portions as soon as I get through."

As John disappeared through the opening down to the hold, Judith got a big grin on her face. Then taking both of Samuel's hands in her hands, they danced around in a little circle and whispered loudly to each other, "The time has finally come! The time has finally come!" After several turns they broke, and hand in hand skipped off down the deck yelling " **Hallelujah!**" at the top of their voices.

ENOCH TRAIN - PASSENGER LIST*
AND HANDCART COMPANY ASSIGNMENT

NAME	Handcart Co.
Ahlstron, John Godfrey***	
Aitken, William K. (35) *Dentist*	2
Cecilia (14) *Spinster*	
____Thomas (10)	
Anderson, Agnes (52) *Wife*	2
Archibald (20) *Collier*	
John (16) *Collier*	
James (14) *Collier*	
Argyle, Joseph (37) *Gas Meter Maker*	1
Jane (33) *Wife*	
*Joseph (14)	
*Benjamin (12)	
*Mary (10)	
*Frances (5)	
*Lorenzo (3)	
*Priscilla (1)	
Ash, John (36) *Gun Maker*	1
Sophia (26) *Wife*	
Joseph (7)	
Ellen (1 2)	
Elizabeth (2 mos.)	
Ash, Sarah (58) *Widow*	1
Bailey, James (53) *Silver Plater*	1
Mary Ann (52) *Wife*	
John (20) *Bass Tap Maker*	
Thomas (19) *Whip Maker*	
Alfred (17) *Silver Plater*	
Mary Ann (15) *Dress Maker*	
Louisa (12)	
Baker, Mary Ann (45) *Widow*	1
John (20) *Groom*	
Emma (17) *Spinster*	
Job (14) *Laborer*	
Harriet (11)	
Wilford (4)	
Baldwin, Hannah (18) *Spinster*	1
Ballam, Anna (45)	–
Charles William (17) *Watchmaker*	
Rachel (8)	
Banks, Mary (45) *Spinster*	–
≈Barker, Mary	–
Bascleo [Sp.?], Henry	–
Bates, Mary Ann (21) *Spinster*	1
Bathgate, Mary (59) *Widow*	2
Mary (12)	

NAME	Handcart Co.
Bauer, Alois (24) *Wheel Wright*	–
Baxter, Henry (49) *Contractor*	–
Agnes (49) *Wife*	
Magdalon (23) *Spinster*	
Catherine (21) *Spinster*	
Jane (17) *Spinster*	
Agnes (14) *Spinster*	
≈Bayham, Elizabeth	–
Bell, John (54) *Mechanic*	2
Maria (55) *Wife*	
James (17) *Wire Worker*	
Samuel (15)	
Birch, James (28) *Moulder*	1
Mary Ann (29) *Wife*	
Thomas (7 1/2))	
Mary Ann (6)	
Edward J. (2)	
Birch, William (68) *Shoemaker*	1
Elizabeth (40) *Wife*	
Elizabeth (17) *Spinster*	
Black, Nicholas (46) *Miner*	–
Elizabeth (45) *Wife*	
Eleanor (17) *Spinster*	
Nicholas (14)	
Elizabeth (2)	
Bleak, James (26) *Silver Smith*	–
Elizabeth (27) *Wife*	
Richard (6)	
Thomas (4)	
James (2)	
Mary (Inft.)	
Boden, Mary (22) *Spinster*	–
Bond, Samuel (61) *Laborer*	1
Elizabeth (55) *Wife*	
William (23) *Potter*	
Bond, Samuel (25) *Potter*	1
Bone, Henry *Stewart*	–
Bone, Mary Ann (10)	–
[See Richardson, P.]	
Bouring, Henry E. (33)	
Coach Trimmer	2
Ellen (18) *Wife*	
Wallace (4)	
Bourne, Thomas (59) *Mason*	1
Margaret (49) *Wife*	

NAME	Handcart Co.
Mary Ann (22) *Spinster*	
Margaret (20) *Spinster*	
James (16) *Mason*	
Priscilla (14) *Spinster*	
Louisa (12) Spinster	
John (6)	
Bowen, David (18) *Pudler*	1
Bowers, James (45) *Collier*	1
Mariah (51) *Wife*	
Sarah (18) *Spinster*	
Abraham (17) *Glass Maker*	
Isaac (14) *Glass Maker*	
Jacob (10)	
Isaiah (8)	
Shadrach (6)	
Boynham, Elizabeth (21) *Spinster*	–
Brazier, George (21)	–
Brazier, John (21)	–
≈Brederick, Richard B.	–
Brenchley, Caroline (24) *Spinster*	–
Bridgers, Charles H. (20)	
Cork Cutter	1
Broderick, Thomas B. (31)	–
Elizabeth *Wife*	
John H. (11 mos.)	
Brooks, Nathan (61) *Plasterer*	–
Betty (53) *Wife*	
Alice (21) *Spinster*	
Brough, Alice (69) *Widow*	1
Brown, Christianer (26) *Spinster*	–
Bruner, Sussanna (66) *Spinster*	2
Bryner, Ulrich (28) *Agriculturist*	–
Marian (27) *Wife*	
Marian (4)	
Burdett, Elizabeth (65) *Widow*	2
Burditt, Emma (19) *Spinster*	2
Carr, John (37) *Cooper*	–
Sarah Ann *Wife*	
Arthur J. (13)	
Henry (7)	
Walter H. (3)	
Marian M. 98 mos.)	
Chambers, David (54) *Weaver*	2
Mary (54) *Wife*	
David, Jr. (14)	

NAME	Handcart Co.
Chapell, Henry E.	–
Chapell, Henry E. (Cook)	–
Chapman, John (58) *Farmer*	1
Chester, Ann (20) *Spinster*	1
Francis	–
William (14)	–
Chetwynd, Maria (21) *Spinster*	–
Chetwynd, Maria (24) *Spinster*	–
Clark, George (53) *Laborer*	1
Mary A. (51) *Wife*	
Charlotte (18)	
*William (14)	
*Hannah (6)	
Clark, Thomas (18)	–
Clotworthy, Hugh (29) *Miner*	2
Jane (36) *Wife*	
Janet (9)	
Mary (7)	
Thomas (3)	
Jean (2)	
Margaret (2 mos.)	
Clough [Sp.?], Moses	–
Commander, James (35) *Seaman*	1
Mary (25)	
Cooper, John (21) *Boot Maker*	–
Crandall, Spicer (33) *Farmer*	2
Crawford, James (23) *Wool Spinner*	2
Crump, Charles (53)	–
Charles (33) *Cooper*	
James (39)	
Sarah Taylor (20)	
Elizabeth Taylor (18)	
Dale, Ann (36)	–
Emma (14) *Spinster*	
Eliza (12)	
Sophia (8)	
Anne (1)	
Darroch, Elizabeth (4)	
[See E. Maxwell]	–
Davis, Elias (44) *Laborer*	–
Ann (46) *Wife*	
Devereux, John (51) *Waggoner*	1
Esther (61) *Wife*	
Donald, John W.	–
Doney, John (34) *Laborer*	1
Ann (23) *Wife*	
Ann T. (1)	

NAME	Handcart Co.
Downie, Margaret (30) *Spinster*	2
Dreaney, John (31) *Miner*	2
Mary Jane (28) *Wife*	
Samuel (2 1/2)	
Isabella (4 mos.)	
Duncan, Catherine (24) *Weaver*	–
Durham, Thomas (27) *Bobbin Turner*	–
Mary (27) *Wife*	
Eardley, Benson (23) *Potter*	2
Louisa (27) *Wife*	
Edwick, William (17)	
Telegraph Clerk	–
Eldridge, Thomas (25) *Agriculturist*	1
Charlotte (24) *Wife*	
Charlotte (1)	
Eliker, Heinrich (59) *Shoemaker*	2
Margaretha (54) *Wife*	
Heinrich, Jr. (26) *Agriculturalist*	
Barbara (24) *Spinster*	
Elizabeth (22) *Spinster*	
Konrad (20) *Spinster*	
Margaretha (18) *Spinster*	
Susanna (14) *Spinster*	
Jonannes (13) *Spinster*	
Ellsworth, Edmond (36) *Farmer*	1
Fairclough, Ann (18) *Spinster*	–
Ferguson, James	
(Pres. Enoch Train Co.)	–
Ferney [Sp.?], William (20) *Laborer*	–
Findlay, Mary (59) *Widow*	–
Fowler, Thomas (19) *Laborer*	1
Franklin, Elizabeth (59) *Widow*	1
Franks, Sarah (23)	–
Frew, John (30) *Engine Keeper*	2
Jean (35) *Wife*	
James (8)	
Janet (7)	
Mary (1 ½)	
Frisby, Absalom (21)	
Tin Plate Worker	1
Frost, Edward (33) *Turner*	1
Eliza (26) *Wife*	
Isabella (7)	
John F. (4)	
≈Furrer, Anna	2
Galbraith, John (Cook)	–
Gale, Mary (47) *Spinster*	2

NAME	Handcart Co.
≈Galloway, Andrew	–
Galloway, Andrew (28) *Engineer*	1
Jane (24) *Wife*	
*Annie Eliza (3)	
Gardener, Ann (40) *Wife*	2
Agnes (20) *Spinster*	
James (18) *Dresser*	
Alex.[ander] (16) *Cotton Twister*	
Elizabeth (14) *Spinster*	
Walter (8)	
Gardner, William (26) *Gardner*	–
Emily G. (3)	
Goble, William (39) *Green Grocer*	–
Mary (41) *Wife*	
Mary (12) *Spinster*	
Edwin (10)	
Caroline (8)	
Harriett (5)	
James (3)	
Fanny (1)	
Godsall, John (45) *Shoemaker*	–
Mary (50) *Wife*	
Louisa (18) *Spinster*	
Susanna (16) *Spinster*	
Frances A. (8)	
John (5)	
≈Godsall, Mary	–
≈ 4 Children	
Goodworth, Hannah (44) *Widow*	1
Richard (10)	
Joseph (6)	
Frederick (5)	
Granger, Catherine (20) *Spinster*	–
Granger, Walter (34) *Weaver*	2
Catherine (36) *Wife*	
Robert (14) *Rivet Boy*	
Alexander (9)	
Catherine (7)	
Walter (5)	
John (4)	
Grant, Elanor (26) *Spinster*	–
Grant, Susan (56) *Wife*	–
Thomas (17) *Miner*	
Elizabeth (11)	
≈Gray, Jane	–
Gray, John (51) *Leather Cutter*	2
Jane (52) *Wife*	

NAME	Handcart Co.	NAME	Handcart Co.	NAME	Handcart Co.
Jane (22) *Spinster*		Charlotte J. Rowe (7)		Johnston William (29) *Miner*	2
Franklin (4)		Charlotte E. (33) *Spinster*		Elizabeth (21 *Wife*	
Mary (2)		Hicks, Thomas (21)		David (7)	
William (5 wks.)		*Black Ornament Maker*	–	Richard (5)	
Green, William (30) *Miner*	1	Hillhouse, William (46) *Miner*	2	William (3)	
Haley, John M. (28) *Butcher*	–	Margaret (52) *Wife*		Jones, Daniel (41) *Farmer*	1
Hannah (28) *Wife*		Janet (24) *Spinster*		Ann (36) *Wife*	
Amelia (51)		John (22) *Miner*		Rachel (16) *Spinster*	
Hall, William (29) *Laborer*	2	Mary (15) *Spinster*		Ann (14) *Spinster*	
≈Halley, James	–	Robert (13)		Daniel (12)	
≈ Wife		David (11)		Marion (7)	
≈ 2 Children		Elizabeth (6)		Richard J. (3)	
Ham, Ann (31) *Spinster*	1	William (2)		Sarah (1)	
Hanna, Henry (29) *Miner*	–	Janet (1 mo.)		Jones, Esther (28) *Spinster*	–
Catherine (22) *Wife*		Hodgetts, Hannah (18) *Spinster*	2	Jones, Hannah (45) *Spinster*	–
Agnes (1)		Hollsworth, James (38) *Shoemaker*	–	Jones, James (35) *German Fork Maker*	1
Hanson, George (26) *Gun Maker*	1	Holly, James (31) *Laborer*	–	Sabrina (35) *Wife*	
Frances (25) *Wife*		Lucy (21) *Wife*		Jones, Mary Ann (19) *Spinster*	1
Clara (11 mos.)		Ann (3)		Jones, Thomas (21) *Waggoner*	–
Hardie, Janet (45) *Widow*	2	James (11 mos.)		Jones, William (45) *Mariner*	–
Phillis (23) *Clock Maker*		Holt {Sp.?}, Robert (42) *Shoemaker*	–	Mary Ann (50) *Wife*	
Agnes (21) *Spinster*		Ellen (44) *Wife*		Robert (21) *Laborer*	
John (15)		Margaret (23) *Spinster*		Louisa (19) *Spinster*	
Grace (13)		James (22) *Shoemaker*		Frederick (14)	
James (10)		Daniel (16) *Shoemaker*		Kcors [Sp.?], Mary Ann (22) *Spinster*	–
Hargraves, Samuel (39) *Weaver*	2	Alice (13)		Kelly, John (31)	–
Agnes (33) *Wife*		Joseph (11)		Mary (30)	
Jane (16) *Spinster*		Martha (5)		John C. (1)	
Mary (13) *Spinster*		Hughes, Samuel (31) *Polisher*	–	Kettle, John (53) *Cottager*	1
Janet (10)		Emma (28 *Wife*		Inda (43) *Wife*	
John (8)		Hunt, Abraham (30) *Laborer*	1	Mary Ann (18) *Spinster*	
Elizabeth (3)		Eliza (30) *Wife*		Robert (14)	
Margaret (1 1/2)		Hunt, John A. (25) *Farmer*	–	Eliza (12)	
<>Enoch Train [Born 24 March]		Ipsom, Niels (24) *Shoemaker*	2	James (9)	
Harmon, William (52) *Miner*	1	Georgina (27) *Wife*		Samuel (5)	
Harvey, Emma *Wife*	–	Ivins, Thomas (70) *Gardner*	1	Anna (1)	
Hawkins, William (39) *Farmer*	–	Jackson, George (43) *Miner*	–	Kennington, Richard (52) *Laborer*	2
Elizabeth (39) *Wife*		Ruth (47) *Wife*		Mary (47) *Wife*	
Hay, Mary (34) *Spinster*	2	Herbert (15) *Miner*		Sarah J. (17) *Spinster*	
Heaton, William (28) *Wool Comber*	2	George (15) *Miner*		William (14)	
Esther B. (25) *Wife*		Ellen (13) *Spinster*		Eliza (12)	
Christopher B. (3)		Sarah Ann (3)		Richard (10)	
William McD. (3 mos.)		Susanna (18) *Spinster*		Mary A. (1½)	
Hemming, Jane (20) *Spinster*	–	Jeffries, Eliza (21) *Spinster*	1	Lacing, Elizabeth *Widow*	–
Hicks, John (30 *Shoemaker*	–	Johnston, George (36) *Engine Driver*	2	Langman, Rebecca (22)	
Harriet (24) *Wife*		Janet (14) *Spinster*		Lawrence, Samuel (41) *Shoemaker*	–
Robert Rowe (9)		Isabella (4)		Harriet *Wife*	

NAME	Handcart Co.	NAME	Handcart Co.	NAME	Handcart Co.
Henry (14)		Ann (40) *Wife*		Mary (2)	
Harriett (12)		Mary (8)		Jean (1)	
George (24) *Shoemaker*		Noah (5)		Nash, William (23) *Gardner*	–
Lawson, William (29) *Miner*	2	>McAllison, Mr.	–	Newman, Henry (27) *Farmer*	
Lee, John (33) *Pot Maker*	1	>McAllison, Mrs.		Mariah L. (26) *Wife*	
Sarah (32) *Wife*		McAllister, John D. T. (29) *Carpenter*	–	Maria L. (4)	
William (12)		McArthur, Daniel P. (35) *Minister*	2	Henry I. (2)	
Fanny (11)		McAuslin, Elizibeth (24) *Wife*	–	Oakley, John	1
Elizabeth (9)		McDonald, Alex[(26) *Miner*	2	Olive, Ann (30)	–
Samuel (4)		McDonald, John (24) *Engine Keeper*	2	Ord, Thomas (29) *Spring Maker*	
Chauncey (2)		McDougald, Joseph (25) *Miner*	2	Page, William (19)	
Sarah Ann (5 mos.)		McGowan, Mary (29) *Spinster*	2	*Gun Furniture Finisher*	–
Leonard, Truman (35) *Farmer*	2	>McHodgett, Mrs.		Park, Isabella (62) *Widow*	2
Leiseley, Alice (61) *Widow*	–	(Husband took her off ship]		Parker, Mary Ann (24) *Spinster*	
Ann (26) *Spinster*		> 5 Children [2 Went on with ship'sCo.]		Parker, Robert (35) *Warper*	2
≈Lewis, Mary Ann	–	>McLane, Mr.	–	Ann (36) *Wife*	
Lister, James (26) *Butcher*	–	McMannis, Joseph (34) *Cooper*	–	Maximillian (11)	
Ann (32) *Wife*		Margaret (33) *Wife*		Martha A. (9)	
Dinah (10)		Margaret (9)		Arthur (5)	
Lloyd, John Sr. (38) *Shoemaker*	1	Mary (7)		Ada (8 mos.)	
Elizabeth (37) *Wife*		Janet (11 mos.)		Parson, Elizabeth (24) *Spinster*	–
Mary (11)		Margaret (73) *Widow*		Passey, Thomas (18) *Miller*	1
John (10)		≈McMurrin, Joseph	–	Peacock, George (30) *Miner*	2
William (8)		≈ Wife		Mary Ann (7)	
Thomas (5)		≈ 3 Children		George, Jr. (4)	
Jane (2)		Meadows, Mary Ann (21) *Spinster*	1	Peel, Frances (28) *Spinster*	–
Lucas, Mary (47)	–	Meikle, Margaret (57) *Widow*	2	Petty, Edward (53)	
William (18)		William (30) *Weaver*		Pilgrim, Rebecca (30)	
Ludert, Josephine (43) *Widow*	2	Isabella (19) *Spinster*		≈Player, Elizabeth	–
Alphonse (6)		James (17) *Carpenter*		≈Player, Emily	–
Lyons, Thomas (29) *Weaver*	–	Agnes		Player, Joseph (41) *Black Smith*	–
Mary Anna (30) *Wife*		Merchant, Caroline (25) *Spinster*	–	Ann (39) *Wife*	
Jennie (7)		Middleton, William (39) *Laborer*	–	Elizabeth (16) *Spinster*	
Jessie (5)		Ann (43) *Wife*		Emily (14)	
Mary (3)		John (15)		Alfred (5)	
>Christina Enoch [Born 21 March]		Midgeley, Joseph (21) *Draper*	–	Pope, George (27) *Tailor*	
Martin, Eliza (20) *Spinster*	–	Miller, Ann (49) *Spinster*	–	Jane (31) *Wife*	
Mathieson, Mary *Spinster*	2	Sarah Jane (14) *Spinster*	1	Franklin (3 wks.)	
Maxwell, Elizabeth (52) *Widow*	2	Miller, James (21) *Miner*	–	Porter, Nathan T. (36) *Farmer*	
Arthur (30) *Carpet Weaver*		Mirrin [Sp.?], Margaret (61) *Widow*	–	Powell, John (43) *Mason*	1
Catherine (25) *Spinster*		Morris, William (55) *Awl Maker*	1	Elizabeth (35) *Wife*	
Elizabeth (23) *Spinster*		Sarah Ann (54) *Wife*		William (15) *Mason*	
Darroch, Elizabeth (4)		Moss, Henry (19) *Upholster*	1	Mary (13) *Spinster*	
Ralph (23) *Carpet Weaver*		Moss, John (17) *Carpenter*		Margaret (8)	
Ann (14) *Spinster*		Muir, Edward F. (22) *Cabnet Maker*	–	Elizabeth (6)	
Mayo, Mary (65) *Widow*	1	Muir, George (23) *Miner*	2	Hannah (4)	
Mayoh [Sp.?], Peter (40) *Porter*	–	Margaret (26) *Wife*		David (Inft.)	

NAME	Handcart Co.
Pratt, William (31) *Gun Maker*	1
Caroline (30) *Wife*	
Eleanor Salina (11)	
George (8)	
Orson (3)	
Emily (8 mos.)	
Preater, Richard (29) *Lath Cutter*	1
Mary (30) *Wife*	
Salome M. (4)	
Lora I. (2)	
Price, Ann (45), *Widow*	1
Emma (19) *Spinster*	
Eliza (17) *Spinster*	
Ramsey, Ralph (32) *Wood Carver*	2
Elizabeth (33) *Wife*	
John S. (15)	
Son (14)	
Randle, Ann (31) *Widow*	2
Oscar J. (19/12)	
Rasdall, John (20)	
Agricultural Laborer	1
Elizabeth (22) *Wife*	
Mary Ann (Inft.)	
Reid, James (39) *Shoemaker*	2
Elizabeth (31) *Wife*	
Elizabeth (11)	
James (6)	
Mary (4)	
John (1)	
Richardson, Peter (24) *Laborer*	2
Eliza (33) *Wife*	
Richardson, William (27) *Farmer*	–
Maria (29) *Wife*	
William H. (3)	
John H. (1)	
Mary (1 mo.)	
Richins, Thomas D. (31) *Waggoner*	1
Harriet D. (22) *Wife*	
Franklin (1)	
Robinson, Eliza (25) *Spinster*	1
Robinson, John (46) *Pistol Maker*	1
Emma (27) *Wife*	
Elizabeth (21) *Spinster*	
Sarah (19) *Spinster*	
John (16)	
Clara (10 mos.)	

NAME	Handcart Co.
Roper, Charles (34) *Farmer*	–
Catherine (28) *Wife*	
≈Rossen, Charles	–
≈ Wife	
Rowland, William (22) *Ship Wright*	–
Elizabeth (36) *Wife*	
William (4)	
John C. (3 mos.)	
Harriet F. (37) *Spinster*	
Rowlands, Ephrain *Sailor on Ship*	–
Rowley, John (33) *Potter*	–
Isabella (33) *Wife*	
James (23) *Potter*	
William (17)	
Margaret (11)	
Isabella (7)	
Sarah (6)	
Mary (2)	
Joseph (2 mos.)	
George (28) *Potter*	
Russell, Ellen (23) *Spinster*	2
Salisbury, Ann (36) *Wife*	–
William T. (14)	
Henry (12)	
Joseph (4)	
Sanders, Wallis (64) *Carter*	1
Sarah (20) *Spinster*	
Mary (18) *Spinster*	
James (15) *Carter*	
John (12) *Printer*	
Thomas (10)	
Sanderson, Rebecca (41) *Wife*	2
Sarah Ann (11)	
Rhoda (9)	
Schies, Johannes (39) *Weaver*	2
Anna (39) *Wife*	
Senior, Thomas (29) *Miner*	–
Sheen, James [Sr.] (58) *Quarryman*	1
Maria (58) *Wife*	
Hannah (22) [*Spinster*	
Ellen (19) *Spinster*	
Ann E.	
Sheen, James [Jr.] (26) *Quarryman*	1
Mary (23) *Wife*	
Sheen, Robert (27) *Quarryman*	1
Eliza (28) *Wife*	
Mary (8)	

NAME	Handcart Co.
Louisa (5)	
Ann (4)	
Emma (3)	
Ann Eliza (3 mos.)	
Shelton, Richard (18) *Blacksmith*	1
Shields, Elizabeth (26) *Spinster*	2
Smart, Sarah (50) *Wife*	2
Smith, Amelia (18) *Spinster*	–
Smith, Andrew (28) *Tailor*	2
>Smith, Aniki	–
Smith, Isaac (59) *Laborer*	–
Charlotte (54) *Wife*	
Benjamin (15)	
Emily (11)	
Smith, John	–
Smith, Mary (64)	–
Emma (26) *Spinster*	
Robert (34) *Mechanic*	
Ester E. (9)	
Smith, Sarah Ann (22) *Spinster*	–
Smith, William (36) *Gardner*	
Charlotte (30) *Wife*	
William Jr. (11)	
Charles (8)	
George E. (5)	
Sounds [Sp.?], William (36)	
Engineer	–
Sarah (36) *Wife*	
Esther (6)	
Jacob (2)	
Spiers, George (29) *Weaver*	–
Janet (27) *Wife*	
William (7)	
Janet (5)	
Agnes (1½)	
Sprigg, Sarah Ann (18) *Spinster*	1
Stephens, Ann (66) *Widow*	–
Stewart, Nancy (49) *Wife*	–
Jane (17) *Spinster*	
Matilda (15) *Spinster*	
Margaret (12)	
Anne (23)	
Stevenson, Alexander (36) *Carpenter*	1
Magdalene (35) *Wife*	
Isabella (27) *Spinster*	
John (13)	

NAME	Handcart Co.	NAME	Handcart Co.	NAME	
Magdalene (11)		Titt, Richard (66)	–	Wandless, Ellen (28) *Wife*	2
Alexander (7)		Ann (59) *Wife*		Ellen (6)	
Orson (5)		Elizabeth (22) *Spinster*		Warring, George (18) *Boot Closer*	1
Joseph B. (3)		Tranton, Sarah Anne (27) *Wife*	–	Warner, James (60) *Cottager*	1
Marion (1)		Turner, John (29) *Baker*	–	Webster, Frances (25) *Laborer*	–
Stones, James (30) *Coal Miner*	–	Jane W. (23) *Wife*		Westwood, Susan (55)	–
Mary (34) *Wife*		Sarah C. (11 mos.)		White, John (30) *Miner*	–
Hannah (9)		Tweedle, Elizabeth (21) *Spinster*	2	Mary Ann (28) *Wife*	
Sarah E. (7)		Upton, William (22)	–	Wilkie, Isabella (48)	–
John D. (5)		Mary (20) *Wife*?		Williams, Amelia (30) *Spinster*	–
Erastus I. (3)		Vaughn, Elanor (48) *Widow*	1	Williams, George (18) *Lamp Maker*	1
Tanner, Edmund (5)	–	Walker, Emma (21) *Spinster*	1	Wilson, Benjamin (40) *Miner*	–
Tanner, Mary (44)	–	Walker, William (25) *Moulder*	–	Mary (36) *Wife*	
Malinda (17) *Spinster*		Elizabeth (24) *Spinster*	1	Robert (10)	
Jane (15) *Spinster*		Emma (21) *Spinster*	1	William (6)	
Kate (7)		Wall, Joseph (17) *Stone Cutter*	–	John (2 ½)	
Harriet (6)		Sarah (16) *Spinster*		Catherine (59) *Widow*	
Tait, Elizabeth (23) *Wife*	–	Walters, Archer (47) *Joiner*	1	Wiseman, John (53) *Surgeon*	–
Mary Ann (11 mos.)		Harriet (47) *Wife*		Mary Ann (44) *Wife*	
Taylor, Elizabeth (53)	–	Sarah (18)		John Josh (4)	
James (39)		Henry (16)		Henry H. (11 mos.)	
Sarah (20)		Harriet (14)		Wright, John (48) *Miner*	–
Taylor, Joseph (44) *Laborer*	–	Martha (12)		Wright, William (22) *Clerk*	2
Harriet (49) *Wife*		Lydia (6)		Mary (25) *Wife*?	
Eliza (44)				Yumer {Sp.?}, Anna (30) *Spinster*	1

COUNTRIES

	Adults	Children	Infants	Total
England	252	56	14	322
Scotland	107	34	5	146
Ireland	15	1	1	17
Wales	13	5	0	18
Danes	2	0	0	2
Americans	8	0	0	8
Switzerland	17	2	0	19
India	1	0	1	2
TOTALS	415	98	21	534

"Elder Thomas Ferguson a returning Missionary to Utah is included in the above summary of American Emigrants, also Henry E. Chapell and Henry Bone in the English Summary and John Gilbraith in the Scotch Summary."

Class	Adults & 8 Years Up	Children Up to 8 Years	Infants	Total
P. E. Fund	332	84	15	431
Ordinary	79	14	6	99
TOTALS	411	98	21	530

Elder James Ferguson, President of the Company	1
John Gilbraith & Henry E. Chapell: Cooks	2
Henry Bone: Steward	1
	Total 534

"Memorandum, Ephraim Rowlands one of the Sailors, was member of the Church but not included in the above summary."

Elder James Ferguson, President
Edmund Ellsworth & Daniel D. McArthur, Counselors

*Names are from the British Mission Liverpool Passenger List taken from Emigration Records of the Liverpool Office of the Bristish Mission 1855-1856, found in the archives of The Church of Jesus Christ of Latter-day Saints, Libr. No. 1045 (CR 271/25, No. 2).[75] Any exceptions are identified by the symbols below:

* On Hafen's First Handcart Company List, but **not** on Enoch Train Passenger list.
** On Hafen's Second Handcart Company List, but **not** on Enoch Train Passenger list.
– On the Enoch Train Passenger list, but **not** on the lists of Handcart Companies One or Two. They may have remained in the east.

≈ *Deseret News*, "Ship Enoch Train, For Boston, March 23, 1856", published passenger list shows additional names or different spellings.
>From Journals and Diaries of Enoch Train Passengers. See the index to locate the source.

Figure 8: *Enoch Train Passenger List*

For the Passenger List of the *Samuel S. Curling*, please see Appendix D, pp.,143-158.

Figure 9: *Taking An Omnibus to the Train Station*

CHAPTER III

JOURNEY BY OMNIBUS, STEAMSHIP AND TRAIN TO IOWA CITY

BY OMNIBUS TO THE RAILROAD STATION. Soon the transportation for the railway station arrived, and by families the Saints headed down the gangplank through all of the activity on the dock and crowded onto the Omnibuses.

What an experience! People seem to be everywhere, carrying things, selling things, rushing back and forth doing what ever fits the lifestyle into which they have fallen. The noise and bustle is very much like the Liverpool dock, yet vastly divergent. There seems a much greater variety, from the ways in which people dress, to the attitudes they each uniquely radiate. They shine with a light, a message that says, "I'm different, I'm American". And above the noise and bustle can still be heard the music of the Birmingham band, standing on the deck of the Enoch Train, playing a lively tune.[1]

It wasn't hard to find the Omnibuses, once the dock had been reached. They were large, tall, roofed-in wagons with great wheels and bright paint, pulled by a strong team of horses that at present stood quietly and seemed unconcerned with everything around them. At the rear step-up area there was a man with a bushy beard, waving his arm in a circle, pointing at the entry, and calling, "Step lively now or we'll ne'er git' ya' ta' the train station on time! Step along! Step along!" In his waving hand he held a hat with a long feather in it, that trailed across the dock each time it made it's downward sweep. It was a bright and fuzzy feather that seemed to be frayed at every point, except where it stuck securely into the hat.

And every emigrant stepped more lively, herding their family and friends through the throngs of people and up the step into their bus, these special wagons with two long rows of seats, one on each side that ran the length of the bus. As they entered, everyone pushed as closely together as they could, filling every space, as well as resting children on the laps of anyone sitting down. Those who stood in the center isle held onto one of two overhead ropes strung next to the roof from one end of the bus to the other.

By 4 o'clock the first Omnibuses had been loaded and left for the railway station. Flying from the top of the first bus was a small American flag that fluttered in the breeze, as the horses pulled their load through the busy streets. A little flag, with white stars on a blue field in one corner, and alternating red and white horizontal stripes covered the remaining space. It is the symbol of this young nation, and the small beginning of a new way of life that will become greater and stronger as this people, who travel below it, move ever west to Zion.[2]

Five times the Omnibuses were loaded at the dock and driven to the train station. At 5:30 p.m., after all of the *Enoch Train* pioneers had been crowded onto a train at Boston Station, that began the first part of the overland journey that will continue for about 300 miles to Greenbush, New York.[3] Once underway, the passenger train traveled about 12 miles per hour, other than being quite crowded, it really didn't seem much different than the ones used in England.

It was a blessing to the people that the leaders had arranged for the movement and loading of luggage, etc. from the ship and sent it on to the train. The overwhelmed and exhausted emigrants had a hard enough time keeping track of their families and hand luggage in the various moves that were occurring. They were constantly concerned that someone might become lost or left behind as they passed through this strange, wonderful country. Right now it was enough to stay with the Saints, have faith in our leaders, and endure with hope that it will be over in a few days, and all can rest in Iowa City a while before starting the great trek west.

Figure 10: *Pioneer Passenger Train*

TRAVELING PIONEER PASSENGER CLASS ON IMMIGRANT TRAIN CARS

Due to a lack of information on the subject, not much can be described with absolute accuracy about the passenger cars used by the *Enoch Train* pioneers. Depending on the railroad, and the passenger class, the type of car would vary. James Stuart, in *Three Years in North America*, stated:

> "The cars were thirty to forty feet in length with aisles down the middle and seats arranged along the sides. 'The benches are like free seats in a church, with low backs, sometimes of padded velvet,'... ⁴

Charles MacKay, A European, obviously used to private compartments, found railroad travel difficult in the United States. In *Life and Liberty in America; Or Sketches of a Tour in the United States and Canada*, he concluded:

> "Without a proper place to stow away ones hat; with no convenience even to repose the head or back, except to the ordinary height of a chair; with a current of cold outer air continually streaming in, and ...with the constant slamming of the doors at either end of the car ...the passenger must, indeed, be 'dead beat' who can sleep or even doze in a railway car in America."⁵

Such things, however, did not tend to concern most of the Saints this early in their train journey. They were pleased to be moving again, pushing toward the conclusion of the second stage of their journey to Zion.

For the curious, even with a full moon that shone occasionally through the overcast sky, there was not much to be seen of the countryside at night. The daylight hours, on the other hand, revealed a rich green countryside; dark green woods; farms with freshly planted crops; log houses; wood frame houses; varieties of animals; and towns and villages that seemed to be thriving. With each new site, the Saints strained to see all they could out the windows as the train rattled down the track. Each wondered how this would compare with their Zion in the Valley of the Great Salt Lake. Would their woods be as thick and green? Would the ground be as fertile in which to plant their seeds? Would the rivers and streams be as plentiful? Would their houses be as large and grand as those they see out the windows? Would their cities and towns be as settled and polished, or would they be like what they had heard of frontier towns, dirt streets, few shops and stores, and everything built from rough hewed logs or prairie sod?

At Greenbush, New York, the train reached the Hudson River. Since presently there was no bridge over the Hudson to Albany, the Saints and their luggage were removed from the train and loaded onto the Steamer *Plymouth Rock*. The ferry then carried them across to a waiting train, where they would continue by rail to Iowa City, Iowa City.⁶ Successfully transferring all of the Saints from the train to the ferry was a bit of a task. This was minor when compared with the labor required to unload and reload all of the luggage, etc. going with them, only to repeat the process on the other side of the river.

The Saints had only been on board the *Plymouth Rock* a short time when a special visitor greeted them:

3 May 1856 - Saturday
"...At New York Apostle John Taylor came to the boat to talk to the Saints. He impressed us very much standing there so erect and tall. I noticed his long beard; he was ready to address us. Our attention riveted on his countenance, then he turned to our captain and said, `How long since these folks have had any refreshment?' `Two days,' was the answer. `Brothers and Sisters,' said John Taylor, `I should like to see you eat before I speak to you.' In less than half an hour bakers bread, steak and coffee were brought onto the ship. I had not thought about being so hungry until then. How nice this food tasted."

"Apostle Taylor spoke to the Saints and asked God to bless us with a safe journey to Utah...[7]

After receiving instructions and a blessing from the Lord's Apostle, all exited the ferry and loaded onto a train. This train's cars were of less quality than the first, being referred to as "immigrant cars":

"Mormons, because they almost always traveled in 'emigrant cars,' that is the cheap cars, rather than the first class and 'Palace' Cars, experienced most of the discomforts typical of mid-nineteenth century railroading. Among the standard problems were crowding (up to **84** in each car!), uncomfortable cars, poor, heating, ventilation, lighting, and sanitary facilities, inadequate eating conveniences, a lack of drinking water, noise, smells, jolting, shaking, vibration, fatigue, an abundance of dirt, lice, soot, sparks, smoke, fire, gamblers, thieves, tramps, drunks, marauding soldiers, impolite railroad personnel, 'mashers' who tried to 'take advantage' of women, few if any sleeping arrangements, loss of luggage, snow, ice, sickness, deranged saints, bad breaks, derailment, accidents, wrecks, poor equipment, ... deaths, and births–to name a few.

"Most sat up all night, few could afford berths or even rented pillows; some between connections slept in barns and warehouses, Brigham Young Jr. was delayed by snow: eating was catch-as-catch can—grabbing anything handy at short meal stops, buying things from 'butcher boys,' i.e. vendors on the trains, or from farmers and their wives at train stops."[8]

While immigrant cars had definite drawbacks to comfort, they were much preferred to cattle cars, complete with lice, that some companies of Saints were transported in to Iowa City. Those who traveled this way found their only comfort in sitting on luggage or boxes in the open air. Occasionally sparks from the engines caused fires that sometimes destroyed baggage. Then too, if their train happened to jump the track, that greatly increased the possibility of injury or even death.[9]

From Albany it was 350 miles to Buffalo, 180 more miles to Cleveland, a hundred miles to Toledo and 250 miles more to Chicago.[10] Most of the time it seemed like forever. Like time was standing still; that the babies seemed to constantly cry messages at one another from opposite ends of the passenger cars; that people never stopped talking, and some few that never ceased complaining. Rattling down a track that seemed to have no end with 79 others in close proximity caused one to join in with the general chaos of things; unless you were fortunate enough to be next to a window. Then you could loose all thoughts into the countryside, into memories stimulated by what one saw as the train passed. Of course, looking out the window did not always allow for a long escape, for the wind that came whistling in through the loose fitting "windows" was cold, and could in the early morning, late afternoon, and at night, make your body and mind numb quickly.

As the days and the miles rolled by the landscape and the scenery changed, but somehow seemed to blend into one another. Since the train track had been laid using a route that required the least amount of work and still go in the proper direction, it often meant traveling for long distances next to rivers or down areas that looked like they might once have been washes. When the light was just right, sunlight sparkled and exploded in short bursts of illumination that looked like swirling sunbeams. It was not unusual to see fish make great leaps from the water into the air to chomp down a dragonfly or some other insect passing close to the surface. Often boys on banks with willow poles were seen fishing under trees, and where the water was very wide and deep, an old man could be seen rocking back and forth in a boat with a fishing line hanging over the side sporting a bobber. Although it would probably never happen, it was fun to think that while he was asleep, some huge fish would come along and yank the line right out of his hand and scare him half to death. Oh, what tales he would then have to tell at home in front of the fire at night about the one that almost pulled him into the water.

Often stomachs rumbled with loud, empty sounds. It was a long way between stops and not all that much food available for everyone while the train rolled on. At the infrequent stops, people were allowed to get off the train to stretch their legs, and if they could afford it, buy food from the venders that were at the station platform no matter what time it was. Of course most were traveling on the Perpetual Emigration Fund, so they did not have extra money along to pay for food. They were grateful to get what the brethren could distribute, and thankful if they still had any food "squirreled" away from their time on the ship.

And you had to be careful if you got off the train that you did not stray too far away, because you never knew when the conductor would call "All Aboard", wave his lantern and the train would leave, belching huge puffs of smoke and soot. There was also the problem of keeping the women in sight and protected as there were very "low life" type men around the train stops who were constantly looking for a woman to use. Many of them would rob or hurt you and never have a second thought over it. We had been instructed to stay close together and watch out for one another long before we left the Enoch Train.

Then, of course, there was the frantic dash by most at each stop to find the "facilities" to relieve natures needs. Some of the passenger cars had "privy's", but even more did not. This of course was always a challenge when the train was in motion to satisfy such needs, as well as those that became ill and the needs to take care of babies and children not able to control themselves.

Lots of prayers were sent up by the Saints on these journeys, most as silent pleadings to help the individual and his or her family endure: another minute; another hour; another day. And thanks to the Lord for the peacemakers, the storytellers and those who could always make the best of every situation. For those who could sing loud and cheerfully, and were contagious enough to cause others to join in positive thinking and action. For those who were ready to take over the care of a child or a sick family member to allow those bearing the greatest burden and responsibility to rest, even if for a brief time. Double blessed are the obedient that remembered the second of the Lord's great commandments, to love a neighbor as oneself. They are they that will be most happy and comfortable in Heaven, for to live a Celestial life one most live the Celestial law, which is to be strictly obedient to all God's commandments and to be of service at all time and in all places to all people.

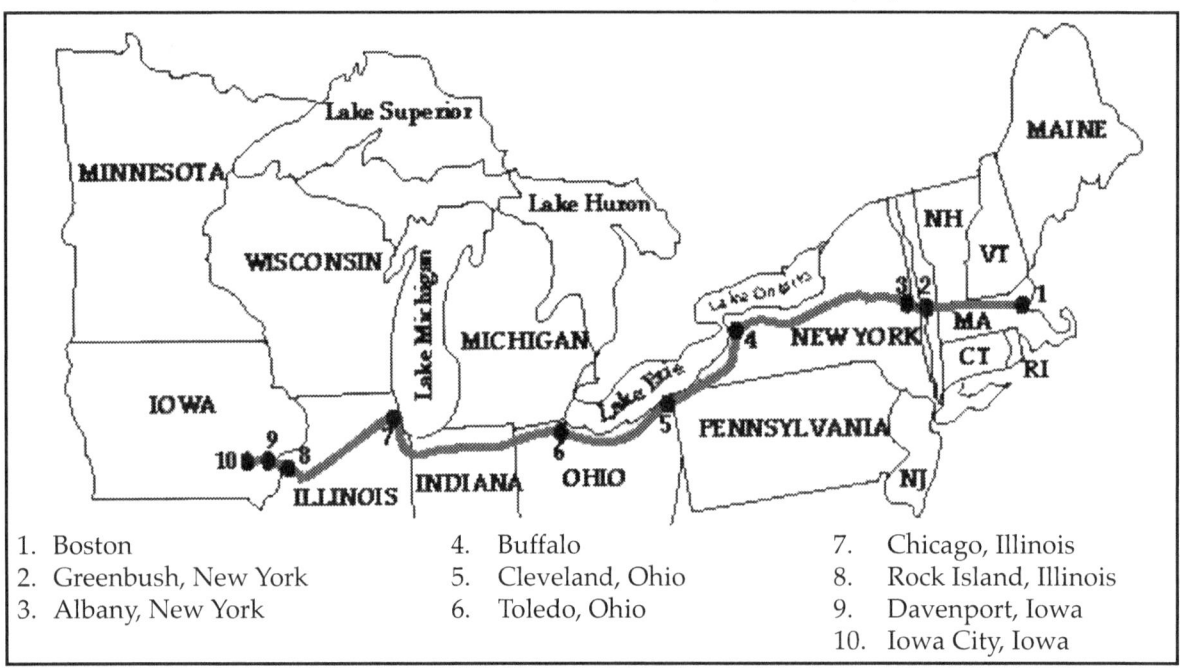

1. Boston
2. Greenbush, New York
3. Albany, New York
4. Buffalo
5. Cleveland, Ohio
6. Toledo, Ohio
7. Chicago, Illinois
8. Rock Island, Illinois
9. Davenport, Iowa
10. Iowa City, Iowa

Figure 11: *Enoch Train Pioneer Railroad Route from Boston to Iowa City*

WAITING TO CROSS THE MISSISSIPPI RIVER

In Chicago the Saints had to change trains for Rock Island, after a rather lengthy lay over. Departing at 11:00 p.m. on the Chicago and Rock Island Railroad, they traveled 246 miles, where they were scheduled to cross the Mississippi River on a bridge at eight o'clock. But the train arrived fifteen minutes late and was stopped. It was learned that a great wreck had broken the bridge with a train that had arrived just ahead of us, and they were unsure how long it was going to take to repair the bridge.[11] [Another report said the bridge had fallen when the previous trained passed over it.[12]] Since the railroad couldn't leave hundreds of people hanging around the station platform in Rock Island, Illinois, they allowed the travelers to stay in a storehouse near the station. After waiting around with no word from about 9:00 a.m. on Saturday, 10 May 1856, notification was received that it would be at least Monday before they would be able to cross the river.

The town of Rock Island, located on the Illinois side of the river, was considered to be a nice community, and a railroad town. It had to be tolerant of the railroad because of the problems with the bridge that began its crossing over the river here, and because it seemed constantly involved with travelers that had to wait whenever the bridge was damaged or some wreck occurred at the island in the river.

"...Rock Island and Davenport...are situated nearly opposite each other. Rock Island being in Illinois, a little below an island of the same name. The island is three miles in length and properly named. On its lower end is situated Fort Armstrong, built in the Black Hawk War in [1832].[13]

"Its [the bridge]... length will be 5832 feet, consisting of spans of 250 feet each, exclusive of bearings. The river is divided into two channels at this point by the beautiful isle, Rock Island. The main channel is on the Iowa side, the second channel upon the Illinois side of the river. That portion of the bridge over the main channel is 1583 feet in length. The circular shaped draw-pier, which stands near the center of the channel, is 40 feet in height, 46 feet in diameter at the foundation, and 37 feet at the top. On each side of the draw-pier is a draw of 120 feet, working on the rotary principle, making, in all, a clear space of 240 feet for the passage of river craft."[14]

Figure 12: *Waiting at the Train Station*

As the weary travelers tried to find some rest in a cold dark storehouse, Archer Walters paced back and forth trying to decide what should be done:

"We were very short of bread for the children, who had been crying for five days for something more to eat. In the storehouse we managed to fix the children some rice we had stored in our box, left over from our ship allowance. It made them a bit more satisfied, but not much. It seems that even with the best of intentions and planning, food shortages plagued the whole company. Of course, those who had money could buy a few things from the venders and farmers that were on the platforms when the train would briefly stop to take on water or passengers for the palace cars. But for most of us, we had a bit of bread that we had been carefully rationing out, and nothing more."

After watching her husband pace back and forth, varying shades of light and shadow dancing across his face, and knowing what was on his mind, Harriet Walters stood up and walked over to where she could put her arms about him. She turned him to her and looked hard into his eyes in the dim light leaking through the broken window. Startled by the boyish look of despair she saw there, she knew it was time to do something to improve the moment.

"Archer, since we will be here, at least until tomorrow, I'm going into town to see what food I can find to buy with our last two cents."

Suddenly tensing, he quietly responded with a firm, but controlled voice, "I'm not sure that would be wise, especially in a strange place that we know nothing of."

"Archer, our children are hungry and we must do something!"

"Then give **me** the two cents and **I'll** go," he said firmly.

"Not likely!" she muttered, and gave him a little poke with her index fingers, " I'm the bargain finder in this family and you know it. Stay here with the children and don't worry—God will protect me."

Just then, Edward Frost stepped out of the dark shadows of the warehouse, and approached the couple:

"Excuse me, I couldn't help but overhear your conversation. Here's fifteen cents to add to what you have. Maybe you can find some meat as well as bread, which will give the children much more nourishment and satisfaction."

"May God bless you forever Edward Frost," Harriet spoke softly with tears welling up in her eyes, "you're such a good and thoughtful man! I'll take your fifteen cents and I'll bring back enough to satisfy my five children and your two as well."

"God go with you Harriet Walters," Edward replied, "be careful, and may you find and deal only with kind souls that will understand and help your need."

Her husband Archer tugged on her arm and asked, "Are you sure that someone shouldn't go with you?"

"No, I shall be fine. Please just care for the children and pray for my success. I'll be back soon."

Turning quickly, she scurried out of sight, but did return in a short time with bread and meat enough to satisfy both families. She had found bread plentiful and cheap, which left more money for the more substantial and satisfying food Edward Frost, had mentioned. There was great joy in the hearts and stomachs of the Walters and Frost families as they had a moonlight picnic. The storehouse may have been dark and cold, but the light of their happiness and love lit up their little corner with a warm and radiant glow. [15]

On Monday, 12 May 1856, the Saints finally crossed the mile wide Mississippi River, but not as they expected, it was on a steamboat, not a train. And instead of staying together, they were divided into two groups, as the tug could only carry half at a time. The first group left at 8:00 a.m. and the second at 2:00 p.m.[16] This of course created a great deal of extra trouble and work, as all of the luggage, etc., safely loaded on the train from Chicago, had to be unloaded, moved to the dock at the river and reloaded on the boat. Then upon reaching the other side of the river, had to be unloaded from the ship and transported back to a train on the Davenport, Iowa side, where it was once again loaded for the remaining distance to Iowa City, the end of track.

LOADED ONTO OPEN BOXCARS TO TRAVEL ON TO RAILS END

The passenger cars for this last leg of the journey were open-air boxcars, where everyone sat on their hand luggage or on the dirty floor. Passengers were not one bit pleased to be in such circumstances and could be heard to complain loudly:[17]

"Please get your elbow out of my side, thank you! This is just awful being stuffed together in these cars like this. I'll bet there must be over 80 people per car. If it weren't for the fact there are no tops on these things, I'm sure we'd suffocate."

"Well they had to do something to get us all into the number of cars that the railroad provided. At least it won't be like this for long."

"Long enough! I understand that we won't be to Iowa City until sometime tonight."

"Yeah, and with those dark clouds overhead it will probably rain on us all the way there."

"Better start praying that the rain holds off, or we'll all end up like drowned rats."

"I don't feel very good, my stomach is churning, and my Mother and Father are back somewhere in the middle of the car!"

"Quick, move 'em to the outside, on the end of the row. Then if he throws up, he can lean over the side of the car!"

The sick passenger, who had been seated in the middle of the row, is pushed into a standing position and shoved along until he reaches the end of the row, where they wedged him back into a seated position. But that only lasted momentarily, as he quickly stands up with one hand over his mouth and the other holding his stomach, and leans over the side of the car. Suddenly a hand came out of the crowd behind him and grabbed the back of his belt to keep him from falling overboard. As his companions hear great retching sounds from over the side of the car, they look at each other and begin to feel a bit "green".

Finally, on Monday evening, 12 May 1856, the second part of the journey came to an end at about 3:00 p.m. with arrival of the first group at Iowa City, Iowa. The second group's train arrived about 10:00 p.m.[18] The 1300 mile trip, under less than luxurious circumstances, had made most everyone weary, but for the price of $10-11.00 per person, the brethren had arranged for the quickest and best transportation possible from Boston to Iowa City. And there were few that complained of the circumstances required in gathering to Zion. Such faith in their leaders now and in the future will bring these Saints to Zion in a shorter period of time, with less illness and loss of life, than any group of Saints that had thus far reached the Valley of the Great Salt Lake.[19]

The rain they had been concerned about was now falling and most of the Saints took shelter in the Iowa City Depot to wait out the storm. A few however, not wanting to wait one minute longer, took their possession in hand and walked the four miles[20] to the camp ground. [Walter's said 2 miles] There they set up tents in the rain and tried to stay dry and warm until the sun would finally come out on Wednesday. On Wednesday and Thursday, 14-15 May, the luggage was moved from the Iowa City depot to the camp using wagons and handcarts.[21]

McAllister said of the emigrant camp:

"...It was located on a beautiful hill about 3 miles from the center of the city. Plenty of food and water."[22]

Of course it was mainly a "tent settlement", with a few wooden buildings. The pioneers passing through stayed in tents, or in wagons, depending on their mode of transportation west, until they were fully supplied, their leadership organized, and all things were in order to depart. The *Enoch Train* pioneers were housed in tents, most of which they had made themselves aboard ship. These tents and the ones yet to be completed, would go with them on their journey across the plains and mountains to Utah.

Figure 13: *Steamer Ferry on the Mississippi*

Figure 14: *Emigrant Camp at Iowa City*

CHAPTER IV

WAITING & WORKING AT THE EMIGRATION CAMP NEAR IOWA CITY

Iowa City, Iowa certainly must be a nice little town, but to the hundreds of weary travelers confined to the railroad depot, because of the rain over the last two days and nights -- only the depot and what can be seen through the dirty windows is all that can be understood of it. Just as it had rained all Monday night, Tuesday, May 13th was no better. With all of the water that had fallen outside of the depot, those that had pressed on to the emigrant camp must be soaked by now to their skin. Several times during the day various people had gone out of the depot with the thought that the rain would let up and they could make it on to camp, only to be driven back to shelter.

Farmer's pray for a good soaking rain like this to help their crops. And it's good to fill up the rain barrels, cisterns, the lakes and ponds. But to the passengers from the Enoch Train who had spent so much hope and energy in reaching the "jumping off point" for their trek across the prairies and mountains to their new homes in Zion, it was just one more aggravation. One more delay. One more disappointment, but there were few that murmured other than the children who were hungry and tired of having to stay indoors. If they only knew how much time they would spend in the "out of doors" that lay before them, they would play more and murmur less.

The adults mainly spent their time discussing handcarts: how big are they, did they roll easy, how much weight could they carry and not be too hard on a man to pull....or was it push? Since this was the first handcart group to test Brother Brigham's challenge, there were none who could really speak with much authority on the subject. Could they move their carts and families at 15 or 20 miles a day? Someone said there would also be some ox driven wagons going along too, to carry the food, equipment and heavy items. However, since they would not be hampered with the usual problems of a wagon train, they should have no trouble in keeping up with the handcarts. But then someone raised the question of how many barrels of water they would carry to see to the thirsts of the handcart movers.... how many times a day they would stop to drink.... would they drink on the move.... how would each family get the water back and forth, and so on.... and so on..... and so on..... And no one had any answers yet, just lots of "I supposes".

Children were assured that they could do it and the elderly were comforted with promises of loving care and assistance. After all, they were the people of Zion. They were of one mind and one heart, and as there would be no poor among them, there would also be none left behind or uncared for.

As morning broke on Wednesday, 14 May 1856, a broad beam of warm sunlight cut between the clouds, bouncing and sparkling off the dew and rain hanging from the edges of the leaves, flowers and blades of grass. A fine mist puffed up from the earth and settled in little pockets here and there at the base of small mounds and higher places among the ever so slightly rolling knolls stretching out into the countryside. Birds were singing their wake up songs and the wind ever so gently shook the limbs and leaves of the trees, sending droplets of water in every direction, almost like mother nature was shaking herself dry. Bees were busy making their trips to the waiting flowers and insects were flitting from place to place doing the things that only an insect can really understand. Even the mosquitos were busy having breakfast at the expense of those who were still too sleepy to stop them. Across the floor of the depot, like fairy dust, shafts of light glistened through clean spots in the windows bouncing here and there like nature's alarm clock.

Then the loud blast of a steam whistle sounded on a train that was pulling away from the station, and no one from the youngest to the oldest was quiet any longer. Everyone was up and bustling about getting ready to leave for the camp. As hopeful as the majority were about reaching camp this morning, as they got underway the clouds moved on ahead of them, closing out the sunlight and replacing it's warm rays with a cold, drizzling rain. But it made no difference, wet or dry, the Enoch Train pioneers pushed on to the campground.

FROM RAILS END TO THE IOWA CITY CAMPGROUND
14 May 1856 - Wednesday
"A. M. Commenced hauling our luggage to camp on wagon and handcart. All were safely lodged in camp by 11 o'clock. Many wet to the skin, for it rained very fast. Brother Ferguson and I overtook a family and carried two of their little fellows into camp. It was located on a beautiful hill about 3 miles from the center of the city. Plenty of food and water."[1]

15 May - Thursday
"...The balance of our luggage came today."[2]

Those that had previously reached the Iowa City camp were already assigned to tents. Those that arrived in the rain were issued tents and set about the task of putting them up in designated areas. Most of the Saints were used to hard work and dealing with adversity, but few had ever put up a large tent before, and especially not during a rain storm. Fortunately there were enough brethren around that understood the process, that assisted the novices. But many a tent pole fell before it reached it's proper anchor spot, and many a tent peg pulled out of the ground that had not been properly set, before those assigned to the tent could go inside and prepare for rest.

The first few days in camp most every family was at one time or another soaked to the skin. The tents provided relief and protection from the storms, but until the luggage reached the camp, and was distributed, they had nothing dry to change into. If their blankets and bedding did happen to get wet, or they somehow managed to find a way to dry them out, they could wrap themselves up in whatever was usable until wet clothes could be wrung out and "dried". For most, it just meant staying wet and shivering everytime a cold wind found its way into the tent. Only the thoughts of a brighter tomorrow and their place in Zion kept them cheerful, along with words of encouragement from parents, family and friends.

The size of the tents were rather large, having been designed to be occupied by up to 20 souls, which generally meant 3-5 families. Each tent was placed under the supervision of a tent captain, and every five tents under the captain of a "hundred". According to Joseph Argyle, Jr., whose father was a tent captain in the first company:

> "The duty of the company captain was to look after everything in general to see that the company was provided with all provisions that they were able to carry and to assist in all that would aid for the betterment of the company. The tent captain was expected to give all of his time and attention to his company, to may sure that all allotments of one pint of flour for each person were given every twenty-four hours and to equalize as nearly as possible all labor, or to act as the father over his family."[3]

LIFE IN AND AROUND TENT CITY
While waiting at the Iowa City campground, regulations and tent life were much more relaxed than they would be once the pioneers hit the trail. Here they had tasks assigned to take care of their daily needs as well as making preparations to leave, such as sewing additional tents, making handcarts, etc., but things were not so centered on tent orientation as it would be on the trail. That didn't mean, however, that there were not some restriction, as Archer Walters explained:

> "Today, Tuesday, May 27th, I once again worked ten hours building handcarts for the journey. It was overcast, as it's been all day, and I remember thinking that we will probably get another big rainstorm; again tonight. Then it struck me as I was walking up the hill, that where the our tent was pitched, if the wind should come from the west tonight, it would flood us out again with a stream of water. I was so tired of waking up wet and listening to my family complain about all the work they would have to go through to get everything dry again, it struck me the problem could be solved by moving the tent to a better location.
>
> "When I reached the tent, I quickly explained my idea and asked who would help, and all said they would. So we hurriedly moved the tent to the new site and got everything in place before the storm began. That night we stayed dry and warm, but the next day I received a severe scolding from the brethren for moving the tent from its assigned spot without permission. I didn't care much for the reprimand, but at least they agreed to let me leave the tent in it's new location, which proved to be a blessing to all until we took it down to leave on the trek.

Of course illness was an occasion that sometimes necessitated tent reassignments to protect the other families in the tent.

15 May - Thursday
"Went to the same tent... Stil slept with the children that had the fever and could not be removed and I thought it hard but took it patiently."[4]

16 May - Friday
"Went to Iowa to seek work. The bosses was short of lumber and got no work. Come back to camp. Tent was down and we was moved to another tent. The children bad with fever still with us and another family of healthy put with us."[5]

17 May - Saturday
"Bro. Godsall was sent to look at the children bad with fever and he agreed with me that we ought to be separated, and I still loved Bro. Lee the same and we was separated. Bro. Lee made a tent to himself and it was better for both of us and all was right."[6]

The time had arrived, these Saints through the use of the Perpetual Emigrating Fund had been brought from England to bring to pass the fulfillment of Brigham Young's prophecy of a quicker and less costly way of gathering to Zion than by wagon train.

Handcarts were not a surprise to any of the Saints that had arrived in America aboard the *Enoch Train* and the *Samuel S. Curling*, for they knew what their means of transportation would be before they left England, and they came willingly and eagerly. They were to make up the first two handcart companies to cross the plains to Utah. What was a surprise, was that the handcarts that they had expected to pack up at the Iowa City campground and quickly depart to Zion, were not ready for them. They had to wait four weeks for their completion.

Because of the need to start their journey as soon as possible, those pioneers who had the skills and were qualified, were put to work making their own handcarts.[7] Others were assigned the tasks of completing and repairing tents; purchasing livestock; etc. Many went into Iowa City and the surrounding farms, seeking work and taking whatever they could find. The money, supplies and equipment that they earned being used to help them while they waited and later on the trail.

19 May - Monday
"Went into the city of Iowa. Short of lumber. Saw a chapel or church burnt down. They say they were preaching against us yesterday but perhaps they will learn better by this purifying by fire. Had some whiskey and water which took all my strength for it was so hot. Got to camp about ½ past 8 o'clock."[8]

20 May - Tuesday
"Went to work to make hand carts. Was not very well. Worked 10 hours. Harriet very poorly."[9]

2 June - Monday
"...Still working at the hand carts."[10]

There were two types of handcarts made, the flat cart and the family cart, both are similar in size and construction. When it's finished it will look something like a two wheeled version of a covered wagon, having the same width as a wide track wagon:

"Some handcarts were built in St. Louis, some in Chicago, and some by Mormon artisans at Iowa City. Their cost varied from $20 to less than $10 each. Lacking uniformity of materials and workmanship, the staunchness of the carts varied."[11]

"The open handcart was made of Iowa hickory or oak, the shafts and side pieces of the same material, but the axles generally of hickory. In length the side pieces and shafts were about six or seven feet, with three or four binding cross bars from the back part to the fore part of the body of the cart; then two or three feet space from the latter bar to the front bar or singletree for the lead man, woman or boy of the team.

"The carts were the usual width of the wide track wagon. Across the bars of the bed of the cart we generally sewed a strip of bed ticking or a counterpane. On this wooden cart of a thimbleless axle, with abut 2 ½ inch shoulder and 1 inch point, we often loaded 400 or 500 pounds of flour, bedding, extra clothing, cooking utensils and a tent. How the flimsy yankee hickory structure held up the load for hundreds of miles has been a wonder to us since then.

"The covered or family cart was similar in size and construction with the exception that it was made stronger, with an iron axle. It was surmounted by a small wagon box 3 or 4 feet long with the side and end pieces about 8 inches high..."[12]

The flat handcarts, instead of having raised sides, have strips of bed ticking or counterpane sewed across bars on the bed of the cart. Items are kept in place on the cart by throwing a cover over them and tying them down with rope.

Usually five people were assigned to each handcart, with two persons assigned to pull it. A father with a son of appropriate age and strength, and several smaller children, were allotted a covered cart. Onto each cart will be loaded 400 to 500 pounds of flour, bedding, extra clothing, cooking utensils and sometimes a tent (Although most tents were carried on the wagons.).[13] So as to not cause extra strain on the handcarts, each individual is only allowed a total of 17 pounds of personal items,[14] which included clothing and bedding, and possibly books, toys, antiques, shoes, a washboard, and tools for the father's trade or repair of the handcarts.

21 May - Wednesday
"A. M. Commenced weighing the handcart luggage. Evening held a meeting of the company, spoke to the saints. Brother J. [?] Hunt, Mr. Heaten[?], and T. Leonard made some very good remarks."[15]

To avoid leaving their extra clothing behind, which they were sure they would not be able to replace for some time in the Utah Valley, there were several people who wore extra clothing on their person until after their things had been weighed, then they planned to sneak them back onto their handcart. It worked for most quite well, but a second inspection, held at another time without any advanced notice, caught the excess weight and they were required to reduce their load to just the seventeen pounds each.

Earlier pioneers heading for Zion had to make choices about what they would take with them in the limited space of the covered wagons they used for travel. Many cherished items brought carefully from home on their ocean voyage, such as china, grandfather clocks, chest-o-drawers, fine clothing, etc., had to be sold in Iowa City and/or along the trail to make room for the real necessities like food, water and supplies desperately needed in the Valley, or to reduce the weight of the load the oxen, horses or mules would have to pull. They of course had much more room to transport their "fancies" than the handcart travelers, not that they really had very much to begin with being basically poor and assisted by the Perpetual Emigration Fund.

In some respects it was really advantageous to have to wait in camp a few weeks, because it gave us an opportunity to learn how to exist in the out of doors. For example, most of the ladies had never before been blessed to cook over an open campfire. To one minute have the flames licking up high around the pot and the next, because the wind shifted, having one half of the stew burning, while the other doesn't cook. Or try to ignite a piece of green wood, or have dinner boil over, causing great puffs of choking white smoke to sweep into the cooks lungs that resulted in coughing and watering eyes.

While it was true many had learned to cook over an open hearth in their homes, it was still different in the out of doors. For those who had used stoves or ovens in their homes, they had to learn how to do most everything "from scratch". How do you get an open-air fire started? What if the wood is wet? What if there is no kindling? What if?...What if?..., When there is no oven, how can bread be baked? When the only food being supplied to eat is not what you're used to eating, how can it be fixed to keep a hungry family happy? When cooking in a hanging pot over a fire, how high should the pot hang, or should it sit right on the flames/coals? What can be used to sweeten or season if nothing comes with the daily issue of food? How far should you go in sharing and/or swapping things with neighbors so that your own don't do without?

For a man who has never had to cut wood, or sharpen an ax, or shaped a handcart part or a new yoke for an ox team, how long does it take to learn to do it right? Or when you're assigned to care for the animals, who wants to look stupid because he's never milked a cow or hooked up a team of horses or oxen to a wagon. Some men were even asked to clean the rifles, when they've never seen one up close before. What happens when the day comes they are asked to use the rifles.... to load and shoot, to go hunting to bring home fresh meat? Or how about having small children around so much each day and night, when in the past you only saw them early mornings before work and the late evening before bed? And living with two or three other families in the same tent, where is privacy found? The other families are great people, but they must get as tired of having me around all the time as I am of them. How long will we be able to stay good neighbors? .....And the outhouses! With all of the complaints about them, what will they all do when they are in the open prairies and there are none? When are they going to explain that to us?

The children, bless their hearts, it's easy to see what a strain it is to have parents and adults around all the time, watching every action, hearing every word, and always wanting something done. Going to school for a part of each day helps, but for those that are older and have never been to school before, they are red faced embarrassed at having to learn to read and write about childish things like cats and dogs and balls and babies, and so forth. Every time they try to get off alone long enough to really be able to explore, or chase frogs, or catch fish, someone comes huntin' for them and then commences to make them feel guilty about being gone too long. And on and on, yaketty-yak......

And if you're at the age when you start discovering an interest in a cute companion, it's hard to find any way to "spark 'em" if you can never get off alone. About the only time you can hold a hand or ask a private question is at a dance when there is so much going on it's hard to watch everyone all the time. Of course a body can always try walking and talking on the side of the tent opposite the "door", but if any one is inside they can hear most every word, and with the sun out or a bright moon they make very interesting silhouettes. What's it goin' to be like on the prairie where they say there's not even a tree to step behind, unless you're close to a stream or a lake? At least in the mountains there will be rocks and gullies.

Another real challenge to the people was in keeping themselves and their clothing clean. There may have been a few tubs around that could be used for such things while at Iowa City campgrounds, but once on the trail it would become a real trial. Soap would not be in great supply, and access to a tub would be an improbability with a handcart company. More than likely any personal baths would be taken in a river or stream fully clothed. If they had some good lye soap they could rub it over their clothes, rinse off real good, and then wait until the sun dried them off. If they didn't get dry before the sun went down, they usually slept in damp clothes and hoped they didn't "sour" overnight.

As far as washing any extra clothing, etc., it would be done at the waters edge using a large rock. They would rub the soap over the cloth, work up a lather, and like the Indians had for centuries, beat the wet soapy clothing against the rock until it was judged to be as clean as possible. Then it would be rinsed several times in the water and rung out until it was felt that all the soap was gone. Wrung out once more it would then be hung on a bush or over a tree limb to dry in the sun. This process usually only took place at the evening camp, when there was enough time to handle the task while the tents and fires, etc. were being taken care of before the evening meal. If the cloth didn't dry before departure the next day, they could be laid over the top of the handcart to dry. If they for some reason got put away while they were still damp, it wouldn't take long until they had "soured" or "mildewed", which would mean they would have to be washed and dried all over again.

Figure 15: *Two Types of Handcarts*

SABBATH IN THE IOWA CITY CAMP

At least one thing never changed in camp and that was the Sabbath and the services held on the Lord's day. At the Iowa City campground they did not have a building to hold Church in, but like it was on board the ship, it wasn't the place but the occasion that was important. The Lord had established His Church and the proper method of worship that brought His Spirit to every righteous gathering at any location and under any circumstance. From some of the Saints journals:

17 May - Saturday
"A. M. Camp was regulated. P. M. President Daniel Spencer arrived, all were very glad to see him."[16]

18 May - Sunday
"Beautiful morning. Very warm. Camp meeting ½ past 10. Opened by singing. Prayer by Elder Ellsworth. Bro. Van Cott introduced Bro. Spencer. He spoke short. Elder Ferguson was called to address the meeting. He spoke some length upon polygamy. Bro. McAllister sung a song, 'The Good Honest Heart'; singing by

the Saints, Upper California. Benediction by Elder Godsall. Adjourned until ½ past 1 o'clock. Very attentive. Bro. Bunker addressed the meeting."[17]

"A. M. Very many visitors in camp. 2 o'Clock had meeting, Brother Spencer spoke a short time. Brother Ferguson then preached on the plurality of wives. Adjourned for one hour. ½ past one assembled again. Brother Ellsworth, Bunker and I addressed the multitude. Evening took a walk with Claude. E. G. Webb, the sisters Hardie, Burdett and Godsell...."[18]

25 May - Sunday

"Morning meeting. Bro. Godsall, from Birmingham, addressed the meeting. Meeting ½ past 2. Brother Webb spoke and someone had been speaking against us. He roared out like a lion and would of slain them with a look of his eyes and if any was honest in heart and had been guilty they must have trembled for he spared none."[19]

"A. M. By appointment from President Spencer, I presided over the meeting. Elder John Dogett?] preached the Gospel. P. M. Johnson T. Webb, very many strangers present, even had a meeting of the Saints, Brother Spencer addressed them. Ellsworth, Leonard and I made some remarks. Bore testamony, the same as Brother Spencer, the Spirit rejoiced exceedingly."[20]

1 June - Sunday

"Meeting ½ past 10. Bro. ___ spoke and Bro. Webb. Sarah still at the farm, Mr. Linley's. Henry went on watch to the cattle. The band played several tunes after the meeting."[21]

"A. M. My hands are so painful I cannot do meetings. Brother Ellsworth presided all day. Brother Daniel Tyler and E. G. Webb addressed the assembly. P. M. Brother J. Ferguson address, Saints and strangers felt well. Evening Elizabeth daughter of Constant and Ann H. Schroder and wife of Elizabeth White, born 26 March 1832, Kentucky, U.S.A., baptized by Elder James Holly, confirmed by Elder John Cooper. Alice Ellen Daughter[?] of Elias and Elizabeth White, born August 2, 1855 blessed by James Holly and John Cooper. [__?] baptized by John Edward Frost, confirmed by Elder John A. Hunt. George [?] and Ellen Bowing were re-baptized by Elder [__?]. After the baptism we had a meeting and President Spencer addressed the Saints. I was released from the Presidency of the handcart company to take charge of the Commesary Department. Brother Daniel D. McArthur succeeded me in the presiding of the company. Brother Daniel Tyler was unanimously chosen as bishop of the stake or campgrounds, Brother Daniel Spencer as first and James Ferguson second counselor. Several of the brethren addressed the Saints, all felt well. By order of President Spencer I married Arthur Maxwell and Elizabeth McArtland[?]."[22]

The Birmingham Band was playing this evening and it made everyone happy and full of joy. No one wanted to go to their tents or do anything else but listen to the music, to sing when they played what could be sung to, and to socialize with the Saints. And there is no group of people better at socializing than this people, for they all seem to want to talk and laugh and expound at about the same time. The elderly have seated themselves on chairs or what ever they could find, in little circles where they seem to bubble over with enthusiasm. And such bragging and carrying on, no one has ever seen the likes of. Lots of the Mommas and Papas have walked off for a stroll in the moonlight, and if they took the time to pay attention, they would find a few young adults and teens doing the same thing. Isn't it nice, just to be alone in your own little world, even for a short time, to experience again the feelings of love and belonging with just one other soul. To forget for even a few minutes responsibilities, chores, children, duties, meals, mending, lessons.....just hold that precious hand and walk in the moonlight, hearing only the sound of your own heart, the words of your special someone, the sounds of the frogs, the crickets, the peaceful creatures of the night on God's good earth.

There just never seems to be enough time for dancing and being carefree. For eating pies and goodies, for playing games and having fun. But when that time does come, the Saints know how to take the fullest advantage of it. And they do love to socialize, even if it's just sitting around the last glow of the campfire and spinning a yarn for people to laugh at or singing a song together before laying down a weary body for a nights sleep. A sleep that will end all too soon with the first rays of morning light when "everything seems to start all over again." It is most needful to take advantage of the warm and happy times to treasure up and think about in the days ahead when the road gets long, the sand gets deep and the sun tries to bake all the moisture out of your body. That will make it easier to sing the "Handcart Song" or "Come, Come Ye Saints" or just to smile and keep putting one foot in front of the other when you're too tired to go on, but know there's water and a resting place ahead, just "a little piece up the road."

WAITING TO CROSS THE PRAIRIE TO FLORENCE, NEBRASKA

On 24 May 1856, an independent **wagon** company was organized at the Iowa City campground. With all of the emphasis on getting the handcart companies going, it might seem a bit unusual that there would also be a wagon company leaving, but there were 6 wagon companies that traveled to Utah during 1856. All a part of the grand plan to gather the Saints to Zion.[23]

24 May - Saturday
"A. M. Brother Ferguson and [__?] left us, the former to Boston, the latter to Saint Louis. A company called the Independent was organized by Brother D. Spencer and [__?] Hodgett and chosen captain, John Cooper Clark, Davis captain of the guard. Brother Spencer addressed the company. Brother French[?] Hodgess[?] and myself made some remarks. All felt to rejoice in Mormonism...."[24]

During the four weeks of waiting and preparation, journals recorded births and deaths in the camp arrivign and departing according to their own schedule, just as they did on the *Enoch Train*. Here there were three births and five deaths:

16 May - Friday
"A. M. 4 o'Clock Sister Catherine, wife of Walter Granger, was delivered of a daughter. [?] was alive the day previously, named Elizabeth [?]. Adopted daughter of John Taylor died of croupe, age five months. The two were buried in the camps graveyard about a quarter of a mile from camp...."[25]

19 May - Monday
"A. M. 10 o'Clock, Sister Maria, wife of James Shinn, died of consumption. Age 60 years... Was very hot during the day and cold at night..."[26]

20 May - Tuesday
"...Sister Shinn was buried at 7 o'clock."[27]

27 May - Tuesday
"...In the evening Sister Jane, wife of John Fruge[?], was delivered of a son about 10 ½ o'clock. He named him William McAllister Fruge[?], Sister Hardie waited on her."[28]

30 May - Friday
"A child born in our tent ½ past one a.m."[29]
"A. M. At 2 ½ o'clock Sister Elizabeth, wife of John Lloyd, was delivered of a daughter named Martha. Waited upon by Sister Hardie."[30]

4 June - Wednesday
"...Made a coffin for a child dead in camp."[31]

6 June - Friday
"Made another child's coffin and a rough table for the Elders to eat upon...."[32]

Sickness in the camp was something that was with the *Enoch Train* Saints from the day they arrived. Many who had not been feeling very well during the train trip, found themselves much worse after being soaked in the rain as they traveled to the campground and had to sleep in wet clothing and bedding for a few days.

22 May - Thursday
"Harriet worse with what we are told is the American Fever. Sometimes like the Ague. Sarah went to Lindley's Farm to work and sent poor Harriet some milk and crust of bread."[33]

26 May - Monday
"Went to work. Harriet still very bad. Lightened very bad; began about 8 o'clock until 11 o'clock. Never saw it so in my life and it rained hard and our beds began to swim. I was wet on my side as I laid until I found it out."[34]
"... Evening we experienced a dreadful storm from the N.W."[35]

31 May - Saturday
"Martha began to be ill. Still at work at the handcarts. A meeting at night and we are to prepare for off."[36]
"Very busy all day. Suffered very much with boils which gave me great pain. Brother Spencer arrived at noon. Had a meeting in the evening...."[37]

For those mentioned above, as well as many others, the greatest of care was provided. They used whatever helpful herbs, foods and nursing techniques they possessed. But best of all was the administration of the priesthood and the marvelous cures and healings that took place because of this great power and the strong faith of the people.

On Sunday, 1 June 1856, another group of Saints arrived from Liverpool by way of Boston. They had traveled aboard the sailing ship *Samuel S. Curling*, and then had followed by train and ferryboat to Iowa City.[38] The Curling had 707 Saints on board and they too were scheduled to travel by handcart to Zion.[39] [Crandal put the number at 770.[40] One of the passengers, Mary Brannigan Crandal recorded in her journal:

2 June - Monday
"Busy all day. P. M. Captain Daniel Jones company which left Liverpool by the "S. Curling" arrived about 6 o'clock. The following returning missionaries were with him [J] L. Woodward and William Butler. The company generally healthy and excellent spirits, Brother David Grant came also."[41]

"We found tents pitched, men making handcarts, and women cooking out of doors. While waiting for the handcarts to be finished, three or four of us went to Florence and got sewing to do at five dollars a week and board."[42]

The *Curling* Saints were also very surprised to find that they were going to have to wait because the handcarts were still not finished. Some of them [74], however, did not have to wait four weeks, instead they were combined with those of the *Enoch Train*, being organized with 16 families with 47 people in the First Company and 7 families with 27 people in the second handcart company.

Two missionaries returning from England were called to lead these pioneers. Edmund Ellsworth was designated as captain of the First Company, and John D. McAllister, captain of the Second.

19 May - Monday
"...Evening a meeting was called, Brother Spencer presides. The company was divided into two handcart companies, Brother Edmund Ellsworth was chosen captain of one and I captain of the other. Several of the brethren spoke, all felt well and happy."[43]

20 May - Tuesday
"A. M. Called my company together and appointed Captain of the Guard and a clerk of the company, Henry Borin to the former office and William Wright to the latter. P. M. Brother G. D. Grant and William W. Kimballs arrived with cattle for our company...."[44]

It wasn't long before it was decided that John D. McAllister was needed more in Iowa City to handle the commissary for all of the groups and companies coming in, than he was as the Captain of the second company. As a result, Daniel D. McArthur, also a returning missionary from England, was appointed Captain in his place.[45] In a written report McArthur made to Wilford Woodruff once the company reached Salt Lake City, he stated:

"On the 19th of May, 1856, our company, which had crossed the sea with us, were divided, by President Daniel Spencer, into two handcart companies, Brother Edmond Ellsworth to take charge of the first and I, Daniel D. McArthur, to take charge of the second company. Then every move was made to get our carts ready, which job was a tedious one, but by using all our efforts, the first company was enabled to start on the 9th of June, and the second on the 11th, about 11 o'clock. This second company numbered 222 souls, and were bound for Florence, and from thence to the Valley.... Our carts, when we started, were in an awful fix. They moaned and growled, screeched and squealed, so that a person could hear them for miles. You may think this is stretching things a little too much, but it is a fact, and we had them to eternally patch, morning, noons and nights.... Our train consisted of 12 yoke of oxen, 4 wagons, and 48 carts; we also had 5 beef and 12 cows; flour, 55 lbs. per head, 100 lbs. rice, 550 lbs. sugar, 400 lbs. dried apples, 125 lbs. tea, and 200 lbs. salt for the company."[46]

FIRST HANDCART COMPANY

Edmund Ellsworth, Captain

Argyle, Joseph (37):
    Jane (33) (wife)
    Benjamin (12)
    Mary (10)
    Frances (5)
    Lorenzo (3)
    Priscilla (1)
Ash, John (36):
    Sophia (26) (wife)
    Ellen (1 2)
    Elizabeth (2 months)
Ash, Sarah (59) (widow):
    Joseph (8)
Bailey, James (53):
    Mary Ann (52) (wife)
    John (20)
    Thomas (19)
    Alfred (17)
    Mary Ann (15)
    Louisa (12)
Baker, Mary Ann (48) (widow):
    John (19)
    Emma (17)
    Job (15)
    Harriet (11)
    Wilford (4)
Baldwin, Hannah (18)
Bates, Mary Ann (21)
Birch, James (38):
    Mary Ann (29) (wife)
    Thomas (8)
    Mary Ann (6)
    Edward J. (2)
Birch, William (60):
    Elizabeth (40) (wife)
Bond, Samuel (61):
    Elizabeth (55) (wife)
    Samuel, Jr. (25)
    William (23)
Bourne, Thomas (59):
    Margaret (48) (wife)
    Mary Ann (22)
    Margaret (20)
    James (16)
    Priscilla (14)

    Louisa (12)
    John (7)
Bowen, David (18)
Bowers, James (45):
    Mary Ann (51) (wife)
    Sarah (18)
    Abraham (17)
    Isaac (14)
    Jacob (10)
    Isaiah (8)
    Shadrach (6)
Bridges, Charles H. (21)
Brough, Alice (69)
Brough, William (30)
>Bunney, John (28):
    >Ann (25) (wife)
>Butler, William (28):
    >Emma (25) (wife)
Chapman, John (58)
Chester, Ann (20)
Clark, George (55):
    Mary A. (51) (wife)
    Charlotte (18)
    William (14)
    Hannah (6)
Commander, James (35):
    Mary (25) (wife)
Devereaux, John (51)
    [*wife Esther?]
Doney, John (35) :
    Ann (24) (wife)
    Mary Jane
    (born on plains)
Eldredge[ridge], Thomas:
    *Charlotte (wife)
    –Child's name unknown
Ellsworth, Edmond (37)
Fowler, Thomas (19)
Franklin, Elizabeth (51)
Frisby, Absalom (21)
Frost, Edward (33):
    Eliza (26) (wife)
    Isabella (7)
    John F. (4)
Galloway, Andrew (28):
    Jane (25) (wife)
    Annie Eliza (3)

Goode, Maria (25)
Goodworth, Hannah (43):
    Joseph (19)
    Frederick (8)
    Richard (5)
Green, William (30)
Ham, Ann (31)
Hanson, George (26):
    Frances (25) (wife)
    Clara (11 months)
Harmon, William (52)
>Henwood, John (46):
    >Elizabeth (43) (wife)
    >Richard (19)
    >Elizabeth (16)
Hill, Eleanor (40)
Hunt, Abraham (30):
    Eliza (30) (wife)
Hurst, Abraham:
    –Wife's name unknown
Ivins, Thomas (70)
Jeffries, Eliza (21)
Jones, Daniel (41):
    Ann (36) (wife)
    Rachel (16)
    Ann (14)
    Daniel (12)
    Marion (7)
    Richard J. (3)
    Sarah (1)
Jones, James (56) :
    Sabina (36) (wife)
Jones, Mary Ann
Kettle, John (53),:
    Judith (43) (wife)
    Mary Ann (18)
    Robert (14)
    Eliza (12)
    James (9)
    Samuel (5)
    Hannah (2)
Lee, John (33):
    Sarah (33) (wife)
    William (12)
    Fanny (11)
    Elizabeth (9)
    Samuel (5)
    Chauncey (3)
    Sarah Ann (9 mon.)

>Lewis, Jane (29) Mrs.
Lewis, John (33):
    John S. (8)
Lloyd, Benjamin (23)
Lloyd, John (38):
    (dropped out, June 20)
    Elizabeth (38) (wife)
    Mary (11)
    John (10)
    William (8)
    Thomas (5)
    Jane (2)
    Martha (4 weeks)
>Lloyd, Thomas (24):
    >Benjamin
>Marshall, Sarah (34):
    >Lavinia (12)
    >Selina (10)
    >Tryphena (8)
    >Louisa (6)
    >George (4)
    >Sarah (2)
Mayo (Mays), Mary (65)
Meadows, Mary Ann (21)
>Miller, Sarah T. (or J.)
Morris, William (53) :
    Sarah Ann (53) (wife)
Moss, Henry (19)
>Moyle, John (48):
    >Philippi (40) (wife)
    >Elizabeth (19)
    >Stephen (15)
    >Henry (12)
    >Alfred (9)
    >John (5)
Murray, James
Nappriss, George (23)
>Oakley, John (36)
Passey, Thomas (18)
>Phillips, John A. (22)
Powell, John (43):
    Elizabeth (35) (wife)
    William (15)
    Mary (13)
    Margaret (8)
    Anna (4)
    David (infant)
Pratt, William (31):

Caroline (31) (wife)
Eleanor Saline (12)
George (9)
Orson (3)
Emily (1)
Preater, Richard (29):
　Mary (31) (wife)
　Salome M. (4)
　Lora I. (2)
Price, Ann (46):
　Emma (19)
　Eliza (17)
Rasdell, Joseph (John) (20):
　Elizabeth (22) (wife)
Richins, Thomas (30):
　Harriet Devereaux (22) (wife)
　Albert Franklin (1 mon.)
Robinson, Eliza (26)
Robinson, John (46):
　Emma (27) (wife)
　Elizabeth (21)
　Sarah (19)
　John (16)

Clara (10 months)
Sanders, Walter (65):
　Mary (19)
　James (15)
　John (13)
　Thomas (10)
Sheldon, Richard (19)
Shinn, James, Sr. (60):
　Hannah (22)
　Ellen (19)
Shinn, James, Jr. (26):
　Mary (24) (wife)
　Sidney (6 weeks)
Shinn, Robert (28):
　Eliza (28) (wife)
　Mary (7)
　Louisa Eliza (6)
　Ann (4)
　Emma (3)
Sprigg, Sarah Ann (18)
Stalley, Peter
Stevenson, Alexander:
　Magdalene (35) (wife)

Isabella (27) (dropped out July 10)
John (13)
Magdalene (11)
Alexander (7)
Orson (5)
Joseph B. (3)
Marion (1 2)
>Stoddard, Robert (51):
　>Margaret (44) (wife)
　>James (14)
　>Mary (10)
　>Dinah (5)
>Stoddard, William (42):
　>Margaret (37) (wife)
　>Caleb (18)
　>Robert (16)
　>Jane (12)
　>Sarah (10)
　>Hannah (8)
　>Mary (3)
　>Margaret (1)
>Taylor, Elizabeth (24)

Vaughan, Eleanor (78)
Walker, Elizabeth (17)
Walker, Elizabeth (24)
Walker, Emma (21)
>Walker, Henry (58):
　>Isabella (50) (wife)
　**Children, unknown #
Walters, Archer (47):
　Harriet (47) (wife)
　Sarah (18)
　Henry (16)
　Harriet (14)
　Martha (12)
　Lydia (6)
>Warner, James (60):
　**Ann (49) (wife)
　**Sarah Ann (14)
Wareing, George (18)
Welling, Job (23):
　Frances E. (25) (wife)
　Job (1 2)
Williams, George (18)
>Yeo, William

TOTALS:
Families..............................95
Individuals....................278+

*On Enoch Train's Passenger list, but not on Hafens First Handcart Company list.

**Taken from Journals not found on Hafen's list.

>Passengers from Samuel S. Curling

**On Hafen's list, not on Liverpool Passenger List

[Taken from Appendix M, Roster of Members of the Handcart Companies, First Company Roster, Hafen's Handcarts To Zion, pp. 277-281. Their list was compiled from information found in the L.D.S. Historian's office and other sources.]

Stanley B. Kimball in Historic Resource Study Mormon Pioneer National Historical Trail, page 143 shows: 275 people; 52 handcarts; a few wagons [probably 4]; 9 Jun 1856 – left Iowa City, Iowa; 26 Sep 1856 – arrived Salt Lake City;

Figure 16

SECOND HANDCART COMPANY

Daniel D. McArthur, Captain

Aitken, William K. (35):
    Cecilia (14
    Thomas (10)
Anderson, Agnes (52):
    Archibald (20)
    John (16)
    James (14)
**Arthur, ——, and family
    (dropped out June 30)
Baranigan, Mary
Bathgate, Mary (59):
    Mary (12)
Bell, John (54):
    Maria (55) (wife)
    James (17)
    Samuel (15)
>Bermingham, Patrick (26):
    >Elizabeth Kate(24) (wife)
    >Mary Katherine (4)
    >Edward J. (3)
    >Jane E. (infant)
Bone, Mary Ann (10)
Bowring, Henry E. (33):
    Ellen (18) (wife)
    Wallace (4)
Bruner, Susannah (66)
Burdett, Elizabeth (65)
Burdett, Emma M. (19)
Chambers, David (54):
    Mary (54) (wife)
    David, Jr. (14)
Clotworthy, Hugh (29):
    Jean (36) (wife)
    Janet (9)
    Mary (7)
    Thomas (3)
    Jean (2)
    Margaret (2 mon.)
Crandall, Spencer
Crawford, James (23)
**Dechman, James
Dorrech, Elizabeth
Downie, Margaret (30)
Dreaney, John (31):
    Mary Jane (28) (wife)
    Samuel (22)
    Isabella (4 months)
Eardley, Bedson (23):

    Louisa (27) (wife)
Elliker, Heinrich (59):
    Margarethe (54) (wife)
    Heinrich, Jr. (26)
    Barbara (24)
    Elizabeth (22)
    Konrad (20)
    Margarethe (18)
    Susanna (14)
    Jonannes (13)
>Finlay, William (49):
    >Lindsay (48) (wife)
    >Ann (17)
Frew, John (30):
    Jean (35) (wife)
    James (8)
    Janet (7)
    Mary (12)
**Furrer, Anna
Gale, Mary (47)
**Gallop, Thomas (39):
    Agnes (36) (wife)
Gardner, Ann (48):
    Agnes (20)
    James (18)
    Alex. (16)
    Elizabeth (14)
    Walter (8)
Grainger, Walter (34):
    Catherine (36) (wife)
    Robert (14)
    Alexander (9)
    Catherine (7)
    Walter (5)
    John (4)
Gray, John (51):
    Jane (51) (wife)
    Jane (22)
    Franklin (4)
    Mary (2)
    William (5 weeks)
Hall, William (29)
Hardie, Janet (45):
    Phyllis (23)
    Agnes (21)
    John (15)
    Grace (13)
    James (10)

Hargraves, Samuel (39):
    Agnes (33) (wife)
    Jane (16)
    Mary (13)
    Janet (10)
    John (8)
    Elizabeth (3)
    Margaret (12)
    *Enoch Train (infant)
Hey, Mary (34)
Heaton, William (28):
    Esther B. (25) (wife)
    Christopher B. (3)
    William McD. (5 mon.)
Hillhouse, William (46):
    Margaret (52) (wife)
    Janet (24)
    John (22)
    Mary (15)
    Robert (13)
    David (11)
    Elizabeth (6)
    William (2)
    Janet (1 month)
Hodgetts, Hannah (18)
Ipson, Niels Peter (22):
    Georgina Keller (27) (w)
Johnstone, George (36):
    Janet (14) [?24] (wife?)
    Isabella (4)
    *Hamilton (infant)
Johnston, William (29):
    Elizabeth (21 [?]) (wife)
    David (7)
    Richard (5)
    William (3)
Kennington, Richard (52):
    Mary (47) (wife)
    Sarah J. (17)
    William (14)
    Eliza (12)
    Richard (10)
    Mary A. (1 2)
>Lawrensen, William (55):
    Ann (50) (wife)
    Jane (18)
    Maragaret (11)
Lawson, William (29)

Leonard, Truman
>Lucas, Anthony (58):
    >Mary (57) (wife)
    >Eliza (26)
    >Ann (21)
    >Mary (14)
>Lucas, Thomas (25)
Ludert, Josephine (43):
    Alphonse (6)
McArthur, Daniel D. (36)
    [Company Captain]
>McCleave[McClane], John (48):
    >Nancy (40) (wife)
    >Margaret (17)
    >Mary Jane (15)
    >Isabella (13)
    >John T. (11)
    >Joseph S. (8)
    >Eliza (6)
    >Alexander (2)
McDonald, Alexander (26)
McDonald, John (24)
McDougall, Joseph (25)
McGowan, Mary (29)
*McLane, Mr.
Mathiasen, Mary (21)
Maxwell, Elizabeth (52):
    Arthur (30)
    Catherine (25)
    Elizabeth (23)
    Ralph (18)
    Ann (14)
Meikle, Margaret (57):
    William (30)
    Isabella (19)
    James (17)
>Morehouse, Elizabeth (30)
Muir, George (23):
    Margaret (26) (wife)
    Mary (2)
    Jean (1)
    *Unnamed son (infant)
Park, Isabella (62)
Parker, Robert (35):
    Ann (36) (wife)
    Maximillian (11)
    Martha A. (9)

Arthur (6)	>Reed, Elizabeth (20)	Sanderson, Rebecca (41):	Unnamed child
Ada (8 months)	Reid, James (39):	Sarah Ann (11)	Unnamed child
Peacock, George (30):	Elizabeth (31) (wife)	Rhoda (9)	Tweedle, Elizabeth (21)
Mary Ann	Elizabeth (11)	Schies, John (39)	Wandles, Ellen (28):
George, Jr.	James (6)	**Anna	Ellen (6)
Ramsay, Ralph (32):	Mary (4)	Unnamed wife	Wright, Maria (25)
Elizabeth (33) (wife)	John (1)	Shields, Elizabeth (26)	Wright, William (22)
John S. (15)	Richardson, Elizabeth (or Eliza) (33)	Smart, Sarah (26)	
*Unnamed daughter (infant)		**Smith, Anaki	TOTALS:
	Richardson, Peter (24)	Smith, Andrew (28)	Families............................80
Randall, Anna M. (31):	Russell, Ellen (23)	>Stewart, Agnes:	Individuals..................221+
Oscar J. (12)		Unnamed child	

[Taken from Appendix M, Roster of Members of the Handcart Companies, Second Company Roster, Hafen's Handcarts To Zion, pp. 277-281. Their list was compiled from information found in the L.D.S. Historian's office and a few other sources.]

>Were not on the Enoch Train passenger list. They are assumed to be from the Samuel S. Curling.

>Passengers from Samuel S. Curling

**On Hafen's list, not on Liverpool Passenger Lists.

Standley B. Kimball in Historic Resource Study Mormon Pioneer National Historical Trail, page 143 shows: 222 people; 48 handcarts; 4 wagons; 11 Jun 1856 – left Iowa City, Iowa; 26 Sep 1856 – arrived Salt Lake City

Figure 17

PREPARING THE HANDCART COMPANIES TO LEAVE

There seems to be some disagreement with the number of covered wagons that accompanied the two handcart companies. McArthur states above that he had 4, other sources list 3 per company, while others give 5 for both companies. What we do know for certain is that they were pulled by oxen and that a number of them were assigned to accompany each handcart company, to carry food, tents, supplies and equipment. These wagons were also used to carry those that become extremely sick or might be injured along the way. There was some concern voiced by the leadership that the wagons would tend to slow them down, but there was no other ways to transport their supplies. The wagons of the first company likely also carried instruments for the Birmingham Band which was a part of their company, as there was not be room for on them on the handcarts. The men who are responsible for the wagons also had the assignment of supervising the livestock, which was another reason they were not always able to move as quickly as the Captains of the companies wished.

The new experiment, however, did not present a picnic prospect to some. There are those who weaken and withdrew from the ranks along the way, while others hesitated on the borders of the plains to undertake the journey at all. One family proclaimed at the sight of the handcarts:

"We think it will be better to remain here [Iowa City] or at St. Louis for a time until we are able to help ourselves to a wagon. Mother says that she must have a revelation before she can see this right. Why we would have to sell nearly all our clothes! And what shall we do for things to wear when we get to the Valley? Seventeen pounds weight each is but very little."[47]

But most did not hesitate, they were anxious to leave, to get away quickly to Zion.

Throughout the 4 week period of waiting, there were frequent downpours of rain and thunderstorms, sickness, babies born, deaths and all the usual things that occur when over 800 people are quartered together in a "tent village" in a waiting situation.[48] All were anxious to be on their way, but through no fault of their own, were required to wait patiently. Here begins some of the trials and tempering of the first handcart companies of Saints, as they are shaped and polished in the Refiners fire .... all a part of God's people being gathered and proved as they pass through the wilderness to Zion.

3 June - Tuesday

"A. M. Captain Ellsworth and McArthur [?] very pressing to leave for the bluff on their way to the valley. Brother Olsey[?] and Butler were appointed to go with Brother Ellsworth. Brother Leonard and Crandall with Brother McArthur. Brother Joseph France was appointed to go ahead and make all necessary arrangements between Iowa and the bluffs for provisions. [?}"[49]

5 June - Thursday

"All expect to go with our hand carts. I was liberated from working and my tools to go with us to do repairs on the road."[50]

Those Listed On Liverpool Mission Office Enoch Train Passenger List
NOT SH0WN AS BEING IN THE FIRST OR SECOND HANDCART COMPANIES

Ballam, Anna
Banks, Mary
Bascleo, Henry
Bauer, Alois
Baxter, Henry
   Agnes
      Magdalon
   Catherine
   June
      Agnes
Black, Nicholas
   Elizabeth
   Eleanor
   Nicholas
   Elizabeth
Bleak, James
   Elizabeth
   Richard
   Thomas
   James
   Mary
Boden, Mary
Bone, Henry
Boynham, Elizabeth
Brazier, George
Brazier, John
Brenchley, Caroline
Broderick, Thomas
   Elizabeth
   John H.
Brooks, Nathan
   Betty
   Alice
Brown, Christianer
Bryner, Ulrich
   Marian
   Marian
Carr, John
   Sarah Ann

   Arthur J.
   Henry
   Walter H.
   Marian M.
Chapell, Henry E.
Chetwynd, Maria
   [Listed twice]
Clough {Sp.?], Moses
Cooper, John
Crump, Charles
   Charles
   James
   Sarah Taylor
   Elizabeth Taylor
Dale, Ann
   Emma
   Eliza
   Sophia
   Anne
Darroch, Elizabeth
   [See E. Maxwell]
Davis, Elias
   Ann
Donald, John W.
Duncan, Catherine
Durham, Thomas
   Mary
Edwick, William
Fairclough, Ann
Ferguson, James
Ferney [Sp.?], William
Findlay, Mary
Franks, Sarah
Galbraith, John
Gardner, William
Goble, William
   Mary
   Mary

   Edwin
   Caroline
   Harriett
   James
   Fanny
Godsall, John
   Mary
   Louisa
   Susanna
   Frances A.
   John
Granger, Catherine
Grant, Elanor
Grant, Susan
   Thomas
   Elizabeth
Haley, John M.
   Hannah
   Amelia
Hanna, Henry
   Catherine
   Agnes
Harvey, Emma–
Hawkins, William –
   Elizabeth
Hemming, Jane–
Hicks, John –
   Harriet
   Robert Rowe
   Charlotte J. Rowe
   Charlotte E.
Hick, Thomas–
Hollsworth, James–
   James
Holly, James –
   Lucy
   Ann
   James

Holt [Sp.?], Robert –
   Ellen
   Margaret
   James
   Daniel
   Alice
   Joseph
   Martha
Hughes, Samuel –
   Emma
Hunt, John A.–
Jackson, George –
   Ruth
   Herbert
   George
   Ellen
   Sarah Ann
   Susanna
Jones, Esther–
Jones, Hannah–
Jones, Thomas–
Jones, William –
   Mary Ann
   Robert
   Louisa
   Frederick
Kcors [Sp.?], Mary Ann–
Kelly, John –
   Mary
   John C.
Lacing, Elizabeth–
Langman, Rebecca–
Lawrence, Samuel –
   Harriet
   Henry
   Harriett
   George
Leiseley, Alice –

Ann
Lister, James –
   Ann
   Dinah
Lucas, Mary –
   William
Lyons, Thomas –
   Mary Anna
   Jennie
   Jessie
   Mary
     Christina Enoch
     (born 3/21)
McAllister, John D. T.–
McAuslin, Elizabeth–
McMannis, Joseph –
   Margaret
   Margaret
   Mary
   Janet
   Margaret
Martin, Eliza–
Mayoh [Sp.?], Peter –
   Ann
   Mary
   Noah
Merchant, Caroline–
Middleton, William –
   Ann
   John
Midgeley, Joseph–
Miller, James–
Mirrin [Sp.?], Margaret–
Moss, John–
Muir, Edward F.–
Nash, William–
Newman, Henry –
   Mariah L.
   Maria L.
   Henry I.
Oliver, Ann–
Ord, Thomas–
Page, William–
Parker, Mary Ann–
Parson, Elizabeth–
Peel, Frances–
Petty, Edward–
Pilgrim, Rebecca–
Player, Joseph –
   Ann
   Elizabeth
   Emily

Alfred
Pope, George –
   Jane
   Franklin
Porter, Nathan T.–
Richardson, William –
   Maria
   William H.
   John H.
   Mary
Roper, Charles –
   Catherine
Rowland, William –
   Elizabeth
   William
   John C.
   Harriet
Rowlands, Ephrain–
Rowley, John –
   Isabella
   James
   William
   Margaret
   Isabella
   Sarah
   Mary
   Joseph
   George
Salisbury, Ann –
   William T.
   Henry
   Joseph
Senior, Thomas–
Smith, Amelia–
Smith, Isaac –
   Charlotte
   Charlotte
   Benjamin
   Emily
Smith, John–
Smith, Mary–
   Emma
   Robert
   Ester E.
Smith, Sarah Ann–
Smith, William –
   Charlotte
   William Jr.
   Charles
   George E.
Sounds [Sp.?], William

[Family]
   Sarah
   Esther
   Jacob
Spiers, George –
   Janet
   William
   Janet
   Agnes
Stephens, Ann–
Stewart, Nancy –
   Jane
   Matilda
   Margaret
   Anne
Stones, James –
   Mary
   Hannah
   Sarah E.
   John D.
   Erastus I.
Tait, Elizabeth –
   Mary Ann
Tanner, Edmund–
Tanner, Mary –
   Malinda
   Jane
   Kate
   Harriet
Taylor, Elizabeth–
   James
   Sarah
Taylor, Joseph –
   Harriet
   Eliza
Titt, Richard –
   Ann
   Elizabeth
Tranton, Sarah Anne–
Turner, John –
   Jane W.
   Sarah C.
Upton, William –
   Mary
Walker, Emma–
Wall, Joseph –
   Sarah E.
Webster, Frances –
Westwood, Susan–
White, John –
   Mary Ann

Wilkie, Isabella–
Williams, Amelia–
Wilson, Benjamin –
   Mary
   Robert
   William
   John
   Catherine
Wiseman, John –
   Mary Ann
   John Josh
   Henry H.
Wright, John–
Yumer {Sp.?}, Anna–

TOTAL
   316 People
   131 Families

Figure 18

Phase Three:

CHAPTER V

HANDCARTS WEST TO FLORENCE (WINTER QUARTERS) THE GREAT HANDCART EXPERIMENT BEGINS

THE FIRST HANDCART COMPANY LEAVES FOR FLORENCE, NEBRASKA. **On Saturday, 7 June 1856, all was in readiness and the 264+ souls of the First Company commenced their journey of 1,300 miles to the Valley of the Great Salt Lake.[1] After getting everyone placed in their assigned traveling position, the Saints stepped off with great strength and excitement. On this first day they managed to travel 60 yards before they stopped to camp for the night, a camp at which they remaining for a part of Sunday. After the meetings were over, being anxious to make up for their poor showing of the first day, they loaded up, lined up, and journeyed 3 miles before again stopping to set up camp. But their travel efforts on the Sabbath turned out to be non-productive, as they set up camp among the brush where they did not rest very well. Their cattle wandered off during the night and became lost taking them until Tuesday night to track them down, as they had gone all the way back to the old campground.[2]**

When the men had not returned with the cattle by 5:00 p.m. Monday afternoon, it was decided the company should move on without them. The searchers could follow their trail and catch up with them at the next campsite.

9 June - Monday
"At 5 p.m. the handcarts were in motion, proceeding Zionward (from the camp ground west of Iowa City). The Saints were in excellent spirits. The camp traveled about 4 miles and pitched their tents for the night."[3]

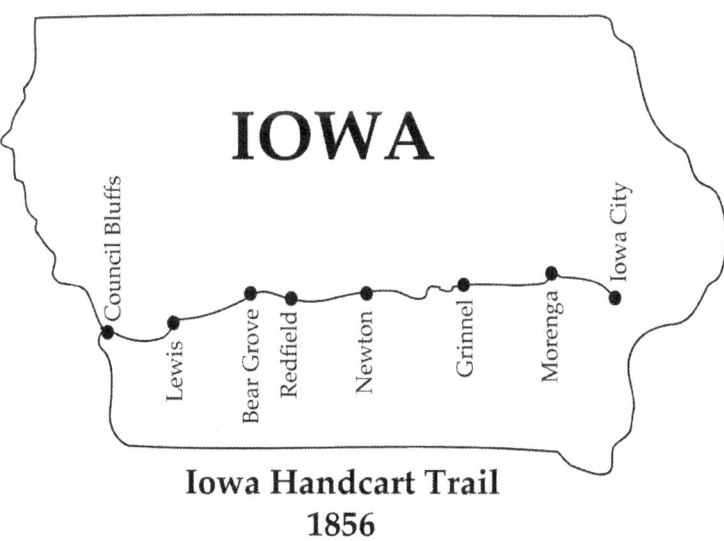

Figure 19: *Iowa City, Iowa to Florence (Winter Quarters), Nebraska*

Tuesday, the immigrants remained in camp all day, partly because the men had still not returned with the missing cattle, but also because three yoke of oxen had strayed away. Several more brethren were assigned to hunt for the oxen. It might seem like some type of "bad luck" had attached itself to the first handcart company, but none of the pioneers looked at it in that light. They had been told by their leaders that there were many things that they would need to learn in their journey across Iowa to prepare them for the more difficult part of their trek from Florence, Nebraska [Winter Quarters] to the Salt Lake Valley. This was the "shake down" part of their sojourn and they would learn many valuable lessons. It appeared the first lesson would be about better stewardship over their animals.[4]

During the wait, several of the Saints were given the assignment of tightening and adjusting items on the new handcarts. There were also many discussions and demonstrations on more effectively packing the handcarts; starting and caring for cookfires; more efficient ways of setting up and taking down tents; and picking good campsites. Of the latter there was not such a great concern, as they were traveling a trail that frequently passed by homes and small settlements in Iowa, and from Florence to Salt Lake they had a copy of *The Latter-day Saints' Emigrants' Guide: Being a Table of Distances, showing all the Springs, Creeks, Rivers, Hills, Mountains, Camping Places, and All Other Notable Places, From Council Bluffs, to the Valley of the Great Salt Lake*.[5] (See the Appendix for the full text.) This publication having been available and in use by pioneers since it's first printing in 1848.

Early on Wednesday morning, 11 June, the oxen were brought into camp, and by 8:00 a.m. the company had moved out on their daily trek. Instructions were carefully given to those who would be caring for the animals on the move, as there was no desire to be held up again by repeating the same mistakes. The brethren who brought the strays in didn't get a chance for any rest, but they did not complain. They seemed to be happy that everyone was enthusiastic about moving on.

There, uncoiling before me, and moving off down the trail, was a long line of handcarts. It's funny how much they remind me of a beautiful snake I once watched slithering away at my approach. The snake was sectioned in different colored band that rippled in its sway from one side to the other. The handcarts too were in sections, but their colors all seemed pretty much the same and the noise that came from the carts would have driven any snake in its right mind a long ways away in a hurry. It must be because the wheels and axles are all so new they are rubbing against places that in a few days should be worn smooth. But then, it might be because there had been no grease put on them to make them run smoothly.

It's a very dusty day and every wheel that's turned, and every foot that's moved, causes fine particles of dirt to fly up and be pulled back down by gravity to rest on anything that is available. Those in the front are not having such a hard time, but the farther back one moves in the long train, the more dust there is to fly. The smaller children try to walk out to the side of their handcart, as far away from the dirty trail as possible to keep from coughing and choking, but worried parents won't let them get to far out for fear of having some mischief befall them. Those who have bandannas around their necks, scarf's in their pocket or a large handkerchief soon tie them over their nose and mouth to cut down on breathing the ever present dust. I once remember reading a western story about how bandits did much the same thing when they were out to rob a bank or a stagecoach and I had to chuckle with the thought of 274 bandits walking in a line pulling handcarts that weighed 400-500 pounds. That would be enough to turn a bandit from crime forever!

11 June - Wednesday

"Journeyed 7 miles [Galloway, p. 444 and Ellsworth, p. 96 say 5 miles]. Very dusty. All tired and smothered with dust and camped in the dust or where the dust blowed. Was Captain over my tent of 18 in number but they were a family of Welch and our spirits were not united. Had a tent but Elder Ellsworth would not let me use it and have to leave my tent poles behind me."[6]

"....About 8 a.m. the camp started forward and traveled five miles. Pitched tents. Brothers Robinson's and Jones' carts broke down."[7]

THE SECOND HANDCART COMPANY LEAVES FOR FLORENCE, NEBRASKA

It was on this same Wednesday that Captain McArthur and the 211+ Saints of the Second Company left Iowa City. By nightfall they had caught up with Captain Ellsworth's company and made camp close by. From this point on, across the whole of Iowa to Florence, Nebraska, it could be said that the two companies "traveled together." That was not to say the two handcart trains were merged into a single group, but rather that they stopped for their camps at the same places at about the same times. This wasn't always pleasing to Captain Ellsworth, but seemed to bring a great deal of pleasure to Captain McArthur.

11 June 1856

"This day started from Camp D. D. McArthur, T. Leonard and Spicer W. Crandle as his Counselors, Walter Granger as one of the Comisaries & Wm. Heaton the other, as those at the head of each hundred too under us. 117 persons in my hundred and 100 in Bro. Cradles. It being put upon me to take charge of the Oxen or teams at present I done so; yoked them and was ready for a start at 12 o'clock. When we started out under heavy shouts from those who remained Bro. Spencer at their head. Brothers Ferguson & McAllister went a mile or to and comforted our hearts by singing the hand cart song and 3 cheers for all who aided in this operation.

"Traveled about 2 miles when our head cart was broken which for a moment put a damper on many but Bro. Dan and myself had it fixed in 25 minutes by putting in a new Axle in place of the one that had broken.

"It was quite warm and dusty but still traveled 8 miles and camped after Breaking an ox yoke which was replaced by the next morning in time to start I had bot. a stick from one Holler by Name who was kind to me also listened to my testimony in favor to Mormonism etc & lent me an orger to use for the purpose of making the yoke. Got into camp with the 1st company at sundown, the sick improving. All tired yet in good spirits."[8]

"Captain D. D. McArthur left on the 11th with 221 souls, accompanied by Elders Crandall and Leonard as assistants. These numbered in all 497 souls, embraced 104 of the 'Curling's Company', and their fit out was, together, 100 handcarts, 5 wagons, 24 oxen, 4 mules, 25 tents, and provisions to Florence. [He is giving **reference** to the **combined totals** of **both companies** here.] Brother Ferguson visited their camp 35 miles out, and accompanied them during a portion of a morning's march. He reports that though their first two days travel were good marches for men, considering the sandy roads, he never visited a camp of traveling Saints so cheerful and universally happy."[9]

In the second company Mary Brannigan Crandal made a request to have her own handcart to pull and Captain McArthur agreed. The Church has always pointed with pleasure to the fact that they were the first to recognize women and their rights in our nation. This is a good example of how early the equality of women was being practiced.

"On the 11th of June we commenced our journey westward, with D. D. McArthur as captain. The day we started the dust flew into our eyes until we could hardly see. I went to the captain and told him if he would let me have a handcart I would haul it myself. He said he would let me try, so I started with my bedclothes, provisions, cooking utensils and clothes strapped on the cart. Soon two other girls were with me...."[10]

Thursday at 6:00 a.m. the journey resumed and because the wind calmed, they were able to travel faster, in spite of very dusty roads. Everyone in the First Company were in good spirits when they stopped to pitched tents at 2:00 p.m.[11] Unfortunately the same could not be said for everyone in the Second Company, as Truman Leonard recorded in his journal:

12 June - Thursday
"Day a dreadful one, dust beyond anything I think I ever saw. Traveled 12 miles and camped with Brother Edmond again. Many were very tired, but most took it without murmuring. One family, however, were dissatisfied. They had broke the order by taking to shun the dust and lost the Spirit of the Camp and one lad took plenty of the spirit of liquor. Had my hands full in driving the cart teams and taking care of the sick. Never was more worried in my life..."[12]

SOME TURNED BACK

Those who didn't take it "without murmuring" decided that they had gone far enough. Ten people, "... with Bermingham [Probably Patrick and Eliza Birmingham and their 3 children], and List [Probably James and Ann Lister] at their head, left or refused to go further with us, so we took their carts and left them on the ground." That may sound a bit harsh, but they had agreed to complete the journey under certain specified commitments and their refusal not only to go on, but to encourage others to do the same, left them without compensation of any sort. It is however, probably good that their decision was made here rather than somewhere in the great wilderness of the western frontier.

Friday, 8:00 a.m., the camp started again. Today traveling for 7 miles over good roads and all went well. A number of curious strangers stopped to visit. They had their questions answered and many had an opportunity to hear Mormonism preached.

FIRST COMPANY

13 June - Friday
"The journey was continued about 8 a.m., over good roads, and all went well. During the day a number of strangers visited with the Saints, who traveled that day 7 miles."[13]

"The camp started about 8 a.m. Traveled seven miles. Good roads. All went off well. Visited by a good (many) strangers."[14]

SECOND COMPANY

13 June - Friday
"Traveled about 7 miles and stoped at 2 o clock. Marked the cattle on the right hip with tar the figure was No 1; then fixed a lot of hand carts in connection with Capt. McArthur, found many arms much worm which we remedied by putting double boxing of tin. In the evening had meeting, and had sanctioned by the company by vote McArthur myself and Bro. Crandel also the Presidents of each 20, who were stand as head to look after the interests of each tent, I was called upon to open by prayer and after much was said by Elders Dan & Spicer I spoke upon the propriety of going on foot instead of riding in the wagons as it would be no honor so to do, and again it was the salvation of the Camp to preserve the teams, also for the weakly ones when they were traveling among the gentiles not to

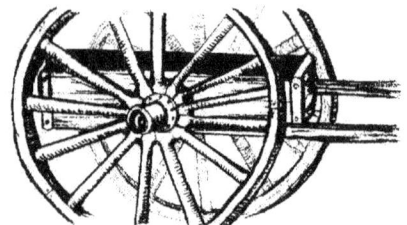

complain or murmur but to preach Mormonism and bear a faithful testimony of the truth for the sake of the cause and others who were destined to follow us.

"I also advised the sisters to take of their extra baggage and trade it off for provisions as I had done getting more than the things were worth.

"I also had the privelege of preaching Mormonism to several who listened attentively."[15]

On Saturday, June 14th, the companies were once again up at first light and resumed their journey at 6:00 a.m. The advantages of starting so early allowed for making an earlier stop for the evening. If the camping area had plenty of water, wood and game there was much that could be done before dark while camp was being set up. With the temperatures getting quite warm at midday, it also meant more miles could comfortably be traveled in the cool of the day. Also, if it happens to be a long distance between watering stops, it was easier to do when a great thirst had not been worked up under a baking sun. If it was a Saturday, stopping early gave the Saints extra time to prepare for the needs of the Sabbath.

Of course departing by 6:00 a.m., not everyone was able to get everything packed up and all their family fed. Often the adults and older children would have to leave with the carts, bread or a biscuit in their hand for breakfast, or just do without until the afternoon break. It didn't take many of the Saints long to realize that it was a good idea to fix a bit of food at the evening meal and set it aside for the next morning. They learned from those daily experiences what was needed so as to be as prepared as possible for every eventuality.

DEATH AND BURIAL ON THE TRAIL

This particular Saturday they had traveled 7 miles over good roads, stopping at 9:00 a.m. to pitch their tents. About 6:00 p.m. two major events took place, William, the 12 year old son of John Lee, died of consumption. And at about the same time Elder James Ferguson arrived from the general camp to check on the progress, health and general welfare of the companies.[16] Later on that evening, Lora Pratter, daughter of Richard Pratter, also died.

SECOND COMPANY
14 June - Saturday
"Started early went 7 miles and camped again with Bro. Elsworths Company But about 12 o Clock Broke a yoke and false tongue and bearly escaped great danger from wild cattle etc; got into camp procured a stick for a ox yoke and made it before night; Just as James Ferguson an Birminhams and Lucus's folks came into camp who had been persuaded so to do by the former, we gave them 3 cheers each although they did not deserve it by any means."[17]

Thus, seven days had passed since the First Company had started a journey that would not end until the 26th of September. Ahead of them were adventure, drudgery, joy, pain, anguish and determination. But never was there a doubt that the Lord was not with them. As in the days of the ancient exodus of Israel, He was their pillar and light through the wilderness. They knew He had called them to gather to Zion and would do His part, as they would need to do theirs. So some pushed, some pulled and the sands of the plains were passed over as they followed the trail that had been marked for them by many wagonloads of Saints now dwelling in the Valley.

"It may be Sunday, but I still need to get up and take care of building a coffin." Archer Walters muttered to himself as he stumbled out side of the tent before lighting his candle. With the breeze that was blowing, it was a good thing the candle was inside a lantern case.

"Building coffins is far from being my favorite job, especially at 4 o'clock in the morning, but I promised I'd have it done as soon as possible and this whole thing is hard enough on them as it is. Good thing I put that lumber in the shed with tools last night." And a little breeze blew up the back of his coat, feeling like cold hands sliding up his spine.

"Oh, Father In Heaven, please help me. Guide my feet to my work and my hands in their labors. May I shape and plane the wood to make it a fit place for the mortal resting place of this boy. Help his momma and daddy to accept thy will, and carry on, remembering the promises of Zion and Thy Kingdom. And Father, I love Thee, and I pray Thou will always remember and love me and my family. Help us too, to carry on and to reach Thy Zion with hills surrounding. Amen and amen....." And the moon came out from behind a cloud and shone down on Brother Archer, and the North Star beamed a little brighter. There was peace all around in the campground of the Saints.

That night Archer Walters recorded in his journal:

"Got up about 4 o'clock to make a coffin for my brother, John Lee's son named William Lee, aged 12 years. Meetings as usual, and at the same time had to make another coffin for Sister Prator's child. Was tired with repairing handcarts the last week. Went and buried them by moonlight at Bear Creek."[18]

FIRST COMPANY

15 June - Sunday

"Today is Sunday. The Saints remained in camp and held two meetings. The morning meeting commenced at half past ten. Singing. A prayer by Elder Heaton. Elder Joseph France addressed the meeting. Afternoon meeting commenced at half past one o'clock. Singing with prayer by Elder Leonard. Elder Edward Frost addressed the meeting. A great many strangers attended the meetings. Good attention by all present. At nine o'clock this morning Lora Pratter, daughter of Richard Pratter, died of whooping cough, age 3 years. At half past seven the sacrament was administered to the two companies. It was a time or rejoicing for all. Elder Ferguson addressed the Saints. About 9 p.m. the above named two children were interred at Little Bear Creek [35 miles from Iowa City.]."[19]

16 June - Monday

"Travelled 19 miles ... pitch tent ... mended carts."[20]

"At half past six a.m. the camp moved off in good spirits. Traveled thirteen miles and rested from half past eleven a.m. until four p.m. at Big Bear Creek. The camp moved two miles and camped for the night. About nine we had a storm of rain."[21]

17 June - Tuesday

Travelled 17 miles...pitched tent. "Made a little coffin for Bro. Job Welling's son and mended a hand cart wheel." [22]

"At four a.m. the bugle was blown for all to turn out, and at quarter to seven the camp moved off. Traveled ten miles and rested two hours. At twenty past two we pitched our tents. The journey was performed without an accident. No wood, plenty of water. About twenty minutes past three, Job Welling, son of Job Welling, died, age one year and seven months. Died of canker or inflammation of the bowels."[25]

SECOND COMPANY

15 June - Sunday

"35 miles from cart camp at Iowa City. Had meeting Bro. France preached to the gentiles who had assembled to the Nos of I think 150. At half past one had another meeting which was opened by me when Bro. Frost preached upon the first principles. A good spirit prevailed. In the evening had meeting partook of the Sacrament. J. Ferguson too gave us much good instruction. Two deaths in Bro Edmonds com."[23]

16 June - Monday

"Traveled 15 miles, tolerable good road; but the day was warm and many were very tired, sick improving fast. Bro James after going about 2 miles with us took his leave for camp 45 miles, bought about 60 lbs lard for cart use and other purposes, Good Spirit in Camp. Camped on Bear Creek."[24]

17 June - Tuesday

"Day fine and roads good. Went 15 miles further and camped on the Prarie, had much the appearance of rain. A goodly No of strangers present for whom the band plaid for them and received some pay."[26]

With the death of little Job Wellington, many parents in the company were becoming very worried about the increasing mortality rate of the children. Were they doing something wrong to cause their suffering and death, or was it just that the Almighty missed their presence or had some important calling for them in the world of spirits? Times like this made those with eternal marriages less forlorn, though no less sad. But the thought that a worthy mother could still raise her little one from childhood into manhood in the next life did give greater comfort. And to have a sure knowledge of their child's assurance of a Celestial judgement and Eternal blessings with the Father and the Son was the greatest comfort of all.

At such moments of sorrow, the love, compassion and care of the Saints was a great blessing. These fellow citizens of Zion, there without any need for a request, were as much like family as those born of the same blood, and often more understanding and compassionate. God bless the gentle hearts and the helping hands.

EARLY STARTS AND USUALLY SHORT DAYS OF TRAVEL ACROSS IOWA
FIRST COMPANY

18 June - Wednesday

"Rose before sun rise; ... Very hot Harriet still very ill but hope she will soon be better if it please my Heavenly Father."[27]

"At 4 a.m. the bugle sounded for all to rise and at 5:20 the company resumed the journey, traveled 10 miles without accident, and pitched tents at 8:35 a.m., in order to give the sisters an opportunity of washing their clothes. During the day, the remains of Job Welling's little son were interred at a point 3 feet from the north-east corner of Mr. Watson's farm, in Section 25, Township 80, Range 17 West."[28]

SECOND COMPANY

18 June - Wednesday

"Wednesday went 10 miles starting early, the day was warm & many gave out for want of food and water, Arrived at Dixons about 10 O clock and his well supplied all our 2 companies, the woman did not like it but the man was a gentleman I told him he was doing the greatest favor he ever done in his life and I said God bless all who feel well towards this people Arrived in camp about 11 and fixed hand carts till dark. put a tin and iron on nearly all the arms to our carts.

"Mr Gideon Gardner heard of me and came 4 miles with his Wife and 3 others to see me. we had a long talk and parted with the best of feelings. He plead hard for me to go home with him but I could not In the evening had meeting"[29]

After rising so early on Wednesday, traveling so far, and accomplishing so much, it seems a bit unusual that on Thursday the First Company rose late and did not leave until almost 8:00 a.m., but they still managed to travel 13 miles [Galloway & Ellsworth say 15 miles][30] and make camp by noon at Bear Creek. Several of the Saints were ill and were rebaptized in the afternoon for their health by Elder John Oakley.[31] Rebaptism at that time in the Church being an accepted practice when approved by priesthood leaders.

The Second Company evidently rose at first light to pursue their journey. After a somewhat lengthy break at Skunk Creek, they stopped for the night in a grove of trees on Elk Creek about 3:00 p.m. They also had traveled 15 miles before camping .

19 June - Thursday

"Day warm at noon passed over North Skunk a beautiful stream. stoped to rest an hour or two; then had to rise a tremendous hill before which however I had to with 3 yokes cattle drove a balky team up loaded with 2 That for which the drive gave me 50 cnts. Traveled in all through the day 15 miles which caused us to be very tired at night. Camped on Elk Creek in a beautiful grove at 3 O Clock, when I fixed up my rifle with some balls went out and the first shot I ever made with her I cut a gray squirrel nearly in two the 2nd I centered a single pigeon and then tried it at a mark with success and satisfaction The little game I got was made good use of by the sick and feeble who are all improving."[32]

DISCONTENT AND HARRASMENT AT NORTON, IOWA

After having traveled several days on a rather flat terrain, the handcart pioneers found themselves in a hilly and rather rough environment. John Lloyd and his family of the First Company had been showing signs of discontent for some time, but decided on Friday, June 20th, they had enough and were "backing out." According to Galloway, Lloyd had been drinking whisky quite heavily as they traveled along the road. So with the company about an hour away from Norton at about 9:00 a.m., they stopped beside the road and watched the rest of the Saints walk by.[33]

20 June - Friday

"...Traveled sixteen miles [Walters says 14 miles[34]]. The road was very hilly and rather rough. It was rather a hard day's travel. About a quarter of eight this morning John Lloyd, wife and family, backed out. .... We rested by a stream from ten until twelve. Pitched our tents at four p.m. along side a beautiful stream of water. Plenty of wood Several were baptized for their health by Elder Oakley."[35]

The Second Company also traveled through the town of Norton, but some very vocal anti-Mormon hecklers greeted them. Truman Leonard, in particular, was singled out by two men, Uvel and Wilson by name, to receive their abusive attitudes. Uvel, who was loud and belligerent, pushed up close behind Leonard to where he could almost feel his hot breath on his neck. At Uvel's side stood Wilson, wearing a large smirk on his face.

"You say your name is Leonard?" Uvel bellowed, "Well Mr. Leonard, my name's Uvel, and I know all about you Mormons. You're not Christians and you're disloyal and troublesome to everyone and everything you come in contact with!"

Leonard, hearing such a charge, stopped suddenly and turned to look into the face of his critic. "I don't wish to have trouble with you Mr. Uvel, so I'll not bother to answer your lies and slander.

Being taken somewhat off guard with Leonard's quick and calmly stated reply, Uvel looked quickly at Wilson for a visual sign of support and then back at Leonard. "I mighta' known that anyone who would believe that someone like that money digger, Joe Smith could be a prophet, would be too much the coward to stand up to anything." and he continued with a belligerent tone of voice, "I repeat! You're **no** Christian and you're disloyal to your country, going off into Utah so you 'kin stir up Indians to fight against **true** Americans."

Wilson laughed sarcastically, and moved to Leonard's side, to make him feel boxed in. "You tell 'em Uvel, and did you know they even want to make Utah a state of **our** nation?"

"That'll be the day!" Uvel mocked.

"When I heard they were comin' by, I traveled 2 ½ miles to get a good look at 'em," Wilson whined as he looked Leonard up and down, shaking his head back and forth in an exaggerated way, "an' ya' know what? There's no doubt that Mormons and Indians are a lot alike.... The only **good** ones are **dead** ones!" and he grinned real big and cackled like a chicken, hat in hand, slapping it against his leg. He then danced a little two step and firmly set his hat back on his head.

Leonard, although becoming more and more agitated, controlled himself and looked Wilson directly in the eyes. "You sir, are wrong! You know nothing of us or what we believe or do."

Holding his nose, Wilson turned and crossed to the left side of Uvel. Then using a know-it-all tone of voice said, "Oh, you don't have to pick up a pole cat to know of its nature. All those people in Illinois that made a **good** Mormon outta' Joe Smith knew what needed to be done and they **did it**. Now all **us Christians** would all be better off if'n the rest of ya' followed your false prophet to the same end!"

Almost at the boiling point, Leonard clenched his teeth together and in a low cutting voice proclaimed most emphatically, "You sir, are a **liar**!"

Uvel, with a toss of his head, ignored the remark and turned to face Wilson. "I agree Wilson, there never was a Mormon ever lived that could be trusted to be anything but trouble. I'm gonna' get on home right now, an' any Mormon that trys to stop on or go though my land will **die** on the spot!"

Turning quickly, without a backward glance, Uvel walked down the street, mounted his horse and rode rapidly out of town. Left standing all alone, Wilson took a step toward Leonard and proclaimed in a loud voice, so the people watching across the street could clearly hear, "You Mormons are so ignorant, why it's a well known fact that there's not half a dozen of ya' can read or write. That's why your leaders can dupe ya' inta' believin' anything they say. I lived for a short time in Missouri and I know **all about ya'**. You Mormons don't even **dare** put your foot in that state cuz' they have a standin' order from the governor to kill ya' on sight. They don't even need ta' give ya' a trial. What does that say for Ole' Joe Smith and the Mormons?"

Rising up to his full height, Leonard leaned forward putting his face almost against Wilson's face. In a quiet, cutting voice that rang out at his adversary like the roar of a lion, he exclaimed, "I'll tell you what it tells me. That you are an **unmitigated liar** and I have made up my mind to **beat the fear of the Lord into you!**" Stepping forward with the tensions of a panther about to pounce, Wilson stepped back. Each step Leonard took was followed by a reaction of retreat by his now cowering foe. Each word pounded on his soul like a ten-pound hammer. "Now stand right there and face me like a man, if you're more than mouth and have the stomach for it.... No? You won't stand firm? Then let me explain to you in simple language the Gospel of the Lord Jesus Christ, so that even a **small** mind like yours can understand it...."

And Brother Leonard, with fists clenched at his sides, began to preach the Gospel to him. He poured forth truth and understanding so quickly, and with such power, that Wilson was confounded. Those watching the proceedings yelled to him that he had better keep his peace, as the Mormon was too much for him. At which he begged Leonard's pardon and walked away sheepishly trying to hide himself among his friends.[36]

Leonard, among other things, wrote in his journal that night:

> "...I saw another man Hammer by Name and a Mason who told me not to mind anything about what that fellow had said as he was a mean fellow at Noon we stoped at a creek where we stoped about 2 hours rested ourselves caught some fish then went on and in crossing a prarie in the heat many gave out with fatigue and want of water. I had I think high as 25 in my wagons at a time Mathew Hardy for the first time give out"[37]

AND THE HANDCARTS MUST KEEP MOVING

Water was always a major concern to the handcart Companies on the march, because there was no way to carry large quantities. The usual practice was to press on from water source to water source without stopping. Rest periods were generally taken when a river, creek or spring was reached. Fortunately, they had a guidebook[38] that showed them how far it was between water and camping places and they were able, for the most part, to effectively pace themselves. Of course wise individuals usually tried to keep at least a small amount of stored water with them on their person or on the handcart for emergencies. If a person were to fall, or stop for want of water, there was usually a brother or a sister who would share. For this was the way of it. Of course there were some that were mean spirited and stingy, but fortunately they were few and far between.

FIRST COMPANY

21 June - Saturday

"Travelled about 13 miles. Camped at Indian Creek. Bro. Jas. Bower died about 6 o'clock; from Birmingham Conference. Went to buy wood to make the coffin but the kind farmer gave me the wood and nails. It had been a very hot day and I was never more tired, but God has said as my day my strength shall be. For this I rejoice that I have good health and strength according to my day."[39]

"At 6:30 a.m. the camp moved on, ... rested 30 minutes by the side of a stream, and later an hour on the top of a hill. About 1 p.m. tents were pitched for the night in a grove where there was plenty of wood and water. At 4:45 p.m. James Bowers died of quick consumption, aged 44 years."[40]

SECOND COMPANY

21 June - Saturday

"Hard roads traveled 13 or 14 miles, and on the way broke 2 axeltrees out of Frews and Kennsington sustained the loss, we had one whole one and splised the 2nd & all was fixed up without delaying the company above what was necessary for their good. At 2 O Clock we crossed over South Skunk bridge at which we rested and I changed our cattle by putting a raw pair of steers on the lead to get from the tongue an ox that would hold back and stop the wagon and team Got into camp at 3 O Clock and at 5 Bro. Bowers died by whose side I had sat from nearly the time I had come into camp I closed his eyes amid great mourning among his family and friends, In the evening Capt Dan and myself went back to the Tavern and bought 3 rails which Mr. Reith gave us turned to axeltrees 8 in No of the best kind of Hickory. He said we had helped him to raise a bent to his barn and he would not charge us anything."[41]

Some Sundays on the trail were spent in formal worship and rest. Others were filled with a wide variety of activities, such as traveling on to the next camping place; repairing handcarts, wagons, tents or equipment; or making caskets and/or digging graves for those who had graduated from mortality. Frequently large number of strangers attended the meetings, where they heard the major principles of Mormonism taught. Most of the visitors paid good attention, and always when the sacrament was administered, it was a time of rejoicing for all.

22 June - Sunday

"Got up at day break and made the coffin for Bro. James Bowers by 9 o'clock and he was buried at 11 o'clock. Ages 44 years, 5 months, 2 days. His relatives cried very much after I liften him in the coffin and waiting to screw him down. 11 o'clock washed in the creek and felt very much refreshed. Meeting 2 o'clock until seven. Bro. MacCarter spoke about being driven and he did walk into the Gentiles first rate and told them that they did not mean to be driven again and not to be excited by the priests to come against us as a people again for they would fine them a terrible people."[42]

"The remains of James Bowers were buried near two other graves, a quarter of a mile east of the main line for Fort Des Moines, in Section 26, Township 79, Range 22.

22 June - Sunday

"This morning James Bowers was burried. The day was very warm; had one meeting in the afternoon, I was called upon to pray and was nearly overcome by foul Air etc. Bro. Heaton preached a noble sermon, the Gentiles of a [?] a goodly No. were present paid good attention After this Elders Elsworth & McArthur spoke to the saints as dictated by the spirit of God. We then administered to several who were sick indeed."[44]

The camp was called together for meeting at 4:20 p.m. Elders Wm. Heaton, Daniel D. McArthur and Edmund Ellsworth preached and gave good instructions."[43]

Another new week is upon us, with little that seems different than last Monday or the Monday before, or the weeks before for that matter. Today we didn't leave until 7:25 a.m., but after ten or so miles and a few breakdowns, the first place that looks good to camp will be our stopping place for the night. The people with few or no children that are in good health seem unhappy when we stop so early each day. They claim we should be making around 20 miles a day, but then they don't have little ones that tire out so quickly, or sick souls that need constant care --while the handcarts just keep right on moving; or something that needs to be fixed on the cart; or a body that is old and worn out from years of constant use. The healthy don't seem to be bothered so much by the sun when it heats up, or having loved ones that constantly pester them with questions like, "When can I have another drink?" or "Will we eat soon?" or "Why does William keep bothering me all the time?

When the dew has burned off of the prairie sod, the sun climbs steadily in the sky, and the traveler begins to feel like a loaf of bread being slowly baked in an oversized oven. Little beads of sweat start to form on your head, right under your hat, that quickly become droplets and then widens until they form a stream trickling down over the forehead. Once a stream, now a river, that soaks into eyebrows, creating a waterfall of salty fluid crashing into the chasms of the eyes and rushing down over the cheeks. Then, as each of these rivers and waterfalls converge, the whole of the body turns into a lake that floods the clothing and sticks to the skin. Even the little breeze that seems to constantly be blowing over the prairie, while warm enough to dry your mouth and eyes does little to offset the results of the torrents of sweat. And if you happen to be in the last two-thirds of the handcart column, you are blessed with a thin brownish blanket of dust, blown up into the air that settles like a gentle mist from the turning handcart wheels and shuffling feet.

FIRST COMPANY

23 June - Monday

"Rose early and travelled 10 miles; then repaired the hand carts. Harriet a little better."[45]

"The camp resumed the journey at 7:25, traveled 10 miles and pitched tents at 10 a.m. The roads were rather rough and dusty part of the way and led through a hilly country. During the day, the company crossed two good sized streams. Encampment was made for the night, 4 miles from Fort Des Moines, where wood and water was plentiful. In the morning the company passed through a small town 7 miles from the Fort."[46]

SECOND COMPANY

23 June - Monday

"Rose early hewed out 8 axiltrees; at half past 7 started went 10 miles so staid and camped on 4 mile Creek. On the way saw a Mr. Clafton a Mason and County Surveyor; also a friend to Mormons. He employed many of them at the drive from Nauvoo; one Barker in particular and family. I bought 13 lbs of lard for 105 cts for cart grease, In arriving in camp a man was stalled & I hitched on 4 yoke of cattle broke 2 chain hooks but hauled the load of 5000 out his Name was Smith. I also went to the sawmill near by bought a piece of stuff to make false tongue and put in in. I also preached Mormonism to several men who listened attentively and acknowledged our doctrine. We are now within 4 miles of Fort Demoin and have flour and Bakon to buy."[47]

Tuesday started out like most days, today departing from camp about 6:30 a.m. There was some grumbling about the speed of travel in the Ellsworth Company:

"Travelled 18 miles. Very hot. Bro. Ellsworth being always with a family from Birmingham named Brown and always that tent going first and walking so fast and some fainted by the way. Bro. Frost worn out by going so fast and not resting and many more."[48]

After 11 miles of "somewhat rough and dusty road." and the "rather hard pulling for the handcart boys," the company stopped at about 1:30 p.m. at a place where there was plentiful wood and water. After setting up camp, the brethren set about the unhappy task of burring James and Mary Schinn's son, Sydney, who had died in the morning and was carried on to the campsite on a handcart, so as not to slow down the march. He was laid to rest "30 yards south of the bridge on the bank of Four Mile Creek, under an elm tree."[49]

McArthur's company faced several trials and frustrations on this June 24th. They had to pass over a ferry bridge at Fort Demoin, but before they did so a price was agreed upon for those that would cross. Brother Leonard, who was the last in the company to pass across was stopped and had demanded of him 20 cents more than had been agreed upon. Obviously it was an effort to provide some provocation for causing trouble, so the amount was paid rather than raise any aggitation. As Leonard put it:

"...there were 20 or 30 together asking for a fuss but we outwitted the Devil & his imps..."[50]

During the evening Captain Ellworth had a visitor come into the First Company's camp that he described as an "old mobocrat" that wanted to make a fuss.[51]

While in the area they managed to purchase a ton of flour at $6.00 per hundred, which was an acceptable price. That evening, many visitors came into camp, so the brethren took the opportunity to preach the Gospel to them until about 10:00 p.m. And at that point the owner of the land on which they were camped, a Mr. Bennett, got mad about something that was said and ordered the companies to leave immediately. Captain Ellsworth replied that they would be happy to oblige him, but not until morning.[52]

FIRST COMPANY

25 June - Wednesday

"Travelled about 13 miles. Sold some files to a carpenter; repaired some hand carts."[53]

"The camp resumed the journey at 6:25 a.m. and traveled 19 miles. A gentle, refreshing breeze blew nearly all day. The roads were good. There was plenty of water at Six Mile Creek and at Nine Mile Creek. Tents wer pitched at 1:45 on the bank of a river, where there was plenty of wood."[54]

SECOND COMPANY

25 June - Wednesday

"In the morning made an axeltree; & started about 7 O Clock went 18 or 19 miles; many gave out & we had all we could draw without using up the cattle. Camped at 4 on Coon River and took a bathe. In the evening had a meeting and heard from several of the Brethren who bore testimony of the power of God in strengthening them thus far. Some are ready to apostatize or stop among the Gentiles Sister Ludert & Reed are among the No. Sister Hannah Forres fainted and fell while pulling the cart Bro Ramsey's child is very sick and by some not expected to live. at even a goodly No of Gentiles came in to the camp so I preached Mormonism to several of them for some time."[55]

During Thursday's travel, little Emma, the daughter of Robert and Eliza Shinn [Sheen], died of whooping cough. She was 2 years and 8 months old. In spite of this tragedy, they were still able to cover ten miles, fording the Raccoon River twice. Their travels took them past the town of Bailey, but they did so without incident.[56] Those who had money were able to pick up some additional supplies, but most had to make due with what was the daily issue.

FIRST COMPANY

26 June - Thursday

"Travelled about 1 mile. Very faint for the (lack) of food. We are only allowed about ¾ of lb. of flour a head each day and about 3 oz. of sugar each week. Tea good and plenty; about a ¼ of lb. of bacon each a week; which makes those that have no money very weak."[57]

SECOND COMPANY

26 June - Thursday

"In the morning made another axile had prayers and started at 7 O, Clock went half a mile forded the Coon river the water one foot deep and 60 feet wide about the women walked over boldly. Went 12 miles and camped at 4. Just in time to escape a shower.

"During the day Bo Cunningham from the Bluffs came to meet and give us much good news especially some from my family as he had seen them in Sept last."[58]

It's a Friday morning, and while most were still asleep in their tents, Archer Walters left his tent and walked across the camp to the spot where he had placed the little roughwood casket Emma's body had been laid to rest in till her resurrection. So early in the morning, the air is fresh and cold. It shocks the eyes open and alerts the senses to the sounds of the wind in the trees, the crack of branches and leaves underfoot, and the smells from the first morning fires. Archer always enjoyed these special treats, but like so many mornings; he was once again hurrying from one task to another. Reaching his destination he picked up a piece of wood took out his knife and carefully began to cut Emma's name into it. Another pioneer tombstone. It was always hard to make the caskets and fix the markers, but when it's for a child, there seems to be an ever present lump in the throat that just doesn't want to go down. The head knows that all such children receive the fullest blessings of the Savior, but the heart always seems to have an ache that doesn't go away for a long time. This little angel will be placed into the arms of mother earth 12 feet south of a walnut tree on the west bank of the Raccoon River, just across from the saw mill.

Now he had to hurry on, as there were several handcarts that had yet to be repaired before breakfast. Pulling his coat up over the back of his neck and yanking his hat down on his head a little tighter, Archer bent over to pick up his tools and sank down onto one knee with fatigue. After a moment he raised his head and whispered

Figure 20: A *Coffin For Little Emma*

softly to the skies, "Father, I need some help getting up and going on. Thou art my strength. I can only do what you bless me to do." Then without a second thought, he took his tools in hand and stood up straight and strong. "Once again I work with your strength and not mine own. I thank Thee my Father for Thy help in assisting this people." And off he walked, with a spring in his step, going from tent to tent, and cart to cart, repairing the first company's transportation for the days travel.[59]

That evening after camp had been made, John Ramsey, a child in the second company died.

27 June - Friday
"Traveled 9 miles and after getting in at 12 O Clock on South Coon whare I mad a [__?] and then was oblizeged to do the painful necessity of getting some lumber from a Mr France for 10 cents worth 15 cents to make a coffin for John Ransay aged 19 months who died at 6 O'Clock. I made the coffin and finished it at dark and put the body into it."[60]

FIRST COMPANY

SECOND COMPANY

<u>28 June - Saturday</u>
"We think Harriet a little better. Rose soon after 4 o'clock. Started with high wind. Short of water and I was never more tired. Rested a bit after we camped then came on a thunderstorm and rain blowed our tent down. Split the canvas and wet our clothes and we had to lay on the wet clothes and ground. I thought of going through needful tribulation but it made me cross. I took poor Harriet into a tent and fixed the tent up again as well at Bear Creek Station."[61]

"The camp moved off at forty past five and traveled sixteen miles. The road was good with the exception of some parts of it being rather hilly. The water rather scarce for about thirteen miles. We got supplied with water at Bear Station. Pitched tents at 1 p.m. Pretty good camping ground; plenty of water; wood rather scarce. We had heavy thunderstorm about six p.m. One of the tents was blown down and another rent from top to bottom."[62]

<u>28 June - Saturday</u>
"Left early after digging a grave on the west bank of the stream under a beautiful oak where we buried the child at half past 6 after a prayer by myself we placed a head and foot board to let the people know of the circumstances, it being the first death in our company. During the day had many in the wagons but got along very well although almost entirely without water, at one point went more than a mile to get some. Went into camp near Dalmanuta and on Middle River where soon after a heavy rain attended with strong wind came on tearing one of our tents to ribons and left its inmates to get severely wet but they bore it patiently."[63]

> Each Sabbath day,
>   with peace is blessed,
>   with lots of worship,
>   but not much rest.

Figure 21: *But Not Much Rest* by Robert O. Day

Such was the case on June 29th, when both companies remained in camp all day. The morning was spent doing mending, repairs, and all of the little things that could not be done early in the morning when the camp was rushing to move out, nor in the evening when camp had to be set up, nor while the column was moving.

It would be nice to say that all enjoyed a satisfying feast, but the truth of the matter was that provisions were becoming somewhat limited and all are forced to do with what they get from their daily issue of food. The adults and older teens understand the situation, but the children do not, and they cry for their meals and for "just a little more to eat." And what's a parent to do when there is no more? They can always give the children part of their food, but then where will they get the strength they will need to pull the handcarts early tomorrow morning through the deep sand and over the hills that seem to get harder to climb with each step? So ways must be found to take their minds off of food and redirect it to other things. Work, stories, errands, scripture reading, quiet games, washing, mending, repairing, gathering firewood, whatever works, until it's time for the next meal or to attend Church services.

Oh Lord, my God, please give me strength,
Do not mind my weak complaints.
Overlook my moans and groans,
Help me reach my mountain home.
Zion...ever on to Zion....

Figure 22: *Ever On To Zion* by Robert O. Day

FIRST COMPANY

29 June - Sunday

"Rather stiff in joints when we rose and thought, as thy day thy strength shall be, was fulfilled upon us for which I feel thankful to my Heavenly Father. Busy all day. My wife and Sarah mending. Short of provisions. ... Got the tent up and slept comfortable."[64]

"We remained in camp all day and rested our bodies. The day was fine. Several strangers were in the camp. At twenty past four p.m. the saints met together for meeting, singing, and prayer by Elder [Spicer W.] Crandall. The meeting was addressed by Elders [Samuel] Hargreave, [Edmund] Ellsworth, [Daniel D.] McArthur, [Truman] Leonard, and [Spicer W.] Crandall on a variety of subjects for the benefit of the Saints."[65]

30 June - Monday

"Rose in good health, except Harriet, and started with our hand carts with but a little breakfast as only 3½ lbs. of flour was served out over night, but never travelled 17 miles more easily. Got 5 lbs. of flour and bacon about 1¼ lb., ¾ lb. rice, sugar ¾ lb. and was refreshed after satisfying nature. Sleep very well after prayers in tent."[67]

"The camp moved out at fifty-five past six a.m. Traveled sixteen miles. We traveled twelve miles without resting. The roads were but middling. part of the way somewhat hilly. No water for twelve miles. Pitched tents at ten past one p.m. All in good spirits. Plenty of wood and water."[68]

SECOND COMPANY

29 June - Sunday

"Day most beautiful some strangers came to our tent to whom we preached to for an hour or two. Meeting at 4 O'clock I was called upon to take the charge of the same, prayer by Bro. Elsworth & then after singing again called upon Elder Hargeaves to come forward & address the congregation which he done to great satisfaction the gentiles to a considerable number paid good attention. I also bore a strong testimony to what had been said and added a few ideas upon the gathering. The strangers were then released and the Saints requested to remain where they were instructed by Elders Crandle Elsworth Mc Arthur and myself as dictated by the spirit of God and surely there was some most cutting instructions unto murmurers disobeyers of counsel and women who were dictating & finding fault with their husbands all of which had a good affect we also told them what they might depend upon when they got upon the other side of the River about riding in those Wagons, etc. The Saints felt first rate."[66]

30 June - Monday

"Made an axile in the morning and started out at half past six; traveled 16 miles over a fine road with great ease very few in the wagons nearly off hill the walk after the severe lecture they had received. In the afternoon Bro. Crandle drove the teams. while I conversed for miles on Mormonism with Mr Lockwood a reasonable man. We camped on the head waters of Turkey Creek. by ourselves."[69]

Of course, non-believers were not the only cause of anger or frustration. After almost a month on the trail across Iowa, other things were raising concerns among some of the Saints. Archer Walters, of the First Company, with a wife and 5 children, wrote in his journal on Tuesday, July 1st:

> "Travelled about 15 miles in the rain. Walking very fast, nearly 4 miles an hour. Brother Brown's family and some young sisters with Brother Ellsworth are going first again, as they always seem to do, and it causes many of the brothers to have hard feelings. I have heard them called Brother Ellsworth's, as he always walks with them and looks after them, being in the same tent."[70]

Walters also expressed himself on the food rations and a damaged tent:

> Our food issue is a ½ lb. of flour each and 2 oz. of rice. Such a very little causes my children to cry with hunger, which grieves me and makes me cross. I can live upon green herbs or anything, and do go nearly all day without any, being strengthened with a morsel, but not my children.
> Repaired hand carts again. Then a storm came up about 11 o'clock that lasted an hour and a half. It split our tent and there's not a dry thread on any of us. [71]

Galloway, on the other hand with only a wife and 1 child to care for, viewed the day as rather routine:

> "The camp moved out at 7:10 a.m., traveled 15 miles over a rather rough road, passed a creek and camped for the night on the bank of a creek; wood was plentiful about half a mile from camp. About 10:30 p.m. a thunder storm visited the camp, during which one tent was blown down and another one rent."[72]

LITTLE ARTHUR PARKER IS LOST

On that same day, July 1st as the storm suddenly came up, Robert and Ann Parker hurriedly made camp with their children, but then faced what parents feared most. Little six year old Arthur Parker was missing. Sometime earlier in the day, unknown to them and unnoticed by anyone, Arthur had sat down under a tree to rest while the company moved on.

A frantic search of all the families with children in the Second Company revealed that he was not with anyone traveling in McArthur's Company. The last time anyone remembered seeing him was at least 2 miles back, as they were moving along the trail.

Then an organized search was begun at once. Several of the brother's lead by McArthur and Leonard, immediately traveled back along the trail to look for him.

> SECOND COMPANY
> **1 July - Tuesday**
> "...during the day lost Arthur Parker. He was not mised over 30 minutes before one of the drivers was dispatched after him but without success. he arrived in camp and another man was sent on a mule he staid out till after midnight and through the most dreadful storm I ever witnessed on the plains. The rain poured in torrents and the wind blew almost a gale, one of our tents was riven to tatters and all in it drenched we got them into the wagon and our tent till morning. Our team that we sent for provisions came with 700 pounds of meat one death in Eds camp."[73]

After a second day of fruitlessly waiting, watching, hoping and praying, Robert and Ann Parker knew they had to do something more than rely on others to find their son. It was apparent that only the God and Father of us all could help. Leaving their children in the care of friends, they walked hand in hand far out beyond the camp looking for a private place where they could kneel in prayer.

There in the moonlight, with their knees pressing hard against the prairie grass, Ann looked hard into Robert's face. She remembered the smooth, handsome face of the young man she met and fell in love with so many years ago. It was now ruddy, weather-beaten and filled with stress. His eyes, still soft and dark, looked deeply into her eyes as if searching for her very soul. How she loved him and how much she needed his tender strength to cope each day with common tasks, but now with a little son lost in the wilderness, how much more she needed him as an anchor to keep her from being dragged deeply into an ocean of despair.

Robert, holding Ann's rough and leathery hands tenderly in his, bowed his head and softly poured out his heart to Heavenly Father. Aware that God already knew his thoughts and needs, he spoke them anyway as it somehow gave comfort to speak each need and desire aloud. Pleading for direction and strength, he soon ceased his utterances and let his companion now pour out the feelings of her heart.

There in the stillness of the night, with the solemn pronouncement of amen, neither spoke nor moved. They remained on their knees and waited, expecting divine intervention, but not being sure how it would come. A soft wind blew up from the west, and in that wind like the movement of the Spirit, a calm assurance settled on this humble couple. No word had been spoken, no sound had been heard, yet both knew all would be well with little Arthur.

The time had come for Robert to head back along the trail in search of their little lost lamb. Following the direction of the Spirit, he would search for his son until he was found. Ann would go on with the handcart company and care for their other 3 children until they returned. Gathering up a few supplies to sustain him on his quest, Robert knelt down and one by one kissed his children good-by. Wiping tiny tears away from their concerned faces, he told each one how much he loved them and asked them to please keep Daddy and Arthur in their prayers.

As he was about to leave, Ann took her bright red shawl from around her shoulders, pinned it about Robert's thin shoulders and said to him softly:

> "If you find Arthur, and he has gone on to live with the Lord, use my shawl to wrap him in, as I would wrap him in my arms if he were here. If, God willing, he is alive, then as you approach the camp, use the shawl as a flag to signal me so that I may know as soon as possible, and rejoice."

She hugged him tightly, giving him two kisses, one to give to Arthur from her when he is found, and the other for her husband to save and use whenever he might need it on his journey. Then she turned him to face the trail he would travel and sent him on his way with the words, "Go with God, my beloved. Go with God!"

As the company continued the search the following were recorded in journals:

FIRST COMPANY

2 July - Wednesday
"Rose about 5 o'clock after sleeping in wet clothes, and made a coffin for Bro. Card belonging to the Independent Company but travels with us, for his daughter named ____ Card, aged ____. 5 miles from Indian town.

"Brother Parker's boy, from Preston, England, aged 6 years, lost. 2 miles gone after him which make us stop today and we hope the brothers will find him. No found; travelled about 14 or 15 miles."[74]

"We remained in camp till fifty past three p.m. owing to Brother McArthur's company having lost a boy by the way. At the above hour we started and traveled ten miles. Rested about half an hour on the bank of the river Nishnabotna. Camped two and one half miles west north-west of an Indian town on the banks of a river. Plenty of wood. A most delightful camping ground."[75]

SECOND COMPANY

2 July - Wednesday
"Capt Dan and myself started early on mule and horse in pursuit of the boy went 14 miles back enquiring of all we saw but not a word could be hear from him We then traversed the Creek for miles looking for some sign of the wanderer but not a single trace could be found. We were as well as our animals very tired, so we stoped at Peter Conhauwers took something too eat for which we paid 50 cts. We then went to Lockwoods who was quite stiff thinking we ought to stop & hunt till the boy was found dead or alive Brother Parker staid to get help and search still longer but we were obliged to abandon it or hasard the lives of hundreds who might be without provisions in a country where it could not be had"[76]

McArthur and Leonard did returned that day to the company. Then the next day they started the Second Company early, so as to overtake Ellsworth's company, who had started out the day before. Traveling 12 miles, they stopped to noon at Indian Town, and soon after came to where Brother Ellsworth had camped. Here they found several of their company, including Sister Parker and her children: Max age 12, Martha Alice 10 and Ada 1, who were determined to stay where they were until Brother Parker returned with Arthur. But Captain McArthur prevailed on her to remain with the rest of the company while she waited. After 12 more miles of travel, at about 5 o'clock, they caught up with the Ellsworth's company camped on Prairie Creek, and were greeted by loud cheers.

FIRST COMPANY

3 July - Thursday
"Ever to be remembered. Bro. Card gave me ½ dollar for making his daughter's coffin. Start with my cart before the camp as others had done but was told not and had to suffer for it. Went the wrong way; about 30 of the brothers and sisters and went 10 ½ miles wrong way. We put our three handcarts together and made beds with all the clothes we had and all layed down about ½ past 10 o'clock. 11 o'clock Bro. Butler, who had charge of the mule teams, came with the mules and wagon to fetch us. Got to camp when they were getting up. Laid down about an hour and started with the camp."[77]

"The camp moved out at forty-five past nine a.m. and traveled fourteen miles. Rested at the side of a creek six miles from where we started. Very little water as we came along. After traveling twelve miles, we turned down a road to the right two miles and camped by the side of a creek with plenty of water. Little wood. About twenty of the camp lost the road, but returned about midnight."[78]

SECOND COMPANY

3 July – Thursday
"Started early to overtake Bro Elsworth who had started out the day before. Traveled 12 miles by Indian town and stoped to noon and soon after came to where B E. Camped, here we found several of our crowd whom Bro Butler had taken in the muleteam here Sister Parker was determined to stop but we prevailed on her finally to come on with us; while her husband was still back in pursuit of his son which was truly a lamentable case. We then went 12 miles further (and after stoping at 5 O'Clock taking tea) camped on Prairie Creek with Bro Edmonds company mid loud cheers. But some of this crowd was out all night some of them on another road."[79]

Meanwhile, Brother Parker continued his search, retracing miles of forest trail, calling, and praying for his helpless little son. At last he reached a mail and trading station where he learned that little Arthur had been found and was being cared for by a woodsman and his wife. Arthur had been ill from exposure and fright, but God had heard and answered the prayers of his family and friends.

FIRST COMPANY

4 July - Friday

"About 20 miles. Tired out. Tied my cart behind the wagon and we got in after 3 nights. 1st night, thunder, lightning and rain and our tent splitting and blowing over. All wet to the skin. 2nd night; wind blowing; had hard work to hold the tent up and this last night no sleep. Went to bed; slept never better and rose refreshed."[80]

"The company moved out at 7:10 a.m. and traveled 20 miles. During the day, they crossed two creeks. The first ten miles they had plenty of water, but the last ten there was none. The roads were good. At 3:15 p.m. encampment was made by the side of a good creek where there was plenty of wood. This place was 14 miles from Council Bluffs. All the emigrants were in good spirits."[81]

SECOND COMPANY

4 July - Friday

"Struck our tents at 7, & was soon upon our way, traveled 17 miles, passing the Mishenebotany. - after stoping 2 hours and taking some refreshments at half past 2, came into camp at 6, on Silver Creek There Bro. Arguyle shot a tame elk for which had to be paid twelve Dollars we had the half of it."[82]

During the day Ann and her children took up their handcart and struggled on with the company, but after camp was made each night, she went out on the trail to keep watch with her children. Ever looking, ever hoping to catch sight of her red shawl:

"Oh my little son, my Arthur, has your father found you yet? I just know you are alive and well. You just have to be! Zion won't be the same if you're not there with the rest of us. Oh! Father in Heaven, Thou who has called us forth into this wilderness and who loves us, spare my son. Let my husband find him..."

Then out on the far distant horizon she thought she saw something moving against the skyline. Cupping her hands around her eyes she strained to see what it was. Hoping upon hope that this would be the day. Shadows did little dances here and there across the horizon, mirage's that teased the eyes and caused the blood to race in anticipation and uncertain agony. Then her gaze fixed on shades that seemed different from the constant movement of fading silhouettes. Images that seemed to have some form and substance. As the object got closer, she tried to continue her prayer:

"...Please let him...let...what? Did I see... no... yes...**yes**! It's my red shawl; I can just make it out in the rays of the setting sun. **Praise God**! it is my bright red shawl being waved by Robert. My Arthur...my son, you're **alive**!

Figure 23: Little *Arthur Parker Returned To His Mother*

The whole camp came running to her side as they saw her jumping up and down and dancing around. Then they too rejoiced in the news, as this brave little mother, so full of joy, sank in a pitiful heap on the sand. That night, for the first time in 6 days, Ann slept. Her son Arthur beside her wrapped in her arms and covered by a bright red shawl.

FIRST COMPANY

5 July - Saturday

"A deer or elk served out to camp. Brother Parker brings into the camp his little boy that had been lost. Great joy right through the camp. The mother's joy I cannot describe.

SECOND COMPANY

5 July - Saturday

"Laid in camp all day done a good deal of washing, and at 5 O Clock went out on a hunt and after a good deal

Expect we are going to rest. Washing, etc. today, Jordan Creek. Make a pair of sashes for the old farmer. Indian meal; no flour. Slept well."[83]

"The company remained in camp all day to rest, wash clothes, etc."[84, 85]

of tramping started 2 deer, one of which I had as fair a chance as ever I had in my life but in cocking my rifle it drew off the camp and when I pulled on the [?] bellow of course it was without effect although broad side & within a stones throw Taylor killed a hug doe to be dealt out in the morning." [86]

STRANGERS IN THE CAMP

On this last Sabbath day before the companies would reach Florence, Nebraska, once again there were several strangers in the camp. Some were curious about the handcarts and just what was going on, while others were more interested in the doctrines of a religion that could inspire such a large number of people to cross a wilderness this way. They had seen may wagon trains go by heading west, even Mormon wagon trains, but this was the first pushing and pulling carts and traveling by foot.

FIRST COMPANY

<u>6 July - Sunday</u>

"Made 2 doors for the farmer, 3 dollars and boarded with the farmer."[87]

"Today is Sunday. We remained in camp. Had meeting at twenty past four p.m. Singing and prayer by Brother Crandall. The meeting was addressed by Elders [Andrew] Galloway, [John] Oakley, [Edmund] Ellsworth and [Daniel D.] McArthur. A good many strangers present. Some were attentive, others could not bear the doctrine and walked off grumbling."[88]

<u>7 July - Monday</u>

"Harriet better. Lydia poorly. Travelled about 20 miles." [90] [Walters]

"The camp rolled out at 7 a.m. and traveled 15 miles through a hilly country; rested 30 minutes on the bank of a good creek. For a distance of about 8 miles, there was little of no water. A few houses were passed about 2 miles from the camping ground, where several old 'Mormons' were staying. Tents were pitched about 5 o'clock p.m."[91]

SECOND COMPANY

<u>6 July - Sunday</u>

"Camp Israel on Silver Creek Sunday July 6th 1856. In camp all day rested well, laid hands on Father Holihue and daughter, great faith was exercised At 5 had a meeting, Elders Galloway Oakley Elsworth and McArthur preached to us much instruction was given after which we laid hands on Father Ivins was mouth & pronounced a great blessing upon his head Although of great age I told him he should arrive safe in the Vallie of the Mountains and receive a blessing from the Prophet Brigham."[89]

<u>7 July - Monday</u>

"Left at half past 7 Traveled to Musketoe Creek 7 miles on our way saw several old Nauvoo Mormons Charles Alen, Joseph Walker who gave me *The Mormon, New York Tribune* and the *Banner of Liberty*. I also saw Mr Morcer from Portage Co Ohio he knew several of my friends in those parts especially in Akron. I preached Mormonism to him and he bid us God speed."[92]

Finally, on Tuesday, July 8th, the two companies reached the Missouri River and after crossing on the steam ferryboat *Nebraska*, camped at the City of Florence. Here they would rest for two weeks, while they made major repairs on the handcarts, wagons, and other equipment, and make arrangements for the food and supplies they would need for the 1,031 miles remaining in their trek to Zion.

FIRST COMPANY

<u>8 July - Tuesday</u>

"Travelled around-about road about 20 miles. Crossed the river Missouri and camped at the City of Florence. Very tired; glad to rest. Slept well. Lydia better and Harriet. All in good spirits. Expect to stop some time. Old Winter Quarters."[93]

"The camp moved out at 7 a.m. and traveled sixteen miles over a very rough road up and down hills. One handcart broke down by the way. The camp rested at Pigeon Creek for two and a half hours. Cooked dinner and got nicely rested. Crossed the Missouri by the steam ferryboat a little below Florence. Got to the camping ground at Florence at fifty past four p.m."[94]

SECOND COMPANY

<u>8 July – Tuesday</u>

"This morning several of the old mormons came to see us among others was old Hetherington who gave us considerable. The day was very warm and the roughest road I ever traveled went 17 miles stoping on or near Pigeon took some dinner then went to the Ferry crossed the River in an hour & a half on the steam Ferry *Nebraska* arrived in camp at half past 7 O'clock felt first rate. Saw McGow & F. Wooley."[95]

Figure 24: *Steam Ferry the 'Nebraska"*

Figure 25: *Mother Bathgate leads pioneers towards Devil's Gate*

Phase Four:

CHAPTER VI

TRAVELING FROM FLORENCE TO THE SALT LAKE VALLEY

REST AND PREPARATION AT FLORENCE. The settlement that at one time had been called Winter Quarters, was now known as the town of Florence, Nebraska. For some time this had been used by the Church as a stopover, repair and restocking point for the Latter-day Saint Pioneer companies heading west. Here they would remain for days or weeks, as circumstances would require, before they would resume their journey that would take them over a much more challenging terrain than their trip across Iowa. It was also a place to reevaluate needs and just plain rest, when time could be found to do so.

For those with the skills and willingness, this pause gave many handcart Saints an opportunity to work and make some money for items they presently were in need of [like shoes], or items they would require for the remainder of their journey to the Valley. Most found wages to be quite good, many getting work at $1.50–2.50 per day, while others earned from $2.00–3.00 dollars per week. It just depended on their skills and the immediate availability of jobs.

Men, such as Archer Walters and Truman Leonard that could have easily been employed at-$3.00–4.00 per day instead devoted their time to repairing handcarts and wagon equipment for the journey ahead. Their faithful care for their stewardship clearly illustrating the great faith and devotion of those being gathered to Zion. Poor in the material things of the world, they were rich beyond measure in matters of the Spirit, receiving an abundance of Love from their Heavenly Father and His Son, Jesus Christ.[1]

John Powell secured work in Omaha at a rate that was almost unheard of among the members of the two companies. "He laid the foundation and also dressed the cornerstones for the first courthouse in Omaha. He received eight dollars per day." With this princely sum he purchased new shoes for his family that would see them to the Valley, an act which his children appreciated, except that they considered the shoes "ugly".[2]

FIRST COMPANY

9 July - Wednesday

"Rested. Florence City."[3]

"July 9th to 12th. We were busily engaged repairing the handcarts."[4]

10 July - Thursday

"Repairing hand carts. Could of got 3 or 4 dollars per day had I not engaged with Brother Spencer to repair the carts. Harriet better."[6]

SECOND COMPANY

9 July - Wednesday

"Florence In camp all day dealing out provisions etc. also took a bathe in the Mill Pond, changed our clothes and administered to the Germans & Prophesied good concerning them ... In the evening took a walk into old winter Quarters, Many curious reflections came across my mind saw old man Davenport just from the Vallie receiving much hard news about want of provisions I selected a mule for our use on the plains."[5]

10 July - Thursday

"Busy getting together timber and materials for repairing the hand carts, for operations. In the evening held a counsel meeting Brigam at its head took into consideration the propriety of buying cattle and wagons to let us off as those at Kansas bot at Wm Kimball would not be here in time; all present seemed to urge the propriety of such a move we all spoke warmly upon the subject."[7]

On July 10th, Isabella Stevenson of the First Company, with the encouragement of "an old apostate", decided that she had gone through enough and announced she would go no further.[8] There were also a goodly number of others from the two handcart companies that dropped out here to wait for what they considered the easier method of transportation, by wagon train.[9]

> "The new experiment, however, did not always present a picnic prospect. There were those who weakened and withdrew from the ranks along the way, and those who hesitated on the borders of the plains to undertake the journey at all. An interesting contrast in the feelings of some who face the prospects of a thousand mile overland journey on foot appears in current correspondence. Writes one of a family that hesitated at the sight of the handcarts, 'We think it will be better to remain here or at St. Louis for a time until we are able to help ourselves to a wagon. Mother says that she must have a revelation before she can see this right. Why we would have to sell nearly all our clothes! And what shall we do for things to wear when we get to the Valley? Seventeen pounds weight each is but very little.'"[10]

There were also others that were offered a great deal to remain in the Florence area that refused to do so. A good example comes from the journal of Mary Powell Sabin:

> "While in Florence, Nebraska a gentleman came in our camp, said he to the captain, "Is there any man here from Whales with the name of John Powell, that is the man I want. I have been on the lookout for him for the last five years. My wife wants to see Brother Powell; she thinks the world of him. He gave her a home in the old country." This man offered father eighty acres of land if he would settle in Nebraska. He was also willing to help erect a house for us."[11]

It had only taken the handcart companies one month to travel across Iowa, even with all of the little delays along the way. This greatly outdistanced what the wagon trains were capable of, but some pioneers just did not take to the physical exertion of pushing/pulling a loaded handcart. Of course if they could have just walked and let all of their goods be brought along by some other means than a slow wagon, that would be ideal. Most everyone would then be very happy, but if it came to the choice between what they considered unreasonable exertion with a handcart at a fast pace and less strain with a wagon at a slower pace, Zion could wait. Fortunately, the discontented were in the minority.

From the 9th of July when they arrived in Florence, until the 20th of July when the First Company was finally underway again, a great deal had to be accomplished. Journal entries reflect the efforts made to repair and upgrade the handcarts, outfitting wheels with iron hoops and boxing areas around the axles with copper to make them move easier and result in fewer future breakdowns. Tents were repaired and replaced as needed, as were ox yokes. There was even some spare wood stored in the wagons. Flour and other food staples; cattle for beef and milk; and additional oxen and stock for the wagons were acquired for the journey.[12] There were even some rifles and their accrudiments purchased to enable the brethren to shoot game along the trail to supplement their food supply. They would be especially useful in buffalo country, where one animal would supply a great quantity of meat, and they would only shoot what they would need which would keep it fresh.

While the flour and sawmills that had been built by early Saints could supply many finished products, not everything that was needed was at Florence. Several of the men were sent down the Missouri to trade and purchase what was required. All such activities being under the direction of the commissary and other Church officials at Florence.

On Sunday, July 13th Church services were held at which Elders McGraw, Ellsworth and McArthur spoke. Meetings on this Sabbath were somewhat different because several rowdies and apostates attended that were expected to cause trouble. In spite of the possible threat, the speakers "spoke heavy upon apostates" and were feeling that all in attendance needed the message. However, purely as a precaution, the brethren had earlier cut about 20 heavy walking sticks that were distributed to select men to carry with them throughout the day. Fortunately nothing occurred to hinder the Sabbath or the Saints.[13]

In the midst of all the preparations, two deaths occurred:

SECOND COMPANY
15 July - Tuesday
> "This morning a child died which was born during the night, belonging to Peter and Eliza Richardson from Liverpool I made the coffin; and at 12 O'clock to our great surprise Eliza Haliker a German Sister about 20 years died very suddenly in camp, great mourning ensued for she was a lovely and noble girl as we had in our

division we obtained lumber and Bro. Ramsey made the coffin mostly. I also obtained some ox yoke timber and in the afternoon made one yoke. Today George Grant came here with upwards of 50 head of cattle and over 50 head of calves"[14]

Eliza Holiker [Not on any passenger or handcart company list.] was buried the next day by Spencer Crandall and some brethren from the Second Company in the Winter Quarters cemetery.[15] Although no mention is made as to where the baby was laid to rest, it is probably safe to assume it was buried there as well, probably by its father. While there may have been some type of funeral, it is more likely that it was a graveside service, with a dedication of the graves.

FIRST COMPANY

17 July - Thursday

"Left Florence City and we travelled about 3 miles. Went to ___ to seek work by buy a pair of shoes for Sarah but got no work for want of tools. Stopped there all night; slept in a stable. Came back to camp Friday morning."[16]

"The camp rolled out at 11 a.m. Traveled two and one-half miles to Summer Quarters."[17]

18 July - Friday

"Harriet very ill. Bought her some little niceties but she could not eat the pickles. Had a piece of buffalo beef given to me."[19]

"July 18th and 19th. We remained in camp till Saturday, finishing the carts and getting the balance of our outfit."[20]

SECOND COMPANY

17 July - Thursday

"Bro. Elsworth Co. rolled [?] to Cutters Park, Capt. Dan and myself helped McGow & Grant to separate and mark as also to turn over to the Church the cattle which George had bought. Made one ox yoke; helped to get Bro. Crandel and Dickman off after some yoke and berie timber. In the evening had a meeting. Bro George Capt Dan myself and Crandl spoke to the people as the spirit dictated & truly we had a time of rejoiceing. A great many of the Brethren and Sisters all out to wash so that we cannot go out to camp in a new place which would be very agreeable in consequence of a great quantity of dust in this place."[18]

18 July - Friday

"In connection with Bro. Dan made 8 pair of Ox Beaux and much other work a part of which was to help to select cows and cattle for our outfit to the Vallie. George Grant Preached to us in the evening."[21] ___

On Saturday, July 19th, the Third Handcart Company arrived in Florence. They all seemed to be in good spirits as they set up camp and prepared for the Sabbath day.[22] So far three handcart companies had crossed Iowa without any major problems, and the Church leadership were very pleased with the whole concept.

THE FINAL PUSH TOWARD THE MOUNTAINS OF THE LORD

Finally on Sunday, July 20th at 6:00 a.m., the First Company, having completed their preparations, left Florence and traveled seven miles before pitching their tents at half past nine. All agreed that it was good to be under way again.[23] It would be four more days before the Second Company would depart Florence.[24]

FIRST COMPANY

21 July - Monday

"Travelled about 18 miles. Harriet better."[25]

"The camp rolled out at nine a.m. and traveled eighteen miles. Crossed the Elk Horn by the Ferry Boat and camped about five p.m. Before all the tents were pitched we had quite a thunder storm, and continued more or less all the night."[26]

SECOND COMPANY

21 July - Monday

"Florence Nebraska This morning the Genoa landed and left 800 sacks of flour with sugar apples etc etc. We onloaded 3 wagons and yoked 6 yokes of oxen and Capt. Dan Crandel and myself took charge of them and drove 4 loads apiece, or at least 2 of us. Bunkers teams also helped. In the evening had another tin— with the cows. In the afternoon Baptised a Prusian by the name of Heffing also rebaptised Ludert and Mother Lourermore Brother Crandel went with me."[27]

Out on the trail once more, there were some that began to have second thoughts. Most paid no attention to their internal doubts, but one brother did. From Mary Powell's journal:

"One afternoon father notice Brother Jones pull away and halt by the side of the road. "What's the matter Brother Jones?" asked father. "I see danger ahead," said Brother Jones. "I promised Ann's father I wouldn't

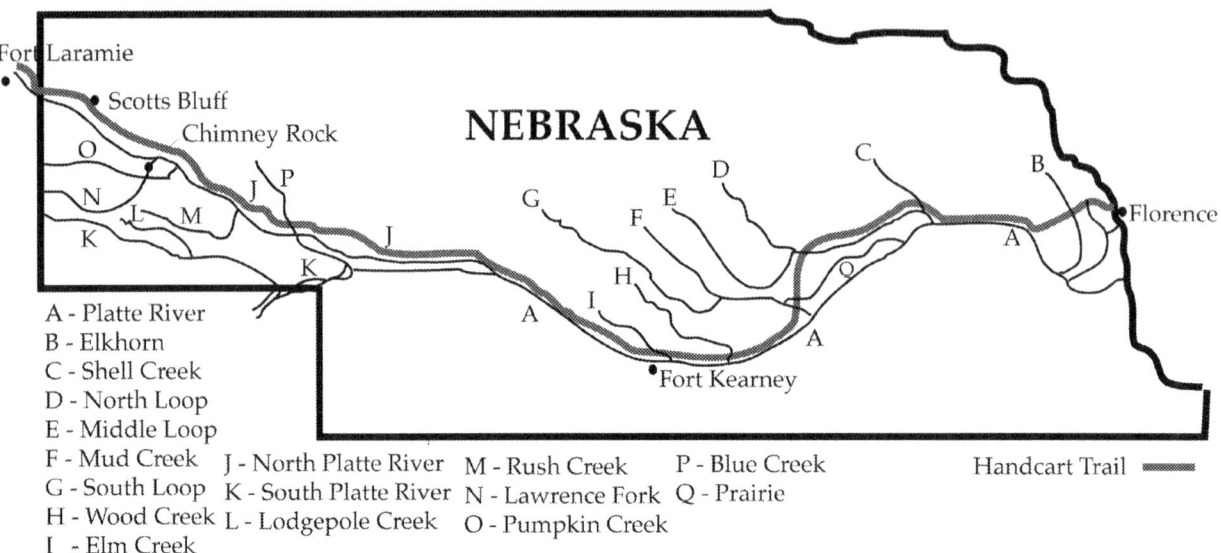

Figure 26: *From Florence, Nebraska to Fort Laramie, Wyoming*

lead her into suffering. I see danger ahead." Brother Jones and his wife remained behind in Omaha. Brother Jones being a butcher by trade, likely secured good work. Father said, We should give him due credit for keeping his word to Ann's father."[28]

FIRST COMPANY

22 July - Tuesday

"Passed off the ferry at elk Horn. Travelled about 12 miles. Thunder storm."[29]

"The camp rolled out at twelve p.m. and traveled seventeen miles along a good road. Passed five dead oxen. Camped at half past seven p.m. at Liberty Pole camping ground close to the Platte River."[30]

23 July - Wednesday

"Very hot day. Travelled about 14 miles. Harriet much better."[32]

"The camp rolled out at half past seven a.m. and traveled fourteen and one half miles. Camped at Loop Fork at four p.m. An excellent camping place. Good feed for cattle. The roads were rather heavy and the day very warm. Water scarce."[33]

SECOND COMPANY

22 July - Tuesday

"Capt Dan and myself made some ship lashes, I also bought some pant stuff, and some hickory for shirts paid 1.70 Elizabeth [?] ooddle made the pants and Sister Wanless the shirts of Hickory busy in getting ready as also waiting for McGowe, got Haples and sings"[31]

23 July - Wednesday

"This morning had a wagon bought for us at 75 dollars, which we had to make beaux for we also got our out fit on the wagons and guns [?] lected with a limited portion of amunition, I also had the mule shod and staples furnished and fret in In the evening had a meeting Capt Dan put it upon Bro. Crandle and myself to talk to the people. much good and powerful instruction was given. after which Bro James Reed by his own carlessness was shot by some scoundrel through the thigh; he cannot go on the wound is so serious."[34]

The Second Company finished their preparations for leaving on July 24th. They took with them; "12 yoke of oxen, 4 wagons, and 48 carts; ... 5 beef and 12 cows; flour, 55 lbs. per head, 100 lbs. rice, 550 lbs. sugar, 400 lbs. dried apples, 125 lbs. tea, and 200 lbs. salt for the company."[35] It had taken them a bit longer, as they had to wait for supplies to show up by steamboat and cattle to be purchased. Traveling 7 miles, they camped on the little Papoose. Their handcarts had covered the distance without incidence, but the wagons were so heavily loaded, it took 5 to 7 yoke of oxen to draw each of them up the hill out of Florence. Needless to say, the wagons were the last ones to the campsite.

Then, as if the Second Company hadn't had enough challenges for one day, during the night one of their mules ran off with a heavy ox yoke attached to him. The next day Captain McArthur and Brother Bowering left at daybreak to bring him back. The wagon teams were obliged to make do with one less yoke of cattle, and did fairly well for 16 miles, until they became bogged down at Horn crossing when they tried to cross big Pappy.

FIRST COMPANY

25 July - Friday
"Travelled about 18 ½ miles."³⁶

"The camp rolled out at seven a.m. and traveled nineteen miles. The roads were pretty good with the exception of about five miles. Rather sandy. Camped at six p.m. two miles from Loop Ferry Fork." ³⁷

SECOND COMPANY

25 July - Friday
"...where we become bog down we also left one at the camp ground When he arrived at 5 o'clock but not in time to get over and to a good camp ground. At 8 Capt Dan came in with the mule but Bowering was down and 2 or 3 miles back having traveld over 40 miles on one meal of vietuals. Quite a number of Omahas upon the ground, and in the night 1 of them was wounded in a [__?]"³⁸

Figure 27:
Indian Chief Pulling a "Little Wagon"

Patrick Birmingham found personal contact with Indians to be a bit different than what he had expected:

"Traveled 20 miles, to Elkhorn River, where we found a camp of Indians, many of whom came to meet us and were very friendly. The chief took my cart and drew it into camp about ¼ mile and although a tall strong looking man, it made the perspiration run down his face until it dropped on the ground. Many of the Indians got drunk in the night and commenced fighting among themselves, but not knowing what they were at we were all called out of our beds and ordered to load our guns. After watching for some time, all became quiet and we returned again to the arms of Morpheus. In the morning we heard that one of the Indians had been shot in the arm by one of his fellows, which we soon verified, their sending over to our camp to know if we had a doctor amongst us. Brother Eatkin went and dressed it."³⁹

As the days went by on the trail, except where unusual circumstances arose, a daily routine more or less developed:

"Each morning at daybreak the bugle sounded, up we rose and assembled for prayer. We then ate a scanty breakfast of dough cakes, fried in the frying pan. Once in a while we would have a few stewed apples. Then we were ready for our march. At ten o'clock we rested one-half hour, then we traveled until we came to water. At the next meal we would eat what was left over from breakfast. At night we often went to bed without supper. There was very little food to cook and we were too tired to cook it. There were twenty-one persons in father's big round tent when we pitched every night. We spread out quilts and blankets and went to sleep.⁴⁰

Figure 28: *Struck By Lightening On The Trail*

STRUCK BY LIGHTENING

Today is Saturday, July 26th. After six hours the First Company has finally finished unloading the last group that crossed over the Ferry at Luke Fort. Under the trees by the river people can rest in comfort, but the temperature unloading handcarts and wagons in that sun must be 100 degrees. It's bound to be a long haul before we stop to camp for the day; it would sure be nice if the wagons could keep up.

Walkin' down this trail is just what was expected, hot and dusty. Havin' a broad brimmed hat keeps off the sun real good, but it doesn't take long before it builds up a dam of sweat under the band, until the hair on your head feels like a mop in a bucket that slops over your face and down your neck. Clothing soon gets soaked, and that breeze that always seems to be blowing is so warm it never leaves anyone feelin' anything but hot and sticky.

Overhead clouds that have been just long wispy fingers scattered here and there move across the sky at a great speed like hands rushing to clap. But the nearer they approach, the more they begin to twist and turn, folding into fists that bang against one another. The sky begins to churn like milk being poured into a bucket, frothing and splashing, but instead of staying white it turns darker and darker, a shade at a time. Low rumbling sounds begin to echo in the distance and the wind pushes harder against each traveler. The Swiss would say that ole' Rip Van Winkle is bowling a game with some of the little men, the loud thunder being the noise of the pins being hit and flying across the heavens

The overcast sky has calmed the direct effects of a scorching sun, but the clouds that have formed are now sure enough rain clouds that might bring a gully washer of a storm. With the handcarts strung out across the prairie, like a long winding snake, experience has taught the handcart pushers and pullers to move a little faster. If things do not change soon, a storm will be upon them and they hope not to be caught out in the open if they can prevent it.

A sky now churned to black, hangs over the column and as the thunder moves closer to the company, so also does the lightning, tearing jagged wounds in the sky. Suddenly great amounts of rain fall, instantly soaking everyone to their skin. A crack of thunder peals across the sky accompanied by a sudden flash of lightening that arks down, grounding itself in the middle of the train with a great explosion. Those closest to the site of the thunderbolt are pounded against the ground, while others leap to hoped for safety under a cart or wagon, instinctively fleeing from such a destructive power.

After a second or two in eternal suspension, during which the scene is forever etched into the minds of all present, people again begin to move, to recover their composure. The thunder and lightening having passed quickly, each now looked to the welfare of their own. During the head count it is discovered that 58 year old Brother Henry Walker had received a direct hit and lay dead on the ground from the blast. While Walker's wife and children were physically unharmed, a little boy named James Studard had been hurt. He was so badly burned, he was not expected to live, but those who administered to him felt that not only would he recover, but would again be able to walk. His father William, Betsy Tay [lor] and several others that were close by in the column, had also been knocked to the ground by the blast but they seemed to recover rapidly. [41]

With the help of some of the brethren, Brother Walker's body was placed on Archer Walters handcart, and once again he resumed his place in line as the company moved on for another 2 miles before making camp. [42] As Walters moved his burden along, he carefully studied those around him. Everyone looked shaken and uncomfortable, but still they rolled on as if nothing had happened. And Archer began to ponder the matter:

> "Look at them, they seem to be acting like nothing has happened. I don't know! It just doesn't seem right that this good man should be dead, and everyone just acts as if there's nothing they can do."

Well, just how would you have them act? Should they fall down on the ground, tear their clothes as the ancient Jews would, and put on sackcloth and ashes?

> "No, that wouldn't help anything, but why is it that **I** seem to be the only one that ever makes the effort to take care of problems as they arise? Why didn't Captain Ellsworth call up the wagons and have Brother Walker's body put on one of them? It doesn't seem right for him to be laid across the top of my cart like an oversized rag doll, in plain view of his family and all of the sisters who worry that such a thing might happen to their husband or children."

Then Captain Ellsworth is wrong and he doesn't care? Maybe it should have been him hit by that lightening bolt, instead of poor Brother Walker?

> "No! Such thoughts are wrong. Why would I even think such an evil thought? It's just that...that it would be nice if someone **else** would take the responsibility for making coffins, digging graves, repairing handcarts and wagons, and all the thousand other things I always seem to end up having to do. I'm just so weary...."

I guess that you feel then that someone else needs to be trusted as much as you, so that you won't have to be burdened with such heavy responsibilities? You who have always gone out of your way to help anyone in need. Now that they have come to trust you and rely upon you, it's now just too much of a burden.

> "What? Just what am I thinking of? Of course I'm happy that I can be of service to my brothers and sisters. Of course I don't want them to go elsewhere as long as I have the strength and ability to help, it's my duty and a way of showing the real love that I have for each of them. Where do I get such thoughts? Maybe singing will lift my spirits." And he began to sing:

> > Come, come, ye Saints, no toil nor labor fear;
> >   But with joy wend your way.
> > Though hard to you this journey may appear,
> >   Grace shall be as your day.
> > 'Tis better far for us to strive
> >   Our useless cares from us to drive;
> > Do this and joy your hearts will swell—
> >   All is well! All is well!
> >
> > Why should we mourn or think our lot is hard?
> >   Tis' not so, all is right.

Why should we think to earn a great reward
    If we now shun the fight?
Gird up your loins; fresh courage take.
    Our God will never us forsake;
And soon we'll have this tale to tell—
    All is well! All is well!

We'll find the place which God for us prepared,
    Far away in the West,
Where none shall come to hurt or make afraid;
    There the Saints will be blessed.
We'll make the air with music ring,
    Shout praises to our God and King;
Above the rest these words we'll tell—
    All is well! All is well!

And should we die before our journey's through,
    Happy day! All is well!
We then are free from toil and sorrow, too;
    With the just we shall dwell!
But if our lives are spared again
    To see the Saints their rest obtain,
Oh, how we'll make this chorus swell—
    All is well! All is well! [43]

Finally the campsite is reached, where tomorrow Brother Walker's body will be laid to rest on a sandy rise on the right hand side of the road. He'll have to be buried without a coffin, as there are no boards to be had. [44]

FIRST COMPANY

26 July - Saturday

"At nine a.m. the camp rolled towards the ferry, where we were detained five hours in crossing. At half past five p.m. the camp again moved on about three miles, where we were overtaken by a most terrific storm of thunder and rain. In the open prairie without tents. Two brothers and two sisters were knocked down by lightening. Brother Henry Walker from Carlisle was killed. Age fifty-eight. He was a faithful man to his duty. We again moved on for one and one quarter miles and camped for the night. Traveled six miles."[45]

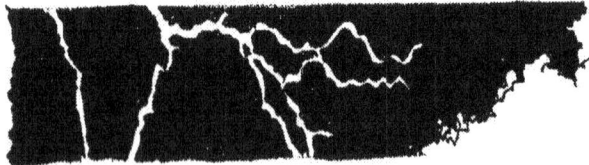

27 July - Sunday

"... four miles west of Luke Fort Ferry. Rose about 4 o'clock. Put a new axletree to a cart that was brok yesterday. Travelled about 2 miles to a better camping ground."[48]

"...At twelve noon the camp rolled out and traveled two and a half miles to a better camping ground, where we remained for the rest of the day. A beef was skilled at night for the camp. About eight p.m. a meeting was called Brothers Oakley, France, and Ellsworth addressed the meeting."[49]

SECOND COMPANY

26 July - Saturday

"Elkhorn At half past 7 was at the ferry ready to cross before this I had bot a chain to supply one that we had lost paid 2 dollars for it, we the teams [?] 1/2 dollar each. got all across safely in little less than 2 hours, I worked very hard; swam our cattle and were ready to start at 10 O'clock across to the Platte 14 miles without water, heavy sand a part of the way, arrived a 5 O'clock greatly rejoiceing a getting water, the day was cool or we should suffered severely; arrived just in time to escape a heavy shower of rain."[46]

"Crossed Elkhorn River by means of a very roughly constructed ferry. For the conveyance of us over, the company had to pay $6. Travelled 15 miles without water until we came to the Platte River, where the water was a joyful sight to many, being 6 or 7 hours under the burning sun without a drop to cool our tongues."[47]

27 July - Sunday

"Fine day took a bathe in the Platte changed our clothes and rested all day. took good care of the cattle salted them and on yoked all the wild steers In the evening had a meeting Capt. Dan Crandel and myself as usual spoke to the people and that too most satisfactorily. In the evening [?] some bullets, there also collected at our tent some girls and sang for us. The people felt first rate and nearly all are well or improving very fast. one boy however cut his foot."[50]

"Camped all day on the north bend of the Platte. Took a dose of castor oil which sickened me very much and kept me cantering for a long time."[51]

THE TRIAL OF FAITH AND ENDURING TILL THE END

Many members of the handcart companies had personal problems, illnesses and afflictions they privately dealt with each day. But still they went on, exercising their faith and hoping, always trusting God was with them. From Patrick Bermingham's journal:

> "Monday ... Rather weak this morning and terribly annoyed by two boils, one on my jaw about as big as a pigeon egg and another on the calf of my leg which greatly torments me when pulling the handcart. With such sores at home I would lie upon two chairs and never stir until they were healed."[52]

..... It seems like we've been travlin' forever today. Must be about 20 miles since we last paused for water, but we've finally stopped to make camp and I'm so grateful. I don't know if I could've gone another step. Right now I've got to lie down for a while, just gotta' have a little rest, then I'll get on with helping set up the camp. Between these miserable boils and pulling the cart all day, I'm totally exhausted. So's Kate, she's also worn out, I'll just pull her down beside me. The children...I'm sure the children... u'll be alright, just a little rest.... a short nap.... then.... some dinner.... It's so good just to rest.....

And like so many other weary travelers, he falls into an exhausted sleep, intended to last but a few short minutes, but in reality lasts a few hours. During such times the children are left in the care of the Saints in the Company and the Savior for protection. Birmingham suddenly aroused from sleep by the mournful cries of his child, blurts out....

> "…. why are you crying my sweet baby, are you hungry my little one? Can't wait one more minute? What time is it?" What did I do with that watch...I've been asleep two hours and Kate's still asleep. "Oh my dear ones, forgive me, Papa just can't cook tonight and Momma needs to sleep, I'll see what's left in the cart from breakfast."
>
> Struggling to move, he uses the wheel on the handcart to pull himself up, every movement is one of agony... ...It hurts so much to move, but I've got to. If I can just pull myself up a little bit more, there. Now where would it be...got to be here some where, ah there it is. It's not much, just a bit of bread, but with the pint of milk they brought us this evening, it'll have to do. "I thank Thee Father for this food for our children to eat, please let it nourish them and satisfy their hunger...it'll just have to, for we have no other."

Figure 29: *Handcarts Pioneers Heading To A Home In Zion*

The week passes on, day by day, footstep after footstep, mile after mile, ever closer to the valley and home.

The calendar shows we've finally reached Sunday, but right now it doesn't seem any different than any other day of the week. We got up, broke camp and left at five o'clock without any breakfast. We've been stugglin' through miles of heavy sand, where in some places the wheels were buried up to the boxes. With every movement I'm reminded of the rest this Sabbath was set aside for. I'm so weak from thirst, hunger and exhaustion, and the pain of these cursed boils that never seem to give up. If we just didn't pull out of line from time to time so I could to lie down, I don't think I could go on. But I'm not the only one that's had to rest frequently, I see more and more all the time having to do the same thing. Many didn't make the choice to lie down; they just fell down on the trail in utter exhaustion.

Earlier today when I turned to look behind me, to see how my family was doing, I thought my heart would burst. There was poor, sick Kate down in the sand crawling on her hands and knees behind the cart, trying to keep up. And the children were walking along beside her, crying and pulling on her to get up. They too were greatly struggling, being bone tired and hungry. All I could do was give them a moment's rest, then put the little ones on the handcart and urged the others along the road so we would keep up. Oh God and Father of us all, have mercy on us, please help us to keep up. Don't let us be left behind in this wilderness. Strengthen us in our efforts and bless us with our needs, if not for me, at least for Kate and the Children...

Strengthened by the exercise of his faith and a fresh surge of energy to his family and their resolve, they once again begin to pick up the pace...

At about 12 o'clock a thunderstorm blew in that cracked open the overcast skies like an egg, suddenly dumping torrents of rain. Quickly the column halted and set about the task of pitching tents in the rain, which didn't happen very fast since the wagons are at the tail end of the company. With the tent poles finally available the tents were raised despite the heavy winds, but once up it did little good as we were still standing up to our knees in water, and every stitch we had was the same as if it had been dragged through the river. It will probably rain all night, but surely God will then send us sunshine and a beautiful day to take a walk. In the meantime we can get some rest, even in our wet clothes, we'll have no trouble sleeping...[53]

FIRST COMPANY

28 July - Monday
"Travelled about 18 miles. Harriet much better; for such we feel thankful."[54]

"At fifteen past seven a.m. the camp rolled out and traveled twenty miles. The roads in many parts were heavy. We rested two hours and had dinner. We turned up to the right about half a mile and camped for the night at half past six p.m."[55]

29 July - Tuesday
"Travelled about 15 miles. Met a Company coming from California. A child born in camp. Sister Doney. My birthday."[57]

"At nine a.m. camp rolled out and ascended a bluff to the right of the camping ground. Traveled fifteen miles. The roads in some parts a little sandy. Camped at quarter to three p.m. about four miles from the upper crossing. Plenty of wood and water. Two good springs on the west side of the camp ground. One of them dug out by Brother Card."[58]

30 July - Wednesday
"Travelled 22 miles."[60]

"The camp rolled out at seven and traveled twenty-five miles. A great part of the road very sandy and heavy for handcarts and wagons. No wood, no water till we camped, and that not very plentiful. Still plenty for camping purpose. Camped at fifteen past six p.m."[61]

SECOND COMPANY

28 July - Monday
"Rose early and was ready to start at half past 6 O Clock, traveled on nicely tho, some sand, traveled 12 miles and came to the North bend of the Plat here we were made glad again to get water as we had suffered considerable. Stoped 2 hours became refreshed and went about 5 or 6 miles further, and camped at a settlement whare a man by the Name of McNaughton joined us with family a team 6 cows, he promised to haul some of our people ones that does not belong to the Church."[56]

29 July - Tuesday
"Left our Camp at half past 8 as it rained severly we [s]tarted our wagons and passed Shell creek at 12 O'clock and then went a long stretch of 13 mi made a grass bridge and crossed by doubling teams, rolled on till dark over a heavy and wet road, camped again on the Platte 18 miles."[59]

30 July - Wednesday
"Started at half past 6, went 7 miles and stoped at Turkey Grove a while, and then went on to the Ferry 2 miles further where we arrived at 3 O'clock. Birch the Ferryman said we would get across this evening, because the water was low and we would have to move the Ferry, but Capt. Dan and I went in a canoe with Birch and found where we could ford nearly all the way and push the load and by

hard work and about 40 of us wet to the neck nearly we got over and at camp about dark. We with some difficulty swam the cattle I got on the back of one I called Lou my near shirl at and led the band, the water was swimming dirt for a short distance. The Ferryman treated us with the best of Brandy and his charge was nine dollars giving us a bottle of the oratter into the bargain. Camped with a lot of return California Emigrants. Good news in the Vallie the 20th of July they were harvesting rye, Capt Edmond is about 55 mile ahead of us doing his best, had a man killed by [__?]"[62]

"Started early this morning and travelled 12 miles to Loup-fork ferry, over which we had to ferry the cars and wagons and women and children. It was really funny to see some 50 of the Brethren hauling a large ferry boat over this ferry and when they would come to a deep place in the stream, all make a rush to get on the boat, some succeeding, some tumbling in and others obliged to swim for it. It took 32 hours to ferry all over. Camped on the other side."[63]

For the few that always seemed to be looking for an easier way, there was always ample opportunity, even in the wilderness, to turn down a different road and travel a different direction. The handcart companies encountered many going to or returning from the gold fields of California. They always had yarns to spin and lots of reasons why it would be better in gold-filled California than in rock filled Utah. For example, the McNaughton family that had joined up with the Second Company July 28th had promised to haul some of the company's people when they stopped at a settlement. Instead they quickly dropped out:

"This morning the California Gold diggers persuaded McNaughton to go back, which we were glad of because he was of no account."[64]

FIRST COMPANY

31 July - Thursday
"Travelled 18 miles. Heavy thunder-storm."[65]

"The camp rolled out at seven a.m. and traveled eighteen miles. The road leading from the camp is a heavy sandy road and continued so for about thirteen miles. It is also very hilly. Camped about fifteen minutes past six p.m. alongside of Prairie Creek. No wood, but plenty of buffalo chips. There is a well about seven miles from where we camped last night on the right hand side of the road."[66]

SECOND COMPANY

31 July - Thursday
"...Started out and went about 8 miles at a good camp ground, plenty of wood etc. 14 or about 15 miles further without water making about 23 in all in good spirits only 2 or 3 gave out. Camped on the Loup Fork in a beautiful place, got in at 7 O'clock looked much like rain but passed off."[67]

The next morning as with every morning, at the call of their leaders, the Saints rose up and pressed on toward the Zion a prophet of God had called them to. For these, the faithful, there was no problem too large or any obstacle too great. Just as there is nothing too hard for the Lord, could there be anything to hard for His gathering Israel?

On the trail the pioneers were always on the lookout for food to supplement their dwindling supplies. On rare occasions when berry bushes were found, the children were sent out to pick all they could find while the handcart train kept on moving. At night, where appropriate, some men were sent out with rifles to find any game that might be available. From time to time, buffalo would be encountered, sometimes one or two, sometimes large herds, but they were always welcomed as a good meat source. On August 1st, the First Company passed a buffalo herd and Captain Ellsworth went out with his rifle. He managed to wound two buffalo, but failed to bring either one down. The herd ran off before anyone else could be found to try. The men for the most part had learned where they had to hit a buffalo to bring him down with a rifle shot, but unfortunately most were not good enough marksmen to always hit the spot.

FIRST COMPANY

1 August - Friday

"The camp rolled out at eight a.m. Traveled sixteen miles. The road is in good condition. Crossed Prairie Creek twice. The second crossing, the handcarts had to be carried over by the brethren. There was a little difficulty in getting the wagons over, the banks of the creek were so steep. We also crossed Wood River by means of a good bridge. At thirty past six p.m. we camped alongside of Wood River. Plenty of wood and water. A good camping ground."[68]

2 August - Saturday

"Crossed over 2 creeks, forded them. Stop dinner. Camped by Wood River. We saw many buffalo. Travelled about 18 miles."[71]

SECOND COMPANY

1 August - Friday

"Left camp at half past 6 traveled 8 miles and came to where the road left the Loup fork, over a heavy sand hill which we raised by doubling teams heavily after going a mile to the river to supply us and our cattle with water. We left at one O'clock and for some time the roads were sandy traveled about 12 miles & camped on the South fork again about a mile distant and near where the old road came in. It looked much like rain but it again passed off."[69]

"23 miles over a bad road. No water, only what we carried. Sister Hardy from Scotland fainted on the road today."[70]

2 August - Saturday

"Day cool and beautiful traveled 5 miles & came to a fine spring of water, here Capt Elsworth com. camped and had a child come leaving notice to that effect as also stating it was 25 miles to water, we put in a good supply and traveled till dark over a heavy road & camped without water The day was a very fatiguing one to us"[72]

"Started early this morning and travelled 28 miles over a very bad road, having to pull the carts through heavy sand, sometimes for miles. We were obliged to carry water with us today. Camped on the open prairie without either wood or water and consequently had to go to bed supperless."[73]

For the First Company, the Sabbath of August 3rd was mainly restful. Captain Ellsworth reported that they "remained in camp all day and attended such duties as we were necessitated to do." They had a worship meeting at 7:00 p.m. "Brothers Oakley, Butler and Ellsworth addressed the Saints."[74] Archer Walters journal showed his mind to be mainly on other things:

3 August - Sunday

"Rested but mended hand carts. Got shell fish out of the creek for we was very hungry. Only ¾ lb. of flour; 1½ oz. of sugar; a few apples; tea plenty."[75]

The Sabbath of the Second Handcart Company that had stopped at another campsite was totally different. The previous day they had received a message from Ellsworth's company that it was 25 miles from the spring at which McArthur was presently camped, to the next water supply. With this information, they loaded up on water and traveled on Saturday until dark over a heavy road and camped with only the water they had left, being worn out with their long day's journey.

On Sunday morning they rose early and were ready to start, when they had a mishap with one of their mules:

3 August - Sunday

"Up early and just as we were ready to start, the mule stumbled threw its rider got away and ran about 16 miles. This gave Capt Dan and me a hard pull. I ran most of the way and finally caught the animal before I knew that McArthur was within 5 miles of me as I had out run him & supposed he had gone back. The mule appeared to be bound for water & determined to make the main Platte 28 miles distant, but coming to a dry slew he stacked up and with some difficulty I got hold of the lasso & then I saw at a distance Capt Dan swinging his hat for joy. We then both got upon the mule & come back to the joy of the camp and I think my legs was as lame as ever I had them, at this time Crandel was getting on 5 or 6 miles after which we went to Prairie Creek in all about 16 miles, though at 10, we found a slew out of which we watered our animals and had some refreshments. In the evening we killed a beef creature, a muley I shot her and it was dressed in less than an hour."[76]

By the time they finally got back to camp at 11:00 p.m. and had just settled down for the evening, the alarm was given that the cattle were gone and the guards were asleep. Needless to say, the rest of the night was spent hunting down the cattle and returning them to the camp.[77]

FIRST COMPANY

4 August - Monday
"At quarter to eight a.m. the camp rolled out and traveled eighteen miles. Good roads. Camped at quarter to three p.m. near the Platte."[78]

SECOND COMPANY

4 August - Monday
"In the morning heavy rain which detained us till 1 O'Clock. we then hitched up and crossed Prairie Creek 2 rods wide and 2 feet deep, and went 10 miles and camped on the same creek again good feed and water, though heavy road to it"[79]

On Tuesday, August 5th, the Second Company decided to not leave until afternoon to allow the women to wash and the men to repair handcarts, etc. As it turned out, it also became a time to say good-by to dear Brother Aniki Smith, who died a few minutes before noon. He knew he was dying and asked as many as possible to gather round him to hear his last words:

"My time has come to meet my maker, but before I do I want as many of you as possible to witness that I did with my last breath bear testimony that I know Brigham Young is a prophet of God and that this Church we have been baptized into is Christ's true Church on the earth, and without a doubt, Mormonism is true.... true. I have lived my life as best I could according to what God has given me understanding to know and because of it, I will come forth in the first resurrection and be with Christ as He rules upon the earth. Please remember me to Brigham Young, his counselors and my friends in the valley.

"Now, dear friends, come forth and shake my hand and bid me a fond farewell. That I might feel your spirit and your love and have that memory to take with me into the world of spirits where I shall wait for you when your time comes to lay your mortal by. Thank you brother... Thank you sister.... Thank you all. **HALLELUJAH! Hallelujah!** Hallelujah...."[80]

At 15 minutes before 12 o'clock he died. His body was wrapped in sheets and he was buried within 12 feet of where he died. Brother Leonard got a heavy post, attached a wide board and had Brother Henry Bowering cut Aniki Smith's name, age, date of death, the camp he belonged to, etc., into it. Captain McArthur said a few appropriate words at the graveside, and by 3:00 p.m. the handcart train departed.

THE HANDCART SONG
Day by day and mile by mile, the Saints found a variety of things to fill their time and thoughts. One of their favorite things to do was to sing, especially when the way was flat and there was not so much chance of being out of breath. They especially sang the "Handcart Song" by J.D.T. McAllister.

Ye Saints that dwell on Europe's shores,
Prepare yourselves with many more
To leave behind your native land
    For sure God's Judgments are at hand.
Prepare to cross the stormy main
Before you do the valley gain
And with the faithful make a start
    To cross the plains with your hand cart.

The land that boasts of liberty
You ne'er again may wish to see
While poor men toil to earn their bread
    And rich men are much better fed,
And people boast of their great light.
You see they are as dark as night
And from them you must make a start
To cross the plains with our handcarts.

But some will say it is too bad
The Saints upon their feet to pad
And more than that to push a load

As they go marching up the road.
We say this is Jehovah's plan
To gather out the best of men,
And women too, for none but they
Will ever gather in this way.

As on the way the carts are hurled
'Twould very much surprise the world
To see the old and feeble dame
    Lending her hand to push the same.
The young girls they will dance and sing,
The young men happier than a king,
The children they will laugh and play
Their strength increasing day by day.

But ere before the valley gained
We will be met upon the plains
With music sweet and friends so dear
    And fresh supplies our hearts to cheer.
Then with the music and the song,
How cheerfully we'll march along
So thankfully you make a start
To cross the plains with our handcarts.

When we get there amongst the rest
Industrious be and we'll be blessed,
And in our chambers be shut in
    While Judgment cleanse the earth from sin.
For well we know it will be so,
God's servants spoke it long ago,
And tell us it's high time to start
To cross the plains with our handcarts.

CHORUS   Some must push and some must pull
        As we go marching up the hill,
    As merrily on the way we go
        Until we reach the valley, oh. [81]

McArthur's Second Company was now about three days journey behind Ellsworth's First Company, and for a little over one month the two groups stayed separated by two or three days. However, McArthur had liked being almost side by side with Ellsworth as they crossed Iowa, and was determined that it should be that way again. As a result, according to some in his company, McArthur pushed everyone at a faster than necessary pace, slowing down only when he had no other choice. His persistence finally paying off on September 11th, three days past Independence Rock. From that point on McArthur pushed his people to stay up with Ellsworth, with the latter determined to keep the lead, which he believed was supposed to be his proper position.

SECOND COMPANY
    6 August - Wednesday
    "Traveled 17 miles and camped on Wood river, passed several lots of Emigrants on their return from the gold mines They gave us good news about the Vallie and also told us that Bro. Elsworth was only about 40 miles ahead of us; our road today was rather bad over many deep slews, dry creeks and hollows etc. The day was very warm and fatigueing, several or quite sick too, and our teams are complaining of their loads as they are nearly as heavy as they were when we started. Crossed Wood River Bridge about 5 O 'Clock and camped about 6 on the same stream"[82]

7 August - Thursday

"Opposite to Fort Kearney, crossed a dry Prairie 18 miles and arrived at a Branch of the Platte at 2 O'Clock, day cool and beautiful, rested 2 hours and went on 6 miles and camped on deep dry creek good feed and buffalo chips with water."[83]

BUFFALO

During the long walk across the open plains between Florence and the turnoff over the mountains toward the Valley of the Great Salt Lake, those gathering to Zion encountered a new animal of great size and number. During the early and mid-nineteenth century, the plains were blanketed with herds of buffalo that were so large that it often took more than a day for one herd to pass.

6 August - Wednesday

"Saw thousands of buffalo. 4 was killed. So thick together that they covered 4 miles at once. Camped by Buffalo Creek. Travelled 10 miles."[84]

"At nine a.m. the camp rolled out and traveled twelve miles. Roads good. Camped about two p.m. on Buffalo Creek four miles from the crossing of B. Creek. We killed four buffaloes today. The camp got quite a good supply of meat."[85]

"One day we saw a speck like a cloud of dust miles behind us. The cloud kept moving toward us and increasing and within two hours an immense herd of buffalo passed us. It looked as if the whole prairie was moving, and it took more than an hour for them to cross the road before we could go on. They didn't seem to notice in the least, but moved right along solid and dumb in one great mass. They passed us at a steady trot and not one soul was harmed.[86]

For many centuries buffalo had been a major food source and mainstay for those that lived in the plains of the North America, especially the Native Americans. Indians spiritual training and life style did not allow them to waste animal life. As a result they learned to use every part of the buffalo from his horns to his tail. His flesh nourished their bodies; his hide kept them warm in the winter and covered their living quarters; his bones held tent sections together and were shaped into various tools; and his intestines were used to carry and store water. Even their dry waste droppings [manure] were used to make hot odorless fires for cooking, known to the pioneers as "buffalo chips," which were very valuable as they trudged across the treeless plains of western Nebraska.

On many occasions, the buffalo also proved to be the physical salvation of the white man traveling through the Midwest. In many ways they imitated their Indian neighbors in the animals uses, especially the mountain men and explorers. It was a sad and wicked day when the greed of the white man began to wantonly destroy such a valuable natural resource. Killing these great beasts for their hides and leaving everything else to rot on the plains was one of the main reasons that the Indians tried so hard to drive the white man from their lands. It also accounted in part for their eventual surrender that ended the Indian wars, as their main food source had been eliminated.

Although a great source of fresh meat, buffalo were not always the easiest creatures in the world to deal with. To kill them required knowledge of where they should be shot to bring them down and the marksmanship to hit the spot. An injured buffalo might run for miles before it would die, or it might turn and charge the hunter. If they got in with the domestic animals, they could easily cause them to stampede, or injure them. If they decided to run where people, equipment or supplies were placed, they would trample them down and crush them like so much prairie grass. They were big, strong, excitable, and quite stupid.

"One day three men went out to shoot a buffalo. The buffalo attacked a horse and ripped its side. We didn't get any meat that day. Later a crowd of boys went out and shot a steer, that day we had beef. Our big kettle now came in handy, we put twenty pieces of meat, each piece about fifty cents worth of beef, into our bake kettle. In this way we cooked for about twenty families. There being no wood, we gathered buffalo chips and built a hot fire under the kettle.[87]

Buffalo also occasionally caused problems with the places the Saints expected to stop for water, as when a herd would drink up or ruin streams, springs, or water holes. Each of the pioneer companies had a copy of the Emigrant's Guidebook88, which they followed closely. Since the Guide explained how far it was between usable camping areas and water sources, the Captains of the handcart companies tried to pace the movement of their people each day to accommodate their needs. Some places were good to stop for water and a rest, while others were better suited for camping. But unexpected actions by the buffalo, or a change in the weather, often caused water sites to be re-dug or passed by.

FIRST COMPANY

7 August - Thursday

"Thousands of buffalo. Travelled 25 miles. Camped late at night. Had to dig for water and it was very thick. Our hungry appetites satisfied by the buffalo. Got up soon to repair hand carts."[89]

"At fifteen to nine a.m. the camp rolled out, and traveled twenty-five miles. The roads good, with the exception of about two miles which is rather sandy. There is no water after leaving the crossing. Camped at about thirty past eight p.m. No water but by digging for it. No wood. Plenty of chips."[90]

"Some days we traveled more than thirty miles to reach water. Often we would come into a place where the springs had dried down. It might be near midnight and then little children would form a circle of eager watchers while the men dug down several feet to water. At last when they saw the chunks of wet mud, they would lay it on their face and hands. Some of them would suck the water from the mud. When the water burst forth it was very thick, the children drank heartily straining it through their teeth. Next morning it looked quite clear."[91]

Straining muddy or thick water through your teeth, or sucking it through a handkerchief or piece of cloth was also used when the only water available was what was left after buffalo had wallowed [walked, rolled and/or urinated] in it. Although such things might seem unthinkable, it took water and food to survive in the wilderness and pioneers did what they had to.

"Some stomachs may reject a supper cooked with water taken from a buffalo wallow, on a fire made from buffalo chips, but to us, the food was good."[92]

FIRST COMPANY   SECOND COMPANY

8 August - Friday

"Rose soon to repair carts. Travelled about 15 miles. Camped by the side of Flat River. Repaired handcarts. Harriet getting round nicely and I feel truly thankful. ...."[93]

"At fifteen to nine a.m. the camp rolled out from this place of desolation and traveled thirteen miles without water. The roads good. Camped about thirty past two alongside the Platte. By turning off to the left about one half mile you will find a good camping ground but no wood. There is another camping ground about two miles ahead."[94]

8 August - Friday

"drove about 9 miles and came to Elm creek here we were among the buffalo in earnest. Stoped and several of us went in pursuit of them, after a long walk I succeeded in getting several shots but only succeeded in killing one old bull which I shot through the spine of the back which brought him down immediately. Capt Dan shot and wounded one severly but still lost him. We took what we were able to pack and went to the train for It had started on. Peacock had killed an old cow near the road which we saved, by dark and then drove on and camped in the prairie without water. trouble with cattle"[95]

After finishing what can be described with pleasure as a rather easy journey today, it's nice to just sit down here by the Platte River to soak my feet, and drink my fill of cool water. Since it's only the middle of the afternoon, what's the rush to set up tents and gather wood or chips for a while. I think I'd just jump right into the river and float there like a log, but as sure as I did, someone would come along with a "if ya haven't got anything ta' do right now but swim, I could sure use your help." It just never fails. There's narry a soul in sight right now, but just as soon as I got in there, there would be 20 people appear out of nowhere. Gadsooks!

I do believe I'm getting some feeling back into my feet. Wish I had a fishing line and a hook, maybe I could get some nice fresh fish for dinner. I like buffalo, but I keep remembering how Momma used to lightly bread fish and fry it to a golden brown at home in Liverpool. There in her tidy little kitchen on her sparkling clean cook stove she was so proud of. And then there was the chips [no, not buffalo chips] and the fresh bread and butter and jam and even sometimes a pie or cake and lots and lots of milk to wash it all down in the greatest of ways. Oh, how that makes my mouth water. Wonder what great food delight will be cooked tonight, probably roasted buffalo. If we only had the potatoes and onions and other necessaries, we could have a great stew in that big pot, instead of just heating water.

Someone said that by some means ole' Father Sanders got left behind somewhere on the trail today. The brethren went back on foot and horseback, but as of yet they haven't found him. I guess no one noticed he was gone because he always seems to stay to himself. He's a nice enough ole' man, but he sure don't talk much. I guess he just must feel tired and a bit unnecessary. I notice that people in trying to be kind to him and keep from burdenin' him down, mostly don't ask him to do much. That can sure make a fella' feel useless, and if you're as old as he is, he might just wonder if there isn't better reason for finding the spirit world than Zion. But, who knows? I hope when they find him he's all right. I'll have to make a greater effort to spend more time with him so he feels needed.

FIRST COMPANY
9 August - Saturday
"Found the old brother Sanderson on a hill about 6 o'clock. Brought him into camp on a mule. Travelled about 15 miles after repairing hand carts until 12 o'clock."[96]

"The camp rolled out at ten past 1 p.m. and traveled thirteen miles. Brother Thomas Fowler found Father Sanders this morning about five miles ahead of the camp. The road for about seven miles is very very heavy, sandy road; hard pulling for handcarts and ox teams. Camped beside the Platte about two miles from Skunk Creek about fifteen eight p.m."[97]

SECOND COMPANY
9 August - Saturday
"Started at 5 O'clock and drove to Buffalo creek— here we stoped, and Capt Dan and I with some others went to waylay some buffalo at the watering place & killed a dry fat heifer and a young Bul both first rate beef and weighed about 800 pounds, got it secure on the carts etc and drove on about 6 miles crossing the Buffalo creek in a very bad place. feed good but water very scarce dug for it but got it the next morning. Several buffalo made an attempt to get among the cattle but we kept them at bay by firing at them. Lawson and myself shot at one and he was found dead near in the morning..."[98]

Once again the Sabbath came, and once again it seemed more or less like every other day in the journey that just seemed to go on and on. In the wilderness there are signposts to look for as described in the Emigrant's Guide, but since only a few have ever seen them before, one days scenery seems very much like every other days scenery. And the camps are put up, and the camps are put down. Sometimes there's an abundance of food and occasionally even a little variety, but after pulling and pushing handcarts all day, every soul is weary. Were it not for occasional songs and dancing, there could almost be an air of despair that Zion would never be reached. But still we push on.

But on Sunday, one would expect that things would be different. A time of worship and rest, of discussion and pleasant conversation, but here on the trail almost anything can happen. The First Company had a meeting at nine A.M., with lots of good instruction, then at about eleven moved out and traveled 14 miles,[99] with all, or most, suffering from "diarrhea or purging, Don't know whether it was the buffalo or the muddy river water."[100] They finally stopped and made camp at six P.M.

The Second Company stopped for the day, which they spent in killing a buffalo and drying its meat all about the camp, instead of traveling. They were visited by some Californians from the mines that gave them news of good crops in Salt Lake Valley. They also mentioned that about 35 miles ahead the company would run into some bad feed. A meeting was held in the evening that was addressed by Captain McArthur and Brother Crandel. Several of the sick were administered to and faith was exercised in their behalf for a full recovery.[101] Of course cooking and cart repairs were also a part of the days activities.

It had become a regular occurrence to have people visit the handcart companies both on the move and in their evening camps. Most were very curious as to why such large bodies of people were crossing the wilderness using handcarts. When they learned it was part of a religious activity that was gathering believers from all over the world; they were usually interested in hearing about the message. There were, however, some that visited because of what they thought they might be able to get, not knowing how little of worldly goods this people really had. Although many miles apart, both companies had visitors on August 11th.

The First Company met a man who claimed he was heading for the States, having traveled all this way alone.[102] The visitor to the Second Company was much more creative claiming to be starving to death and begging for provisions. He claimed his companions near Fort Bridger had robbed him as they were heading back toward the States from California. The man was fed and given bread and meat to last him four or five days.[103]

From the 11-15th of August, both companies traveled many miles through heavy sand, made even worse if it had rained the day before — which it did one day so hard that it took 2-3 more days just to get everything dry again. Meat became a major portion of their diet with buffalo or beef being killed and distributed each day. But with an average of two animals a day per company, divided between 200+ people in each, the rations could not be described as abundant. For the most part they had plenty of water and forded many creeks and streams, on some days several times. Over the five day period the First Company traveled 61 miles, averaging 14+ miles a day, fording 9 creeks or streams. The Second Company traveled 97 miles, averaging 19+ miles a day, but forded no streams.104

MOTHERS BATHGATE AND PARK

While there were many who had a tendency to move a bit slower as the days and miles rolled by, there were others like old Mother Mary Bathgate of the Second Company, a native of Scotland, that never seemed to run out of steam. She was upwards of 60 years old and without hesitation told everyone that she had been in the coal-pits for forty of those years. It was her practice to travel about a half mile ahead of the company, as "the ring leader of the footmen or those who did not pull the handcarts"105, where she would swinging her cane and shout, "Hurree for the handkerts."106

One Saturday, 16 August 1856, 147 days since the Enoch Train left Liverpool and 24 days since departing Florence, the company was traveling over 18 miles of what seemed to be the worst road on the plains, being mainly sand. The sun seemed extra hot and the prairie breeze very dry, so Mother Bathgate stopped to take a short rest. She must have been talking, instead of looking, and she sat down next to a rattlesnake that promptly bit her on the back part of her leg, just above the ankle. As soon as her companions realized what had happened they began to scream and beat the grass in fear, but it was the snake that was probably the most frightened. It must have left with great haste, as it was never reported found.107

Mother Bathgate was aggravated more than frightened, and took immediate action. First, she sent a little girl back to get Brothers McArthur, Leonard and Crandall to come "with all haste" and to bring the oil to administer to her. Then she tied her garter tight around her leg above the wound to try to stop the circulation of the poison.108

When the brethren got the word, they dropped everything and came running. By the time they arrived, her leg had swelled to four times it normal size and she was quite sick.109 They cut the wound open with a pocketknife, then squeezed out all the bad blood they could, and there was considerable because she had the forethought to apply the garter so tightly. All the time they were working on her, she kept repeating that "there was power in the priesthood, and she knew it." Then they anointed the wound and her head with consecrated oil and laid hands on her head in faith giving her a blessing and rebuking the influence of the poison. They fully believed she would be healed, and she was.110

Upon being told that she must be put into one of the wagons until she was recovered, Mother Bathgate called witnesses "to prove that she did not get into the wagon until she was compelled to by the cursed snake." She and Mother Isabella Park, both over 60 years of age, had never ridden one inch since leaving Iowa City, a fact they were proud of. There was no doubt if an alternative would have been available to riding in the wagon; she would have taken it.111

Once she was comfortably laid in a wagon, the company moved on for another two miles, before stopping to take some refreshment. But because she continued to be quite sick, the company waited about an hour and one-half before hitching up the teams to push on. As the word was given to start, old Mother Park ran in front of the wagon to see how her friend and companion was doing, just as the driver yelled to start his team. The team lurched forward where the fore wheel knocked her to the ground and rolled over both hips. Brother Leonard, who was standing close by, quickly grabbed Mother Park to pull her out of the way before the rear wheel reached her, but he was not fast enough and it caught her, running over both ankles.112

It was commonly thought that she had been hopelessly crushed, but to everyone's amazement, not a bone was broken, "although the wagon had something like two tons [of] burden on it, a load for 4 yoke of oxen." Immediately the brethren anointed and blessed her as they had Mother Bathgate, and placed her in the wagon next to her friend.113

FIRST COMPANY
16 August - Saturday
"Forded over 5 or 6 creeks. Travelled 17 miles. Camped by Wolf Creek."[114]

"The camp moved off at quarter to eight a.m. and traveled sixteen and three quarter miles. A good part of it heavy sandy traveling. Other parts of the road was good traveling. We crossed small creeks, had dinner on the banks of Camp Creek. Camp about seven p.m. on the east bank of Wolf Creek. Buffalo chips no so plentiful here. Good feed for the oxen."[115]

SECOND COMPANY
16 August - Saturday
"Traveled 18 miles over the worst road I ever passed on the plains. Almost everything worked against us to. In the first place Mother Bathgate was bitten by a rattle snake... At a stopping soon after Mother Park went to see Sister Bathgate and my wheels run over her ... two others ... also were obliged to ride so by at about 2 we were out our wagons which made it the hardest day we had"[116]

It was the ninth Sunday spent on the trail, since leaving the Iowa City Campground, and every Sabbath seemed to take on a unique existence. Ancient Israel traveling in the wilderness was required by commandment to stop and do nothing on the Sabbath but worship and rest. Even the manna that made up their food for that holy day was gathered on the day before. Yet restored Israel didn't seem to have such absolute requirements. On most Sundays the Saints usually traveled at least a few miles, and even when they stayed in camp the whole day, it was used for laundry, repair and preparation for the next days journey. And what was also strange, before they would reach the valley, there would be some Sabbath's where no worship service was held at all.

Journals from the two companies show a total of three deaths occurring August 17th, Brother Missel Rossin from Italy who was found dead by the side of the road;[117] Brother Peter Stalley also from Italy;[118] and one of Father Elakers daughters of the 2nd company.[119] The First Company traveled 12 miles, crossed Wolf Creek, ascended a sandy bluff and had no worship service. The Second Company, didn't travel, but instead spend the day hunting, repairing, mending, washing, bathing and writing. They did, however, manage to have a worship service they referred to as a "meeting."[120]

Over the next week, from the 18th to the 23rd of August, nothing spectacular seemed to have taken place. Sixteen to 24 miles a day were being traveled over "tolerable" to "very sandy" road. The First Company had one day that they had to travel 142 miles without water, and a second day they were detained 3 hours by a thunderstorm, but still had to travel 12 miles after that without water. Both companies noted a shortage of buffalo chips for fires and good feed for the animals were in unusually short supply.[121]

Both companies were now in the area of Chimney Rock, and the Second Company had visitors that told them of good crops in the Salt Lake Valley, but reported some relatives were down with sickness. Brother Leonard also mentioned in his journal that they had killed 4 rattlesnakes and had gained some on the First Company, now being only about 25-30 miles behind them. He also reported that they "gained some of Captain Elsworth Company" which seemed to imply that some from the First Company had been either left behind or had not bothered to keep up. No clarification was provided.[122]

On Saturday, August 23rd, both companies managed to get some meat for the weekend and a bit for the following week. The First Company killed a buffalo and the Second Company killed one of its beef. All the Saints were thankful to have the extra food and nourishment.[123]

ANOTHER SUNDAY ON THE TRAIL
Woke up to another Sunday on the trail. Thought we would probably be walkin' again, but was relieved to find it was to be a day of rest. The brethren told the tent captains that there would be a Sacrament Meeting at 6 this evening, and until then we could do what we found necessary or pleasant. There were several in the tent that just laid back down and went to sleep. Of course the Mothers, with a few exceptions, got up and fixed some food for their families, mostly biscuits and what ever else they had to go along with the family's issued daily ration of flour and a pint of milk. A couple of the fathers let their wives rest while they took over the cookin', but then they joined the other men working on handcart and wagon repairs.

Today there seems to be several working on shoe repairs. Some were cutting pieces from hides to put in their shoes to cover the holes from the inside, while others, deciding the hole was too large, were cutting thicker hides and fastening them around the shoes. They cut the hide wide enough to more than cover the hole, then split it on top so it could be tied in two different knots to keep it from working off too soon. Some of their attempts seem somewhat futile, but it's a matter of finding a way, or just goin' barefoot. And between the hot sand now and the rocks of the mountains they would reach in the near future, it was very necessary to cover the feet in some way.

Some wash and mend clothes, others fixed tents, some are even taking everything off of their handcart and rearranging the items on the cart so it will pull more evenly. The children, of course, went off to play as they were allowed to, and some of the young adult couples took the opportunity to take a quiet stroll to have some time alone. All in all, it was nice to just have the time to do the little things.

At 6:00 p.m. everyone was called to a Sacrament meeting. As usual, some brought blankets or coats to sit on, while others just sat on the ground or available flat rocks. There was lots of singing and words of counsel, in addition to renewing our covenants through the Sacrament. But what I remember most were Captain Ellsworth's, comments:

> "I want to compliment you on your general overall conduct during the last week. There has been less quarreling, which is a great improvement. However, those that robbed the handcarts or wagons, unless you repent quickly, your flesh will rot from your bones and you surely will go to Hell!"[124]

It was real interesting watching everyone looking around at each other in amazement. It was impossible to tell if they were looking to see who might know what they had done, or if they were wondering who of these fellow Saints Brother Ellsworth could possibly be talking about. Guess we'll never know, unless they decide to "fess up".

Company Two, camped at Chimney Rock, spent their Sunday very much like the other company, doing everything from shoeing oxen, washing and mending clothes, baking, and repairing handcarts, to holding Church services. It had been a difficult week and the Saints were glad to have a break. As Brother Bermingham put it:

> "Camped all day at Chimney Rock. Spent the day mending my clothes and baking and cooking while Kate was washing and mending the children's clothes. On the 22nd while we were on the road travelling, we were overtaken by a very heavy thunderstorm which wet us all to the skin, but as soon as it was over we went at it again and made a journey of 7 or 8 miles before we camped and then we had to lie on the wet grass all night, and go to bed supperless, there being no firewood to cook, the Buffalo chips being wet. We had to ford 20 streams this week."[125]

On Monday, Captain McArthur started his company early and traveled 26 miles over road that Leonard labeled good and having lots of water. That night while camped near Scotts Bluff one of their girls, Catherine Granger, was discovered to be missing and had to spend the night by herself.[126]

The closer the First Company came to Fort Laramie, the more Indians they encountered. On Monday, August 25th, approximately 19 miles from the fort, Archer Walters reported seeing a large Indian camp. Then on the 26th, traveling 19 miles toward the fort over very sandy roads, then eventually forded the Platte River and camped 3 miles from the fort.[127] In making that river crossing Sister Watt was hurt by falling from the wagon half way across, but Brother John Lee came to her assistance and all ended well.[128] Mary Powell, while not very impressed by the river crossing, was excited by the Indians she saw. She recorded in her journal:

> "At Fort Laramie there was an encampment of 16,000 Indians. They were holding a treaty. They were camped for a distance of thirty miles up the river. We camped near the river that night without a fire. The next morning we met 500 Indians on the road, they were on their way to the treaty. Father presented some of them with beautiful peacock feathers; this pleased them very much. They stopped and looked at our handcarts. "Little wagons, little wagons" said they. How the squaws laughed."[129]

When the First Company finally settled for the day, several went into the fort to do some trading and buying. The trading post was reported to have most everything a person could need on the trail or in the wilderness, but the prices were very high. Walters, for instance, took a couple of daggers [knives] with him, trading one for a piece of bacon and salt, and sold the other for $1.25, which he used to purchase bacon and meal for his family.[130] Only a few of the Saints had the funds to buy some flour and bacon to supplement their normal rations.

Meanwhile, the Second Company was expending their days and energy in traveling as fast and far as they could over very sandy, or as they often referred to it "heavy" road. From the 25-27th of August they

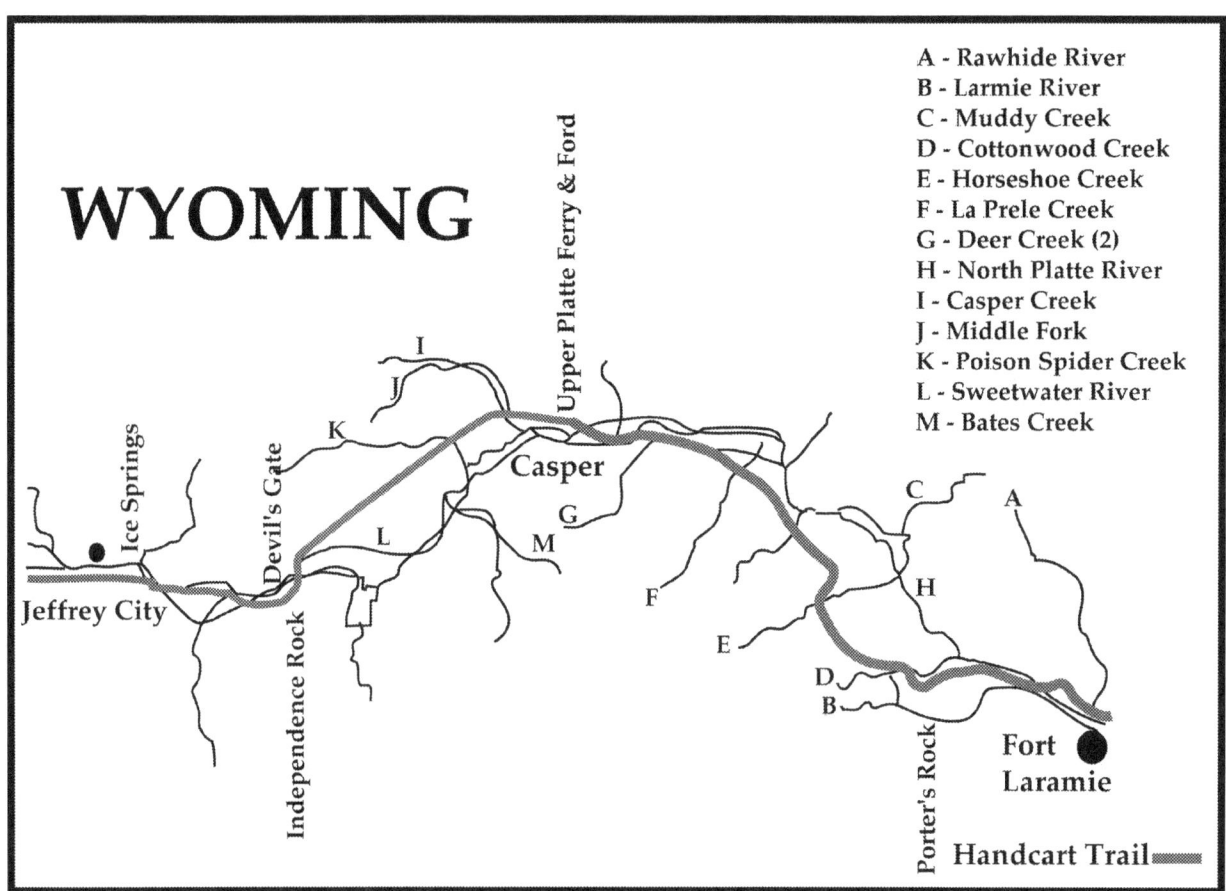

Figure 31: *Handcart Trail – Fort Laramie to Jeffrey City, Wyoming*

averaged about 19 miles a day under very warm skies, except for the 16th when they had a heavy storm while camped on the Platte River. Sandy or "heavy roads" are not easily described. To do justice to understanding the term, one must experience the struggle. The normal easy road efforts in moving a handcart is to have the man/woman pushing on the front cross rod, at the same time lowering the handle just enough to keep the load over the cart bed level. This put the smallest amount of resistance possible on the wheels and the 300-500 pound load would roll right along. Of course it always made it easier if the load on the cart bed was properly distributed so it was not heavier on one side or the other.

As the road level changed to be going on a greater/lesser incline/decline, it might prove necessary to have another in the cart group, usually, but not always, a member of the same family get behind the cart to push or pull as needed. The more difficult things became, the more people were added to the back of the cart and then to the sides. On heavy roads, the deeper the wagon sank into the sand, the more people had to join in, and if as in some cases the wheels were almost up to their hubs, people were put on each wheel to help turn the wheel by hand. Since most of the time the metal rim around the wheel was very hot from the sun and the sand, it usually meant holding onto the spokes of the wheels and pushing/pulling them to make each turn. The ability to travel 19-20 miles through heavy sand each day was a great accomplishment. Upon reaching rocky and unlevel roads or trails, they would still follow the same pattern of moving the cart, people behind or on the side, and moving the wheels by physical force.

In particularly difficult terrain, it was a common practice for cart groups to help other cart groups move first one handcart and then go back and move the other. The unity of the Saints became very strong when it came to neighbor helping neighbor, and it usually did not even require a request being made. It only took an awareness that the need existed and the help was offered spontaneously. Of course this type of brotherly or sisterly help took place on the Saints wagon trains too, but not to the same extent as those with handcarts.

Leaving the Fort Laramie area, the First Company traveled 18-21 miles August 27th, stopping to camp at 5:00 p.m. at Bitter Cottonwood where the wood and water were plentiful, but the feed for the animals was scarce.[131] The pioneers had a good meal that night of bacon and meal porridge, which according to Archer Walters, was "the best supper for many weeks." Their journey had now brought them 5462 miles from Winter Quarters and left them 4844 miles to travel to reach Salt Lake City. In other words, they were just over half way from Winter Quarters and about three-quarters of the way from Liverpool.[132] Traveling 15 miles on the 28th brought them to Horse Shoe Creek, which had both a good spring and good feed for the animals. While the stock filled up with food, the women took the opportunity to wash some clothes.[133]

Thursday, August 28th brought the Second Company to Fort Laramie. During 11 miles of travel that day on sandy roads, they passed many Indian camps, which they were relieved to learn were filled with peaceful inhabitants. After crossing the river, the handcart train stopped at the fort.[134] Brothers' McArthur, Leonard and several others went in to the fort trading post to pick up some "necessaries". While they found the trading post to have many useful items available for purchase, they also found that they were very expensive. For example, Leonard wrote:

28 August - Thursday

"traveled 11 miles and arrived at Laramy crossed the River; went to the Fort in com with Capt. Dan to get some nails &c Ox nails were 2 dollars per pound I bot .50 cents worth. Quite a No of our people bot. flour Bacon etc. Came a mile and a half and camped with but little feed."[135]

FIRST COMPANY

29 August - Friday

"Travelled 25 miles. Camped Platte River. Met some Californians."[136]

"The camp rolled out at fifteen past seven a.m. and traveled twenty-five miles. The road was pretty good. Sixteen miles to the Platte where we took dinner. Traveled two miles and forded the Platte. Camped about thirty past six p.m. on the Platte. Plenty of wood; feed pretty fair."[137]

DEER CREEK AND WAGONS OF FLOUR

FIRST COMPANY

30 August - Saturday

"Travelled 22 miles. Met some Californians and they told us the wagons was waiting at Deer Creek for us."[139]

"The camp rolled out at twenty-five past seven a.m. and traveled nineteen miles. The road pretty fair. Forded the Platte again. Traveled about six miles and camped by the side of a creek. Plenty of wood, water, and feed. We passed two emigrants from California. By them we were informed that five wagons were waiting on us at Deer Creek. Camped at about thirty past six p.m."[140]

SECOND COMPANY

29 August - Friday

"travelled 21 miles and camped on the creek almost without feed except brush, one of our oxen sick came 12 miles in the afternoon, some of our camp did not get on till near 8 O clock"[138]

SECOND COMPANY

29th —30th AUGUST:

These two days we travelled 50 miles. The 30th we crossed the Platte again to the north side. Remained in camp all day."[141]

30 August - Saturday

"Started early and traveled 25 miles and struck [?] the catle, passing two small lots of water, one at 4 miles the other [__?]"[142]

Supplies were running very low, so when the First Company reached Deer Creek about 5:30 p.m., everyone rejoiced to find five wagons from the Valley waiting, each containing 1000 pounds of flour. This Sabbath night we were blessed with full bellies not only from an abundance of bread, but a cow was killed and distributed. We may have come into the campground faint and hungry after 22 miles on the road, but now there was contentment. There was plenty of water and wood, and even the cattle had all they wanted to eat for their feed was plentiful. There was only one thing that distracted from our happiness, the death of 54 years old Brother Robert Stoddard from the Carlisle Conference, who died from consumption. He was buried at the camp, 400 yards from the left side of the road.[143]

Things were mighty pleasant in camp, and the company was so tired, it was decided to not travel on Monday, September 1st. We just stayed right there, mended carts, and did a lot of little things. And another thing, it was right nice to have wood to burn rather than buffalo chips. The air smelled cleaner and the food sweeter, even though it was really only a figment of the imagination.

A meeting was held to decide about whether we should pay 18 cents a pound for some extra flour to take with us. The brethren from Salt Lake had brought extra flour for just such a purpose, if we were interested, If not they would take the flour elsewhere and sell it. There wasn't much money left in most Saint's pockets to afford such an opportunity, so the outcome became obvious.

At times like these, with an opportunity to sit alone quietly or take a solitary walk amongst the trees, hearts swell in gratitude for the love and care our Father in Heaven gives us. That great sacrifice of our Savior, which applies to all who love Him, and what a wonderful blessing it really is, especially the new and everlasting covenant. He is calling us now to Zion, even those of us that are too poor to ever be able to afford to do it on our own. Every step on this trail, every strain with the handcarts and wagons, every challenge, great or small, is worth the blessings we now have and those that we will receive in the valley of the mountains of the Lord. The rest is sweet, but still we are anxious to be on our way, each day closer and closer to home.

Sunday, August 31st, was neither what could be described as a restful or holy for the Second Company. They were faced with a 29 mile trek on a rainy day over a sandy road, a crossing of the Platte River, and the loss of 4 cows and 2 oxen.[144] Leonard wrote that they, "expected to have a meeting but were to busy." Monday didn't turn out to be much better:

1 September - Monday
"Traveled 25 miles, crossing the River to the North side at 11 O'clock, done very well for water but feed none as it was after dark before we got into [__?] Met Cushombo a Mt-eer who gave us some beef."[145]

Father Walter Sanders, age 65, died last night and was buried this morning before we left, about 300 yards from the South side of the road. His four children: Mary, 19; James, 15; John, 13; and Thomas, 10 were in attendance at the short graveside service, along with his many friends of the First Company.146 While Mary and James said they would be able to take care of the wagon and the family, they will never be left to fend against things alone. Most everyone will keep an eye out for them and their needs, even though they will be credited with doing for themselves in every way they can to keep them strong, and with a feeling of independence. It is always strange, that no matter how much one knows and believes from the Gospel about death and the life that follows, there is still always a sense of loss. A wish that such a thing did not have to come to pass, mixed with a surety that the lost love one expects you to go on, to live for them in Zion what they had hoped to live for themselves.

The horn is sounded, the carts fall into line, and once again the pioneers move on. This September 2, 1856, 19 more miles of sandy road to be traveled and one creek to be crossed before the next camp is made. With every step and every turn of the wheel, down deep inside each soul is the knowledge and joy of being one step closer to Zion. Soon journey's end will be reached and with the Saints we will dwell. No more hunger, no more thurst, no more persecution, only peace and happiness under the laws of God and the direction of His prophet. No more poverty, no more struggles with the wicked world, only Zion!

For the first 3 days of September, the Second Company averaged about 25 miles a day.[147] They were making good mileage each day, but the constant push was beginning to tell on the Saints. Leonard wrote in his journal:

2 September - Tuesday
"Rose early drove our cattle accross the river and staid by them and the mule till near 7 O Clock when we drove them in, again drove 25 miles crossing the River to the South at one O'clock In the afternoon had no water for 12 miles, after dark when we got into camp again on a large creek wood plenty but feed poor; about 45 sick and lame in the wagons."[148]

With 45 sick and lame in the wagons, that was about one-fourth of the company. It was fortunate that they met a provision wagon from the valley with 1000 pounds of flour. The additional food alone "caused the hearts of the saints to be cheered up greatly."[149]

FIRST COMPANY

3 September - Wednesday

"Met 4 wagons; Henshaw from Nottingham; John Barns from Sheffield. Travelled 15 miles."[150]

"The camp rolled this morning at thirty past eight a.m. and traveled eleven miles. It was very heavy pulling owing to the dust and a heavy wind. Crossed the Platte a mile and a half below the upper crossings. A good place to ford. Camped beside of the Platte at thirty past four p.m. Plenty of wood. Feed middling."[151]

SECOND COMPANY

3 September - Wednesday

"Rose early greased the wagons, which we made an every two days job, at noon to our joy met with the Vallie boys with flour from the Mountains, they were at deer creek. at 2 O Clock started out went 11 miles the Brethren going with us, & in the evening we held a meeting to learn if the companys were willing to pay 18 dollars per hund for flour they said sis. Bro. Nealy had the charge of the flour"[152]

In early September the weather began to alternate between rain and snow, making it difficult to cook anything.[153] During such weather if clothing, bedding, etc. got wet, it was a difficult thing to ever get it totally dry again, and the wood being wet was difficult, if not impossible to light. This meant being cold and often going without food because there was no way to cook it.

There was also a problem in the Second Company with wolves, having killed an animal each night for five nights in a row; they were a real threat to the cattle. A guard was organized to build large fires to keep them away, but the weather did not always cooperate. Because of so many cattle being lost to wolves and previous sickness, Brothers McAntire and Chester Snider were appointed to return with us with two poor teams and 1400 lbs. of flour."[154]

FIRST COMPANY

4 September - Thursday

"The camp rolled out this morning and traveled twenty-six miles. The roads were very good for traveling. Had dinner by the side of Mineral Spring Creek. Camped at Little Stream Creek at thirty past five p.m. About a half an hour after getting to camp it got very cold and rained for several hours so that we could not light a fire."[155]

5 September - Friday

"We remained in camp today owing to the inclement state of the weather. It rained and snowed alternately for the whole of the day so that we could not cook hardly anything."[157]

SECOND COMPANY

4 September - Thursday

"Crossed Muddy Creek and travelled 20 miles and late in the evening forded the Platte again for the last time. For five days we were not in camp for an hour after night and we were always up at daybreak preparing to start at 5. We met the wagons at Deer Creek which were sent with flour from the Valley to meet us. There were 5 wagons, one for each Company and each wagon had 1000 lbs. of flour in them. Two started for the Valley with our Company. German boys father died."[156]

5 September - Friday

"Very cold and rainy all day laid in camp, much snow near us on the Mountains, kept our Cattle together with some trouble."[158]

"Very wet today. Could not start it rained so much. Snow four feet deep on the mountains all around us."[159]

About four o'clock this morning of the 6th, the weather finally settled enough that the camp of the First Company was about to be gotten up to pack up and move on. This notion didn't last very long for it was soon discovered that 24 head of cattle were missing. Robert and James Sheen had been left on duty during the bad weather last night[160] and they evidently thought it was more important to try and stay as warm and dry as possible, because they surely didn't pay much attention to the animals. It was hoped the cattle had just wandered off, but there was still the real possibility that the wolves got some of them. How can people be so thoughtless of the whole company as to think of their own comfort before they remember the needs of their fellow travelers? Everyone is praying they will find all the missing stock, as it will be a real problem to have to go on without them.

There can be no attempt at travel today until we see if they can be found.161 All of the available brethren of the company have been organized to search for them. We hope to at least find the oxen so we won't have to do without the wagons and what they carry. With a hope in our hearts and a prayer on our lips, each of the groups head out to look in their assigned areas. It really "stinks" that we have to go through all this, just because those two didn't do their job. One more morning without breakfast, and with the wood as wet as it is from all the rain, there will be no fires and therefore no dinner either when we finally get back. What a rotten job!

It took until 3:00 p.m. before the last of the stock could be rounded up and herded back to the campsite. Even though the next day was the Sabbath, it was determined to start as early as possible in the morning and try to make up for lost time, if the weather held.

Since the weather had basically cleared enough for travel, the Second Company who had been very careful to keep their cattle together during the storms, was able to use Saturday the 6th for travel. They still encountered some snow on the sides of the trail, but the path was only passable even though it proved to be very heavy from the damp sand following the rain. Their progress was greatly slowed, but they managed to make 15 miles before stopping "at the last point of the river".[162] After setting up camp, they had several handcarts to repair because of the day's struggle. Since they were now able to build fires, they killed a beef to cook for the evening meal to strengthen the Saints from the day's struggle, as well as prepare for the unknown needs of the morrow.[163]

FIRST COMPANY

7 September - Sunday

"The camp rolled out this morning at thirty past seven a.m. and traveled twenty-two miles. The road was good for the first fourteen miles. Camped to have dinner beside a most beautiful creek of water. For the next eight miles the road is very sandy and heavy. Camped at thirty past six p.m. by side of Sweetwater, two miles from the crossing. A good camping ground. Good feed for the cattle. George Neappris died this evening. Age 24. Emigrated from Cardiff in Dan Jones' company."[164]

SECOND COMPANY

7 September - Sunday

"Traveled 20 miles, lost a German boy at noon, camped at 4 O Clock on horse creek near greese wood and among a lot of Indians Capt Dan and Bro. McAntire were out all night but found not the young man. Came to where Capt Elsworth had camped the night before, as he had [?] to let the snow get out of the way before him as there had been considerable; roads quite heavy at the Willow Spring and [?] up those heavy hills, no wood but sage brush where we camped."[165]

A Sabbath passed with no worship service, just strain and tragedy. On Monday, September 9th, George Neappris of the First Company was laid to rest, being:

"...buried on a sand ridge directly east of three rocky mounds. Two and a half miles from the crossing on the bend of the north side of the river..."[166]

In the hunt for the young man from the Second Company, the searchers had no luck:

"...Capt. Dan came up near night without the lost man, and the conclusion is that he was taken back by some men on their return from the Vallie of the Merchant train, they tried to get a boy to go back with them."[167]

FIRST COMPANY

8 September - Monday

"11 miles. Had dinner at Devil's Gate."[168]

"...Crossed Sweetwater by a good bridge. The roads were in many parts rather rough. Had dinner beside an old trading post close by the Devil's Gate. Camped beside Sweetwater at thirty past five p.m. not far from a company of apostates."[169]

SECOND COMPANY

8 September - Monday

"Traveled about 20 miles and camped near Independence Rock passed the Solaraties beds about 4 O Clock, but the rain had nearly spoiled it, lived on greece wood creek feed good..."[171]

9 September - Tuesday

"The camp rolled at thirty past seven a.m. and traveled sixteen miles. The roads continued rather rough with a heavy headwind. Camped at five p.m. beside Sweetwater. An excellent camping ground. Killed a cow."[170]

10 September - Wednesday

"The camp rolled out at forty past seven a.m. and traveled eighteen miles. The roads tolerably good to Sweetwater crossing. After that it was sandy for seven miles. Camped at six p.m. on Sweetwater. A very indifferent camping ground. Poor feed."[173]

11 September - Thursday

"The camp rolled out at forty past seven a.m. and traveled nineteen miles. The first part of the journey the roads pretty good. No water for twelve miles. You will then come to a good stream of water and good feed. Take the left hand road. Traveled eight miles to a creek. A poor camping ground. Middling feed. Camped at six p.m. Brother McArthur's company came up. They had traveled nearly night and day to overtake us."[175]

9 September - Tuesday

"Again went 18 or 20 miles, but a about 4 O Clock Mariott drove into a chuck hole and broke a hind wheel all to pieces, Crandel concluded that we had to have the wagon but I fixed up the wheel temporarily and loaded it, so as to get it into camp a little after dark, we had an Indian with us when we made to sleep in our tent, to preserve him as we supposed from stealing a horse. The mail passed us a dark saying that Capt Elsworth is only 4 miles ahead."[172]

10 September - Wednesday

"Cold night heavy frost, up early repaired the wheel that was broken, 5 new spokes and done some other repairs and traveled 18 or 20 miles, over some dreadful sand road, at night camped near Rev. Brackenbury... who gave me some news about the Vallie and the road camped at the 2nd crossing on Independence Rock good feed... night cold and winds frost quite severe."[174]

11 September - Thursday

"Started at 7 traveled about 11 miles, made the 5th crossing at noon or a little before, here most of the people took dinner while we drove about 3 miles to good feed, started at half passed one, and after going 6 miles over heavy roads, struck the cut off a little after dark and then went about 12 miles over good road... traveled till 11 O Clock at night and came upon Capt, Elsworths company..."[176]

MC ARTHUR'S COMPANY FINALLY CATCHES UP WITH THE FIRST COMPANY

Tuesday, September 11th, at 11:00 p.m., while Ellsworth's company was stopped for the night at a poor campsite, McArthur's Company overtook them. Brother Leonard described the encounter:

"11 O'clock at night and came upon Captain Ellsworth's company, under a heavy hill. The moon shone beautifully, and we unobserved, paraded our company and gave them 3 loud cheers, which was returned by a tune or two from their band. We were soon among the saints who mingled together in happy groups till near midnight. Captain Edd rather hated our coming upon him, but we had it to do in order to obtain feed for our cattle."[177]

Much to Captain Ellsworth's dismay, the Second Company would regularly overtake the First Company for the rest of their journey to Salt Lake City, in what appeared to be a competition. Ellsworth felt that his company had left Florence first, had maintained a good rate of travel, and therefore should not have to compete with McArthur and the Second Company for campgrounds, stock feed, water, etc. He saw McArthur as someone driven to show that his company was better in every way and deserved to pass the first company and lead out because of it. Of course McArthur was never quoted by anyone as having said or felt this way, but one must wonder with the long days that were put in by his company to gain the extra miles. There is no doubt that McArthur and his counselors knew their actions bothered Ellsworth, as it is mentioned in Leonard's journal several times during this part of the journey.

It appears that the pioneers of the two companies did not join in the practices of "one-ups-manship" that appeared to occur between the leadership. They enjoyed the camaraderie of their fellow Saints, the relationship of the majority going all the way back to the sea crossing of the Enoch Train. Everyone enjoyed the music of the Birmingham Band, which traveled as a part of the First Company, and the time they had in the evening for socializing made the journey less of a routine.

FIRST COMPANY

12 September - Friday

"The camp rolled out at forty-five past seven a.m. and traveled twelve miles. The greatest part of the road very hilly and rough. A good spring of water about six miles from where we started this morning. Camped at forty-five past one p.m. Good camping ground. Feed pretty fair. Plenty of good spring water, about two hundred yards from the road, right side."[178]

SECOND COMPANY

12 September - Friday

"Started late and traveled not more than 14 miles, and again camped with Elsworth who in company with several others came to our tent where we had a jolly good time."[179]

After traveling 28 miles September 13th, the First Company camped at Pacific Springs. They had taken a cutoff that led them over good roads and by good water and feed. The Emigrant's Guide: Table of Distances [180] shows this Pacific Springs to be 8022 miles from Florence (Winter Quarters), and 2282 miles from Salt Lake City. Here they came upon Captain Bank's Wagon Company, which had left Florence ten days ahead of the handcart company. Bank's group was quite surprised at the speed of their travel. It would have been a joyous occasion all around had it not been for the death of 65 year old Mary Mayo, who was buried closed to the mountain on the left hand side of the road.[181]

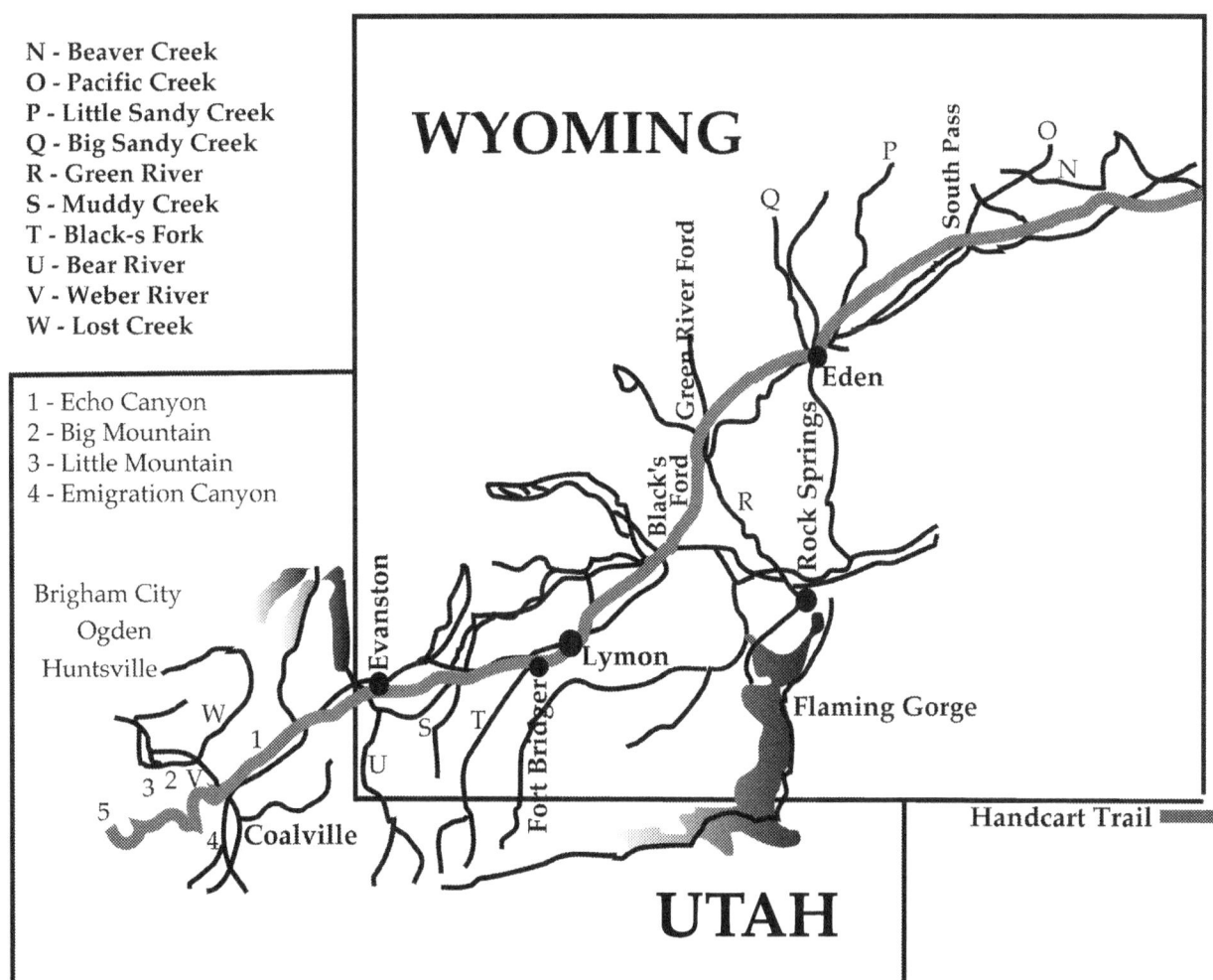

Figure 31: *Handcart Trail – Jeffrey, Wyoming to Salt Lake City, Utah*

The Second Company did not fair so well, and never caught up by nightfall. They did however, make it a point to catch up on the 14th. Then they had a rather unusual circumstance take place, when David Chambers' son came into camp from Salt Lake City to get his father, mother and brother and took them back with him to the valley.[182]

A journal entry implies their delay was somehow the fault of the First Company:

13 September - Saturday
"A late start in consequence of waiting for Capt Edd. Started drive over the balance of the cut off, & camped on or near sweet water, killed a beef... Capt Edd on 12 miles"[183]

FIRST COMPANY

14 September - Sunday
"Travelled 3 miles. Camped to mend hand carts and women to wash. Sister Mayer died."[184]

"The camp rolled out at nine a.m. and traveled three miles where there was plenty of feed for the cattle."[185]

15 September - Monday
"The camp rolled out at seven a.m. and traveled twenty-six miles. A creek of water twelve miles from where we started. Also feed. Here we rested two hours. Sixteen miles we camped at Little Sandy. We got plenty of water by digging for it. Plenty of wood and pretty good feed. Camped at nine p.m. Very good roads."[188]

16 September - Tuesday
"The camp rolled out at thirty past eight a.m. and traveled twenty-three miles. Good roads. Crossed a splended creek of water five miles from Little Sandy. Camped on the banks of Big Sandy at seven p.m. Plenty of wood on the opposite side of the river. Poor feed for cattle."[190]

SECOND COMPANY

14 September - Sunday
"drove about 15 miles and camped at Pacific creek 3 miles from the Springs, here we came up with Capt. Elswoth again we also had the pleasure of seeing Patriarch John Smith, Wm Smith who gave me news from my family Hinderson, Peter Vanorden was also with him we held meeting in the evening where Capt Dan put it upon me to take charge of the same; Bro. John gave us some good advise, exhorted the saints to faithfulness, secret prayer etc, several from Edds camp were at our meeting especially the girls."[186]

"On the 14th we camped at Pacific Spring Creek, and there I took in 1000 lbs. of more flour, so as to be sure to have enough to do me until we got into the Valley, for I was told that that would be the last opportunity to get it."[187]

15 September - Monday
"Traveled 27 miles after a severe rain and hail storm, shod the mule etc. Camped at 10 in the evening on little Sandy to the anoyance of Capt. Elsworth, [?] but [?]"[189]

16 September - Tuesday
"On account of confusion with Elsworth we laid by all day drove our cattle up the stream 4 miles as his were they good good feed, in the evening Capt. Bank came up with the Band who gave several lively tunes for the benefit of our company."[191]

During the morning of Wednesday, September 17th, James Birch, age 38, of the First Company died of diarrhea. His wife Mary Ann and three children Thomas, age 8; Mary Ann, age 6; and Edward J., age 2; were left to move their handcart and meager belongings on to Zion. He was:

"...Buried on the top of sand ridge east of Sandy. The camp rolled at eight and traveled eleven miles. Rested four hours by the side of Green River. Forded the river about four p.m. and camped about six p.m. Good feed and camping ground."[192]

In an effort to catch up, the Second Company:

"Traveled 23 miles and camped on big Sandy. Saw the grave of James Birch of Elsworths company, road gravelly and hard on our cattles feet [some?] feed at noon for our animals."[193]

Thursday, September 18th, both companies give a record of their travel for the day and camping spots, but no reference is given to any unusual occurrence of passing a group of seventeen missionaries from the valley bound for Britain and elsewhere. Elder Thomas Bullock wrote of this historic event from Florence, Nebraska on 28 October 1856, which was later published in the Millennial Star.[194]

"We were very agreeably surprised by suddenly coming upon the advance train of handcarts, composed of about 300 persons, travelling gently up the hill west of Green River, led by Elder Edmund Ellsworth. As the two companies approached each other, the camp of missionaries formed a line, and gave three loud Hosannahs with the waving of hats, which was heartily led by Elder P. P. Pratt, responded to by loud greetings from the Saints of the handcart train, who unitedly made the hills and valleys resound with shouts of gladness; the memory of this scene will never be forgotten by any person present. They were very cheerful and happy, and we blessed them in the name of the Lord, and they went on their way rejoicing. The same day we met a [second] company of handcarts, led by Elder D. McArthur."[195]

A rather basic day with the First Company, Friday, September 19th,[196] Leonard's diary reports of the Second Company, that there were "a good many riding McCleve very sick as also the old German."[197] Since it was a policy of the companies that the pioneers only be allowed to ride in the wagons when they were sick or injured, a problem obviously existed. When it is found that on the 16th Captain McArthur pushed his company 30 miles so they could catch up with the First Company already at Fort Bridger, it begins to look like the Saints were just plainly worn out.

FIRST COMPANY

20 September - Saturday

"The camp rolled out at forty-five past six a.m. and traveled nine miles to Bridger. The road rather rough and rocky. Camped at Bridger for the day. At fifteen past ten a.m. Killed a first rate fat ox. Shod several of the oxen."[198]

21 September - Sunday

"At seven a.m. the camp rolled and traveled twenty-two miles. The roads were good. Crossed several creeks. Passed a sulphur and soda spring. Camped at six p.m. Plenty of wood and feed, but no water."[200]

SECOND COMPANY

20 September - Saturday

"This morning Honrick Elaker 56 years of age [died] I took the charge of his burial a solemn scene took place as he was the 3rd who had died beside one that had been lost since leaving Winters Quarters. Traveled upwards of 30 miles arriving of Fort Bridger where we over took Capt Elsworth, in a great stun to be sure. Two of our cattle are rather tired and we have concluded to leave them with Square Robinson to recruit and save them"[199]

21 September - Sunday

"Rested a half day killed a fat cow that Robin turned out as church property he also let Elsworth have an ox. Obtained a few pair of mocasins for the lame, traveled 10 miles and camped on rocky run, picked up two of Edds com who had been left."[201]

"...Henry Bouning fell down and fainted yesterday under the hand cart from fatigue. Had to be carried into camp which we did not reach until 10 o'clock at night."[202]

22 September – Monday

This has been a day that will never be forgotten. We left camp by 5:30 a.m., but most had to get up by 4:00 a.m. to be ready. I was so cold this morning, I must've wore my teeth down a half an inch from shivering and clattering them together. I was hopen' we might get a fire built to warm up a bit before leaving, but then they said we would eat breakfast later on the trail. After we had traveled 6 miles we finally got to build a fire and eat. I was just startin' to thaw my bones out, when we had to put out the fires and move on. As the sun got higher and the pace of the First Company got steadier, everyone finally got warm enough to shed some of the blankets and things we were wearing.

About 3 in the afternoon two young men met the train. It turned out they were Brother Brigham and Heber's sons, who seemed down right glad to see us. Never got it straight if they had been sent out to look for us or were on some other business, but makin' their acquaintance was a real treat. As the company moved on there was plenty to talk about, and the excitement grew knowing we were gettin' so close to Salt Lake. A thunderstorm about 5:30 p.m. stopped the conversations short. Captain Ellsworth must have thought the rain would let up, I guess, because we pushed on through that gully washer and didn't make camp until 6. The campsite had plenty of water and feed for the animals, but it was scarce on wood to burn, and what we did find was for the most part wet.

We started settin' up camp, but couldn't get very far with it as the wagons with the tents didn't arrive until midnight. Everything we had on and everything we had with us was wet, and a cold wind did its best to turn us into ice. There was some grumblin' while we waited for the wagons to show up, but still we felt all right. And when we finally got the tents up we thought we had died and gone to heaven. No more wind right on us, and we could get some of the wet things hung up in the tents to hopefully dry a bit.[203]

Excitement in the Second Company, September 22nd, seems to have been limited to the birth of a son to Margaret and George Muir, the parents of Mary, age 2; and Jean, age 1.[204]

The next day Ellsworth's Company didn't leave camp until noon, probably to give everyone a chance for a little extra rest and to dry clothes after the problems of the night before. Once started, traveling over roads that were considered good, they forded the Weber River about 1:00 p.m. and camped about 6:30 p.m., logging 18 miles for the day. That evening they were visited by a few Indians, who evidently were friendly.[205]

McArthur's Company on the 23rd, traveled to the mouth of Echo Canyon and camped, not to far from where Ellsworth had been on Monday. Somehow they learned of the circumstances of the tents arriving late as Leonard recorded in his journal:

23 September - Tuesday

"Traveled to the mouth of Echo Kanion late when we arrived and a very cool night was near a camp who thretened Capt Edd as he had left some persons out all night who had suffered much as it rained very hard and they were wet so as to be obliged to lay in camp till near noon"[206]

Now, somewhere between 50-60 miles from Salt Lake City, the excitement of the pioneers of the handcart companies increased with each mile traveled and each camp made. With the Emigrants Guide [207] listing so many good places they could stop to make camp each day, it seemed to focus the distance of daily travel to stopping whenever the captains felt the absolute need to do so.

PROMINENT POINTS AND REMARKS	Dist. miles	From W Qrs. miles	From C of GSL miles
Kanyon creek, 1 rod wide, 1 foot deep: You have to cross this creek thirteen times, besides two bad swamps. The road is dangerous to wagons, on account of dense, high bushes, trees, and short turns in the road. Good place to camp. (See Note 9)	2 ¾	1001 ¼	29 ¾
Leave Kanyon creek. – – – – Here you turn to the right, and begin to ascend the highest mountain you cross in the whole journey. You travel through timber, some on side hills, and cross the creek a number of times.	8	1009 ¼	21 ¾
Small spring, left of the road. – – – You will probably find water in several places, but it is uncertain where, as it runs but a little way in a place and then sinks in the earth.	3	1012 ¼	18 ¾
Summit of mountain: Altitude, 7,245 feet.	1	1013 ¼	17 ¾

PROMINENT POINTS AND REMARKS	Dist. miles	From W Qrs. miles	From C of GSL miles
You have now a view of the south part of the Valley of the Great Salt Lake. The descent is steep, lengthy, and tedious, on account of stumps in the road.			
Bridge over a deep ravine. – – –	¾	1014	17
This is dangerous to cross, and a wagon may be easily upset. The road lays through a forest of small timber, and is unpleasant traveling.			
Brown's creek and spring. – – –	¾	1014 ¾	16 ¼
Not a bad place to camp, but there is a much better one half a mile lower down.			
Cold spring on Brown's creek. – – –	2 ¾	1017 ½	13 ½
Within a rod of the road, on the east side, under a grove of Black Birch bushes. Good place to camp, but some miry. Good camping any where for two miles lower.			
Leave Brown's creek. – – –	1 ¾	1019 ¼	11 ¾
You now ascend another high mountain, by a steep and crooked road. On both sides this mountain, there are many Serviceberry bushes.			
Summit of last ridge. – – –	1	1020 ¼	10 ¾
The descent is very steep, all the way, till you arrive on the banks of Last creek.			
Last creek. – – – – –	¾	1021	10
You cross this creek nineteen times. Several of the crossings are difficult. There are several side hills which require care in teamsters. Three camping places on it, but the road is rough.			
Mouth of the Kanyon. – – –	5	1026	5
You now enter the Valley of the Salt Lake. The road at the mouth of the Kanyon bad, and rough with stumps. Afterwards, descending and good.			
City of the Great Salt Lake. – – –	5	1031	

Figure 32: [Emigrant's Guide, pp. 19-20]

FIRST COMPANY

24 September - Wednesday
"The camp rolled out at seven a.m. and traveled twenty miles. The roads were rather rough and rugged. Camped about thirty past six p.m. Wood, water, feed, plenty."[208]

25 September - Thursday
"The camp rolled out at seven a.m. and traveled twenty miles. Crossed canyon eleven times. The roads a little rough. Had dinner at the bottom of Big Mountain. Crossed Big Mountain in two hours and fifty-five minutes. Camped at the foot of the Little Mountain at six p.m."[210]

SECOND COMPANY

24 September - Wednesday
"Made a heavy days drive and camped on the Weber, during the day broke 2 hand carts in Echo Kanion I also shod 2 lame oxen at noon"[209]

25 September - Thursday
"Traveled about 25 miles and camped after dark near the top of the big Mt dome more shoeing of cattle as also picked up one of Capt Edds company who was left on East Kanion creek Sanders by name nearly dead we let him sleep in our tent Pat. Linch came and staid all night and told us that Capt Edd were at or between the mountains 10 miles ahead."[211]

26 September - Friday

"The brethren from the city sent us a wagon with provisions as we were rather short. At thirty past ten a.m. the camp rolled and traveled thirteen miles. About eight miles from the city we were met with Governor Young and his counselors the Nauvoo brass band, the Lancers, and a great many others. We were first rate received in the city. Provisions of all kinds came rolling in to us in camp. The brethren of the city manifested great interest towards us as a company, which caused our hearts to rejoice and be glad."[212]

26 September - Friday

"Started early although our cattle were much scattered I found a number of them on the top of the big Mountain. got them together and started without breakfast. came near the foot of the little Mountain where we overtook Capt. Elsworth company turned our cattle our to feed got breakfast receiving some beef from the city, we also gave the people a chance to clean up before going into the city, at 11 O'Clock started and came over the little Mt without doubling teams. Capt. Elsworth had started before us and it was reported that he intended to rush into the city before us' but Brigham heard that we were near and gave instructions that we all should come in together..."[213]

In the last few journal entries made by the Second Company, from September 21–26th, there are several comments and inferences that imply Captain Ellsworth is not being as careful as he should in looking out for the welfare of his company, being mainly concerned with getting into the valley first. For example, the 21st they "picked up two people Edds com who had been left"; the 23rd "Capt Edd ... had left some persons out all night who had suffered much as it rained very hard and they were wet so as to be obliged to lay in camp till near noon"; the 25th "picked up one of Capt Edds company who was left on East Kanion creek Sanders by name nearly dead we let him sleep in our tent"; and on the 26th "Capt. Elsworth had started before us and it was reported that he intended to rush into the city before us' but Brigham heard that we were near and gave instructions that we all should come in together".

It is difficult to understand why such an apparent rivalry should arise between the leaders of these two handcart companies. With the exception of a few Saints from the ship, the Samuel S. Curling, all were companions on the Enoch Train, had crossed an ocean and almost half a continent together, helping and encouraging one another all along the way. But from Florence, Nebraska there seemed to be a driving force that made Ellsworth want to maintain his lead and position as the First Company to leave and the first into the Salt Lake Valley, and McArthur's driving ambition to catch up to him at all costs and not to be second crossing the wilderness nor be found even one day behind him on entering the valley. It would be difficult to specifically point at injury or death caused by this competition, but there is no doubt it was a source of hardship on some.

ESCORTED BY PRESIDENT YOUNG AND PARTY INTO SALT LAKE CITY

As we were just about to an area called "Mouth of the Canyon" we noticed a large gathering of people. As we got closer Captain Ellsworth stopped the column and was introduced to President Young, President Kimball and a whole lot more leaders that had come up out of Salt Lake to meet us. They even brought a whole parade with them, a band, a Marshall, a group of Lancers and all kinds of people. There was so much excitement going on, hugging, kissing, and talking like never before witnessed. We were treated like we was someone real important. Why, they even brought a bunch of melons with them that they sliced up and handed around to the group. 214

While all the excitement was going on, Captain McArthur and the Second Company arrived, and darned if they weren't given the same kind of greetin'. We were not really expectin' McArthur's company, as last we heard they were still at the east base of Big Mountain. They must have really pushed hard to get here this quick. But I kinda' think it's wonderful that all of the Enoch Train people could get to Zion at the same time, since everyone left at the same time. Now that's not to forget those from the Samuel S. Curling who can just be thankful they got to come with this group and be with the first handcart companies to travel to Zion.

After all of the greetin' and eatin' and adjustin' a few last things on the handcarts and wagons, President Young had the two companies line up, one behind the other, and follow what he called the escort down the rest of the canyon and into Salt Lake City. I couldn't help but remember the part in the Old Testament about the long procession following King David bringing the Ark of the Covenant into the Holy City. Not that we were in any way bringing the Ark, but we were in a long procession with music and gladness, and as we reached the streets of Salt Lake there was even some dancing that went on by some. Our carts were our arks, but we carried what few belongings we had in the world in them and not the Ten Commandments and things. Our arks weren't holy, but the people pulling and pushing them had surely been molded and shaped in the Refiners Fire so they would be hard and strong in the building of the Kingdom of God here in Zion. The bodies were indeed tired, but the spirits were strong. Every handcart pioneer had earned their right to a place in the Valley of the Mountains.

President Young's prophesy and call to bring the poor and honest in heart quickly to the Valley by the use of handcarts had proven true. With the help of the Perpetual Emigration Fund, many more such Saints, not just hundreds, but thousands, would now be able to follow the handcart journey until the Lord should provide a better way. There were now no doubters in the companies, nor in the councils of the Church about the use of this type of transportation. We did beat the wagon train, and we would have been able to travel even faster had we not had problems with the carts not being properly prepared before departure and having to wait on the wagons that carried our heavy supplies and equipment.

I noticed the faces of the Saints that lined the streets of the city, many cried with joy at our arrival, and many wept with tears of sympathy for the condition they saw us to be in. Our shoes were worn out, the clothes on our backs for the most part were rags or close to them, hats and bonnets were broken down from long weeks of use. But it was the little children of the companies that drew the greatest attention, those that walked beside their parents and those that rode on top of the carts. You could see in the eyes of the beholders great empathy and desire to immediately take these precious souls into their arms, to pat their heads and fill their stomachs, but they refrained. They knew their opportunities would soon come to give a helping hand.

As sunset was coming upon us, the procession arrived at the public square, where the lancers and the bands and carriages were formed into a line facing the line of handcarts. President Young made a few remarks to the gathering, ending with a blessing, and the valley Saints went to their homes while the handcart Saints pitched their tents and made ready for the nights activities.[215]

Of these events, Gustive Larson wrote in his journal:

"As they came down the bench you could scarcely see them for the dust. When they entered the City the folks came running from every quarter to get a glimpse of the long looked-for hand carts. I shall never forget the feeling that ran through my whole system as I caught the first sight of them. The first Hand Cart was drawn by a man and his wife. They had a little flag on it, on which were the words, 'Our President, may the unity of the Saints ever show the wisdom of his counsels.' The next Hand Cart was drawn by three young women...The tears ran down the cheeks of many a man who you would have thought would not, could not, shed a tear."[216]

Wilford Woodruff's account said:

"One of the most interesting scenes that was ever witnessed in our Territory, was the arrival of two of the handcart companies on the 26th. Having heard the night previous that they were camped between the two mountains, President Young and Kimball, and many citizens, with a detachment of the Lancers, and the brass bands, went out to meet and escort them into the city. They met the companies at the foot of the Little Mountain. Elder E. Ellsworth led the first company, and Elder Daniel D. McArthur the second."[217]

Assignments were made to take the handcart Saints temporarily into the homes of the valley Saints, until arrangements and accommodations could be made for each of the families to have their own homes and farms. Much kindness was given and much gratitude expressed. Clara Hanson wrote of the event:

"It was a long weary march from Emegration Canyon across the bench and through the city to the old Square camping place, we were to tired to realize that we had arrived at the end of our journey, but we were in a strange place withoute a home money or frinds, only such as the Br. and Sisters in there sympathy could bestow who where living at S.L.C. and as a general thing there were many.

"The Saints had been instructed to take the Emegrants home for the night, so it fell to our lot to be taken to the home of Br. & Sister Mikesell. Oh what a blessed privelage it was to sit upon a chare and to lie upon a bed under a roof. We remained there two days, than we moved to Br. Evans as they had milk that we could have a little for the baby."[218]

The next morning as the pioneers were gathering the animals, they found they were missing a steer. It was not just any animal, but one that came to them under most unusual circumstances. Weeks before, while camped at the Platte River, one of the oxen used to pull the wagons, died. While in somewhat a state of confusion about how they should balance the wagon team, they were considering the possibility of replacing the fallen ox with a cow. No one seemed sure that such a match up would work, but they didn't know of any other way to handle the problem. As the discussion went on, one of the brothers looked up on the side of the hill and saw a large fat steer just standing there looking at them. Brother Ellsworth, upon seeing the beast, said that he was sure the Lord had provided the animal to help them move on to the mountains. And though he appeared to be wild, they had no trouble catching or using him. He worked as well in the yoke as the others that pulled the wagons.

Now that the Saints were in the valley and he was no longer needed, he was gone. No one bothered to search for him, instead they uttered quiet prayers of thanksgiving for the Lord's help in their great time of need.[219]

On Saturday, 27 September 1856, there was great activity in the camps of the handcart pioneers. Brethren and sisters from Church were busy from early in the morning helping the Saints needs to be met. One of the things that happened was the rebaptism of some of the pioneers, a practice that was used occasionally during this period of time as a means of blessing the lives of the Saints. Truman Leonard wrote in his journal of one such assignment:

27 September - Saturday

"Great Salt Lake City With the company most of the day in setling up matters and advising the poor and administering to the sick I was requested by the order of Brigham to baptize two individuals one a Dane sick and crazy and a Bro. Ellise a good but worn down sick man, took the Dane in a hand cart had him hauled to City Creek where I Baptised the two and confirmed them in connection with Bro Maxwell, who assisted me. Bro. Lorenzo Young sent some toast and tea which the poor fellows refished exceedingly well The Dane walked a goodly distance back, even further than he had done at any one time from the Upper Crossing of the Platte, at one time, the point where he had been taken crazy. Towards night my Wife came to meet me in a carriage drive by one Shepherd. We went to Levi Riters and staid all night"[220]

The Sabbath of September 28th, with everyone able to meet with an established congregation in a permanent structure, was never to be forgotten. The Spirit of the Lord was poured out in abundance and the handcart pioneers enjoyed a Sunday that had not been available to them since before the Enoch Train left Liverpool.

And surely there could not have been a more joyous people of the Lord found anywhere in His creation, for they had reached the Valley of the Mountains of the Lord and had joined those who were building day by day His Zion!

> Oh where have ye' been my Bonnie Boy,
>   Where come ye' from I say?
> I've sailed across an ocean blue
>   from many miles away.
> And since you're here my loving son,
>   Oh, have ye' come to stay?
> You've gathered me from out the world,
>   I'll never leave-no nay!
> My daughter sweet, I see you've come,
>   What are you here to do?
> You've called me here from out-the world,
>   To build a Zion true.
> Over prairies thick with grass,
>   Over mountains high –
> Through the rivers, cross the sands –
>   With carts a trail did ply –
> Till at last we reached this land
>   That God to us did give,
> To learn the fullness of His love
>   And all His laws to live.
> Here we rolled our handcarts–
>   Here we brought out faith–
> Here we shall be happy–
>   Zion gathered to this place! [221]

Figure 33: *Zion Gathered To This Place* by Robert O. Day

Appendix A

A BRIEF ACCOUNT OF THE
Apostasy, Restoration & Gathering of Modern Day Israel & The Perpetual Emigration Fund

Between 1850 and 1878, during a time of a great religious awakening in the world, over 85,000 people joined The Church of Jesus Christ of Latter-day Saints. Willingly leaving their old lives behind them, they traveled to a place know to them as Zion, because God had called them to this holy task through His living prophet.

To understand why in 1856 men, women and children would be willing to sacrifice so much to get to a modern day Zion, it is essential to understand the reality of "the gathering" as members of The Church of Jesus Christ of Latter-day Saints did in the 19th century. The gathering was, and still is, a holy responsibility for the faithful of Christ's restored Church to prepare all things for His Second Coming to the earth, in this the Dispensation of the Fullness of Times.

Ancient Israel of *Old Testament* times was scattered to the four quarters of the earth because of their disobedience. The most notable scattering being the "lost ten tribes" into the north county, leaving mainly the descendants of the tribes of Judah and Levi. Of course some of each of the twelve tribes have been found scattered throughout the world, but they all presently refer to themselves as Jews. By the time that Jesus was born in Bethlehem, the Holy Land was again in bondage, this time to Rome. The pure in heart accepted Him as the Messiah, but for personal and political power the Sanhedrin pushed the rejection of Jesus as a fraud and convinced the Jews they must still wait for their Savior.

THE APOSTASY

The Holy Scriptures taught that there would be a falling away of the people of Christ's Church into apostasy in the "Meridian of Time", and then a full restoration of all things as they were at first in the "dispensation of the fullness of times."

> "Now we beseech you, brethren, by the coming of our Lord Jesus Christ, and by our gathering together unto him, That ye be not soon shaken in mind, or be troubled, neither by spirit, nor by word, nor by letter as from us, as that the day of Christ is at hand. **Let no man deceive you by any means: for that day shall not come except there come a falling away first** ..."[1]

Apostle Bruce R. McConkie, commenting on this subject, said:

> "Between the original day of our Lord's ministry among men and his glorious Second Coming, there was to be a universal falling away from the faith once delivered to the saints. Darkness was to cover the earth and gross darkness the minds of the people, until the earth would be 'defiled under the inhabitants thereof.' **Men were to transgress the laws, change the ordinances, break the everlasting covenant**. It would be 'as with the people, so with the priest.' (Isaiah 24.) There were to be false Christ's, false prophets, and false doctrines, deceiving, if it were possible, even the very elect.[2]
>
> "Blessings have always attended conformity to true principles, while cursings have been the fruit of apostasy. The **scattering of Israel**, for example, **took place because that people forsook their God and the true principles he had revealed to them**. Their **gathering takes place** as they **return to him** and **begin to live his laws**."[3]
>
> "This **universal apostasy began** in the **days** of the **ancient apostles** themselves[4]; and it was **known to and foretold by them**. Paul recorded specifically that the Second Coming would not be until this great falling away took place.[5] He warned of the 'perilous times' that should come 'in the **last days**'; times when **men would**

have '**a form of godliness**,' but would **deny 'the power thereof'**; times when they would **be 'Ever learning, and never able to come to the knowledge of the truth**'[6]; times in which they would be turned 'from the truth . . . unto fables.'[7] Our Lord foretold the perplexities, calamities, and apostate wickedness of these same days."[8]

For seventeen centuries the world had waited and hoped for the promised restoration that would occur just before the great Millennium of Christ's personal reign upon the earth.

"In the **meridian of time** our **Lord personally restored his gospel** and, through the ministry of his apostolic witnesses, offered its saving truths to all men.[9] ... The **great apostasy** which is of importance and concern to men in **this day** is the one which **took place when men departed from the pure Christianity** which was **restored** in the **meridian of time**."[10]

THE RESTORATION

After centuries of Catholicism, many within the ranks of the clergy began to question what they saw as changes in the doctrines of their church; added to this dissension came the period of the renascence, the invention of the printing press, and for the first time people other than the clergy and those selected from the ranks of nobility began to master the ability to read and to think for themselves. This was followed by a great protest against practices, which were now understood to be contradictory to Scriptures:

"Members of the various sects of that portion of Christendom which broke off from the Roman Catholic Church during the Reformation in the 16th century, as also the members of those sects which have since broken off from these original dissenting groups, are called Protestants. Martin Luther and others, for instance, first remonstrated and protested in the most solemn manner against the practices and doctrine of the Roman Church, and then finally, in good conscience, had no choice but to sever their affiliation with this organization. **This Protestant revolution was inspired of God**; it was **one** of the **necessary occurrences** which **prepared the way** for the **restoration of the gospel**."[11]

Martin Luther stated, "I have **sought nothing beyond reforming the Church in conformity with the Holy Scriptures**. The **spiritual powers** have been not only **corrupted by sin**, but **absolutely destroyed**; so that there is **now nothing** in them **but a depraved reason** and a will **that is** the **enemy and opponent of God**. I simply say that **Christianity has ceased to exist among those who should have preserved it**."[12]

John Wesley said, "It does not appear that these **extraordinary gifts of the Holy Ghost** were **common in the Church** for **more** than **two or three centuries**. We seldom hear of them after that fatal period when Emperor Constantine called himself a Christian; ... From this time they **almost totally ceased**; ... The **Christians had no more** of the **Spirit of Christ than** the **other heathens** ... This was the real **cause** why the extraordinary gifts of the Holy Ghost were **no longer to be found** in the **Christian Church**; because the Christians were **turned Heathens again**, and **had only a dead form left**."[13]

Roger Williams commented, "There is **no regularly constituted church on earth**, **nor** any **person authorized to administer** any **church ordinance**; nor can there be **until new apostles are sent** by the **Great Head of the Church** for whose coming I am seeking."[14]

Thomas Jefferson remarked, "The **religion builders** have **so distorted and deformed** the **doctrines of Jesus**, so **muffled them in mysticisms, fancies and falsehood**, have **caricatured them** into **forms** so **inconceivable**, as to shock reasonable thinkers ... **Happy** in the **prospect** of a **restoration of primitive Christianity**, I must leave to younger persons to encounter and lop off the false branches which have been engrafted into it by the mythologists of the middle and modern ages."[15]

The masses, having been made of aware of so many truths that they had not had known before, wanted to be the masters of their own spiritual and temporal lives, then and in the future. And, with the era of global exploration and colonization by the great powers of the Old World, many eventually found themselves in North America. After several years of submission to a tyrannical king and the government that supported him, they engaged in a revolutionary struggle that won 13 English colonies freedom from their mother country.

As a means of providing the people a guarantee of freedom they had not before enjoyed, great leaders of the young United States of America, under divine inspiration, forged first the Articles of Confederation, then later a Constitution for the nation, with a carefully thought out set of guarantees for freedoms they called the Bill of Rights. Amendments inspired by the All Mighty were added to the Constitution insuring the foundations and fundamental freedoms that allowed the coming forth of a great religious awakening in the nation. Thus fulfilling ancient prophecy and setting the stage for the coming forth of the full restoration of the Gospel of Jesus Christ.

Nephi having seen this day in vision, prophesied regarding the Churches of the time:

> "In the **last days**, or in the **days of the Gentiles** — yea, behold **all** the **nations** of the Gentiles and also the Jews, both those who shall come **upon this land and** those who shall be upon **other lands,** yea, even upon all the lands of the earth, behold, they **will be drunken with iniquity** and **all manner of abominations.**' (2 Nephi 27:1.) He spoke in detail of the **many churches**; of their **pride, worldly learning,** and **denial of miracles**; of their '**envyings,** and **strifes,** and **malice**'; of the **secret combinations** of the **devil** which commit murders and iniquities; of their **priestcrafts and iniquities** (2 Nephi 26:20-29); of the **ministers** who 'shall **teach with their learning,** and **deny the Holy Ghost, which giveth utterance**' and of their '**false** and **vain** and **foolish doctrines.**'" [16]

Likewise, Mormon saw and wrote of the people of these last days:

> "O ye wicked and perverse and stiffnecked people, why have ye built up churches unto yourselves to get gain? Why have ye transfigured the holy word of God, that ye might bring damnation upon your souls? Your churches, yea, even every one, have become polluted because of the pride of your hearts. For behold, ye do love money, and your substance and your fine apparel, and the adorning of your churches, more than ye love the poor and the needy, the sick and the afflicted. O ye pollutions, ye hypocrites, ye teachers, who sell yourselves for that which will canker, why have ye polluted the holy church of God? Why are ye ashamed to take upon you the name of Christ? Why do ye not think that greater is the value of an endless happiness than that misery which never dies — because of the praise of the world? Why do ye adorn yourselves with that which hath no life, and yet suffer the hungry, and the needy, and the naked, and the sick and the afflicted to pass by you, and notice them not? Yea, why do ye build up your secret abominations to get gain, and cause that widows should mourn before the Lord, and also orphans to mourn before the Lord, and also the blood of their fathers and their husbands to cry unto the Lord from the ground for vengeance upon your heads?"[17]

The Lord had caused all things to be put in order to bring about the restoration, in this the dispensation of the "Fullness of Times." It was a part of the Lord's Gospel plan for man.

> "**Since** the **gospel** was **first given to Adam, each time** it was **thereafter lost by apostasy** and then **revealed to man again** there has **been a restoration of the gospel.** Our **Lord** in his **personal ministry**, for instance, **restored the original gospel,** the same plan of salvation, which he had revealed to Adam in the beginning. But when men in this day speak of the restoration of the gospel, they mean the final great restoration, which has now taken place as part of the restoration of all things. This dispensation is the age of restoration to which all the ancient prophets look forward. In it all things are to be restored 'which God hath spoken by the mouth of all his holy prophets since the world began.'[18] **All things** are **being gathered together in one in Christ.**"[19]

THE GATHERING

With the prayer of a fourteen year old boy, Joseph Smith, Jr., who was pure in heart and prepared from before the foundation of the world, the final Gospel dispensation of the "Fullness of Times" was ushered in. One by one all things were put in order that would allow God's Saints to be gathered to a central location. There they would be taught eternal truths; build a temple to receive God's endowment; learn what they will need for exaltation of themselves, their ancestors, and their progeny; and go forth to preach the Gospel to all nations. A place from which the Gospel could roll forth as "a rock cut out of the mountain that would roll forth and fill the whole earth." A place where the "pure in heart" would dwell, with "no poor among them", a land called Zion.

Some of the key events that made up the restoration of the Gospel are:

- Spring 1820: In answer to a young boys fervent prayer an **absolute knowledge** of God The Eternal **Father** and His **Son** Jesus Christ was **restored** again to the **earth**.

- 22 September 1827: Joseph Smith the prophet **received the gold plates** of the *Book of Mormon* from the angel Moroni at the hill Cummorah and **translation began**.

- 15 May 1829: the **Aaronic Priesthood** and its authority are **restored by John the Baptist** to Joseph Smith and Oliver Cowdrey.

- Between May & June 1829: the **Melchizedek Priesthood** and its **authority** are **restored by** the **Apostles Peter, James and John** to Joseph Smith and Oliver Cowdrey.

- In June 1829 the **translation** of the *Book of Mormon* is **completed** and on the 11th day of that month it is copyrighted.

- 26 March 1830: The *Book of Mormon* is made **available for sale** in Palmyra.

- 6 April 1830: The **Church of Jesus Christ** is **officially organized** in this dispensation at Fayette, New York.

- April-July 1830: a **public ministry** of the **Church is begun**.

- December 1830: a **revelation**, later known as *Doctrine and Covenants* 37, is received by the prophet **commanding** the **membership** of the **Church** to be **gathered to "the Ohio."**

- 2 January 1831: a **revelation** detailing **why** the **Church must move to Ohio** is given, along with a promise that there His law and an endowment would be given.

- 9 February 1831: the **law is received by revelation**, which we now recognize as *Doctrine and Covenants* 42.

- 19 June 1831: **Joseph** Smith **starts for Missouri** to designate the **"land of Zion."**

- 20 July 1831: Joseph has **revealed** to him that **Independence, Jackson County, Missouri** is designated as the **center place for Zion** and a **great temple** is to **built there.**

- 22 November 1833: **Joseph learns** of the **expulsion of the Saints from Zion** and the mob action in Jackson County, Missouri.

- 14 February 1835: the **Quorum of the Twelve Apostles is organized**; and on 28 February, the **Quorum of the Seventy**.

- 28 March 1835: a **revelation**, now known as *Doctrine and Covenants* 107, is received **on priesthood.**

- 29-30 March 1836: the prophet **Joseph presides** in the **Kirkland Temple** as an **endowment** of power **from on high fell upon** a large **group of priesthood leaders.**

- 3 April 1836: the **Lord appears to Joseph** Smith **and Oliver** Cowdery and **accepts** the **Kirtland Temple**. At that time **Moses restored the keys of the gathering of Israel; Elias** restored the **keys of the gospel of Abraham;** and **Elijah restored the priesthood keys and sealing powers.**

- June 1837: the **first missionaries** are **sent to England**, arriving 19 July. On 27 July **Joseph leaves for Toronto, Canada** to preach the Gospel and the gathering.

- Early January 1838, J**oseph and** the **remaining faithful escape** the **apostates and mob violence** in **Kirtland** and **move to Far West**, Caldwell County, Missouri where converts had been gathering for some time. More problems, an **extermination order**; the Saints escape from the mob; unlawful and unjust imprisonment for the prophet and his companions; followed by their escape; and eventual **sanctuary** and a **new place of gathering at Commerce, Illinois, renamed Nauvoo**. There from May of 1839 to 1845 the Saints **built a great city and another temple**. Here the **full use and purposes of temples** were revealed; the **full endowment given; Celestial marriage** and **eternal families; vicarious work for the dead;** etc. Here also the **Twelve Apostles** were **trained** and had the **full authority of their office** and **calling bestowed** upon them, placing the responsibilities of the Kingdom upon their shoulders. All this and so much more.

- And yet **Joseph knew** the **gathering of Zion** would have to **continue elsewhere**. On February 20, 1844 he **instructed the Twelve** to **oversee** the **organization and outfitting** of **exploring parties** for a **new location in the west**. The **stone** had been **cut out of the mountain without hands** and was already rolling forth upon the earth. The **gathering of Zion had begun** and **all things** had been **put in motion** for the **last time before Joseph and** his brother **Hyrum** were **martyred at Carthage Jail.**

Peter taught anciently that the Second Coming of the Son of Man could not take place "until the times of restitution of all things, which God hath spoken by the mouth of all his holy prophets since the world began."[20]

> "It should be noted that **Peter does not say that all things must be restored before Christ comes**, but that the age, era, period, or **times** in the earth's history in **which restoration** is to **take place must** itself **commence**. That era **did begin in the spring of 1820**, but **all things** will **not** be revealed until **after Christ comes**."[21]

By the time Joseph Smith, Jr. was martyred at age 38, all things of the Kingdom of God had been divinely restored and the final "Gathering of Zion" had begun.

Of course some things that are a part of the restitution of all things have to do with events that will not take place until the Lord's Second Coming:

> "Now the **great restoration of all things** is the **return of the earth**, and **all that pertains to it**, including every form of life, **back to the primeval and perfect state** which prevailed **when all things first rolled from their Creator's hands** and were pronounced, 'Very good.' [22] The **most important part** of this great restoration of all things is, of course, the **restoration of the gospel**, but in the eternal sense **all of the Lord's dealings are part of his gospel plan**."[23]

> "We believe … that **the earth will be renewed and receive its paradisiacal glory**."[24] Thus conditions, which prevailed in the Edenic day, forecast similar conditions that will again prevail during the millennial era; and a revealed knowledge of millennial conditions gives an understanding of analogous conditions that prevailed when the earth enjoyed its first paradisiacal status. The same conditions will not prevail in every detail, but certain basic things will be similarly arranged.

> "When the **earth was first created all the land was in one place** and there were no mountains and valleys of the kind that now exist. At the **Second Coming of Christ the sea** will **be driven back to its place in the north**, the **continents shall become one land again**, every valley shall be exalted, every mountain shall be made low, and the earth shall cease bringing forth thorns and noxious weeds, but **shall become as the garden of the Lord**."[25]

THE GATHERING IN THE LAST DAYS

One of the great *New Testament* parables taught by the Lord had to do with the wheat and the tares. The ancient apostles understood what was meant by the parable, but not many others did. While most today would understand that it had to do with last day judgment, the saving of the righteous and punishment of the wicked that had to exist together until their final separation, few understand that the gathering of the wheat is first and foremost the **gathering** of the righteous to Zion in the last days.

> "Therefore, **I must gather** together **my people, according** to the **parable** of the **wheat and** the **tares**, that the **wheat** may be **secured in** the **garners** to **possess eternal life**, and be crowned with celestial glory, when I shall come in the kingdom of my Father to reward every man according as his work shall be;"[26]

It was a call to bring His people out of Babylon to Zion:

> "Wherefore, prepare ye, prepare ye, O my people; sanctify yourselves; **gather** ye **together**, O ye people of **my church, upon the land of Zion**, all you that have **not been commanded to tarry**. **Go ye out from Babylon. Be ye clean** that bear the vessels of the Lord… Yea, verily I say unto you again, the time has come when the voice of the Lord is unto you: **Go ye out of Babylon; gather** ye out **from among** the **nations, from** the **four winds**, from **one end of heaven to the other**.[27]

Judah will gather to Jerusalem, but all other tribes will gather to the New Jerusalem, the Zion of America.

> "The Book of Mormon is a record of the forefathers of our western tribes of Indians; having been found through the ministration of an holy angel, and translated into our own language by the gift and power of God, after having been hid up in the earth for the last fourteen hundred years, containing the word of God which was delivered unto them. By it we learn that our western tribes of Indians are descendants from that Joseph which was sold into Egypt, and that **the land of America is a promised land unto them, and unto it all the tribes of Israel will come with as many of the Gentiles as shall comply with the requisitions of the new covenant. But the tribe of Judah will return to old Jerusalem. The city of Zion spoken of by David, in the one hundred and second Psalm, will be built upon the land of America**, 'And the ransomed of the Lord shall return, and come to Zion with songs and everlasting joy upon their heads'[28]; and then they will be delivered from the overflowing scourge that shall pass through the land. But Judah shall obtain deliverance at Jerusalem.[29] **These** are **testimonies** that the **Good Shepherd** will **put forth His own sheep, and lead them out from all nations** where they **have been scattered in a cloudy and dark day, to Zion and to Jerusalem**, besides many more testimonies which might be brought."[30]

> "…The **whole of America is Zion** itself **from north to south**, and is described by the Prophets, who declare that it is the **Zion where the mountain of the Lord should be**, and that it should be in the **center of the land**."[31]

The gathering of the last dispensation is unique; in as much as the Lord says He will gather together all things in heaven and earth.

"Unto whom I have committed the keys of my kingdom, and a dispensation of the gospel for the last times; and for the fullness of times, in the which **I will gather together in one all things,** both which are **in heaven, and** which are **on earth;** And **also with all those** whom **my Father** hath **given me out of the world.**[32]

"And **righteousness** will I send **out of heaven;** and **truth** will I send forth **out of the earth, to bear testimony** of mine **Only Begotten;** his resurrection from the dead; yea, and also the resurrection of all men; and **righteousness and truth** will I cause to **sweep the earth** as with a flood, to **gather** out **mine elect** from the **four quarters of the earth, unto a place** which I shall prepare, an **Holy City**, that my people may gird up their loins, and **be looking forth** for the time of **my coming;** for **there shall be my tabernacle**, and it shall be **called Zion**, a New Jerusalem.

"And the Lord said unto Enoch: Then shalt thou and all thy city meet them there, and we will receive them into our bosom, and they shall see us; and we will fall upon their necks, and they shall fall upon our necks, and we will kiss each other; And there shall **be mine abode**, and it shall be Zion, which shall come forth out of all the creations which I have made; and for the space of a **thousand years** the **earth shall rest.**"[33]

"And **he that receiveth these things receiveth me**; and they shall **be gathered** unto me **in time and in eternity**."[34]

All who are gathered to Zion from all nations will live there in peace, having mutual protection, spiritual reinforcement, instruction, and equality.[35]

"And it shall be **called the New Jerusalem**, a **land of peace**, a city of **refuge**, a place of **safety for** the **saints** of the Most High God; And the **glory of the Lord shall be there**, and the terror of the Lord also shall be there, insomuch that the **wicked will not come** unto it, and it shall be **called Zion**. And it shall come to pass **among the wicked**, that **every man that will not take** his **sword against his neighbor** must **needs flee** unto **Zion for safety**.

"And there **shall be gathered unto it out of every nation under heaven**; and it shall **be the only people** that shall **not** be **at war one with another**. And it shall be **said among the wicked**: Let us **not** go up to **battle against Zion**, for the inhabitants of Zion are terrible; wherefore we cannot stand. And it shall come to pass that the **righteous** shall be gathered out from among all nations, and shall <u>come</u> to **Zion, singing** with **songs** of **everlasting joy**."[36]

A primary responsibility of the gathered Saints is to build a temple where they can stand in holy places and the Lord can reveal unto His people the ordinances necessary for their exaltation. When they were first gathered to Kirtland, one of their first tasks was to build a temple. After it was learned through revelation that Independence in Jackson County, Missouri was to be Zion, the New Jerusalem, the prophet Joseph marked the spot for the temple and plans were made for its construction. After being driven out by the mobs to northern Missouri, another site for a temple at Far West was designated. When they were driven from Missouri and settled in Illinois, again one of the first tasks was the designation of a spot for a temple at Nauvoo. That temple was barely completed, and used but a very short time, before the Saints were driven out again, into the wilderness of Iowa. After Brigham Young was shown the place for the settlement of Zion in the valleys of the mountains of Utah, the first item of business was to designate the site for the temple in Salt Lake City. A temple which took many years to complete and with other temples in Utah being completed and used first for temple ordinances.

"Verily this is the word of the Lord, that the city **New Jerusalem shall be built by the gathering of the saints**, **beginning** at **this place**, even the place of the **temple**, which temple **shall be reared in this generation**."[37]

"Behold, it is my will, that **all they** who **call** on **my name**, and **worship me according** to mine **everlasting gospel**, should **gather together**, and **stand in holy places**;"[38]

It is absolutely essential that the Lord have a temple in which he can teach His people, bless them, and provide ordinances that form binding eternal covenants with Him that bring exaltation. There are certain holy forms of worship that can only rightly be performed in the House of the Lord.

"The **main object** was to **build** unto the **Lord a house** whereby He **could reveal** unto **His people** the **ordinances of His house** and the **glories of His kingdom**, and **teach** the people the **way of salvation**; for there are **certain ordinances and principles** that, when they are taught and practiced, **must be done** in a place or **house built for that purpose**.

"It was the **design** of the **councils of heaven** before the world was, that the **principles and laws** of the **priesthood** should be **predicated upon the gathering of the people in every age of the world. Jesus did everything to gather the people, and they would not** be gathered, and He therefore poured out curses upon them. **Ordinances instituted in the heavens** before the foundation of the world, in the priesthood, **for the salvation of men, are not to be altered or changed.** All must be saved on the same principles.

"It is **for the same purpose that God gathers together His people in the last days**, to **build unto the Lord a house** to **prepare** them for the **ordinances and endowments, washings and anointings, etc**. One of the ordinances of the house of the Lord is **baptism for the dead**. God decreed before the foundation of the world that that ordinance should be administered in a font prepared for that purpose in the house of the Lord."[39]

"...The declaration this morning is, that as soon as the Temple and baptismal font are prepared, we calculate to give the Elders of Israel their washings and anointings, and attend to those last and more impressive ordinances, without which we cannot obtain celestial thrones. But there **must be a holy place prepared for that purpose**. There was a proclamation made during the time that the foundation of the Temple was laid to that effect, and there are provisions made until the work is completed, **so that men may receive their endowments and be made kings and priests** unto the **Most High God, having nothing to do with temporal things**, but their whole time will be taken up with things pertaining to the house of God. There **must**, however, **be a place built expressly for that purpose**, and for men to be baptized for their dead. It **must be built** in this the **central place; for every man who wishes to save his father, mother, brothers, sisters and friends**, must **go through** all the **ordinances for each one** of them separately, the same as for himself, from baptism to ordination, washings and anointings, and receive all the keys and powers of the Priesthood, the same as for himself."[40]

Many aspects of the restoration of all things in this dispensation could not take place until the Kirtland Temple was dedicated and those holding the keys of the various ordinances and dispensations of the earth delivered those keys to the prophet Joseph Smith. For example:

"After this vision closed, the heavens were again opened unto us; and **Moses appeared** before us, and **committed unto us** the **keys** of the **gathering of Israel** from the **four parts of the earth, and** the **leading** of the **ten tribes** from the **land of the north**."[41]

When all things are taken into consideration regarding the Second Coming, there had to be a means for spreading Christ's Gospel for the last time to the four quarters of the earth. To accomplish this task the authority of God's priesthood and powers had to be restored to the earth, by calling the prophet Joseph Smith, Jr. Then a tool for restoring the fullness of the gospel had to be made available, in the *Book of Mormon*. Missionaries had to be sent forth to find the faithful and a place had to be established where converts could come to prepare more missionaries. Then to be able to bless the lives of the converts and to fulfill prophecy, the Saints had to be gathered to one place where they could be spiritually and temporally strengthened and blessed. To provide them with the fullness of the Gospel and restoration of all blessings, a Temple would be needed to restore all keys, and a dedicated place separated from the ways of the world where the worthy could be trained and prepared for exaltation. Hence, the gathering prophesied in the *Old and New Testament, The Book of Mormon*, and modern revelation was a necessity.

"The greatest temporal and spiritual blessings which always flow from faithfulness and concerted effort, never attended individual exertion or enterprise. The history of all past ages abundantly attests this fact. In addition to all temporal blessings, there is **no other way for the Saints to be saved in these last days, [than by the gathering]** as the concurrent testimony of all the holy Prophets clearly proves, for it is written—'They shall come from the east, and be gathered from the west; the north shall give up, and the south shall keep not back.' '**The sons of God shall be gathered from far, and His daughters from the ends of the earth.**'"[42]

"**Take away** the **Book of Mormon** and the **revelations, and where is our religion**. We **have none**; for **without Zion**, and a **place of deliverance**, we **must fall**; because the **time is near** when the sun will be darkened, and the moon turn to blood, and the stars fall from heaven, and the earth reel to and fro. Then, if this is the case, and **if we are not sanctified** and **gathered** to the **places God** has **appointed**, with all our former professions and our great love for the Bible, **we must fall**; we cannot stand; we cannot be saved; **for God will gather out His Saints from the Gentiles, and then comes desolation and destruction, and none can escape except the pure in heart who are gathered.**"[43]

THE PERPETUAL EMIGRATING FUND

By the middle of the nineteenth century, missionary work and the gathering to Zion were well underway. With very few exceptions, all of the newly converted Saints desired to gather to Utah, but there were many of the poor that could not. President Young and the Brethren spent much time agonizing over what could be done. Finally a decision was reached and in 1849 a new program was initiated:

"In the work of gathering their co-religionists from the Missouri frontiers—their fellow exiles from Illinois, too poor to make the journey to the valleys without the assistance of their more fortunate brethren—the saints in the valleys of Utah contributed both time and means on a large scale; but in this they were reminded that they were but fulfilling the obligations entered into at Nauvoo before the exodus began. It was in this year of grace, 1849, however, that what was known afterwards as "The **Perpetual Emigration Fund**" was **established**. It had for its **purpose, first**, the **removal to** the **mountains of all the worthy Latter-day Saints exiled from Illinois**, who **desired to gather** to the main body of the church, and **after** that to **extend aid to the worthy poor among the saints** throughout the **world**.

"The '**perpetual**' feature of the plan was to be **maintained by those** who **received aid** from this emigrating fund **returning** "**the same, in labor or otherwise**, as **soon** as their **circumstances will admit**," and "with interest if required," in order that the **means might be used again** to **aid others**;..."[44]

"...The council approved this suggestion, and a committee was appointed to raise a fund by voluntary contribution to effect this purpose. "The October conference (1849) sanctioned the doings of the committee," says the epistle of the presidency, bearing date of **October 12th, 1849**, and **appointed Edward Hunter,** a tried, faithful and approved bishop, **as general agent** to bear the **perpetual emigration funds** to the states, to superintend the **direction and appropriation** thereof, and return the same to this place with such poor brethren as (it) shall be wisdom to help.

"We wish all to understand, that this **fund is perpetual**, and is **never to be diverted** from the object of **gathering the poor to Zion while** there are **saints to be gathered**, unless He whose right it is to rule shall otherwise command...."

"The subject at the **October conference** was brought up by **Heber C. Kimball**. Referring to the Nauvoo covenant he said: "**Shall we fulfill** that **covenant**, or shall we not?" The **vote was unanimous** to fulfill the covenant. "Now let every man and woman take hold," said Elder Kimball, "and **do not send** your **agent to the states with less than $10,000**; and then you will cause a day of rejoicing among the poor in Illinois." The conference **appointed** a **committee** of five to **gather contributions** for the fund. The names of the committee follow: Willard **Snow, John S. Fulmer,** Lorenzo Snow, John D. Lee and Franklin D. Richards. **Bishop Edward Hunter** was appointed to be the **agent to go east** and **expend** the funds thus raised,—amounting that year to **six thousand dollars**, in gathering the poor to the valleys. It was moved by Elder John Taylor that the whole business pertaining to the **fund** be placed under the **direction** of the **first presidency** of the church, and his motion was carried unanimously."[45]

On 12 October 1849, the First Presidency wrote of the general manner for the use of the funds in an epistle to the Church:

"... therefore, ye poor, and meek of the earth, lift up your heads and rejoice in the Holy One of Israel, for your redemption draweth nigh; but in your rejoicings be patient, for though your turn to emigrate may not be the first year, or even the second, it will come, and its tarryings will be short, if all the saints who have, [means] will be as liberal as those in the valley."[46]

While the Church leadership had taken on the task of raising funds to start the PAF [Perpetual Emigrating Fund], it needed a means of impressing on those who were blessed by the fund, that they had an obligation to repay the fund as soon as possible. A written contracted was signed by the recipients, including the payment of interest where possible, as a means of keeping the fund solvent. Of course the brethren responded to individual circumstances regarding the recovery of interest.

"It will be observed that the **obligation** in the **signed contract** concerning interest was an **agreement** to **pay interest 'if required.'** Whenever there was anything like promptness in the payment of the principal, or where **misfortune** had been **encountered**, it was the **policy** of the company **not to require interest**; indeed the policy of the company was very generous in respect of the payment of both principal and interest. This fund conceived in such noble spirit was the means of bringing tens of thousands of the landless poor from Europe—for its operations were not confined to America and the British Isles—to the unoccupied lands of the Great Basin, where in a few years, they and their descendants became landed proprietors, independent and prosperous citizens of the intermountain west.[47]

During the 1880-Year of Jubilee, many of the poor with pressing circumstances had half of their debt forgiven, others were totally forgiven at the direction of President John Taylor.

"The discourses delivered during the conference were spirited, hopeful, and breathed assurances of the triumph of the work of God, and prophetic of future achievement that should be larger than in the past. But more important than what was said, was what was done at this conference. The **church authorities** acted in the **spirit** of the **old Israelitish Jubilee**, if not precisely in its form and letter. In the first place there was an **accumulated indebtedness** on the part of the **community** to the **Perpetual Emigration Fund of $704,000 in principal**; with accumulated **interest** of **$900,000**; the whole **amounting** to **$1,604,000**. **One-half** of this sum, $802,000, was **stricken from the account**, and f**orgiven to the poor** who had been struggling with the difficulties of life, and who had **not** been **able** to **meet** their, **engagements** to the fund. 'Not half the amount that was due by them,' explained President Taylor, "but the whole;" and to those who are forgiven the debt, it will be blotted out, and the remainder will be **left** to **those to pay** who are **able to** and **have not done it**. "And we shall **expect** that those who have not met their engagements," said he, "**to meet them;** * * * for in **former times they did not release the rich (from debt) it was the poor**." This was carried into effect by the local authorities in the respective wards and stakes designating the parties worthy to be forgiven their debt to the fund."⁴⁸

Of course the first use for the PEF was to gather the poor from Illinois, but by January of 1852 its scope was widened:

"... the **presidency** of the **British Mission** was **also authorized** to **introduce this system** for the gathering of the saints out of that country, and by January, 1852, **1,140 English pounds**, equal to about $5,700.00 had **been subscribed**; and in the **emigration of that year from England, 251 persons were sent by the "fund."** Special arrangements had been made to conduct this company from Liverpool to Salt Lake City..."⁴⁹

Eventually the PEF was expanded to assist the poor of the world in gathering to Zion.

In an effort to give the fund greater stability, it was sanctioned by the Utah Territorial government:

"...In order to give this charity stability and perpetuity its promoters were **organized** into **a company by** the provisional **government** of the "**State of Deseret**," September 14, 1850; under the style and title of "**The Perpetual Emigration Fund Company**." This act was **legalized** by the **Utah territorial government**, Oct. 4th, 1851; amended by the same authority in January 12, 1856.⁵⁰

The first suggestion of using the Perpetual Emigration Fund to gather Saints to Zion using handcarts, was made by First Presidency in 1851:

"This method of emigrating the saints was first suggested by the **presidency** of the church in their **sixth general epistle**, addressed "to the saints scattered throughout the earth," and bearing date of September 22nd, 1851. In that epistle **great emphasis** was laid upon the subject of the **saints "gathering to Zion**," as may be judged by the following excerpt:

"O ye saints in the United States, will you listen to the voice of `the Good Shepherd'? **Will you gather**? Will you **be obedient** to the **heavenly commandments**? **Many** of you have been looking for, and **expecting too much**; you have been expecting the **time would come** when you could j**ourney across the mountains** in your **fine carriages**, your **good wagons**, and have **all the comforts** of life that heart could wish; but **your expectations are vain**, and if you wait for those things you will never come, * * * and your faith and hope will depart from you. How long shall it be said in truth `the children of this world are wiser in their generation than the children of light.' **Some** of the **children of the world** have **crossed** the **mountains and plains,** from Missouri to California, with a **pack** on **their back** to **worship** their god—**gold**! Some have performed the same **journey** with a **wheel-barrow**; some have accomplished the same with a **pack on a cow**. **Some** of the **saints, now** in our **midst, came** hither **with wagons or carts made of wood, without a particle of iron,** hooping their **wheels** with **hickory, or rawhide, or ropes**, and had as **good** and **safe a journey** as any in the camps, with their well **wrought iron wagons**; and **can you not do the same?** Yes, **if** you **have** the **same desire**, the **same faith**. Families might **start** from the **Missouri river, with cows, handcarts, wheel-barrows,** with **little flour**, and **no unnecessaries**, and **come** to this place **quicker**, and **with less fatigue, than** by following the **heavy trains**, with their cumbrous herds, which they are often obliged to drive miles to feed. **Do you not like this method** of traveling? **Do you think salvation costs too much?** If so, it is not worth having. **Sisters, fifty and sixty** years old, have **driven ox teams** to this **valley**, and are **alive and well** yet; true they **could have come easier** by **walking** alone, than by driving a team, but by driving the oxen, they helped others here; and **cannot you come the easier way**? There is **grain** and **provision enough** in the **valleys for you** to come to; and you **need not bring more** than enough **to sustain you one hundred days**, to insure you a supply for the future."⁵¹

In 1855, PEF pioneers were informed that the following year their only means of gathering would be restricted to the use of handcarts, once they reached Iowa City, Iowa.

"We propose sending men of faith and experience, with suitable instructions, to some proper outfitting point to carry into effect the above suggestions; **let the saints**, therefore, who **intend** to **immigrate** the **ensuing year,** understand that they are **expected to walk and draw their luggage across the plains**, and that they **will be assisted by** the **fund in no other way**."[52]

"...**let them pursue the northern route from Boston, New York, or Philadelphia**, and **land at Iowa City** or the then terminus of the railroad; there let them **be provided** with **handcarts** on which **to draw** their **provisions and clothing**, then **walk and draw them**, thereby saving the immense expense every year for teams and outfit for crossing the plains."[53]

"**We are sanguine** that such a train will **out-travel any ox train** that can be started. They **should have a few good cows** to furnish **milk**, and a **few beef cattle** to drive and **butcher as** they may **need**. In this way the **expense, risk, loss and perplexity of teams will be obviated**, and the saints will more effectually **escape** the **scenes of distress, anguish** and **death** which have often **laid so many** of our brethren and sisters in the **dust**."[54]

The *Millennial Star* reported that in 1856, a total of "4,326 souls" immigrated to Zion, 2,012 of which were funded by the Perpetual Emigration Company.[55]

B. H. Roberts, in his *Comprehensive History of the Church*, reported PEF totals as:
1850—432	1856—1,273	1859—54
1852—298	1857—1	TOTAL—4,769
1853—400	1858—0 "(owing to Utah difficulties)"	

The cost was "about three hundred thousand dollars," which was "but a small portion of the yearly 'Mormon immigration,' no record of which, so far as I am acquainted, has ever been [kept], not could there be, [kept such record], as persons emigrating on their own means have come and gone at pleasure."[56]

The Congress of the United States of America brought the Perpetual Emigration Fund to an end in 1887 in a bill known as the Edmunds-Tucker Act. As a means of forcing the Church to end its practice of Polygamy, the act dissolved the Perpetual Emigration Fund Company as well as The Church of Jesus Christ of Latter-day Saints and seized all assets. For the PEF, that amounted to over $800,000. Of course the matter was appealed to the Supreme Count of the United States, and in the meantime differences with the government were worked out to return Church assets with the guarantee that polygamy would no longer be practiced nor permitted.[57]

Between 1850 and 1887, over 85,000 Mormon emigrants make their way across an ocean and two-thirds of a continent to reach a valley in the high deserts of the Rocky Mountains. Because a prophet said it should be done, between 1856–1860, some 3,000 of the 30,000 men, women and children helped by the PEF, were willing to push and pull handcarts across 1,300 agonizing miles to gather to Zion.[58]

Surely this was the literal fulfillment of Isaiah's prophecy centuries earlier:

> "And it shall come to pass in the last days, that the mountain of the Lord's house shall be established in the top of the mountains, and shall be exalted above the hills; and all nations shall flow unto it. And many people shall go and say, Come ye, and let us go up to the mountain of the Lord, to the house of the God of Jacob; and he will teach us of his ways, and we will walk in his paths: for out of Zion shall go forth the law, and the word of the Lord from Jerusalem."[59]

[Emphasis Added throughout Appendix A]

Appendix B

"PERPETUAL EMIGRATING FUND COMPANY
"Organized at Great Salt Lake City, Deseret, U.S.A., October 6th, 1849

"We. the undersigned, do hereby agree, and bind ourselves to the PERPETUAL EMIGRATING FUND COMPANY, in the following conditions, viz–

"That, in consideration of the aforesaid Company emigrating or transporting us, and our necessary luggage, from [Name of Country] to Utah, according to the Rules of the Company, and the general instructions of their authorized Agents;

"We do severally and jointly promise, and bind ourselves, to continue with, and obey the instructions of, the Agent appointed to superintend our passage thither, that we will receipt for our passages previous to arriving at the port of disembarkation in the United State, at the point of outfit on the Missouri river, prior to arriving in G.S.L. Valley, and at any intermediate stopping place the Agent in charge may think proper to require it;

"And that, on our arrival in Utah, we will hold ourselves, our time, and our labour, subject to the appropriation of the Perpetual Emigrating Fund Company, until the full cost of our emigration is paid, with interest if required." [*Millennial Star*, 12 Jan 1856, p. 26]

The Latter-day Saint's Millennial Star

SATURDAY, JANUARY 12, 1856

General Instructions.

In view of the approaching departure for America of many of the official members of the Church in the British Isles and Foreign Missions, and the general change that will shortly take place in appointments, we publish the following General Instructions for the benefit of the officers of the Church, and also the members, but especially newly-appointed officers, that they may enter upon the duties of their respective callings with an understanding of the way in which business is conducted by this Office with the Conferences and Missions.

EMIGRATION DEPARTMENT

"*Application for Passage.* — All applications for passage to America must be accompanied by the name, age, occupation, and name of native country, of every individual; and a deposit of £1 for each over ONE YEAR OLD, without which no berths can be secured. The time the applicants wish to embark should also be stated, and they will be accommodated as near that date as possible.

"When a vessel is engaged, we notify such applicants as wish to sail about the time she will be going, by printed circular, giving the date of embarkation, price of passage, and all particulars, to which we require an immediate answer, stating whether the parties notified will embark or not, that in case they are not ready we may have an opportunity to notify others. If we receive a reply that passengers will embark in a certain ship, we immediately secure berths for them; and if they do not embark in that ship their deposits are forfeited, unless they are prevented by sickness or death, when we require to be informed of the fact at the earliest moment, that substitutes may be procured to occupy the berths thus rendered vacant.

"No persons who have recently been exposed to small-pox or other contagious disorders should come forward for embarkation, nor children having them be brought, as the lives of such would thereby be jeopardized, and death probably be sown among all the ship's company. Furthermore, in all cases where it is apparent to the Government Medical Inspector that passengers are in such a situation, they are rejected by him, and cannot proceed on their voyage until free from contagious sickness.

"These regulations respecting passage are necessary to secure the Office from the loss that would accrue from a ship going to sea with a number of empty berths.

"*Provisions and Price of Passage.* —The recent British and American Passenger Acts have very largely increased the scale of provisions formerly allowed, and have made all persons 8 *years of age and upwards statute adults*. Two children over 1 year and under 8 years old count as one statute adult. This, of course, has correspondingly increased the price of passage, but as it necessarily varies more or less on each ship, we cannot here quote a fixed rate. The prices on the first ship sent out by us under the new Acts were £4 5s. for adults, £3m 5s. for children, and 10s. for infants. We hope there will be no particular advance on these prices, but we can scarcely expect they will be much lower.

"THE SCALE OF PROVISIONS AS NOW FIXED BY LAW IS AS FOLLOWS—To each adult, or every two children, weekly—

3½ lbs	Bread,	2	lbs	Potatoes,	2	oz.	Salt,
1 lb	Flour,	1¼ lbs	Beef,	½ oz.	Mustard,
1½ lbs	Oat Meal,	1	lb	Pork,	¼ oz.	Pepper,
1½ lbs	Rice,	1	lb	Sugar,	1 gill	Vinegar,
1½ lbs	Peas,	2	oz	Tea,			

3 quarts of water daily, and 10 gallons daily to every 100 for cooking.

"Ships clearing out between the 16th of January and 14th of October are provided for 70 days, and those clearing out between the 15th of October and the 17th of January for 80 days.

"The new Acts also require each ship to be provided with *Medical Comforts*. The following scale has been fixed upon by the Government Emigration Commissioners for vessels sailing from this Port to North America.

"FOR TWO HUNDRED ADULTS AND UNDER—

14 lbs	Arrowroot,	30 lbs	Sugar,	½	gallon Brandy,
25 lbs	Sago,	12 lbs	Marine Soap,	2 doz. milk. in pints,
20 lbs	Pearl Barley,	2 gallons	Lime Juice,	1 doz. Beef Soup, in lbs,
		3 doz.	Preserved Mutton, in ½ lbs.		

One half of the above scale to be added for every additional Hundred."

"Passengers furnish their own beds and bedding. A straw mattress will answer very well for sleeping upon when they do not bring feather or other beds with them. Each single passenger also requires a box or barrel to hold provisions; and the following articles for cooking, &c.—a boiler, saucepan, fryingpan, tin porringer, tin plate, tin dish, knife, fork, spoon, and a tin vessel to hold 3 quarts of water.

"Where families emigrate together, one boiler, one saucepan, one fryingpan, and one provision box, of suitable size, will be sufficient for all. The water bottles also may be made to convenience in size and number, but they must hold the number of quarts due the whole family per day.

"*Luggage.*—As much as possible of passengers' luggage should be marked "*To go below*," that it may be put into the hold of the ship. Only that which is absolutely necessary during the voyage should be retained on deck.

"*Emigrants for the United States only.*—As we design to have the business of the present season's emigration concluded a month earlier in the year, if possible, than was last season's, we request that intending emigrants for the United States only will apply immediately, as we wish to ship them about the 1st of February, or as soon after as practicable. We cannot, as we did last season, ship this class of emigrants with those going through to Utah.

"*Through Emigrants.*—To such as purpose to go through to Utah on their own means, we have to say that teams can be ordered through us as heretofore, and will be supplied at the point of out-fit for the Plains by our agent. We think £55 will cover the cost of one wagon, with bows, yokes, and chains, four oxen, and one cow perhaps two. All who wish us to order for them must inform us immediately, and send the needful, that we may transmit the same to our agent. The 1st of March will be as late as we can receive orders for this season, but it will be much to the advantage of purchasers and ourselves if we can know by the 15th of February what will be required.

"Tenting and wagon–cover material we also purpose to supply as heretofore. For a tent 44 yards are required, for a wagon–cover 26 yards. The material is a good British Twilled Nankeen, 27 inches wide, and will be 6 ½d per yard.

"*P. E. Fund Emigrants.*—Persons ordered out by the P. E. Fund Company are notified to that effect on our receiving the instructions from the President. The order holds good for *one season only*. Those persons unable to go are requested to state the reasons why, for transmission to the President, after which a new order from him will be required before such parties can be forwarded out.

"P. E. Fun Emigrants, whether ordered out or selected here, are forwarded entirely subject to the regulations of the Company which exist when their embarkation takes place. That portion of the journey between Great Britain and the United States is performed in accordance with the requirements of the Passenger Acts, as set forth at the commencement of this article.

"After landing in America they are forwarded in charge of Agents of the Church from place to place until they arrive in Utah. The mode in which the American part of the journey is conducted varies some little each year. For that which will be pursued the present year, we refer to the *Millennial Star*, No. 51, Vol. XVII, and to further instructions which will shortly be given through the same medium.

"All P. E. Fund passengers are required before embarkation to sign a Bond, of which the following is a copy–

"Perpetual Emigrating Fund Company.

"*Organized at Great Salt Lake City, Deseret, U.S.A., October 6th, 1849.*

"**We, the Undersigned,** do hereby agree, and bind ourselves to the PERPETUAL EMIGRATING FUND COMPANY, in the following conditions, viz.–

"That, in consideration of the aforesaid Company emigrating or transporting us, and our necessary luggage, from [Name of Country] to Utah, according to the Rules of the Company, and the general instructions of their authorized Agents;

"We do severally and jointly promise, and bind ourselves, to continue with, and obey the instructions of, the Agent appointed to superintend our passage thither, that we will receipt for our passages previous to arriving at the port of disembarkation in the United States, at the point of outfit on the Missouri river, prior to arriving in G. S. L. Valley, and at any intermediate stopping place the Agent in charge may think proper to require it;

"And that, on our arrival in Utah, we will hold ourselves, our time, and our labour, subject to the appropriation of the Perpetual Emigrating Fund Company, until the full cost of our emigration is paid, with interest if required."

"Some P.E. Fund passengers are able to pay a portion of the expense of their journey. Such deposit the amount with us prior to embarkation from Liverpool, and we place the same to their credit to apply on settlement in Utah with the P.E. Fund Company.

Exchange.—There is no necessity for exchanging English gold into American money, as the former is almost always at a premium in the United States. English silver cannot be taken without a loss.

"*Drafts on Utah.*—To those persons emigrating, who have more money than they require to consume on the journey, we would say, deposit with us your surplus monies, and take our drafts upon the Trustee in trust for the Church. This is the only safe method of transferring the amount to your new homes, and will also assist in the carrying on of the work of the Lord in these lands. We feel ourselves called upon the more to urge this mode of transferring monies to Utah, from the fact that some who have undertaken to carry their funds with them have been robbed on the way of all they possessed. We are also prepared to issue drafts upon New York or way of all they possessed. We are also prepared to issue drafts upon New York or St. Louis.

"Persons wishing to transmit monies to friends in Utah, New York, or St. Louis, can obtain drafts of us on either of these places.

Tithing.—All Later-day Saints who have more than enough means to carry them to the place of destination, whether in the States or at Utah, are expected to pay their Tithing previously to leaving this country. This is a sacred duty enjoined upon the Saints by the Lord, and is a privilege which cannot be lightly esteemed by those who correctly appreciate the blessings of the Lord's House—the powers of the world to come. No SAINT *will neglect this admonition.*

"*To Saints not prepared to emigrate, but who have a portion of the means by them.*—With this class of the Saints we have a word. Deposit your means, as fast as accumulated, with this Office, where they will not run to waste, but be ready for you when you are prepared to embark, or in the mean time, if you wish them returned. To such depositors we issue acknowledgments, or certificates of deposit, which must be produced when the money is withdrawn, or used for emigration. No transfer of such monies can be made without an order to that effect from the depositor, and the production of the certificate of deposit.

"PUBLISHING DEPARTMENT.

"*Appointment of Book-Agents.*—The attention of the Presidents of all Missions, and the Pastors and Presidents of all Conferences, doing business with this Office, is specially requested to the fact, that we hold the Missions, Conferences, and Branches responsible for the settlement of their accounts, and not the individuals whom they may appoint to act as their agents.

"It is, therefore, of the first importance, that such men be intrusted with their business and have both the desire and the ability to transact it properly.

"Pastors are required to forward us certificates of the appointments of their agents, and votes of Conferences to sustain them and make good any deficiencies which may occur through them. These certificates should bear the date of the Conference at which the votes was taken, and should be signed by both President of Conference and Pastor. It is necessary that this order be carefully maintained that the interests of the Church in this Office, which is now doing business with the ends of the earth, may be properly secured.

"*Book Accounts.*—All Agents in the British Isles, whose accounts with us exceed £15 per quarter, are expected to remit twice a month; those under £15 and over £5, monthly; and those under £5, twice a quarter; taking care to make their last remittance in time to be placed to their credit before the list of debts is published for that quarter. Agents in Foreign Missions should remit as often as practicable.

"*List of Debts.*—On the last day of March, June, September, and December, respectively, we balance our accounts with the Conferences for Books, *Stars*, &c. The "Quarterly List of Debts" appears in the first or second *Star* that goes to press after those dates.

"*Conference or General Agents.*—Each General Book Agent should balance his accounts with the Sub-Agents on those days, and straightway forward to each of them a statement of the debt due by his Branch to the General Agent.

"Each Conference should appoint two Auditors to audit the General Book Agent's Account with us.

"These Auditors should audit the General Book Agent's Account with us on the same days that we balance our accounts with the Conferences.

"In auditing the General Agent's Account, the Auditors should make out a statement of the stock and cash he has then on hand, and the Sub-Agents' debts due to him. The stock should be valued at the price charged from this Office. A copy of this statement should be handed at once to the President of the Conference.

"The Auditors should preserve their statement until they see the *Star* containing the 'Quarterly list of Debts,' due by the Conferences. They should then compare their statement with the amount published in the *Star* as due by their respective Conference. If the amount of their statement equal the amount published by us as due, all is right. The result any way should be reported to the President of the Conference.

"If the amount of the Auditors' statement do not equal the amount published in the *Star* as due by that Conference, the President and the Auditors together should examine the General Agent's Ledger Account with us. The first entry should be an item equal to the amount due this Office the previous quarter. All the invoices sent from this Office to the General Agent during the quarter they are auditing for, should be compared with the credits, and the 'Money List' in the *Star* should be examined to compare with the debits. The last remittance to us in the quarter is acknowledged in the 'Money List' bearing the date of the termination of the quarter.

"If all the mount agree, a balance should be struck. If this balance disagree with ours published in the *Star*, the President should write to us to ascertain if we have made any error in our books. But if their balance agree with ours, and the General Agent has not sufficient in stock, Branch debts, and cash to meet it, then he is a defaulter to the amount deficient.

"If the General Agent represents cash in hand, the amount should be forthwith remitted to us. The Auditors can ascertain whether this is done by referring to the first 'Money List' for the succeeding quarter.

"*Branch or Sub-Agents.*—Each Branch in every Conference should appoint two auditors to audit the Sub-Agents Account with the General Agent.

"These Auditors should audit the Sub-Agent's Account on the same day that the General Agent's Account is audited.

"In auditing the Sub-Agent's Account the Auditors should make out a statement of his stock in hand, and cash if any. The stock should be valued at the price charged by the General Agent. A copy of this statement should be handed at once to the President of the Branch, and another to the President of the Conference. If there be any cash in hand the Auditors should see that it is forthwith sent to the General Agent.

"The Auditors should preserve their statement until they see the balance sent by the General Agent as due by the Branch. Their statement should then be compared with that balance. If they agree, all is right. The result any way should be reported to the President of the Branch, and to the President of the Conference.

"If their statement disagree with the balance sent by the General Agent, the President of the Branch and the Auditors together should examine the Sub-Agent's Account with the General Agent. The first entry should be an item equal to the amount due the General Agent the previous quarter. All the invoices sent by the General Agent during the quarter they are auditing for, should be compared with the credits, and all the receipts from the General Agent during the quarter should be compared with the debts. If the Sub-Agent has not obtained receipts from the General Agent for remittances to him, the President should write to the General Agent for them. If all these amount agree, a balance should be struck. If this balance disagree with the balance sent by the General Agent, the President should write to the General agent to ascertain if he has made any error in his books. But if this balance agree with the balance sent by the General Agent, and the Sub-Agent has not sufficient in stock and cash in hand to meet it, then he is a defaulter to the amount deficient.

"*Selling Books.*—No Book Agent whatever is authorized to sell Books, *Stars*, &c., to individuals on credit. If any Agent does so, he is responsible for the Amount. No such private debt should be taken into consideration in auditing his books.

"*Orders for Books from General Agents to our Office.*—Orders for Books, *Stars*, Pamphlets, &c. from our General Book Agents should reach us by Thursday morning in each week, in order to be executed with the Parcels which leave our Office on the following Saturday.

"DONATIONS.

"*Perpetual Emigrating Fund.*—Branch Perpetual Emigrating Fund Treasurers should make up their books on the last day of March, June, September, and December, respectively, and forward the donations to the Conference Treasurer, who should send them immediately to us, accompanied by a list of the Branches donating, with their respective amounts attached, and his own Christian name, surname, and address in full. Without these particulars, the donations cannot be receipted for, nor the amounts passed into our books.

"Conference Treasurers should lay before the succeeding meeting of the Conference, the receipts they receive from us each quarter, and read to the Conference the amount Each Branch has contributed, that the delegates may know that the total amount forwarded to us, agrees with the amounts they have contributed.

"*Temple Offerings.*—The instructions relating to the Perpetual Emigrating Fund Donations will apply to these also, except that a list of the Branches donating is not required.

"TITHING.

"The full names of persons paying Tithing, with the names of the Branch and Conference in which they reside, must accompany the amount paid.

"STATISTICAL REPORT.

"Two Statistical Reports are required Each Year from the Conferences in the British Isles, and the Foreign Missions under our watch-care—the first Report to be made up from the 1st of January to the 30th of June, and the second from the 1st of January to the 31st of December, the latter to embrace a report of the proceedings of the whole year, without regard to the Half-year's Report.

"The Reports from the British Isles should reach this Office in 10 days after the dates named, and from the Foreign Missions as soon after as practicable. The particulars required are—

"Name of Mission, Name of Conference, number of Branches, Seventies, High Priests, Elders, Priests, Teachers, and Deacons; and the number of persons Excommunicated, Dead, Emigrated, and Baptized, since the date of the last Report; the total number of Members, including Officers and scattered Members; and the names of the Pastor, President, and Secretary.

"APPOINTMENTS.—With a particular view to the prosperity and comfort of our brethren going out to Utah by the newly adopted mode of hand-carts the ensuing season, we deem it advisable to release Elder Edmund Ellsworth from his present field of labour, that he may benefit the approaching emigration by the considerable experience which he has had in journeying across the Plains.

"Elder W. S. Muir is appointed to succeed Elder Ellsworth in the pastoral charge of the Birmingham district.

"Elder William Noble, of Bradford, is appointed to succeed Elder Holt in the Presidency of the Manchester Conference, instead of Elder Muir.

FRANKLIN D. RICHARDS,
    36 Islington, Liverpool,
DANIEL SPENCER,
    January 3, 1856,
C. H. WHEELOCK."
[*The Latter-day Saints' Millennial Star.*, No. 2, Vol. XVIII, Saturday, January 12, 1856, pp. 24-30]

....

"Perpetual Emigration Fund Company, organized at Great Salt Lake City, Deseret, U. S. A., October 6th, 1849.

————————————————————————————

————————————————————————————Agent, Liverpool.

We, the undersigned, do hereby agree with and bind ourselves to the Perpetual Emigration Fund Company, in the following conditions, viz.—

And that, on our arrival in the Great Salt Lake valley, we will hold ourselves, our time and our labor, subject to the appropriation of the Perpetual Emigration Fund Company, until the full cost of our emigration is paid, with interest if required."[B. H. Roberts, *Comprehensive History of the Church*, Vol. 3, Ch. 88, pp.409-10]

Appendix C

COMPOSITE PASSENGER LIST
OF THE
ENOCH TRAIN

CONSOLIDATED LIST Head of Family Dependents	BRITISH MISSION Liverpool Passenger List ENOCH TRAIN	DESERET NEWS Passenger List ENOCH TRAIN
Ahlstron, John Godfrey***		
Aitken, William K.	Aitken, William K.(35) - *Dentist*	Aitken, William
Cecilia	Cecilia (14) *Spinster*	≈ 2 Children
Thomas	Thomas (10)	
Anderson, Agnes	Anderson, Agnes (52) *Wife*	Anderson, Agnes
Archibald	Archibald (20) *Collier*	≈ 3 Children
John	John (16) *Collier*	
James	James (14) *Collier*	
Argyle, Joseph	Argyle, Joseph (37) *Gas Meter Maker*	Argyle, Joseph
Jane (wife)	Jane (29) *Wife*	≈ Wife
Joseph	Joseph (14)	≈ 6 Children
Benjamin	Benjamin (12)	
Mary	Mary (10)	
Frances	Frances (5)	
Lorenzo	Lorenzo (3)	
Priscilla	Priscilla (1)	
Ash, John	Ash, John (36) *Gun Maker*	Ash, John
Sophia (wife)	Sophia (26) *Wife*	≈ Wife
Sarah (widow)	Sarah (58) *Widow*	≈ 3 Children
Ellen	Ellen (1 1/2)	
Elizabeth	Elizabeth (2 mo.)	
Joseph	Joseph (7)	
Bailey, James	Bailey, James (58) *Silver Plater*	Balley, James
Mary Ann (wife)	Mary Ann (52) *Wife*	≈ Wife
John	John (20) *Brass Tap Maker*	≈ 5 Children
Thomas	Thomas (19) *Whip Maker*	
Alfred	Alfred (17) Silver Plater	
Mary Ann	Mary Ann (15) *Dress Maker*	
Louisa	Louisa (12)	
Baker, Mary Ann	Baker, Mary Ann (45) *Widow*	Baker, Mary Ann
John	John (20) *Groom*	≈ 5 Children
Emma	Emma (17) *Spinster*	
Job	Job (14) *Labourer*	
Harriet	Harriet (11)	
Wilford	Wilford (4)	
Baldwin, Hannah	Baldwin, Hannah (18) *Spinster*	Baldwin, Hannah
Ballam[n], Anna	Ballam, Anna (45)	Ballan, Anne
Charles William	Charles William (17) *Watchmaker*	≈ 2 Children
Rachel	Rachel (8)	
Banks, Mary	Banks, Mary (45) *Spinster*	
Barker, Mary		Barker, Mary
Bascleo [Sp.?], Henry	Bascleo, Henry	
Bates, Mary Ann	Bates, Mary Ann (21) *Spinster*	Bates, Mary Ann
Bathgate, Mary	Bathgate, Mary (59) *Widow*	Bathgate, Mary
**Mary	Mary (12)	≈ Child
Bauer, Alois [Alvis]	Bauer, Alois (24) *Wheel Wright*	Bauer, Alvis
Baxter, Henry	Baxter, Henry (49) *Contractor*	Baxter, Henry
Agnes (wife)	Agnes (49) *Wife*	≈ Wife
Magdalon	Magdalon (23) *Spinster*	≈ 4 Children

CONSOLIDATED LIST Head of Family Dependents	BRITISH MISSION Liverpool Passenger List ENOCH TRAIN	DESERET NEWS Passenger List ENOCH TRAIN
Catherine	Catherine (21) *Spinster*	
Jane	Jane (17) *Spinster*	
Agnes	Agnes (14) *Spinster*	
Bayham, Elizabeth		Bayham, Elizabeth
Bell, John	Bell, John (54) *Mechanic*	Bell, John
Maria (wife)	Maria (55) *Wife*	≈ Wife
**James	James (17) *Wire Worker*	≈ 2 Children
**Samuel	Samuel (15)	
Birch, James	Birch, James (28) *Moulder*	Birch, James
Mary Ann (wife)	Mary Ann (29) *Wife*	≈ Wife
*Thomas	Thomas (7 1/2)	≈ 3 Children
*Mary Ann	Mary Ann (6)	
*Edward J.	Edward J. (2)	
Birch, William	Birch, William (68) *Shoemaker*	Birch, William
Elizabeth (wife)	Elizabeth (40) *Wife*	≈ Wife
Elizabeth	Elizabeth (17) *Spinster*	
Black, Nicholas	Black, Nicholas (46) *Miner*	Black, Nicholas
Elizabeth (wife)	Elizabeth (45) *Wife*	≈ Wife
Black, Eleanor	Black, Eleanor (17) *Spinster*	≈ 2 Children
Nicholas	Nicholas (14)	
Elizabeth	Elizabeth (2)	
Bleak, James	Bleak, James (26) *Silver Smith*	
Elizabeth (wife)	Elizabeth (27) *Wife*	
Richard	Richard (6)	
Thomas	Thomas (4)	
James	James (2)	
Mary	Mary (Inft.)	
Boden, Mary	Boden, Mary (22) *Spinster*	Boden, Mary
Bond, Samuel	Bond, Samuel (61) *Labourer*	Bond, Samuel
Elizabeth (wife)	Elizabeth (55) *Wife*	≈ Wife
William	William (23) *Potter*	≈ Son
Bond, Samuel	Bond, Samuel (25) *Potter*	Bond, Samuel
Bone, Henry (Stewart)	Bone, Henry (Stewart)	Bone, Henry (Stewart)
Bone, Mary Ann	Bone, Mary Ann (10)	Bone, Mary A.
	[See under Peter Richardson]	
Bouring, Henry E.	Bouring, Henry E. (33) *Coach Trimmer*	Bowering, Henry E.
Ellen (wife)	Ellen (18) *Wife*	≈ Wife
Wallace	Wallace (4)	≈ Child
Bourne, Thomas	Bourne, Thomas (59) *Mason*	Bourne, Thomas
Margaret (wife)	Margaret (49) *Wife*	≈ Wife
Mary Ann	Mary Ann (22) *Spinster*	≈ 6 Children
Margaret	Margaret (20) *Spinster*	
James	James (16) *Mason*	
Priscilla	Priscilla (14) *Spinster*	
Louisa	Louisa (12) *Spinster*	
John	John (6)	
Bowen, David	Bowen, David (18) *Pudler*	Bowen, David
Bowers, James	Bowers, James (45) *Collier*	Bowers, James
Mariah (wife)	Mariah (51) *Wife*	≈ Wife
Sarah	Sarah (18) *Spinster*	≈ 6 Children
Abraham	Abraham (17) *Glass Maker*	
Isaac	Isaac (14) *Glass Maker*	
Jacob	Jacob (10)	
Isaiah	Isaiah (8)	
Shadrach	Shadrach (6)	
Boynham, Elizabeth	Boynham, Elizabeth (21) *Spinster*	
Brazier, George	Brazier, George (21)	
Brazier, John	Brazier, John (21)	
Brederick, Richard B.		Brederick, Richard B.

CONSOLIDATED LIST Head of Family Dependents	BRITISH MISSION Liverpool Passenger List ENOCH TRAIN	DESERET NEWS Passenger List ENOCH TRAIN
Brenchley, Caroline	Brenchley, Caroline (24) *Spinster*	
Bridgers, Charles H.	Bridgers, Charles H. (20) *Cork Cutter*	Bridges, Charles H.
Broderick, Thomas B.	Broderick, Thomas B. (31)	
Elizabeth (wife)	Elizabeth (22) *Wife*	
John H.	John H. (11 mo.)	
Brooks, Nathan	Brooks, Nathan (61) *Plasterer*	
Betty (wife)	Betty (53) *Wife*	
Brooks, Alice	Brooks, Alice (21) *Spinster*	
Brough, Alice	Brough, Alice (69) *Widow*	Brough, Alice
Brown, Christianer[ainer]	Brown, Christianer (26) *Spinster*	Brown, Christianer
Bruner, Sussanna	Bruner, Sussanna (66) *Spinster*	Bruner, Sussanna
Bryner, Ulrich	Bryner, Ulrich (28) *Agriculturist*	Bryner, Ulrich
Marian (wife)	Marian (27) *Wife*	≈ Wife
Marian	Marian (4)	
Burdett, Elizabeth	Burdett, Elizabeth (65) *Widow*	Burditt, Elizabeth
Burdett, Emma	Burditt, Emma (19) *Spinster*	
Carr, John	Carr, John (37) *Cooper*	
Sarah Ann (wife)	Sarah Ann (33) *Wife*	
Arthur J.	Arthur J. (13)	
Henry	Henry (7)	
Walter H.	Walter H. (3)	
Marian M.	Marian M. (8 mos.)	
Chambers, David	Chambers, David (54) *Weaver*	Chambers, David
Mary (wife)	Mary (54) *Wife*	≈ Wife
David, Jr.	David, Jr. (14)	≈ Son
Chapell, [man]Henry E.	Chapell, Henry E.	Chapman, Henry E. (Cook)
Chapman, John [listed twice]	Chapman, John (58) *Farmer*	Chapman, John
Chester, Ann	Chester, Ann (20) *Spinster*	Chester, Ann
Francis	Francis	
William	William (14)	
Chetwynd, Maria	Chetwynd, Maria (21) *Spinster*	
Chetwynd, Maria	Chetwynd, Maria (24) *Spinster*	Chetwynd, Maria
Clark, George	Clark, George (53) *Labourer*	Clark, George
Mary A. (wife)	Mary A. (51) *Wife*	≈ Wife
Charlotte	Charlotte (18)	≈ 3 Children
William	William (14)	
Hannah	Hannah (6)	
Clark, Thomas	Clark, Thomas (18)	
Clotworthy, Hugh	Clotworthy, Hugh (29) *Miner*	Clotworthy, Hugh
Jane (wife)	Jane (36) *Wife*	≈ Wife
Janet	Janet (9)	≈ 5 Children
Mary	Mary (7)	
Thomas	Thomas (3)	
Jean	Jean (2)	
Margaret	Margaret (2 mos.)	
Clough [Sp.?], Moses	Clough [Sp.?], Moses	
Commander, James	Commander, James (35) *Seaman*	Commander, James
Mary	Mary (25)	
Cooper, John	Cooper, John (21) *Boot Maker*	Cooper, John
Crandall, Spicer	Crandall, Spicer (33) *Farmer*	Crandall, Spier W.
Crawford, James	Crawford, James (23) *Wool Spinner*	Crawford, James
Crump, Charles	Crump, Charles (53)	
Charles	Charles (33) *Cooper*	
James	James (39)	
Sarah Taylor	Sarah Taylor (20)	
Elizabeth Taylor	Elizabeth Taylor (18)	

CONSOLIDATED LIST Head of Family Dependents	BRITISH MISSION Liverpool Passenger List ENOCH TRAIN	DESERET NEWS Passenger List ENOCH TRAIN

Dale, Ann
    Emma
    Eliza
    Sophia
    Anne
	Dale, Ann (36)
	    Emma (14) *Spinster*
	    Eliza (12)
	    Sophia (8)
	    Anne (1)	

Darragh, Elizabeth	Darroch, Elizabeth (4)[See E. Maxwell]	Darruch, Elizabeth

Davis, Elias
    Ann (wife)
	Davis, Elias (44) *Labourer*
	    Ann (46) *Wife*	

Devereux, John
    Esther (wife)
	Devereux, John (51) *Waggoner*
	    Esther (61) *Wife*
		Deaveraux, John
		    ≈ Wife

Donald, John W.	Donald, John W.	

Doney, John
    Ann (wife)
    Ann T.
	Doney, John (34) *Labourer*
	    Ann (23) *Wife*
	    Ann T. (1)	

Downie, Margaret	Downie, Margaret (30) *Spinster*	Downie, Margaret

Dreaney, John
    Mary Jane (wife)
    Samuel
    Isabella
	Dreaney, John (31) *Miner*
	    Mary Jane (28) *Wife*
	    Samuel (2 1/2)
	    Isabella (4 mos.)
		Dreanly, John
		    ≈ Wife
		    ≈ 2 Children

Duncan, Catherine	Duncan, Catherine (24) *Weaver*	

Durham, Thomas
    Mary (wife)
	Durham, Thomas (27) *Bobbin Turner*
	    Mary (27) *Wife*	

Eardley, Benson
    Louisa (wife)
	Eardley, Benson (23) *Potter*
	    Louisa (wife) (27) *Wife*
		Eardley, Benson
		    ≈ Wife

Edwick, William	Edwick, William (17) *Telegraph Clerk*	

Eldridge, Thomas
    Charlotte (wife)
    Charlotte
	Eldridge, Thomas (25) *Agriculturist*
	    Charlotte (24) *Wife*
	    Charlotte (1)	

Eliker, Heinrich
    Margaretha (wife)
    Heinrich, Jr.
    Barbara
    Elizabeth
    Konrad
    Margaretha
    Susanna
    Jonannes
	Eliker, Heinrich (59) *Shoemaker*
	    Margaretha (54) *Wife*
	    Heinrich, Jr. (26) *Agriculturalist*
	    Barbara (24) *Spinster*
	    Elizabeth (22) *Spinster*
	    Konrad (20) *Spinster*
	    Margaretha (18) *Spinster*
	    Susanna (14) *Spinster*
	    Jonannes (13) *Spinster*
		Eliker, Heinrich
		    ≈ Wife
		    ≈ 7 Children

Ellsworth, Edmond (Capt.)	Ellsworth, Edmond (36) *Farmer*	Elsworth, Edmond E.
Fairclough, Ann	Fairclough, Ann (18) *Spinster* [See William Rowland]	Fairclough, Ann
Ferguson, James (Pres. ET)	Ferguson, James (Pres. ET)	Ferguson, James
Ferney [Sp.?], William	Ferney [Sp.?], William (20) *Labourer*	
Findlay, Mary	Findlay, Mary (59) *Widow*	Findley, Mary
Fowler, Thomas	Fowler, Thomas (19) *Labourer*	Fowler, Thomas
Franklin, Elizabeth	Franklin, Elizabeth (59) *Widow*	Franklin, Elizabeth
Franks, Sarah	Franks, Sarah (23)	

Frew, John
    Jean (wife)
    James
    Janet
    Mary
	Frew, John (30) *Engine Keeper*
	    Jean (35) *Wife*
	    James (8)
	    Janet (7)
	    Mary (1 1/2)
		Frew, John
		    ≈ Wife
		    ≈ 3 Children

Frisby, Absalom	Frisby, Absalom (21) *Tin Plate Worker*	Frisby, Absalom

Frost, Edward
    Eliza (wife)
    Isabella
    John F.
	Frost, Edward (33) *Turner*
	    Eliza (26) *Wife*
	    Isabella (7)
	    John F. (4)
		Frost, Ed.
		    ≈ Wife
		    ≈ 2 Children

Furer [Furrer], Anna		Furer, Anna

APPENDIX C: ENOCH TRAIN COMPOSITE PASSENGER LIST

CONSOLIDATED LIST Head of Family Dependents	BRITISH MISSION Liverpool Passenger List ENOCH TRAIN	DESERET NEWS Passenger List ENOCH TRAIN
Galbraith, John (Cook)	Galbraith, John (Cook)	Galbraith, John
Gale, Mary	Gale, Mary (47) *Spinster*	Gale, Mary
Galloway, Andrew		Galloway, Andrew

Galloway, Andrew
    Jane (wife)
    Annie Eliza
	Galloway, Andrew (28) *Enginer*
	    Jane (24) *Wife*
	    Annie Eliza (3)
		Galloway, Andrew
		    ≈ Wife
		    ≈ Child

Gardener [Gardner], Ann
    Agnes
    James
    Alexander [Alex.]
    Elizabeth
    Walter
	Gardener, Ann (40) *Wife*
	    Agnes (20) *Spinster*
	    James (18) *Dresser*
	    Alexander (16) *Cotton Twister*
	    Elizabeth (14) *Spinster*
	    Walter (8)
		Gardner, Ann
		    ≈ 5 Children

Gardner, William
    Emily G. Williams
	Gardner, William (26) *Gardner*
	    Emily G. Williams (3)	

Goble, William
    Mary (wife)
    Mary
    Edwin
    Caroline
    Harriett
    James
    Fanny
	Goble, William (39) *Green Grocer*
	    Mary (41) *Wife*
	    Mary (12) *Spinster*
	    Edwin (10)
	    Caroline (8)
	    Harriett (5)
	    James (3)
	    Fanny (1)	

Godsall, John
    Mary (wife)
    Louisa
    Susanna
    Frances A.
    John
	Godsall, John (45) *Shoemaker*
	    Mary (50) *Wife*
	    Louisa (18) *Spinster*
	    Susanna (16) *Spinster*
	    Frances A. (8)
	    John (5)	

Godsall, Mary
    ≈ 4 Children
		Godsall, Mary
		    ≈ 4 Children

Goodworth, Hannah
    *Joseph
    *Frederick
    *Richard B.
	Goodworth, Hannah (44) *Widow*
	    Joseph (6)
	    Frederick (5)
	    Richard B. (10)
		Goodworth, Hannah
		    ≈ Richard B.
		    ≈ Frederick
		    ≈ Joseph

Granger, Catherine	Granger, Catherine (20) *Spinster*	

Granger, Walter
    Catherine (wife)
    Robert
    Alexander
    Catherine
    Walter
    John
    = Elizabeth
	Granger, Walter (34) *Weaver*
	    Catherine (36) *Wife*
	    Robert (14) *Rivet Boy*
	    Alexander (9)
	    Catherine (7)
	    Walter (5)
	    John (4)
		Granger, Walter
		    ≈ Wife
		    ≈ 6 Children

Grant, Eleanor	Grant, Eleanor (26) *Spinster*	

Grant, Susan
    Thomas
    Elizabeth
	Grant, Susan (56) *Wife*
	    Thomas (17) *Miner*
	    Elizabeth (11)
		Grant, Susan
		    ≈ 2 Children

Gray, Jane		Gray, Jane

Gray, John
    Jane (wife)
    Jane
    Franklin
    Mary
    William
	Gray, John (51) *Leather Cutter*
	    Jane (52) *Wife*
	    Jane (22) *Spinster*
	    Franklin (4)
	    Mary (2)
	    William (5 wks.)
		Gray, John
		    ≈ Wife
		    ≈ 3 Children

Green[e], William	Green, William (30) *Miner*	Greene, William

Haley, John M.
    Hannah (wife)
    Amelia
	Haley, John M. (28) *Butcher*
	    Hannah (28) *Wife*
	    Amelia (51)	

Hall, William	Hall, William (29) *Labourer*	Hall, William

CONSOLIDATED LIST Head of Family Dependents	BRITISH MISSION Liverpool Passenger List ENOCH TRAIN	DESERET NEWS Passenger List ENOCH TRAIN
Halley, James ≈ Wife ≈ 2 Children		Halley, James ≈ Wife ≈ 2 Children
Ham, Ann	Ham, Ann (31) *Spinster*	Ham, Ann
Hanna, Henry Catherine Agnes	Hanna, Henry (29) *Miner* Catherine (22) *Wife* Agnes (1)	Hanna, Henry ≈ Wife ≈ Child
Hanson, George Frances (wife) Clara	Hanson, George (26) *Gun Maker* Frances (25) *Wife* Clara (11 mos.)	Hanson, George ≈ Wife ≈ Child
Hardie, Janet Phillis Agnes John Grace James	Hardie, Janet (45) *Widow* Phillis (23) *Clock Maker* Agnes (21) *Spinster* John (15) Grace (13) James (10)	Hardie, Janet ≈ 5 Children
Hargraves, Samuel Agnes (wife) Jane Mary Janet John Elizabeth Margaret = Enoch Train	Hargraves, Samuel (39) *Weaver* Agnes (33) *Wife* Jane (16) *Spinster* Mary (13) *Spinster* Janet (10) John (8) Elizabeth (3) Margaret (1 1/2) = Enoch Train (born 3/24)	Hargraves, Samuel ≈ Wife ≈ 6 Children
Harmon, William	Harmon, William (52) *Miner*	Harman, William
Harvey, Emma (wife)	Harvey, Emma *Wife*	
Hawkins, William Elizabeth (wife)	Hawkins, William (39) *Farmer* Elizabeth (39) *Wife*	Hawkins, William ≈ Wife
Hay, Mary	Hay, Mary (34) *Spinster*	Hay, Mary
Heaton, William Esther B. (wife) Christopher B. William McD.	Heaton, William (28) *Wool Comber* Esther (25) *Wife* Christopher B. (3) William McD. (3 mos.)	Heaton, William ≈ Wife ≈ 2 Children
Hemming, Jane	Hemming, Jane (20) *Spinster*	Hemming, Jane
Hicks, John Harriet (wife) Robert Rowe Charlotte J. Rowe Charlotte E.	Hicks, John (30) *Shoemaker* Harriet (24) *Wife* Robert Rowe (9) Charlotte J. Rowe (7) Charlotte E. (33) *Spinster*	
Hick, Thomas	Hick, Thomas (21) *Black Orniment Mkr.*	Hicks, Thomas
Hillhouse, William Margaret (wife) Janet John Mary Robert David Elizabeth William Janet	Hillhouse, William (46) *Miner* Margaret (52) *Wife* Janet (24) *Spinster* John (22) *Miner* Mary (15) *Spinster* Robert (13) David (11) Elizabeth (6) William (2) Janet (1 mo.)	Hillhouse, William ≈ Wife ≈ 8 Children
Hodgetts, Hannah	Hodgetts, Hannah (18) *Spinster*	
Hollsworth, James	Hollsworth, James (38) *Shoemaker*	
Holly, James Lucy (wife) Ann James	Holly, James (31) *Labourer* Lucy (21) *Wife* Ann (3) James (11 mos.)	Holly, James ≈ Wife ≈ 2 Children
Holt [Sp.?], Robert Ellen (wife) Margaret	Holt [Sp.?], Robert (42) *Shoemaker* Ellen (44) *Wife* Margaret (23) *Spinster*	

CONSOLIDATED LIST Head of Family Dependents	BRITISH MISSION Liverpool Passenger List ENOCH TRAIN	DESERET NEWS Passenger List ENOCH TRAIN
James	James (22) *Shoemaker*	
Daniel	Daniel (16) *Shoemaker*	
Alice	Alice (13)	
Joseph	Joseph (11)	
Martha	Martha (5)	
Hughes, Samuel	Hughes, Samuel (31) *Polisher*	Hughes, Samuel
Emma (wife)	Emma (28) *Wife*	≈ Wife
Hunt, Abraham	Hunt, Abraham (30) *Labourer*	Hunt, Abraham
Eliza (wife)	Eliza (30) *Wife*	≈ Wife
Hunt, John A.	Hunt, John A. (25) *Farmer*	Hunt, John A.
Ipsom [sen], Niels	Ipsom, Niels (24) *Shoemaker*	Ipsen, Niels
Georgina M. (wife)	Georgina M. (27) *Wife*	≈ Wife
Ivins, Thomas	Ivins, Thomas (70) *Gardner*	Ivins, Thos.
Jackson, George	Jackson, George (43) *Miner*	Jackson, George
Ruth (wife)	Ruth (47) *Wife*	≈ Wife
Herbert	Herbert (15) *Miner*	≈ 5 Children
George	George (15) *Miner*	
Ellen	Ellen (13) *Spinster*	
Sarah Ann	Sarah Ann (3)	
Susannah	Susanna (18) *Spinster*	
Jeffries, Eliza	Jeffries, Eliza (21) *Spinster*	Jeffries, Eliza
Johnston, George	Johnston, George (36) *Engine Driver*	Johnston, George
Janet	Janet (14) *Spinster*	≈ 2 Children
Isabella	Isabella (4)	
Johnston, William	Johnston, William (29) *Miner*	Johnston, William
Elizabeth (wife)	Elizabeth (21) *Wife*	≈ Wife
David	David (7)	≈ 3 Children
Richard	Richard (5)	
William	William (3)	
Jones, Daniel	Jones, Daniel (41) *Farmer*	Jones, Daniel
Ann (wife)	Ann (36) *Wife*	≈ Wife
Rachel	Rachel (16) *Spinster*	≈ 6 Children
Ann	Ann (14) *Spinster*	
Daniel	Daniel (12)	
Marion	Marion (7)	
Richard J.	Richard J. (3)	
Sarah	Sarah (1)	
Jones, Esther	Jones, Esther (28) *Spinster*	Jones, Esther
Jones, Hannah	Jones, Hannah (45) *Spinster*	Jones, Hannah
Jones, James	Jones, James (35) *German Fork Maker*	Jones, James
Sabrina (wife)	Sabrina (35) *Wife*	≈ Wife
Jones, Mary Ann	Jones, Mary Ann (19) *Spinster*	Jones, Mary A.
Jones, Thomas	Jones, Thomas (21) *Waggoner*	Jones, Thomas
Jones, William	Jones, William (45) *Mariner*	
Mary Ann (wife)	Mary Ann (50) *Wife*	
Robert	Robert (21) *Labourer*	
Louisa	Louisa (19) *Spinster*	
Frederick	Frederick (14)	
Kcors [Sp.?], Mary Ann	Kcors [Sp.?], Mary Ann (22) *Spinster*	
Kelly, John	Kelly, John (31)	
Mary	Mary (30)	
John C.	John C. (1)	
Kettle, John	Kettle, John (53) *Cottager*	
Inda [Judith] (wife)	Inda (43) *Wife*	
Mary Ann	Mary Ann (18) *Spinster*	
Robert	Robert (14)	
Eliza	Eliza (12)	
James	James (9)	
Samuel	Samuel (5)	
Anna	Anna (1)	
Kennington, Richard	Kennington, Richard (52) *Labourer*	Kinnington, Richard
Mary (wife)	Mary (47) *Wife*	≈ Wife

CONSOLIDATED LIST Head of Family Dependents	BRITISH MISSION Liverpool Passenger List ENOCH TRAIN	DESERET NEWS Passenger List ENOCH TRAIN
Sarah J.	Sarah J. (17) *Spinster*	≈ 5 Children
William	William (14)	
Eliza	Eliza (12)	
Richard	Richard (10)	
Mary A.	Mary A. (1 1/2)	
Lacing, Elizabeth	Lacing, Elizabeth (73) *Widow*	Lacing, Elizabeth
Langman, Rebecca	Langman, Rebecca (22)	
Lawrence, Samuel	Lawrence, Samuel (41) *Shoemaker*	Lawrence, Samuel
Harriet (wife)	Harriet (wife)	≈ Wife
Henry	Henry (14)	≈ 2 Children
Harriett	Harriett (12)	
George	George (24) *Shoemaker*	
Lawson, William	Lawson, William (29) *Miner*	Lawson, William
Lee, John	Lee, John (33) *Pot Maker*	Lee, John
Sarah (wife)	Sarah (32) *Wife*	≈ Wife
William	William (12)	≈ 6 Children
Fanny	Fanny (11)	
Elizabeth	Elizabeth (9)	
Samuel	Samuel (4)	
Chauncey	Chauncey (2)	
Sarah Ann	Sarah Ann (5 mos.)	
Leonard, Truman	Leonard, Truman (35) *Farmer*	Leonard, Truman
Leiseley, Alice	Leiseley, Alice (61) *Widow*	Lesley, Alice
Ann	Ann (26) *Spinster*	≈ Daughter
Lewis, Mary Ann	Lewis, Mary Ann	
Lister, James	Lister, James (26) *Butcher*	
Ann (wife)	Ann (32) *Wife*	
Dinah	Dinah (10)	
Lloyd, John Sr.	Lloyd, John Sr. (38) *Shoemaker*	Lloyd, John
Elizabeth (wife)	Elizabeth (37) *Wife*	≈ Wife
Mary	Mary (11)	≈ 5 Children
John	John (10)	
William	William (8)	
Thomas	Thomas (5)	
Jane	Jane (2)	
Lucas, Mary	Lucas, Mary (47)	
William	William (18)	
Ludert, Josephine	Ludert, Josephine (43) *Widow*	Ludert, Josephine
Alphonse	Alphonse (6)	≈ Child
Lyons, Thomas	Lyons, Thomas (29) *Weaver*	Lyons, Thomas
Mary Anna (wife)	Mary Anna (30) *Wife*	≈ Wife
Jennie	Jennie (7)	≈ 4 Children
Jessie	Jessie (5)	
Mary	Mary (3)	
<>=Christina Enoch (born 3/21)		
Martin, Eliza	Martin, Eliza (20) *Spinster*	
Mathieson, Mary	Mathieson Mary *Spinster*	Matheison, Mary
Maxwell, Elizabeth	Maxwell, Elizabeth (52) *Widow*	Maxwell, Elizabeth
Arthur	Arthur (30) *Carpet Weaver*	≈ 5 Children
Catherine	Catherine (25) *Spinster*	
Elizabeth	Elizabeth (23) *Spinster*	
Darragh, Elizabeth	Darroch, Elizabeth (4)	
Ralph	Ralph (23) *Carpet Weaver*	
Ann	Ann (14) *Spinster*	
Mayo, Mary	Mayo, Mary (65) *Widow*	Mayo, Mary
Mayoh [Sp.?], Peter	Mayoh [Sp.?], Peter (40) *Porter*	
Ann (wife)	Ann (40) *Wife*	
Mary	Mary (8)	
Noah	Noah (5)	
McAllister, John D. T.	McAllister, John D. T. (29) *Carpenter*	McAllister, John D. T.
McArthur, Daniel D.(Capt.)	McArthur, Daniel P. (35) *Minister*	McArthur, Daniel P.

APPENDIX C: ENOCH TRAIN COMPOSITE PASSENGER LIST   137

CONSOLIDATED LIST Head of Family Dependents	BRITISH MISSION Liverpool Passenger List ENOCH TRAIN	DESERET NEWS Passenger List ENOCH TRAIN
McAuslin, Elizibeth	McAuslin, Elizabeth (24) *Wife*	
McDonald, Alex[ander]	McDonald, Alex (26) *Miner*	McDonald, Alexander
McDonald, John	McDonald, John (24) *Engine Keeper*	
McDougald[al], Joseph	McDougald, Joseph (25) *Miner*	McDongal Joseph
McGowan, Mary	McGowan, Mary (29) *Spinster*	McGowan, Mary
<>McHodgett, Mrs.		
<>5 Children		
<>McLane, Mr.		
McMannis, Joseph	McMannis, Joseph (34) *Cooper*	
Margaret (wife)	Margaret (33) *Wife*	
Margaret	Margaret (9)	
Mary	Mary (7)	
Janet	Janet (11 mos.)	
Margaret	Margaret (73) *Widow*	
McMurrin, Joseph		McMurrin, Joseph
≈ Wife		≈ Wife
≈ 3 Children		≈ 3 Children
Meadows, Mary Ann	Meadows, Mary Ann (21) *Spinster*	Meadows, Mary A.
Meikle, Margaret	Meikle, Margaret (57) *Widow*	Meikle, Margaret
William	William (30) *Weaver*	≈ 3 Children
Isabella	Isabella (19) *Spinster*	
James	James (17) *Carpenter*	
Agnes	Agnes	
Merchant, Caroline	Merchant, Caroline (25) *Spinster*	
Middleton, William	Middleton, William (39) *Labourer*	
Ann (wife)	Ann (43) *Wife*	
John	John (15)	
Midgeley, Joseph	Midgeley, Joseph (21) *Draper*	
Miller, Ann	Miller, Ann (49) *Spinster*	
Sarah Jane	Sarah Jane (14) *Spinster*	
Miller, James	Miller, James (21) *Miner*	
Mirrin [Sp.?], Margaret	Mirrin [Sp.?], Margaret (61) *Widow*	
Morris, William	Morris, William (55) *Awl Maker*	Morris, William
Sarah Ann (wife)	Sarah Ann (54) *Wife*	≈ Wife
Moss, Henry	Moss, Henry (19) *Upholster*	Moss, Henry
Moss, John	Moss, John (17) *Carpenter*	Moss, John
Muir, Edward F.	Muir, Edward F. (22) *Cabnet Maker*	Muir, Edward F.
Muir, George	Muir, George (23) *Miner*	Muir, George
Margaret (wife)	Margaret (26) *wife*	≈ Wife
Mary	Mary (2)	≈ 2 Children
Jean	Jean (1)	
Nash, William	Nash, William (23) *Gardner*	Nash, William
Newman, Henry	Newman, Henry (27) *Farmer*	
Mariah L. (wife)	Mariah L. (26) *Wife*	
Maria L.	Maria L. (4)	
Henry I.	Henry I. (2)	
Oakley, John	Oakley, John	
Oliver, Ann	Oliver, Ann (30)	
Ord, Thomas	Ord, Thomas (29) *Spring Maker*	
Page, William	Page, William (19) *Gun Funiture Finisher*	Page, William
Park, Isabella	Park, Isabella (62) *Widow*	Park, Isabella
Parker, Mary Ann	Parker, Mary Ann (24) *Spinster*	
Parker, Robert	Parker, Robert (35) *Warper*	Parker, Robert
Ann (wife)	Ann (36) *Wife*	≈ Wife
Maximillian	Maximillian (11)	≈ 4 Children
Martha A.	Martha A. (9)	
Arthur	Arthur (5)	
Ada	Ada (8 mos.)	
Parson, Elizabeth	Parson, Elizabeth (24) *Spinster*	
Passey, Thomas	Passey, Thomas (18) *Miller*	Passay, Thomas

CONSOLIDATED LIST Head of Family Dependents	BRITISH MISSION Liverpool Passenger List ENOCH TRAIN	DESERET NEWS Passenger List ENOCH TRAIN

Peacock, George
    Mary Ann
    George, Jr.
	Peacock, George (30) *Miner*
	    Mary Ann (7)
	    George Jr. (4)
		Peacock, George

Peel, Frances	Peel, Frances (28) *Spinster*	Peel, Frances
Petty, Edward	Petty, Edward (53)	
Pilgrim, Rebecca	Pilgrim, Rebecca (30)	
Player, Elizabeth	Player, Elizabeth	
Player, Emily	Player, Emily	

Player, Joseph
    Ann (wife)
    Elizabeth
    Emily
    Alfred
	Player, Joseph (41) *Black Smith*
	    Ann (39) *Wife*
	    Elizabeth (16) *Spinster*
	    Emily (14)
	    Alfred (5)
		Player, Joseph
		    ≈ Wife
		    ≈ 2 Children

Pope, George
    Jane (wife)
    Franklin
	Pope, George (27) *Tailor*
	    Jane (31) *Wife*
	    Franklin (3 wks.)
		Pope, George
		    ≈ Wife
		    ≈ Child

Porter, Nathan T.	Porter, Nathan T. (36) *Farmer*	Porter, Nathan T.

Powell, John
    Elizabeth (wife)
    William
    Mary
    Margaret
    Elizabeth
    Hannah
    David
	Powell, John (43) *Mason*
	    Elizabeth (35) *Wife*
	    William (15) *Mason*
	    Mary (13) *Spinster*
	    Margaret (8)
	    Elizabeth (6)
	    Hannah (4)
	    David (Inft.)
		Powell, John
		    ≈ Wife
		    ≈ 6 Children

Pratt, William
    Caroline (wife)
    Eleanor Salina
    George
    Orson
    Emily
	Pratt, William (31) *Gun Maker*
	    Caroline (30) *Wife*
	    Eleanor Salina (11)
	    George (8)
	    Orson (3)
	    Emily (8 mos.)
		Pratt, William
		    ≈ Wife
		    ≈ 4 Children

Preater, Richard
    Mary (wife)
    Salome
    Lora I.
	Preater, Richard (29) *Lath Cutter*
	    Mary (30) *Wife*
	    Salome (4)
	    Lora I. (2)
		Preater, Richard
		    ≈ Wife
		    ≈ 2 Children

Price, Ann
    Emma
    Eliza
	Price, Ann (45) *Widow*
	    Emma (19) *Spinster*
	    Eliza (17) *Spinster*
		Price, Ann
		    ≈ 2 Children

Price, Edward (note: next ship)
    +9 Unamed Prices (next ship)
	Price, Edward (note: next ship)
	    +9 Unamed Prices (next ship)	

Ramsey, Ralph
    Elizabeth (wife)
    John S.
    Son
	Ramsey, Ralph (32) *Wood Carver*
	    Elizabeth (33) *Wife*
	    John S. (15)
	    Son (14)
		Ramsey, Ralph
		    ≈ Wife
		    ≈ Child

Randle [all], Ann
    Oscar J.
	Randle, Ann (31) *Widow*
	    Oscar J. (1 9/12)
		Randall, Ann
		    ≈ Oscar J.

Rasdall, John
    Elizabeth (wife)
    Mary Ann
	Rasdall, John (20) *Agricultural Labourer*
	    Elizabeth (22) *Wife*
	    Mary Ann (Inft.)	

Reid, James
    Elizabeth (wife)
    Elizabeth
    James
    Mary
    John
	Reid, James (39) *Shoemaker*
	    Elizabeth (31) *Wife*
	    Elizabeth (11)
	    James (6)
	    Mary (4)
	    John (1)
		Reid, James
		    ≈ Wife
		    ≈ 4 Children

Richardson, Peter
    Eliza
	Richardson, Peter (24) *Labourer*
	    Eliza (33) *Wife*
		Richardson, Peter
		    ≈ Wife)

Richardson, William
    Maria (wife)
    William H.
    John H.
    Mary
	Richardson, William (27) *Farmer*
	    Maria (29) *Wife*
	    William H. (3)
	    John H. (1)
	    Mary (1 mo.)	

CONSOLIDATED LIST Head of Family Dependents	BRITISH MISSION Liverpool Passenger List ENOCH TRAIN	DESERET NEWS Passenger List ENOCH TRAIN
Richins, Thomas D.	Richins, Thomas D. (31) *Waggoner*	Richens, Thomas
Harriet D. (wife)	Harriet D. (22) *Wife*	≈ Wife
Franklin	Franklin (1)	≈ Child
Robinson, Eliza	Robinson, Eliza (25) *Spinster*	Robinson, Eliza
Robinson, John	Robinson, John (46) *Pistol Maker*	Robinson, John
Emma (wife)	Emma (27) *Wife*	≈ Wife
Elizabeth	Elizabeth (21) *Spinster*	≈ 4 Children
Sarah	Sarah (19) *Spinster*	
John	John (6)	
Clara	Clara (10 mos.)	
Roper, Charles	Roper, Charles (34) *Farmer*	
Catherine (wife)	Catherine (28) *Wife*	
Rossen, Charles		Rossen, Charles
≈ Wife		≈ Wife
Rowland, William	Rowland, William (22) *Ship Wright*	Rowland, William
Elizabeth (wife)	Elizabeth (36) *Wife*	≈ Wife
William	William (4)	Rowland, William F.
John C.	John C. (3 mos.)	
Harriet F.	Harriet F. (37) *Spinster*	Rowland, Harriet F.
Rowlands, Ephraim	Rowlands, Ephrain *Sailor on Ship*	
Rowley, John	Rowley, John (33) *Potter*	Rowley, John
Isabella (wife)	Isabella (33) *Wife*	≈ Wife
James	James (23) *Potter*	≈ 8 Children
William	William (17)	
Margaret	Margaret (11)	
Isabella	Isabella (7)	
Sarah	Sarah (6)	
Mary	Mary (2)	
Joseph	Joseph (2 mos.)	
George	George (28) *Potter*	
Russell, Ellen	Russell, Ellen (23) *Spinster*	Russell, Ellen
Salisbury, Ann	Salisbury, Ann (36) *Wife*	Salisbury, Ann
William T.	William T. (14)	≈ 3 Children
Henry	Henry (12)	
Joseph	Joseph (4)	
Sanders, Wallis [Walter]	Sanders, Wallis (64) *Carter*	Sanders, Walter
Sarah	Sarah (20) *Spinster*	≈ 4 Children
Mary	Mary (18) *Spinster*	
James	James (15) *Carter*	
John	John (12) *Printer*	
Thomas	Thomas (10)	
Sanderson, Rebecca	Sanderson, Rebecca (41) *Wife*	Sanderson, Rebecca
Sarah Ann	Sarah Ann (11)	≈ 2 Children
Rhoda	Rhoda (9)	
Schies, Johannes	Schies, Johannes (39) *Weaver*	Schies, Johannes
Anna (wife)	Anna (39) *Wife*	≈ Wife
Senior [Sp.?], Thomas	Senior, Thomas (29) *Miner*	Senior, Thomas
Sheen, James [Sr.]	Sheen, James [Sr.] (58) *Quarryman*	Sheen, James
Maria (wife)	Maria (58) *Wife*	≈ Wife
Hannah [Anna]	Hannah (22) *Spinster*	≈ Anna
Ellen	Ellen (18) *Spinster*	≈ Ellen
	Ann E.	≈ Ann E.
Sheen, James [Jr.]	Sheen, James [Jr.] (26) *Quarryman*	Sheen, James Jr.
Mary (wife)	Mary (23) *Wife*	≈ Wife
Sheen, Robert	Sheen, Robert (27) *Quarryman*	Sheen, Robert
Eliza (wife)	Eliza (28) *Wife*	≈ Wife
Mary	Mary (8)	≈ 4 Children
Louisa	Louisa (5)	
Ann	Ann (4)	
Emma	Emma (3)	
Ann Eliza	Ann Eliza (3 mos.)	
Shelton, Richard	Shelton, Richard (18) *Blacksmith*	Shelton, Richard

CONSOLIDATED LIST Head of Family Dependents	BRITISH MISSION Liverpool Passenger List ENOCH TRAIN	DESERET NEWS Passenger List ENOCH TRAIN
Shields, Elizabeth	Shields, Elizabeth (26) *Spinster*	Shields, Elizabeth
Smart, Sarah	Smart, Sarah (50) *Wife*	Smart, Sarah
Smith, Amelia	Smith, Amelia (18) *Spinster*	
Smith, Andrew	Smith, Andrew (28) *Tailor*	Smith, Andrew
<>Smith, Aniki		
Smith, Isaac	Smith, Isaac (59) *Labourer*	
Charlotte (wife)	Charlotte (54) *Wife*	
Benjamin	Benjamin (15)	
Emily	Emily (11)	
Smith, John	Smith, John	
Smith, Mary	Smith, Mary (64)	
Emma	Emma (26) *Spinster*	
Robert	Robert (34) *Mechanic*	
Ester E.	Ester E. (9)	
Smith, Sarah Ann	Smith, Sarah Ann (22) *Spinster*	
Smith, William	Smith, William (36) *Gardner*	Smith, William
Charlotte (wife)	Charlotte (30) *Wife*	≈ Wife
William Jr.	William Jr. (11)	≈ 3 Children
Charles	Charles (8)	
George E.	George E. (5)	
Sounds [Sp.?], William	Sounds [Sp.?], William (36) *Engineer*	
Sarah (wife?)	Sarah (36) *Wife?*	
Esther	Esther (6)	
Jacob	Jacob (2)	
Spiers [Speers], George	Spiers, George (29) *Weaver*	Speers, George
Janet (wife)	Janet (27) *Wife*	≈ Wife
William	William (7)	≈ 3 Children
Janet	Janet (5)	
Agnes	Agnes (1 1/2)	
Sprigg, Sarah Ann	Sprigg, Sarah Ann (18) *Spinster*	Sprigg, Sarah
Stephens, Ann	Stephens, Ann (66) *Widow*	
Stewart, Nancy	Stewart, Nancy (49) *Wife*	Stewart, Nancy
Jane	Jane (17) *Spinster*	≈ 3 Children
Matilda	Matilda (15) *Spinster*	
Margaret	Margaret (12)	
Anne	Anne (23)	
Stevenson, Alexander	Stevenson, Alexander (36) *Carpenter*	Stevenson, Alexander
Magdalene (wife)	Magdalene (35) *Wife*	≈ Wife
Isabella	Isabella (27) *Spinster*	≈ 7 Children
John	John (13)	
Magdalene	Magdalene (11)	
Alexander	Alexander (7)	
Orson	Orson (5)	
Joseph B.	Joseph B. (3)	
Marion	Marion (1)	
Stones, James	Stones, James (30) *Coal Miner*	
Mary (wife)	Mary (34) *Wife*	
Hannah	Hannah (9)	
Sarah E.	Sarah E. (7)	
John D.	John D. (5)	
Erastus I.	Erastus I. (3)	
Tanner, Edmund	Tanner, Edmund (5)	
Tanner, Mary	Tanner, Mary (44)	Tanner, Mary
Malinda	Malinda (17) *Spinster*	≈ 5 Children
Jane	Jane (15) *Spinster*	
Kate	Kate (7)	
Harriet	Harriet (6)	
Tait, Elizabeth	Tait, Elizabeth (23) *Wife*	Tate, Elizabeth
Mary Ann	Mary Ann (11 mos.)	≈ Child
Taylor, Elizabeth	Taylor, Elizabeth (53)	
James	James (39)	
Sarah	Sarah (20)	

APPENDIX C: ENOCH TRAIN COMPOSITE PASSENGER LIST

CONSOLIDATED LIST Head of Family Dependents	BRITISH MISSION Liverpool Passenger List ENOCH TRAIN	DESERET NEWS Passenger List ENOCH TRAIN

Taylor, Joseph
    Harriet (wife)
    Eliza
	Taylor, Joseph (44) *Labourer*
	    Harriet (49) *Wife*
	    Eliza (44)	

Titt, Richard
    Ann (wife)
    Elizabeth
	Titt, Richard (66)
	    Ann (59) *Wife*
	    Elizabeth (22) *Spinster*	

Tranton, Sarah Anne	Tranton, Sarah Anne (27) *Wife*	Tranton, Sarah A.

Turner, John
    Jane W. (wife)
    Sarah C.
	Turner, John (29) *Baker*
	    Jane W. (23) *Wife*
	    Sarah C. (11 mos.)
		Turner, John
		    ≈ Wife
		    ≈ Child

Tweedle[Twaddle],Elizabeth	Tweedle, Elizabeth (21) *Spinster*	Twaddle, Elizabeth

Upton, William
    Mary (?wife)
	Upton, William (22)
	    Mary (20) *?Wife*	

Vaughn, Elanor	Vaughn, Elanor (48) *Widow*	Vaughn, Eleanor
Walker, Emma	Walker, Emma (21) *Spinster*	

Walker, William
    Elizabeth
    Emma
	Walker, William (25) *Moulder*
	    Elizabeth (24) *Spinster*
	    Emma (21) *Spinster*
		Walker, William
		    Elizabeth
		    Emma

Wall, Joseph
    Sarah E.
	Wall, Joseph (17) *Stone Cutter*
	    Sarah E. (16) *Spinster*	

Walters, Archer
    Harriet (wife)
    Sarah
    Henry
    Harriet
    Martha
    Lydia
	Walters, Archer (47) *Joiner*
	    Harriet (47) *Wife*
	    Sarah (18)
	    Henry (16)
	    Harriet (14)
	    Martha (12)
	    Lydia (6)
		Walters, Archer
		    ≈ Wife
		    ≈ 5 Children

Wandless, Ellen
    Ellen
	Wandless, Ellen (28) *Wife*
	    Ellen (6)
		Wandless, Ellen
		    ≈ Daughter

Warring [Wareing], George	Warring, George (18) *Boot Closer*	Warring George
Warner, James	Warner, James (60) *Cottager*	
Webster, Frances	Webster, Frances (25) *Labourer*	
Westwood, Susan	Westwood, Susan (55)	

White, John
    Mary Ann (wife)
	White, John (30) *Miner*
	    Mary Ann (28) *Wife*	

Wilkie, Isabella	Wilkie, Isabella (48)	
Williams, Amelia	Williams, Amelia (30) *Spinster*	Williams, Amelia
Williams, George	Williams, George (18) *Lamp Maker*	Williams, George

Wilson, Benjamin
    Mary (wife)
    Robert
    William
    John
    Catherine
	Wilson, Benjamin (40) *Miner*
	    Mary (36) *Wife*
	    Robert (10)
	    William (6)
	    John (2 1/2)
	    Catherine (59) *Widow*	

Wiseman, John
    Mary Ann (wife)
    John Josh
    Henry H.
	Wiseman, John (53) *Surgeon*
	    Mary Ann (44) *Wife*
	    John Josh (4)
	    Henry H. (11 mos.)	

Wright, John	Wright, John (48) *Miner*	

Wright, William
    Maria (?wife)
	Wright, William (22) *Clerk*
	    Maria (25) *?Wife*
		Wright, William
		    ≈ Wife

Yumer [Sp.?], Anna	Yumer [Sp.?], Anna (30) *Spinster*	
TOTALS 765 FAMILIES 278	739 259	530 189

COUNTRIES

	Adults	Children	Infants	Total
England	252	56	14	322
Scotland	107	34	5	146
Ireland	15	1	1	17
Wales	13	5	0	18
Danes	2	0	0	2
Americans	8	0	0	8
Switzerland	17	2	0	19
India		1	0	12
TOTALS	415	98	21	534

"Elder Thomas Ferguson a returning Missionary to Utah is included in the above summary of American Emigrants, also Henry E. Chapell and Henry Bone in the English Summary and John Gilbraith in the Scotch Summary."

Class	Adults & 8 Years Up	Children Up to 8 Years	Infants	Total
P. E. Fund	332	84	15	431
Ordinary	79	14	6	99
TOTALS	411	98	21	530

Elder James Ferguson, President of the Company		1
John Gilbraith & Henry E. Chapell: Cooks		2
Henry Bone: Steward		1
	Total	534

"Memorandum, Ephraim Rowlands one of the Sailors, was member of the Church but not included in the above summary."

Elders James Ferguson, President
Edmund Ellsworth & Daniel D. McArthur, Counselors

Sailed 23 March 1856; arrived in Boston 1 May 1856, Church Chronology.

British Mission Liverpool Passenger List taken from Emigration Records from Liverpool Office of the Bristish Mission 1855-1856, Libr. No. 1045 (CR 271/25, No. 2).

<> Found in various Journals showing them present on the *Enoch Train*.

= Born or † died: during the journey according to Journals, etc., see index for available data.

≈ *Deseret News*, "Ship Enoch Train, For Boston, March 23, 1856", published passenger list. They show 411 adults, 98 children and 21 infants, for a total of 530 passengers. James Ferguson was the President; Edmund Ellsworth and Daniel D. McArthur, Counselors; John Galbraith and Henry E. Chapmann, Cooks; and Henry Bone, Stewart. [*Deseret News* 6:160]

*** From data found in *Infobases Collectors Library '97*.

APPENDIX D

COMPOSITE PASSENGER LIST OF THE SAMUEL S. CURLING

CONSOLIDATED LIST Head of Family Dependents	BRITISH MISSION Liverpool Passenger List SAMUEL S. CURLING	DESERET NEWS Passenger List SAMUEL S. CURLING
Ajax, William	Ajax, William [23] *Miner*	
Axton, Thomas	Axton, Thomas [80] *Farmer*	
Elizabeth (wife)	Elizabeth [51] *Wife*	Axton, Elizabeth
John	John [11]	≈ Son
Bailey, Ann	Bailey, Ann [49] *Widow*	Bailey, Ann
Abigal	Abigal [15] *Spinster*	≈ 5 Children
Betsy	Betsey [11]	
Sarah A.	Sarah A. [28] *Spinster*	
Bailey, William	Bailey, William [23] *Laborer*	
Sarah	Sarah [3 1/2]	
Barclay, Richard	Barclay, Richard [14] *Collier*	Barclay, Richard
Barker, Margaret (widow)	Barker, Margaret [77] *Widow*	Barker, Margaret
Arbary [Barbara]	Arbary [47] *Spinster*	Barker, Barbara
Robert [F.]	Robert [20] *Weaver*	Barker, Robert F.
Bascomb, Emma	Bascomb, Emma [28] *Spinster*	
Anne	Anne [23] *Spinster*	
Bassett, John	Bassett, John [30] *Miner*	Bassett, John
Mary (wife)	Mary [32] *Wife*	≈ Wife
Elizabeth	Elizabeth [5]	≈ Child
Hyrum	Hyrum [6 mo.]	
John	John [8]	
Birmingham, Patrick [T.]	Birmingham, Patrick [26] *Clerk*	Birmingham, Patrick T.
Elizabeth (wife)	Elizabeth K. [24] *Wife*	≈ Wife
Mary K.	Mary K. [4]	≈ 3 Children
Eda [Sp.?] J.	Eda [Sp.?] J. [3]	
Jane E.	Jane E. [4 days]	
Bradley, Henry	Bradley, Henry [33] *Laborer*	Bradley, Henry
Mary (wife)	Mary [31] *Wife*	≈ Wife
Mathilda [Sp.?]	Mathilda [Sp.?] [8]	≈ 5 Children
Mariah	Mariah [6]	
Henry Wm.	Henry Wm. [4]	
Lorenzo	Lorenzo [2]	
George F.	George F. [5 mo.]	
Branigan, [Brannigan] Mary	Branigan, Mary [21] *Spinster*	Brannigan, Mary
Bridger [Bridge], James	Bridger, James [49] *Shoemaker*	Bridge, James
Brookes [Brooks], Samuel	Brookes, Samuel [65]	Brooks, Samuel
Emma (wife)	*Lighthouse Keeper*	≈ Wife
Mary	Emma [48] *Wife*	≈ 3 Children
George	Mary [17] *Spinster*	
Francis F.	George [11]	
	Francis F. [6]	
Brorgh [Brough], William	Brorgh, William [30] *Sailor*	Brough, William
Brown, George	Brown, George [34] *Miner*	Brown, George

CONSOLIDATED LIST Head of Family Dependents	BRITISH MISSION Liverpool Passenger List SAMUEL S. CURLING	DESERET NEWS Passenger List SAMUEL S. CURLING

Bunney, John
   Ann (wife)
	Bunney, John [28] *Laborer*
	   Ann [25] *Wife*
		Bunney, John
		   ≈ Wife

Butler, Anne[a] (widow)
   Elizabeth
   William
	Butler, Anne [38] *Widow*
	   Elizabeth [13]
	   William [8]
		Butler, Anna
		   ≈ 2 Children

Butler, William
   Emma (wife)
	Butler, William [29] *Farmer*
	   Emma [22] *Wife*
		Butler, William
		Butler, Emma

Casens, John
   Martha (wife)
   William
	Casens, John [23] *miner*
	   Martha [19] *Wife*
	   William [13] *Miner*	

Chapel, Joseph
   Mary (wife)
   Margaret
	Chapel, Joseph [25] *Engineer*
	   Mary [24] *Wife*
	   Margaret [1]
		Chapel, Joseph
		   ≈ Wife
		   ≈ Child

[H]Copla, John
   Catherine (wife)
   Jane
   John
   Lorenzo
	[H]Copla, John [33] *Quarry Man*
	   Catherine [35] *Wife*
	   Jane [7]
	   John [4]
	   Lorenzo [11 mo.]	

≈Cousing, John
   ≈ Wife
		Cousing, John
		   ≈ Wife

Crane, James	Crane, James [45] *Laborer*	Crane, James
Crane, James	Crane, James [24] *Laborer*	
Cutliffe, Mary [J.]	Cutliffe, Mary [22] *Spinster*	Cutliffe, Mary J.
Daniels, Anne	Daniels, Anne [24] *Spinster*	Daniels, Anna
Davies, David	Davies, David [25] *Miner*	
Davies, David	Davies, David [36] *Minister*	

Davies, David
   Mary (wife)
   Mary
   Louisa
   John
	Davies, David [56] *Laborer*
	   Mary [54] *Wife*
	   Mary [16] *Spinster*
	   Louisa [12]
	   John [19] *Tailor*
		Davies, David
		   ≈ Wife
		   ≈ 3 Children

Davies, David
   Esther (wife)
   Rachel
   Lucy
   Richard
   Anne
   Elizabeth
   William
   Mary
	Davies, David [39] *Miner*
	   Esther [39] *Wife*
	   Rachael [18] *Spinster*
	   Lucy [15] *Spinster*
	   Richard [13]
	   Anne [11]
	   Elizabeth [7]
	   William [3]
	   Mary [7 mo.]
		Davies, David
		   ≈ Wife
		   ≈ 7 Children

Davies, Daniel
   Anne (wife)
   Gwenllian [Sp.?]
   Daniel
   Morgan
   Thomas
	Davies, Daniel [37] *Farm Laborer*
	   Anne [35] *Wife*
	   Gwenllian [Sp.?] [9]
	   Daniel [7]
	   Morgan [3]
	   Thomas [8 mo.]
		Davies, Daniel
		   ≈ Wife
		   ≈ 4 Children

≈Davies, Eleanor
   ≈Elizabeth
		≈Davies, Eleanor
		   ≈Elizabeth

Davies [Davis], Gad
   Elizabeth (wife)
   John
   Margaret
   Mary
   Norman
   Anne
   Hannah
	Davies, Gad [36] *Miner*
	   Elizabeth [31] *Wife*
	   John [15] *Miner*
	   Margaret [12] *Spinster*
	   Mary [7]
	   Norman [5]
	   Anne [3]
	   Hannah [15] *Spinster*
		Davis, Gad
		   ≈ Wife
		   ≈ 7 Children

Davies, George W.
   Hannah (wife)
   Joseph
	Davies, George W. [32] *Book Agent*
	   Hannah [23] *Wife*
	   Joseph [1]
		Davies, George W.
		   ≈ Wife
		   ≈ Child

Davies, John
   Jane (wife)
	Davies, John [30] *Miner*
	   Jane [37] *Wife*
		Davies, John
		   ≈ Wife

Davies, John	Davies, John [37] *Carpenter*	Davies, John

APPENDIX D: SAMUEL S. CURLING COMPOSITE LIST 145

CONSOLIDATED LIST Head of Family Dependents	BRITISH MISSION Liverpool Passenger List SAMUEL S. CURLING	DESERET NEWS Passenger List SAMUEL S. CURLING
Mary (wife) ≈3 Children	Mary [39] *Wife*	≈ Wife ≈ 3 Children
Davies, Joseph [listed twice]	Davies, Joseph [19] *Laborer*	Davies, Joseph
Davies, Lewis Sarah (wife)	Davies, Lewis [23] *Miner* Sarah [20] *Wife*	Davies, Lewis ≈ Wife
Davies [Davis], Margaret	Davies, Margaret [65] *Wife*	Davis, Margaret
Davies, Stephen	Davies, Stephen [20] *Miner*	
Davies, Thomas Anne (wife) Hannah	Davies, Thomas [28] *Miner* Anne [28] *Wife* Hannah [15] *Spinster*	Davies, Thomas ≈ Wife
Davies, Thomas Jannessia [Sp.?] (wife) William Amelia Howell	Davies, Thomas [32] *Miner* Jannessia [Sp.?] [30] *Wife* William [9] Amelia [6] Howell [6 mo.]	Davies, Thomas ≈ Wife ≈ 3 Children
Davies, William Elizabeth (wife) Eleanor Elizabeth	Davies, William [42] *Carpenter* Elizabeth [42] *Wife* Eleanor [18] Elizabeth [14]	
Davies, William Margaret David	Davies, William [7] Margaret [5] David [2]	
Davies, William L. [J.] Mary L. (wife) Isachar L. Zebulon Lucretia Naphthali	Davies, William L. [35] *Collier* Mary L. [34] *Wife* Isachar L. [11] Zebulon [6] Lucretia [2] Naphthali [5 mo.]	Davies, William J. ≈ Wife ≈ 4 Children
Davis, Evan Margaret (wife) Margaret Mary Evan George John	Davis, Evan [41] *Miner* Margaret [38] *Wife* Margaret [18] *Spinster* Mary [16] *Spinster* Evan [12] George [3] John [2 mo.]	Davis, Evan ≈ Wife ≈ 5 Children
≈Davis, Hannah		≈Davis, Hannah
Davis, Sarah	Davis, Sarah [30] *Spinster*	
Davis [Davies], William Mary (wife)	Davis, William [26] *Pedler* Mary [22] *Wife*	Davies, William ≈ Wife

Dee, Thomas
Anne (wife)
Hannah
John
John
   Margaret
	Dee, Thomas [23] *Potter*
	Anne [20] *Wife*
	Hannah [12] *Spinster*
	John [8]
	John [55] *Potter*
	   Margaret [55] *Wife*
		Dee, Thomas
		≈ Wife
		≈ 2 Children
		Dee, John
		≈ Wife
		≈ 2 Children

Dodd, Martha David Mary Elizabeth	Dodd, Martha [37] *Wife* David [10] Mary [7] Elizabeth [3]	
Dome [Dorne], Jacob	Dome, Jacob [25] *Drapers Ass't.*	Dorne, Jacob
Doney, John Ann (wife) Ann T.	Doney, John [34] *Laborer* Ann [23] *Wife* Ann T. [1 1/2]	Doney, John ≈ Wife ≈ Child
Edmonds[Edwards], Nathaniel Jane (wife) John	Edmonds, Nathaniel [26] *Miner* Jane [23] *Wife* John [6]	Edwards, Nathaniel ≈ Wife ≈ Child
Edmunds, John	Edmunds, John [66] *Excavator*	Edmunds, John
Edwards, Elizabeth	Edwards, Elizabeth [20] *Spinster*	Edwards, Elizabeth
Edwards, John Esther (wife) Dinah	Edwards, John [55] *Tailor* Esther [36] *Wife* Dinah [23] *Spinster*	Edwards, John ≈ Daughter

CONSOLIDATED LIST Head of Family Dependents	BRITISH MISSION Liverpool Passenger List SAMUEL S. CURLING	DESERET NEWS Passenger List SAMUEL S. CURLING
Edwards, Mary Ann [A.]	Edwards, Mary Ann [11]	Edwards, Mary A.
Eldridge, Thomas	Eldridge, Thomas [25] *Agriculturist*	Eldridge, Thos.
Charlotte (wife)	Charlotte [24] *Wife*	≈ Wife
Charlotte	Charlotte [1]	≈ Child
Ellis, John	Ellis, John [26] *Carpenter*	Ellis, John
Ellis, John	Ellis, John [38] *Joiner*	
Ellis, Thomas	Ellis, Thomas [54] *Shoemaker*	Ellis, Thomas
Elizabeth (wife)	Elizabeth [50] *Wife*	≈ Wife
Elizabeth	Elizabeth [14] *Spinster*	≈ 3 Children
Thomas	Thomas [11]	
John	John [5]	
≈Evans, Abram J.		≈Evans, Abram J.
≈ Wife		≈ Wife
≈3 Children		≈ 3 Children
Evans, David	Evans, David [26] *Miner*	Evans, David
Elizabeth	Elizabeth [26] *Wife*	≈ Wife
Evans, David	Evans, David [37] *Miner*	Evans, David
Elizabeth	Elizabeth [9]	
Evans, David	Evans, David [45] *Laborer*	Evans, David
Anne (wife)	Anne [46] *Wife*	≈ Wife
Moses	Moses [20] *Smith*	≈ 3 Children
Sarah	Sarah [11]	
John	John [9]	
Evans, Evan	Evans, Evan [41] *Miner*	Evans, Evan
Mary (wife)	Mary [45] *Wife*	≈ Wife
David	David [19] *Miner*	≈ 3 Children
John	John [12]	
Joseph	Joseph [8]	
Evans, Gade [Sp.?]	Evans, Gade [Sp.?] [29] *Farmer*	
Evans, Hanna[h]	Evans, Hanna [37] *Spinster*	Evans, Hannah
Thomas	Thomas [19] *Tailor*	
Evans, Isaac		Evans, Isaac
≈ Wife		≈ Wife
Evans, Job	Evans, Job [23] *Laborer*	
Harriet (wife)	Harriet [23] *Wife*	
Evans, John	Evans, John [26] *Weaver*	
Evans, John	Evans, John [65] *Shipright*	
Anne (wife)	Anne [60] *Wife*	
Lelitia	Lelitia [20] *Spinster*	
Evans, John	Evans, John [19] *Miner*	Evans, John
Catherine (wife)	Catherine [20] *Wife*	≈ Wife
Evans, John	Evans, John [42] *Farmer*	Evans, John
Margaret (wife)	Margaret [41] *Wife*	≈ Wife
Esther	Esther [13]	≈ 2 Children
John	John [7]	
≈Evans, Latitia		≈Evans, Latitia
≈Evans, Margaret		≈Evans, Margaret
Evans, Morgan	Evans, Morgan [22] *Shoemaker*	Evans, Morgan
Anne (wife)	Anne [19] *Wife*	≈ Wife
Gwendlian	Gwendlian [7 mo.]	≈ Child
Evans, Prescilla	Evans, Prescilla [22] *Spinster*	
Evans, Samuel	Evans, Samuel [35] *Miner*	
Sarah (wife)	Sarah [48] *Wife*	
Evans, Thomas	Evans, Thomas [19] *Pudler*	Evans, Thomas
Evans, Thomas	Evans, Thomas [19] *Miner*	Evans, Thomas
Jane	Jane [17] *Spinster*	Jane
Petetia [Sp.?]	Petetia [Sp.?] [20] *Spinster*	
Evans, Thomas[listed twice]	Evans, Thomas [45] *Tailor*	Evans, Thomas
Mary Ann (wife)	Mary Ann [37] *Wife*	≈ Wife
Mary Ann	Mary Ann [11]	

APPENDIX D: SAMUEL S. CURLING COMPOSITE LIST

| CONSOLIDATED LIST
Head of Family
Dependents | BRITISH MISSION
Liverpool Passenger List
SAMUEL S. CURLING | DESERET NEWS
Passenger List
SAMUEL S. CURLING |
|---|---|---|
| Evans, Thomas
  Mary (wife)
  Thomas
  Emma
  Joseph
  Hyrum
  Elizabeth
  Hannah | Evans, Thomas [37] *Laborer*
  Mary [33] *Wife*
  Thomas [9]
  Emma [8]
  Joseph [1]
  Hyrum [5]
  Elizabeth [3]
  Hannah [44] *Widow* | Evans, Thomas
  ≈ Wife
  ≈ 4 Children

  ≈ Mother |
| Evans, Thomas | Evans, Thomas [57] *Coal Proprietor* | Evans, Thomas |
| Evans, Thomas | Evans, Thomas [23] *Minister* | |
| Evans, Thomas D.
  ≈ Wife | Evans, Thomas D. [23] *?Yogel Baller* | Evans, Thomas D.
  ≈ Wife |
| Evans, William
  Mary A. (wife)
  Jenkins
  Elizabeth
  Mary Ann | Evans, William [47] *Miner*
  Mary A. [42] *Wife*
  Jenkins A. [21] *Collier*
  Elizabeth [12]
  Mary Ann [7 mo.] | |
| Findley, William
  Lindsay (wife)
  Ann | Findley, William [49] *Miner*
  Lindsay [48] *Wife*
  Ann [17] *Spinster* | Findley, William‡
  ≈ Wife
  ≈ Daughter |
| Fisher, Thomas | Fisher, Thomas [43] *Laborer* | Fisher, Thomas |
| Fisher, William
  Elizabeth (wife) | Fisher, William [42] *Farmer*
  Elizabeth [32] *Wife* | Fisher, William
  ≈ Wife |
Games, Elizabeth	Games, Elizabeth [44] *Wife*	Games, Elizabeth
Gardener [ner], William	Gardener, William [26] *Gardener*	Gardner, William
German, Catherine	German, Catherine [20] *Spinster*	German, Catherine
≈German, Thomas
≈ Wife
≈ 3 Children		≈German, Thomas
≈ Wife
≈ 3 Children
Gibson, Elizabeth
Sarah
Richard	Gibson, Elizabeth [36] *Spinster*
Sarah [10]
Richard [8]	Gibson, Elizabeth
≈ 2 Children
Giles, David	Giles, David [29] *Miner*	Giles, David
Giles, Thomas D.
?Margaret (wife)
Joseph
Hyrum
?Maria	Giles, Thomas D. [35] *Minister*
?Margaret [34] *Wife*
Joseph [7]
Hyrum [6]
?Maria [1]	Giles, Thomas
≈ Wife
≈ 3 Children
Gilles [Gillies], Robert
  Jane (wife)
  John M.
  Ann C.
  Daniel L.
  Christena G.
  John | Gilles, Robert [34] *Cabnet Maker*
  Jane [34] *Wife*
  John M. [10]
  Ann C. [8]
  Daniel L. [6]
  Christena G. [3]
  John [87] *Pensioner* | Gillies, Robert
  ≈ Wife
  ≈ 4 Children

  Gillies, John |
≈Goode, Maria		≈Goode, Maria
Grant, David	Grant, David [39] *Tailor*	Grant, David
Green, Isaac	Green, Isaac [23] *Boiler Maker*	Green, Isaac
Griffith[s], Elizabeth	Griffith, Elizabeth [22] *Spinster*	Griffiths, Elizabeth
≈Griffith, Richard		≈Griffith, Richard
Griffiths, Richard
Elizabeth (wife)	Griffiths, Richard [39] *Miner*
Elizabeth [51] *Wife*	
≈Griffiths, Samuel
≈ Wife		≈Griffiths, Samuel
≈Wife
Griffiths, Sarah	Griffiths, Sarah [21] *Spinster*	
Groom, Robert
Mary (wife)
James
Richard	Groom, Robert [33] *Engineer*
Mary [29] *Wife*
James [12]
Richard [2]	Groom, Robert
≈ Wife
≈ 2 Children
Harris, John
Gwendllian	Harris, John [26] *Miner*
Gwendllian [30] *Wife*	Harris, John
≈ Wife
≈Hart, William		≈Hart, William

CONSOLIDATED LIST **Head of Family** **Dependents**	**BRITISH MISSION** **Liverpool Passenger List** **SAMUEL S. CURLING**	**DESERET NEWS** **Passenger List** **SAMUEL S. CURLING**

Hawkey, Hannah
    James
    Hannah
    Margaret
	Hawkey, Hannah [33] *Widow*
	    James [14]
	    Hannah [4]
	    Margaret [3]	

Hayes [Sp.?], George	Hayes [Sp.?], George [48] *Fireman*	

Heates [Sp.?], James
    Elizabeth
	Heates [Sp.?], James [22] *Plumber*
	    Elizabeth [14]	

Henwood, John
    Elizabeth (wife)
    Richard
    Elizabeth
	Henwood, John [46] *Laborer*
	    Elizabeth [45] *Wife*
	    Richard [19] *Laborer*
	    Elizabeth [16] *Spinster*
		Henwood, John
		    ≈ Wife
		    ≈ 2 Children

Hicks, John
    Harriet (wife)
	Hicks, John [30] *Shoemaker*
	    Harriet [24] *Wife*
		Hicks, John
		    ≈ Wife

Hollsworth, James
    James
	Hollsworth, James [38] *Shoemaker*
	    James [7 1/2]	

≈Hopkins, Mary		≈Hopkins, Mary

≈Hoppla, John
    ≈ Wife
    ≈ 3 Children
		≈Hoopla, John
		    ≈ Wife
		    ≈ 3 Children

Hughes, Elizabeth	Hughes, Elizabeth [60] *Widow*	Hughes, Elizabeth

Hughes, John
    Sarah (wife)
    Ann
	Hughes, John [41] *Laborer*
	    Sarah [41] *Wife*
	    Ann [10]
		Hughes, John
		    ≈ Wife
		    ≈ Child

Hughes [Hughs], Martha	Hughes, Martha [20] *Spinster*	Hughs, Martha
Hughes, William	Hughes, William	

Hughes, William
    Elizabeth
	Hughes, William [49] *Miner*
	    Elizabeth [47] *Wife*
		Hughes, William
		    ≈ Wife

Hughs [Hughes], Ann	Hughs, Ann [15] *Spinster*	Hughes, Ann

James, John [listed twice]
    Catherine
	James, John [27] *Miner*
	    Catherine [58] *Widow*
		James, John
		    Catherine

James, Ruth	James, Ruth [22] *Spinster*	James, Ruth
James, Sarah	James, Sarah [15] *Spinster*	James, Sarah
James, William	James, William [71] *Laborer*	James, William

Jenkins, Harry [Henry]
    Martha (wife)
    Margaret
	Jenkins, Harry [35] *Miner*
	    Martha [45] *Wife*
	    Margaret [18] *Spinster*
		Jenkins, Henry
		    ≈ Wife
		    ≈ Daughter

Jenkins, Janet	Jenkins, Janet [22] *Spinster*	Jenkins, Janet
Jenkins, John	Jenkins, John [25] *Laborer*	
Jenkins, John	Jenkins, John [25] *Shoemaker*	

Jenkins, Morris
    Margaret (wife)
    Elizabeth
    John
    David
    Thomas
    Joseph
	Jenkins, Morris [34] *Miner*
	    Margaret [37] *Wife*
	    Elizabeth [13]
	    John [8]
	    David [7]
	    Thomas [3]
	    Joseph [1]
		Jenkins, Morris
		    ≈ Wife
		    ≈ 4 Children

Jenkins, Rosser	Jenkins, Rosser [21] *Miner*	

Jenkins, Thomas
    Anne (wife)
	Jenkins, Thomas [32] *Tailor*
	    Anne *Wife*	

Jenkins, Thomas
    John
		Jenkins, Thomas
		    John

Jenkins, William
    Margaret (wife)
    Elizabeth
    William
    Thomas
	Jenkins, William [48] *Mason*
	    Margaret [47] *Wife*
	    Elizabeth [12]
	    William [14]
	    Thomas [8]
		Jenkins, William
		    ≈ Wife
		    ≈ 3 Children

Job, Hannah
    Mary
	Job, Hannah [26] *Wife*
	    Mary [8]
		Job, Hannah
		    ≈ Daughter

John, David [Daniel]	John, David [44] *Collier*	John, Daniel

APPENDIX D: SAMUEL S. CURLING COMPOSITE LIST   149

CONSOLIDATED LIST Head of Family Dependents	BRITISH MISSION Liverpool Passenger List SAMUEL S. CURLING	DESERET NEWS Passenger List SAMUEL S. CURLING

Jones, Amos
    Choico
    Edward
    Hannah
    Lewis
	Jones, Amos [18] *Pudler*
	    Choico [16] *Spinster*
	    Edward [13]
	    Hannah [10]
	    Lewis	

Jones, Benjamin
    Lelitia (wife)
    Esther
    Joseph
	Jones, Benjamin [48] *Taylor*
	    Lelitia [45] *Wife*
	    Esther [13]
	    Joseph [7]
		Jones, Benjamin
		    ≈ Wife
		    ≈ 3 Children

Jones, Daniel
    Mary (wife)
    Lewis
    Walter
    William
    Martha
    Richard
    Daniel
	Jones, Daniel [49] *Miner*
	    Mary [43] *Wife*
	    Lewis [20] *Collier*
	    Walter [18] *Collier*
	    William [14] *Collier*
	    Martha [8]
	    Richard [5]
	    Daniel [2]
		Jones, Daniel
		    ≈ Wife
		    ≈ 6 Children

Jones, Elias
    John
    Mary
    Llewellyn
    Anne
    Elias
    Ruth
    Thomas
    Hannah
	Jones, Elias [46] *Coal Mine Owner*
	    John [14]
	    Mary [17]
	    Llewellyn [11]
	    Anne [9]
	    Elias [7]
	    Ruth [5]
	    Thomas [3]
	    Hannah [1]
		Jones, Elias
		    ≈ Wife
		    ≈ 9 Children

Jones, James	Jones, James [27] *Laborer*	Jones, James

Jones, John
    Mary (wife)
    John
    Owen
    Isaac
	Jones, John [55] *Farmer*
	    Mary [56] *Wife*
	    John [26] *Weaver*
	    Owen [21] *Farmer*
	    Isaac [17] *Farmer*
		Jones, John
		    ≈ Wife
		    ≈ 3 Sons

Jones, John
    Hannah Hopkins (wife)
    Mary
	Jones, John [42] *Share Holder*
	    Hannah Hopkins [35] *Wife*
	    Mary [7]
		Jones, John
		    ≈ Wife
		    ≈ Child

Jones, John
    Mary (wife)
    Hannah
    Catherine
    Mary Ann
	Jones, John [40] *Miner*
	    Mary [39] *Wife*
	    Hannah [16] *Spinster*
	    Catherine [14] *Spinster*
	    Mary Ann [4]
		Jones, John
		    ≈ Wife
		    ≈ 3 Children

Jones, John
    Jane (wife)
    John
	Jones, John [33] *Roller*
	    Jane [28] *Wife*
	    John [4]	

Jones, Margaret	Jones, Margaret [30] *Spinster*	Jones, Margaret
Jones, Mary	Jones, Mary [18] *Spinster*	

≈Jones, Mary
    ≈Margaret
    ≈William
    ≈John
		≈Jones, Mary
		    ≈Margaret
		    ≈William
		    ≈John

Jones, Richard
    Eliza (wife)
    Sarah
    Isaac
    Lewis
    Hannah
	Jones, Richard [38] *Founder*
	    Eliza [38] *Wife*
	    Sarah [7]
	    Isaac [2]
	    Lewis [Inft.]
	    Hannah [10]
		Jones, Richard
		    ≈ Wife
		    ≈ 7 Children

Jones, Thomas	Jones, Thomas [60] *Farmer*	Jones, Thomas

Jones, Thomas
    Ruth (wife)
    Eleanor
	Jones, Thomas [58] *Farmer*
	    Ruth [49] *Wife*
	    Eleanor [29] *Spinster*
		Jones, Thomas
		    ≈ Wife
		    ≈ Daughter

Jones, William
    Mary (wife)
    Anne
	Jones, William [24] *Miner*
	    Mary [20] *Wife*
	    Anne [6 mo.]
		Jones, William
		    ≈ Wife
		    ≈ Child

CONSOLIDATED LIST Head of Family Dependents	BRITISH MISSION Liverpool Passenger List SAMUEL S. CURLING	DESERET NEWS Passenger List SAMUEL S. CURLING

Jones, William
   Sarah (wife)
   Francis P.
	Jones, William [22] *Plasterer*
	   Sarah [25] *Wife*
	   Francis P. [4 mo.]
		Jones, William
		   ≈ Wife
		   ≈ Child

Jones, William
   Thomas
	Jones, William [67] *Miner*
	   Thomas [10]
		Jones, William
		   ≈ Son

Jones, William
   Mary Ann (wife)
   Robert
   Louisa
   Frederick
	Jones, William [45] *Mariner*
	   Mary Ann [50] *Wife*
	   Robert [21] *Laborer*
	   Louisa [19] *Spinster*
	   Frederick [14] *Agriculturist*
		Jones, William
		   ≈ Wife
		   ≈ 3 Children

Jorman, Thomas
   Anne (wife)
   Richard
   John
   Margaret
	Jorman, Thomas [45] *Miner*
	   Anne [54] *Wife*
	   Richard [11]
	   John [9]
	   Margaret [6]	

Kettle, John
   Judith (wife)
   Mary Ann
   Robert
   Eliza
   James
   Samuel
   Anna
	Kettle, John [53] *Cottager*
	   Judith [43] *Wife*
	   Mary Ann [18] *Spinster*
	   Robert [14]
	   Eliza [12]
	   James [9]
	   Samuel [5]
	   Anna [1]
		Kettle, John
		   ≈ Wife
		   ≈ 6 Children

Lany [Sp.?], John
   Elizabeth
   Winefred
   John
   Edward
   Elizabeth
	Lany [Sp.?], John [54] *Mason*
	   Elizabeth [47] *Wife*
	   Winefred [18] *Spinster*
	   John [14]
	   Edward [12]
	   Elizabeth L. [6]	

Lark, William
   Mary (wife)
   Maria
   Mary
   Clarissa
   Nerises [Sp.?]
   Erastees
   Isabella
	Lark, William [35] *Shoemaker*
	   Mary [31] *Wife*
	   Maria [12]
	   Mary [10]
	   Clarissa [8]
	   Nerises [Sp.?] [5]
	   Erastees [3]
	   Isabella [5 mo.]	

Laurenson, William
   Anne (wife)
   Jane
   Margaret
	Laurenson, William [55] *Engineer*
	   Anne [50] *Wife*
	   Jane [18] *Spinster*
	   Margaret [11]
		Laurenson, William‡
		   ≈ Wife
		   ≈ 2 Children

Lewis, Daniel	Lewis, Daniel [50] *Miner*	Lewis, Daniel

Lewis, David
   Anne (wife)
   Joshua
   Mary Anne
   John
	Lewis, David [30] *Miner*
	   Anne [25] *Wife*
	   Joshua [5]
	   Mary Anne [2]
	   John [8 mos.]
		Lewis, David
		   ≈ Wife
		   ≈ 3 Children

≈Lewis, Elias		≈Lewis, Elias

Lewis, Enoch
   Jane (wife)
   John
   Martha
	Lewis, Enoch [36] *Miner*
	   Jane [33] *Wife*
	   John [9]
	   Martha [7]
		Lewis, Enoch
		   ≈ Wife
		   ≈ 2 Children

Lewis, Henry
   Mary (wife)
	Lewis, Henry [23] *Miner*
	   Mary [47?] *Wife*
		Lewis, Henry
		   ≈ Wife

Lewis, Jane	Lewis, Jane [22] *Spinster*	

Lewis, John
   Jane (wife)
   John Lamb [Sp.?]
   Pandyel [Sp.?]
	Lewis, John [33] *Miner*
	   Jane [29] *Wife*
	   John Lamb [Sp.?] [8]
	   Pandyel [Sp.?] [Inft.]
		Lewis, John
		   ≈ Wife
		   ≈ 2 Children

Lewis, John
   Elizabeth (wife)
   George
   Elizabeth
   Mary Ann
	Lewis, John [31] *Sadler*
	   Elizabeth [33] *Wife*
	   George [6]
	   Elizabeth [2]
	   Mary Ann [6 mo.]	

APPENDIX D: SAMUEL S. CURLING COMPOSITE LIST 151

CONSOLIDATED LIST Head of Family Dependents	BRITISH MISSION Liverpool Passenger List SAMUEL S. CURLING	DESERET NEWS Passenger List SAMUEL S. CURLING
Lewis, Lewelyn [Llewellyn]	Lewis, Lewelyn [17]	Lewis, Llewellyn
Lewis, Mary	Lewis, Mary [16] *Spinster*	
Lewis, Rufus	Lewis, Rufus [25]	Lewis, Rufus
≈Lewis, William		≈Lewis, William
≈ Wife		≈ Wife
Lewis, William	Lewis, William [24] *Miner*	
Elias	Elias [21] *Miner*	
Daniel	Daniel [21] *Miner*	
Llewelyn, David	Llewelyn, David [24] *Shoemaker*	
Llewllin [Lewellyn], Mary	Llewllin, Mary [47] *Widow*	Lewellyn, Mary
Anne	Anne [17] *Spinster*	≈ 4 Children
Elizabeth	Elizabeth [11]	
Edmund	Edmund [21] *Blocklayer*	
John	John [18] *Blocklayer*	
Llewllyn [Lewellyn], Rees[e]	Llewllyn, Rees [27] *Miner*	Llewelyn, Reese
Anne (wife)	Anne [20] *Wife*	≈ Wife
Lloyd, Thomas	Lloyd, Thomas [24] *Farmer*	Lloyd, Thomas
Benj [Benjamin]	Benj [23] *Shoemaker*	Bemjamin
Lucas, Anthoney	Lucas, Anthoney [58] *Tanner*	
Mary (wife)	Mary [57] *Wife*	
Lucas, Eliza	Lucas, Eliza [26] *Spinster*	Lucas, Eliza‡
Anne	Anne [21] *Spinster*	
Mary	Mary [14] *Spinster*	Mary
Lucas, Thomas	Lucas, Thomas [25] *Grocer*	Lucas, Thomas
≈ Wife		≈ Wife
McClane [McCave], John	McClane, John [48] *Laborer*	McCave, John‡
Nancy J. (wife)	Nancy J. [40] *Wife*	≈ Wife
Margaret	Margaret [17] *Spinster*	≈ 7 Children
Mary Jane	Mary Jane [15] *Spinster*	
Isabella	Isabella W. [15]	
John	John F. [11]	
Joseph L.	Joseph L. [8]	
Eliza L.	Eliza L. [6]	
Alexander	Alexander F. [2]	
McDonald, John	McDonald, John [58] *Cabinet Maker*	McDonald, John‡
McRevey, Benjamin	McRevey, Benjamin [62] *Weaver*	McRevey, Benjamin
Thomas	Thomas [17] *Weaver*	≈ 3 Children
Edward	Edward [11]	
Joseph	Joseph [6]	
Marshall, Sarah	Marshall, Sarah [34] *Widow*	Marshall, Sarah
Lavinia	Lavinia [12]	≈ 6 Children
Selina	Selina [10]	
Tryphena [Sp.?]	Tryphena [Sp.?] [8]	
Louisa	Louisa [6]	
George	George [4]	
Sarah	Sarah [2]	
Matthews, Anne [Ann]	Matthews, Anne [21] *Spinster*	Matthews, Ann
Matthews, Hopkin	Matthews, Hopkin [32] *Miner*	Matthews, Hopkin
Margaret (wife)	Margaret [34] *Wife*	≈ Wife
Elizabeth	Elizabeth [10]	≈ 5 Children
Mary	Mary [9]	
Margaret	Margaraet [6]	
Joan	Joan [4]	
Alma	Alma [3 mo.]	
Matthews, Joseph	Matthews, Joseph [35] *Miner*	Matthews, Joseph
Rachel (wife)	Rachel [33] *Wife*	≈ Wife
David	David [11]	≈ 4 Children
Joseph	Joseph [11]	
William	William [5]	
Mary Ann	Mary Ann [5 wks.]	
Middleton, Edward	Middleton, Edward [43] (Stewart)	Middleton, Edward

CONSOLIDATED LIST **Head of Family** **Dependents**	**BRITISH MISSION** **Liverpool Passenger List** **SAMUEL S. CURLING**	**DESERET NEWS** **Passenger List** **SAMUEL S. CURLING**

Miller, Ann
   Sarah Jane [J.]
	Miller, Ann [49] *Wife*
	   Sarah Jane [14]
		Miller, Sarah J.

Miller, James G.	Miller, James G. [41] *Minister*	(not going, next ship)

Miller, Mercy
   William A.
	Miller, Mercy [26] *Widow*
	   William A. [5]
		Miller, Mercy
		   ≈ Son

Moore, Hannah	Moore, Hannah [17] *Spinster*	Moore, Hannah
Morehouse [Monhouse], Eliza	Morehouse, Eliza [30] *Spinster*	Monhouse, Eliza‡
Morgan, Thomas	Morgan, Thomas [28] *Minister*	Morgan, Thomas
Morgan, William	Morgan, William [25] *Collier*	Morgan, William

Morgan, William
   Elizabeth (wife)
   John
	Morgan, William [24] *Miner*
	   Elizabeth [22] *Wife*
	   John [2]	

Morgan[s], Catherine
   Thomas
   David
   Eleanor
   William
	Morgans, Catherine [50] *Widow*
	   Thomas [29] *Breakman*
	   David [26] *Driver*
	   Eleanor [16] *Spinster*
	   William [15]
		Morgan, Catherine
		   Thomas
		   David
		   Eleanor
		   William

Morgan[s] [Sp.?], James	Morgans [Sp.?], James [28] *Miner*	Morgan, James
Morgan[s], Margaret	Morgans, Margaret [16] *Spinster*	Morgan, Margaret
Morgans, Owen	Morgans, Owen [19] *Weaver*	Morgans, Owen

Morris, Morris N.
   Susan (wife)
	Morris, Morris N. [25] *Potter*
	   Susan [27] *Wife*
		Morris, Morris N.
		   ≈ Wife

≈Morse, William
   ≈ Wife
		≈Morse, William
		   ≈ Wife

Moses, Thomas	Moses, Thomas [27] *Miner*	

Moses, William
   Elizabeth (wife)
	Moses, William [48] *Shoemaker*
	   Elizabeth [58] *Wife*	

Moyle, John
   Phillipi (wife)
   Elizabeth
   Stephen
   Henry
   Alfred
   John Jr.
	Moyle, John [47] *Stone Mason*
	   Phillipi [40] *Wife*
	   Elizabeth [18] *Spinster*
	   Stephen [15] *Stone Mason*
	   Henry [12]
	   Alfred [9]
	   John Jr. [4]
		Moyle, John
		   ≈ Wife
		   ≈ 5 Children

≈Neppres, George		≈Neppres, George
Oakley, John	Oakley, John [36] *Minister*	Oakley, John
Owens, Elizabeth	Owens, Elizabeth [19] *Spinster*	Owens, Elizabeth
Owens, Owen	Owens, Owen [18] *Tailor*	Owens, Owen
Owen[s], William	Owens, William [44] *Joiner*	Owen, William
≈Oxton, Thomas		≈Oxton, Thomas

Parry, Edward
   Anne [a]
	Parry, Edward [29] *Mason*
	   Anne [21] *Spinster*
		Parry, Edward
		   Anna

Parry, Eleanor	Parry, Eleanor [26] *Wife*	Parry, Eleanor

≈Parry, John
   ≈ Wife
   ≈ 4 Children
		≈Parry, John
		   ≈ Wife
		   ≈ 4 Children

≈Parry, John		≈Parry, John

Parry, John
   Harriet (wife)
   Brigham B.
	Parry, John [38] *Stone Mason*
	   Harriet [28] *Wife*
	   Brigham B. [10 mo.]
		Parry, John
		   ≈ Wife
		   ≈ Child

Parry, John
   Martha (wife)
   Elizabeth
	Parry, John [26] *Teamster*
	   Martha [26] *Wife*
	   Elizabeth [3]	

Parry, Thomas	Parry, Thomas [21] *Mason*	Parry, Thomas

Payne, William [O.]
   Annabella (wife)
   Jacob
	Payne, William [28] *Draper*
	   Annabella [20] *Wife*
	   Jacob [6 wks.]
		Payne, William O.
		   ≈ Wife
		   ≈ Child

Perkins, Anne [Ann]	Perkins, Anne [69] *Widow*	Perkins, Ann
Pettry, William	Pettry, William [40] *Clerk*	
Petty, Edward	Petty, Edward [53] *Mariner*	Petty, Edward

APPENDIX D: SAMUEL S. CURLING COMPOSITE LIST 153

CONSOLIDATED LIST Head of Family Dependents	BRITISH MISSION Liverpool Passenger List SAMUEL S. CURLING	DESERET NEWS Passenger List SAMUEL S. CURLING
Petty, William	Petty, William [40] *Clerk*	Petty, William
Hannah (wife)	Hannah [35] *Wife*	≈ Wife
Temperance A.	Temperance A. [10]	≈ 2 Children
Isabella M.	Isabella M. [Inft.]	
Phillips, Edward	Phillips, Edward [48] *Mason*	Phillips, Edward
Elizabeth (wife)	Elizabeth [47] *Wife*	≈ Wife
Elizabeth	Elizabeth [21] *Spinster*	≈ 5 Children
Jacob	Jacob [22] *Laborer*	
Sarah	Sarah [16] *Spinster*	
Margaret	Margaret [14] *Spinster*	
Mary	Mary [9]	
Phillips [Philips], Jonah	Phillips, Jonah [22] *Miner*	Philips, Jonah
Phillips, Louisa	Phillips, Louisa [18] *Spinster*	Phillips, Louisa
Phillips, Sarah	Phillips, Sarah [22] *Collier*	
Powell, Morgan	Powell, Morgan [39] *Miner*	Powell, Morgan
Margaret (wife)	Margaret [36] *Wife*	≈ Wife
Mary	Mary [14] *Spinster*	≈ 6 Children
William	William [11]	
Anne	Anne [9]	
Elizabeth	Elizabeth [7]	
Lewis	Lewis [4]	
Thomas	Thomas [1]	
Price, Ann	Price, Ann [51] *Widow*	Price, Ann
Price, Ctrn (wife)	Price, Ctrn [21] *Wife*	
Mary	Mary [20] *Spinster*	
Margaret	Margaret [18] *Spinster*	
William	William [14]	
John	John [9]	
Price, David	Price, David [24] *Miner*	
Price, David	Price, David [29] *Farmer*	Price, David
Gwenllian	Gwenllian [24] *Spinster*	Gwenllian
Anne [Anna]	Anne [65] *Widow*	Anna
Price, John	Price, John [20] *Miner*	
Price, John	Price, John [35] *Miner*	Price, John
Margaret (wife)	Margaret [23] *Wife*	≈ Wife
John W.	John W. [3]	≈ 2 Children
Joseph	Joseph [11 mo. Inft.]	
≈Rasdall, John		≈Rasdall, John
≈ Wife		≈ Wife
≈ Child		≈ Child
Rees[e], Gwendlian [llian]	Rees, Gwendlian [38] *Widow*	Reese, Gwenllian
Rees[e], Isaac	Rees, Isaac [32] *Miner*	Reese, Isaac
Hannah (wife)	Hannah [28] *Wife*	≈ Wife
Rees[e], Margaret	Rees, Margaret [46] *Widow*	Reese, Margaret
George	George [15]	≈ 3 Children
Anne	Anne [13]	
Lodwick	Lodwick [10]	
Rees[e], Thomas	Rees, Thomas [39] *Miner*	Reese, Thomas
Margaret (wife)	Margaret [37] *Wife*	≈ Wife
Anne	Anne [16] *Spinster*	≈ 7 Children
Alfred	Alfred [14]	
Sarah	Sarah [11]	
Eleanor	Eleanor [9]	
Nephi	Nephi [8]	
Maria	Maria [5]	
Lennah	Lennah [2]	
Reese, Henry	Reese, Henry [18] *Miner*	Reese, Henry
Reese, William	Reese, William [27] *Miner*	Reese, William
Reynolds, Henry	Reynolds, Henry [33] *Game Keeper*	Reynolds, Henry
Mary (wife)	Mary [41] *Wife*	≈ Wife
William	William [10]	≈ 3 Children
Ann	Ann [8]	
Fred [Sp.?] K. G.	Fred [Sp.?] K. G. [5]	

CONSOLIDATED LIST Head of Family Dependents	BRITISH MISSION Liverpool Passenger List SAMUEL S. CURLING	DESERET NEWS Passenger List SAMUEL S. CURLING
Richards, David	Richards, David [30] *Miner*	Richards, David
Jane (wife)	Jane [31] *Wife*	≈ Wife
Elizabeth	Elizabeth [5]	≈ 2 Children
Martha	Martha [2]	
Richards, John	Richards, John [38]*Minister*	Richards, John
Anne (wife)	Anne [27] *Wife*	≈ Wife
Samuel	Samuel [10]	≈ 5 Children
William	William [8]	
Evans, Ann	Evans, Ann [4]	
Evans, Sarah	Evans, Sarah [3]	
Evans, Joshua	Evans, Joshua [1]	
Richards, Shem	Richards, Shem [25] *Miner*	Richards, Shem
Mary (wife)	Mary [27] *Wife*	≈ Wife
Roberts, David	Roberts, David [29] *Weaver*	
Susannah	Susannah [19] *Spinster*	Roberts, Susannah
Roberts, David	Roberts, David [41] *Quarry Man*	Roberts, David
Catherine (wife)	Catherine [48] *Wife*	≈ Wife
Robert	Robert [18] *Slate Quarry Man*	≈ 5 Children
Thomas	Thomas [15] *Slate Quarry Man*	
Daniel	Daniel [13] *Slate Quarry Man*	
Anne	Anne [11]	
Elizabeth	Elizabeth [9]	
Jane	Jane [6]	
Roberts, David	Roberts, David [45] *Joiner*	Roberts, David
Mary (wife)	Mary [31] *Wife*	≈ Wife
William	William [17]	≈ 5 Children
David	David [11]	
Rosa	Rosa [6]	
Mary	Mary [4]	
Roberts, Eleanor	Roberts, Eleanor [23] *Spinster*	Roberts, Eleanor
Eliza	Eliza [21] *Spinster*	
Roberts, John	Roberts, John [33]	
Roberts, John	Roberts, John [32] *Shop Keeper*	Roberts, John
Mary (wife)	Mary [34] *Wife*	≈ Wife
Elizabeth	Elizabeth [8]	≈ 3 Children
William	William [5]	
Robert E.	Robert E. [2 mo.]	
Roberts, John D.	Roberts, John D. [31] *Miner*	Roberts, John D.
Anne (wife)	Anne [33] *Wife*	≈ Wife
Jacob	Jacob [7]	≈ Child
Roberts, Robert	Roberts, Robert [18] *Quarry Man*	Roberts, Robert
Rosser, George	Rosser, George [34] *Miner*	Rosser, George
Rowe, Charlotte E. [J.]	Rowe, Charlotte E. [33] *Spinster*	Rowe, Charlotte E. J.
Robert	Robert [9]	≈ 2 Children
Charlotte J.	Charlotte J. [7]	
Royans, William	Royans, William [46] *Miner*	
Rusdell, John	Rusdell, John [20]*Agricultural Labourer*	
Elizabeth (wife)	Elizabeth [22] *Wife*	
Mary Ann	Mary Ann [2/12 Inft.]	
Sawyer, Joseph	Sawyer, Joseph [39] *Seaman*	Sawyer, Joseph (Cook)
Henrietta (wife)	Henrietta [34] *Wife*	Sawyer, Henrietta
Henrietta	Henrietta [8]	≈ 2 Children
Mary Ann	Mary Ann [7]	
Sinneto [Sinnett], George	Sinneto, George [37] *Laborer*	Sinnett, George
≈ Wife		≈ Wife
Sinnette[Sp.?], Martha(wife)	Sinnette [Sp.?], Martha [50] *Wife*	
Stoddard[t], Robert	Stoddard, Robert [50] *Warfer?*	Stoddart, Robert
Margaret (wife)	Margaret [44] *Wife*	≈ Wife
James	James [13]	≈ 3 Children
Mary	Mary [10]	
Dinah	Dinah [5]	

APPENDIX D: SAMUEL S. CURLING COMPOSITE LIST 155

CONSOLIDATED LIST Head of Family Dependents	BRITISH MISSION Liverpool Passenger List SAMUEL S. CURLING	DESERET NEWS Passenger List SAMUEL S. CURLING

Stoddard [Stodart], William
    Margaret (wife)
    Caleb
    Robert
    Jane
    Sarah
    Hannah
    Mary
    Margaret
	Stoddard, William [42] *Marble Polisher*
	    Margaret [37] *Wife*
	    Caleb [18] *Weaver*
	    Robert [16] *Weaver*
	    Jane [12]
	    Sarah [10]
	    Hannah [8]
	    Mary [3]
	    Margaret [1]
		Stodart, William
		    ≈ Wife
		    ≈ 7 Children

Swancaes [cee], Richard	Swancaes [Sp.?], Richard [55] *Miner*	Swancee, Richard
Taylor, Elizabeth	Taylor, Elizabeth [24] *Spinster*	Taylor, Elizabeth
≈Thain, Margaret R.		≈Thain, Margaret R.
Thayer, Margaret R.	Thayer, Margaret R. [23] *Spinster*	
Thayne [Thain], John T.	Thayne, John T. [26] *Farmer*	Thain, John T.
Thayne [Thain], Susan[ah]	Thayne, Susanah [23] *Spinster*	Thain, Susan
Thomas, Ann Jane	Thomas, Ann Jane [14] *Spinster*	Thomas, Ann J.
Thomas, Anne [Anna]	Thomas, Anne [74] *Widow*	Thomas, Anna

Thomas, Anne[a]
    Margaret
    Daniel
	Thomas, Anne [77] *Widow*
	    Margaret [46] *Spinster*
	    Daniel [44] *Miner*
		Thomas, Anna
		    Margaret
		    Daniel

Thomas, David	Thomas, David [31] *Miner*	

Thomas, Elvina [Elvira]
    Edward
	Thomas, Elvina [46] *Widow*
	    Edward [13]
		Thomas, Elvira
		    ≈ Son

Thomas, James
    Hannah (wife)
    Jane
    Joseph
    John
	Thomas, James [39] *Miner*
	    Hannah [38] *Wife*
	    Jane [10]
	    Joseph [8]
	    John [1]
		Thomas, James
		    ≈ Wife
		    ≈ 3 Children

≈Thomas, Jane		≈Thomas, Jane
Thomas, Thomas	Thomas, Thomas [19] *Shoemaker*	Thomas, Thomas
Thomas, Thomas	Thomas, Thomas [41] *Wheelwright*	

Thomas, Thomas
    Walter
    John
	Thomas, Thomas [52] *Laborer*
	    Walter? [19] *Miner*
	    John [14] *Miner*
		Thomas, Thomas
		    ≈ 2 Sons

Thomas, Thomas
    Mary (wife)
    Jane
    Thomas
    Jeanet
    Nephi
	Thomas, Thomas [27] *Miner*
	    Mary [32] *Wife*
	    Jane [7]
	    Thomas [5]
	    Jeanet [3]
	    Nephi [1]
		Thomas, Thomas
		    ≈ Wife
		    ≈ 4 Children

Thomas, William	Thomas, William [51] *Farmer*	Thomas, William

Thomas, William
    Letetia Alice (wife)
    Stephen
    Elizabeth
    Joseph
	Thomas, William [38] *Thatcher*
	    L. Alice [39] *Wife* Family
	    Stephen [11] listed
	    Elizabeth [6] twice.
	    Joseph [5 mo.]
		Thomas, William
		    ≈ Wife
		    ≈ 3 Children

Tripp, Margaret	Tripp, Margaret [22] *Spinster*	Tripp, Margaret

Vaughn, Phillip
    Margaret (wife)
    Maria
    Elizabeth
	Vaughn, Phillip [44] *Miner*
	    Margaret [39] *Wife*
	    Maria [12]
	    Elizabeth [10]
		Vaughn, Phillip
		    ≈ Wife
		    ≈ 2 Children

Vepprefs [Sp.?], George	Vepprefs, George [23] *Bricklayer*	

Vernon, Joseph
    Ann (wife)
	Vernon, Joseph [36] *Laborer*
	    Ann [31] *Wife*
		Vernon, Joseph
		    ≈ Wife

Walker, Henry
    Isabella (wife)
	Walker, Henry [50] *Laborer*
	    Isabella [50] *Wife*
		Walker, Henry
		    ≈ Wife

Walters, Hannah	Walters, Hannah [29] *Spinster*	

Walter[s] [Sp.?], Hannah
    Maria
    Thomas
    Elizabeth
	Walter [Sp.?], Hannah [28] *Widow*
	    Maria [11]
	    Thomas [6]
	    Elizabeth [4]
		Walters, Hannah
		    ≈ 3 Children

CONSOLIDATED LIST Head of Family Dependents	BRITISH MISSION Liverpool Passenger List SAMUEL S. CURLING	DESERET NEWS Passenger List SAMUEL S. CURLING

Walters [Sp.?], John
   Esther (wife)
   Ady
   Sarah
   Elizabeth
	Walters [Sp.?], John [47] *Tailor*
	   Esther [34] *Wife*
	   Ady [6]
	   Sarah [26] *Spinster*
	   Elizabeth [14] *Spinster*
		Walters, John
		   ≈ Wife
		   ≈ Child
		Walters, Sarah
		Walters, Elizabeth

Warburton, Mary
   Elizabeth A.
   John T.
   Peter
   Mary J.
	Warburton, Mary [44] *Wife*
	   Elizabeth A. [12]
	   John T. [10]
	   Peter [4]
	   Mary J. [2]
		Warburton, Mary
		   ≈ 4 Children

Ward, William	Ward, William [25] *Miner*	

Warner, James
   ≈ Wife
	Warner, James [60] *Cottager*	Warner, James
		   ≈ Wife

Welling [Willing], Job
   Frances E. (wife)
   Job
	Welling, Job [23] *Tailor*
	   Frances E. [25] *Wife*
	   Job [1 1/2]
		Willing, Job
		   ≈ Wife
		   ≈ Child

White, John
   Mary Ann (wife)
	White, John [30] *Miner*
	   Mary Ann [?31] *Wife*
		White, John
		   ≈ Wife

≈Wilks, Ann		≈Wilks, Ann

≈Wilks, Mary
   ≈ Sarah
		≈Wilks, Mary
		   ≈ Sarah

William[s], Richard
   Rachel (wife)
   Richard M.
   Eleanor
   Claudia
   Jane
	William, Richard [42] *Miner*
	   Rachel [38] *Wife*
	   Richard M. [16]
	   Eleanor [9]
	   Claudia [1]
	   Jane [18] *Spinster*
		Williams, Richard
		   ≈ Wife
		   ≈ 4 Children

William, Samuel
   Anne (wife)
   David
   Mary
	William, Samuel [28] *Laborer*
	   Anne [28] *Wife*
	   David [3]
	   Mary [1]	

Williams, Amelia	Williams, Amelia [26] *Spinster*	Williams, Amelia

Williams, Anne[a]
   Sarah
   Mary
   William
	Williams, Anne [43] *Widow*
	   Sarah [12]
	   Mary [9]
	   William [5]
		Williams, Anna
		   ≈ 4 Children

Williams, Anne [a]	Williams, Annie [18] *Spinster*	Williams, Anna
Williams, Emily G.	Williams, Emily G. [18]	Williams, Emily G.
Williams, Hannah	Williams, Hannah [13] *Spinster*	
Williams, Jane	Williams, Jane [18] *Spinster*	

Williams, John
   Sarah (wife)
   John
   Catherine
	Williams, John [28] *Miner*
	   Sarah [21] *Wife*
	   John [1]
	   Catherine [68] *Widow*
		Williams, John
		   ≈ Wife
		   ≈ Child
		   ≈ Catherine Williams

Williams, John
   Mary (wife)
   Elizabeth
   Sarah
   Anne
   Jane
	Williams, John [40] *Farmer*
	   Mary [42] *Wife*
	   Elizabeth [18] *Spinster*
	   Sarah [16] *Spinster*
	   Anne [14]
	   Jane [12]
		Williams, John
		   ≈ Wife
		   ≈ 4 Children

≈Williams, Letitia		≈Williams, Letitia
Williams, Margaret	Williams, Margaret [15] *Spinster*	
Williams, Richard	Williams, Richard [22] *Mason*	Williams, Richard
Williams, Thomas	Williams, Thomas [22] *Miner*	
Williams, William	Williams, William [18] *Miner*	(not going)
Williams, William L.	Williams, William L. [27] *Miner*	Williams, William L.
Williams, William L.	Williams, William L. [27] *Collier*	

Wills, Mary
   Ann
	Wills, Mary [24] *Spinster*
	   Ann [21] *Spinster*	

APPENDIX D: SAMUEL S. CURLING COMPOSITE LIST 157

CONSOLIDATED LIST Head of Family Dependents	BRITISH MISSION Liverpool Passenger List SAMUEL S. CURLING	DESERET NEWS Passenger List SAMUEL S. CURLING

Wilson, John
    Eliza {widow}
Woodward, William
Wordle, Thomas
Yeo, William
TOTALS 853
FAMILIES 321
	Wilson, John [28] *Ship Brokers Clerk*
	    Eliza [66] *Widow*
	Woodward, William [23] *Minister*
	Wordle, Thomas [23] *Miner*
	Yeo, William [18] *Miner*
	790
		Wilson, John
		    Eliza
		Woodward, William
		
		Yeo, William
		701

COUNTRIES

	Adults	Children	Infants	Total
England	121	26	2	149
Scotland	1	0	0	1
Ireland	22	4	2	28
Wales	426	79	23	528
Americans	1	0	0	1
TOTALS	571	109	27	707

"Elder Dan Jones a returning Missionary to Utah included in the above summary of Welsh Emigrants, also David Davies, Cook, and Edward Middletohn, Steward, and Joseph Sawyer in the English Summary."

Class	Adults	Children	Infants	Total
P.E. Fund	354	59	12	428
Ordinary	210	50	15	275
TOTALS	567	109	27	703

Elder Dan Jones President of the Company
John Oakley & David Grant Counselors

David Davies & Joseph Sawyer: Cooks
    Edward Middleton: Steward

Sailed 19 April 1856.   Total   707

British Mission Liverpool Passenger List taken from Emigration Records from Liverpool Office of the British Mission 1855-1856, Libr. No. 1045.

≈ *Deseret News*, "Ship S. Curling, For Boston, April 19, 1856", published passenger list, Vol. 6, page 160, Film Us/Can 0026587, Family History LIbrary. They show 567 Adults, 109 Children, 27 Infants, for total of 703. Dan Jones, President, John Oakley and David Grant Counselors, David Davies and Joseph Sawyer Cooks, and Edward Middlton, Steward.

‡ Members of the Second Handcart Company.

APPENDIX E-1

THE ENOCH TRAIN PIONEERS
1856

BIRTHS–Alphabetical

NAME	DATE
Doney, Mary Jane	29 Jul
Fruge [Frew], William McAllister	27 May
Granger, Elizabeth	15 May
Hargraves, Enoch Train	25 Mar
Johnstone, Hamilton	24 Mar
Lloyd, Martha	30 May
Lyon, Christina Enoch	21 Mar
Muir, Son (of Sister Muir)	22 Sep
Ramsey, Daughter (Elizabeth & Ralph)	31 May
Richardson, Child (of Peter & Eliza)	15 Jul
Schroder, Elizabeth (of Constant & Ann)	1 Jun

DEATHS–Alphabetical

NAME	DATE
Ash, Elizabeth [2 months]	?
Birch, James [28]	17 Sept
Bower, James [44]	21 Jun
[Card, Daughter in Independent Camp]	2 Jul
Clotworthy, Jane [Jean]	24 Apr
Devereux, Amos	?
Devereux, Esther	31 Mar
Elliker's Daughter	17 August
Elliker, Eliza [20]	15 Jul
Elliker, Honrick [59]	20 Sep
Granger, Elizabeth	16 May
Gray, William [5 weeks]	?
Hillhouse, Janet [1 month]	?
Lee, William [12]	14 Jun
Mayo, Mary [65]	13 Sep
McCleve, John	24 Sep
McLane, Male	11 Jun
Neappris [Nappriss], George [24]	7 Sep
Powell, David [infant]	?
Praeter, Lora [3]	15 Jun
Ramsay, John [1½]	27 Jun
Richardson, Child of Peter & Eliza	15 Jul
Richins, Albert Franklin [1 month]	?
Rossin, Missell [Found dead on road]	17 Aug
Sanders, Walter [65]	2 Sept.
Shinn, Emma [2½]	26 June
Shinn, Maria	19 May
Shinn, Sydney	24 June
Smith, Aniki	5 Aug
Stalley, Peter	17 Aug
Stoddard, Robert [51]	31 Aug
Taylor, Adopted Daughter John Taylor	16 May
Walker, Henry [50] (hit by lightening)	26 Jul
Welling, Job [1½]	17 Jun

APPENDIX E-2

THE ENOCH TRAIN PIONEERS
1856

NAME	DATE
Lyon, Christina Enoch	21 Mar
Johnstone, Hamilton	24 Mar
Hargraves, Enoch Train	25 Mar
Granger, Elizabeth	15 May
Fruge[Frew], William McAllister	27 May
Lloyd, Martha	30 May
Ramsey, Daughter (Elizabeth & Ralph)	31 May
Schroder, Elizabeth (Constant & Ann)	1 Jun
Richardson, Child (of Peter & Eliza)	15 Jul
Doney, Mary Jane	29 Jul
Muir, Son (of Sister Muir)	22 Sep

DEATHS–By Date

NAME	DATE
Devereux, Esther	31 Mar
Devereux, Amos	?
Clotworthy, Jane [Jean]	24 Apr
Taylor, Adopted Daughter John Taylor	16 May
Granger, Elizabeth	16 May
Shinn, Maria	19 May
McLane, Male	11 Jun
Lee, William [12]	14 Jun
Praeter, Lora [3]	15 Jun
Welling, Job [1½]	17 Jun
Bower, James [44]	21 Jun
Shinn, Sydney	24 Jun
Shinn, Emma [2½]	26 Jun
Ramsay, John [1½]	27 Jun
[Card, Daughter in Independent Camp]	2 Jul
Elliker, Eliza [20]	15 Jul
Richardson, Child of Peter & Eliza	15 Jul
Walker, Henry [50] (hit by lightening)	26 Jul
Smith, Aniki	5 Aug
Stalley, Peter [of Italy]	17 Aug
Elaikers Daughter	17 Aug
Rossin, Missell [Found dead on road]	17 Aug
Stoddard, Robert [51]	31 Aug
Sanders, Walter [65]	2 Sep
Neappris [Nappriss], George [24]	7 Sep
Mayo, Mary [65]	13 Sep
Birch, James [28]	17 Sep
Elliker, Honrick [59]	20 Sep
McCleve, John	24 Sep
Ash, Elizabeth [2 months]	?
Gray, William [5 weeks]	?
Hillhouse, Janet [1 month]	?
Powell, David [infant]	?
Richins, Albert Franklin [1 month]	?

APPENDIX F

DAYS & DATES OF JOURNEY BREAKDOWN BY TRAVEL SEGMENTS

Enoch Train Sea Voyage Liverpool to Boston		Week Day	Day of Sea Journey	Total Days of Travel
March 23	Left Liverpool by Tug	SUN	1	1
March 24		M	2	2
March 25		T	3	3
March 26		W	4	4
March 27		TH	5	5
March 28		F	6	6
March 29		S	7	7
March 30		SUN	8	8
March 31		M	9	9
April 1		T	10	10
April 2		W	11	11
April 3		TH	12	12
April 4		F	13	13
April 5		S	14	14
April 6		SUN	15	15
April 7		M	16	16
April 8		T	17	17
April 9		W	18	18
April 10		TH	19	19
April 11		F	20	20
April 12		S	21	21
April 13		SUN	22	22
April 14		M	23	23
April 15		T	24	24
April 16		W	25	25
April 17		TH	26	26
April 18		F	27	27
April 19		S	28	28
April 20		SUN	29	29
April 21		M	30	30
April 22		T	31	31
April 23		W	32	32
April 24		TH	33	33
April 25		F	34	34
April 26		S	35	35
April 27		SUN	36	36
April 28		M	37	37
April 29		T	38	38
April 30	Arrived in Port	W	39	39
May 1	Docked in Boston	TH		40

By Omnibus, Train & Ferry From Boston to Iowa City, Iowa		Week Day	Day of Land Journey	Total Days of Travel
May 2		F	1	41
May 3		S	2	42
May 4		SUN	3	43
May 5		M	4	44
May 6		T	5	45
May 7		W	6	46
May 8		TH	7	47
May 9		F	8	48
May 10		S	9	49
May 11		SUN	10	50
May 12	Arrived Iowa City	M	11	51

APPENDIX F: DAYS AND DATES OF JOURNEY BREAKDOWN BY TRAVEL SEGMENTS 161

At Iowa City Campgrounds Waiting For Handcarts		Week Day	Day of Land Journey	Total Days of Travel
May 13	Waiting in Iowa City	T	1	52
May 14	Walked to Campgrounds	W	2	53
May 15		TH	3	54
May 16		F	4	55
May 17		S	5	56
May 18		SUN	6	57
May 19		M	7	58
May 20		T	8	59
May 21		W	9	60
May 22		TH	10	61
May 23		F	11	62
May 24		S	12	63
May 25		SUN	13	64
May 26		M	14	65
May 27		T	15	66
May 28		W	16	67
May 29		TH	17	68
May 30		F	18	69
May 31		S	19	70
June 1		SUN	20	71
June 2		M	21	72
June 3		T	22	73
June 4		W	23	74
June 5		TH	24	75
June 6		F	25	76
June 7		S	26	77
June 8		SUN	27	78

Handcart Journey – Companies 1 & 2 Iowa City to Florence, Nebraska		Week Day	Day of Land Journey	Total Days of Travel
June 9	First Company starts	M	1	79
June 10		T	2	80
June 11	Second Company starts	W	3	81
June 12	2nd Company reaches 1st	TH	4	82
June 13		F	5	83
June 14		S	6	84
June 15		SUN	7	85
June 16		M	8	86
June 17		T	9	87
June 18		W	10	88
June 19		TH	11	89
June 20		F	12	90
June 21		S	13	91
June 22		SUN	14	92
June 23		M	15	93
June 24		T	16	94
June 25		W	17	95
June 26		TH	18	96
June 27		F	19	97
June 28		S	20	98
June 29		SUN	21	99
June 30		M	22	100
July 1		T	23	101
July 2		W	24	102
July 3		TH	25	103
July 4		F	26	104
July 5		S	27	105
July 6		SUN	28	106
July 7		M	29	107
July 8		T	30	108

At Florence, Nebraska Campgrounds Repair & Resupply	Week Day	Day of Land Journey	Total Days of Travel
July 9	W	1	109
July 10	TH	2	110
July 11	F	3	111
July 12	S	4	112
July 13	SUN	5	113
July 14	M	6	114
July 15	T	7	115
July 16	W	8	116

Handcart Journey – Companies 1 & 2 Florence to Salt Lake City, Utah		Week Day	Day of Land Journey	Total Days of Travel
July 17	First Company starts	TH	1	117
July 18		F	2	118
July 19		S	3	119
July 20		SUN	4	120
July 21		M	5	121
July 22		T	6	122
July 23		W	7	123
July 24	Second Company starts	TH	8/1	124
July 25		F	9/2	125
July 26		S	10/3	126
July 27		SUN	11/4	127
July 28		M	12/5	128
July 29		T	13/6	129
July 30		W	14/7	130
July 31		TH	15/8	131
August 1		F	16/9	132
August 2		S	17/10	133
August 3		SUN	18/11	134
August 4		M	19/12	135
August 5		T	20/13	136
August 6		W	21/14	137
August 7		TH	22/15	138
August 8		F	23/16	139
August 9		S	24/17	140
August 10		SUN	25/18	141
August 11		M	26/19	142
August 12		T	27/20	143
August 13		W	28/21	144
August 14		TH	29/22	145
August 15		F	30/23	146
August 16		S	31/24	147
August 17		SUN	32/25	148
August 18		M	33/26	149
August 19		T	34/27	150
August 20		W	35/28	151
August 21		TH	36/29	152
August 22		F	37/30	153
August 23		S	38/31	154
August 24		SUN	39/32	155
August 25		M	40/33	156
August 26		T	41/34	157
August 27		W	42/35	158
August 28		TH	43/36	159
August 29		F	44/37	160
August 30		S	45/38	161
August 31		SUN	46/39	162

Handcart Journey – Companies 1 & 2 Florence to Salt Lake City, Utah		Week Day	Day of Land Journey	Total Days of Travel
September 1		M	47/40	163
September 2		T	48/41	164
September 3		W	49/42	165
September 4		TH	50/43	166
September 5		F	51/44	167
September 6		S	52/45	168
September 7		SUN	53/46	169
September 8		M	54/47	170
September 9		T	55/48	171
September 10		W	56/49	172
September 11	2nd Co. catches 1st Co.	TH	57/50	173
September 12		F	58/51	174
September 13		S	59/52	175
September 14		SUN	60/53	176
September 15		M	61/54	177
September 16		T	62/55	178
September 17		W	63/56	179
September 18		TH	64/57	180
September 19		F	65/58	181
September 20		S	66/59	182
September 21		SUN	67/60	183
September 22		M	68/61	184
September 23		T	69/62	185
September 24		W	70/63	186
September 25		TH	72/64	187
September 26	ALL ARRIVE IN SLC	F	73/65	188

APPENDIX G

*THE EMIGRANT'S GUIDE**

EXPLANATION

In the following table, the *large* [**Bold**] *type* shows the prominent points and places which will naturally be noticed by the emigrant. The first column of figures shows the distance from point to point, in English miles. The second column of figures shows the total distance of each point to Winter Quarters, and the third column the total distance of each point to the Temple Block, in the CITY OF THE GREAT SALT LAKE. As, for example:

How far is it from Winter Quarters to Pappea?

Answer. (page 5 [1], second line) 18 miles.

How far from Pappea to the Elk Horn river?

Answer. (page 5 [1], second and third lines) 9 miles &c.

Again: How far is it from Raw Hide Creek to Fort John?

Answer . (page 11 [8], last line) 12 miles.

How far is Fort John from Winter Quarters?

Answer. (p. 12 [8], first line) 522 miles.

How far is Fort John from the City of the Great Salt Lake?

Answer. (p. 12 [8], third column of figures) 509 miles.

The *small type*, in this table, contains the various *remarks* touching the nature of the road, lands, and its adaptation for camping purposes, &c. For example:

What is said concerning the "La Bonte river?" Page 13 [9], second line.

Answer. "It is a good place to camp—being plenty of timber, egress and water"—the necessaries for camping purposes, and consequently can be depended on. But, if thought advisable to go a little further, "there is a good camping place a mile further," consequently you have choice of the two good places, within one mile of each other.

What is said of a branch of the La Bonte? Page 13 [9], third line.

Answer. "Doubtful about water," consequently not safe to depend on for a camp ground. It is also said that the "banks are steep," which shows that it is not very good to cross, &c.

---

*William Clayton, *The Latter-day Saints' Emigrants' Guide Being a Table of Distances, Showing All the Springs, Creeks, Rivers, Hills, Mountains... From Council Bluffs, to the Valley of the Great Salt Lake.* St. Louis: Missouri Republican Steam Power Press—Chambers & Knapp, 1848.

Prominent Points and Remarks	Dist. miles	From W. Qtrs miles	From CofGSL miles
Winter Quarters, Lat 41° 18′ 53″ - - - - - - - - - - The road good, but very crooked, following the ridges and passing over a continual succession of hills and hollows			1031
Pappea, ten feet wide, high banks. Some timber on the creek, but it is difficult to water teams. After this' the road is crooked and uneven to the Elk Horn.	18	18	1013
Elk Horn, nine rods wide, three feet deep. - - - - - - - - - Current rather swift, and not very pleasant to ferry. Plenty of timber on its banks. (See Note 1.)	9	27	1004
Creek, ten feet wide, steep banks. - - - - - - - - This creek has a good bridge over it but little timber on the banks. There is a high post, erected near the bridge, for a guide to it.	¾	27¾	1003¼
Platte river and Liberty Pole. - - - - - - - - - Plenty of timber, but you will probably have to go to the river for water-distance about a quarter of a mile. The nearest and best road to water is round the east point of the timber.	11¼	42½	992
Small Lake (narrow) south side the road. - - - - - - No timber on the Lake.	3½	42½	988½
Circular Lake, or pond, close to the road, (south.) - - - - - - - No timber. In the neighborhood of this, the road runs alongside a number of small lakes, or ponds, for two miles; but there is little timber near them.	¾	43¼	987¾
R. R. and T., road joins the river, Lat. 41′ 27′ 5″ - - - - - - - This is a point where a branch of the river runs round an island, on which is plenty of timber. Not much water in the channel but plenty for camping purposes.	9	52¼	978¾
Indian Grave, north side the road. - - - - - - - - This is a large pile of earth, about eighty yards north of the road	7½	59¾	971¼
R. R. and T., road joins the river. - - - - - - - - Plenty of timber and water, without leaving the road.	2	60¼	970¾
Shell creek, 12′ feet wide, three feet deep - - - - - - - - This creek is bridged, and a few rods lower is a place to ford. Plenty of timber on it. After this you will probably find no water for twelve miles, without turning considerably from the road.	2	62¼	968¾.
Small lake, south side of the road. - - - - - - - - Plenty of water in the Spring season, but none in Summer. It was entirely dry, October 18, 1847.	5 ¾	68	963
R. and R., road joins the river. - - - - - - - - After this point you will have four or five miles of heavy, sandy road.	6½	74½	956½
Long Lake, south side the road. - - - - - - - - There is a little timber where this lake joins the river, and it is a good camping place.	2	75	956
Forks of road to new and old Pawnee villages. - - - - - - - The left hand road leads to the Pawnee location of 1847; the other to the old village. The latter is your route.	5½	80½	950½

Prominent Points and Remarks	Dist. miles	From W. Qtrs miles	From CofGSL miles
Lake, south of the road. --------- Plenty of timber close to the road. The banks of the lake are high, but there is a small pond near, where teams can water.	2	81	950
Loup Fork—lake and timber. -------- Opposite to where the Pawnees were located, in the Spring of 1847, and is a good place to camp.	5	86	945
Lake and timber, south of the road. ----------	8¼	94¼	936¾
Looking-glass creek, 16 feet wide, 2 deep -------- There is a poor bridge over this creek. It is, however, not difficult to ford. Plenty of timber on and near it.	1	95¼	935¾
Long Lake, south side the road. -------- Some timber on the south bank, but none on the north side.	2	97¼	933¾
Beaver river, 25 feet wide, 2 feet deep: Lat. 41° 25′ 13″; **Long. 98° 0′ 15″.** -------- Plenty of good timber on both There are two fording places. The upper one is good going in, but steep on the opposite side. The lower one not going down, but good on the other side.	6½	103¾	927¼
Plumb creek, five feet wide: Lat. 41° 24′ 29″; **Altitude, 1,090 feet.** --------- On this creek the old Pawnee mission station stands, but is not a very good place to camp, being near the Pawnee cornfields. The creek was dry, October 16, 1847.	6¾	110½	920½
Ash creek, 12 feet wide, one foot deep. -------- Some timber, but not a very good chance to camp.	2½	113	918
Ford of the Loup Fork: Lat. 41° 22′ 37″; Long. 98° 11′ 0″. ---- This is the pioneer's ford, but is considered not so good as the upper ford. River about 300 yards wide.	1¼	114¼	916¾
Old Pawnee village. -------- Formerly occupied by the Grand Pawnee and Tappas bands; but burned by the Sioux, in the Fall of 1846.	2	114¾	916¼
Cedar creek, 8 rods wide, 2 feet deep. -------- Some timber, and plenty of willow. After this, the road runs on the bottom through high grass for some distance, and gradually rises to higher land.	1½	116½	914¾
Road descends to low land again. -------- You will now find some deep ravines to cross, but none difficult.	3	119¼	911¾
Road leaves the river, and turns up a ravine. ---------- After ascending the higher land, the road is good and level, except crossing the deep, dry ravines.	1¾	121	909½
Road descends into a ravine. -------- You travel up this ravine a quarter of a mile, mostly through high grass.	2	121½	909½

Prominent Points and Remarks	Dist. miles	From W. Qtrs miles	From CofGSL miles
Old Pawnee village, south side the road - - - - - - - - On the banks of the Loup Fork, but mostly destroyed.	5½	127	904
Road descends from the bluffs. - - - - - - - - After descending here, you cross a creek twelve feet wide, and one foot deep— banks soft, but not difficult. You then travel through high grass and small bushes.	2	127½	903½
Road ascends the bluffs. - - - - - - After travelling about four miles, then turning left from the road, so as to strike the timber you see ahead where it meets the river, the road can be shortened at least a half mile.	4	127 ¾	903¼
Upper ford of the Loup Fork. - - - - - - - - You will find the water in some places near 3 feet deep, and will have to travel down the river about half a mile, to avoid deep holes, and find a good place to get out. (See Note 2.)	6	133	897¼
Road ascends the bluffs. - - - - - - - - After ascending the bluffs you will find a heavy, sandy road for five or six miles.	5¾	139½	891½
Prairie creek, 12 feet wide 1½ feet deep. - - - - - - - - Plenty of water and grass, but no timber. Banks some soft and miry. By taking a southwest course from this creek, you would strike Wood river six or eight miles above the old crossing place, and thence crossing to the Platte, by a course a little west of south, the road may be shortened at least five miles.	18	157½	873½
Dry creek. - - - - - - - - - - - - - - -	1	158½	872½
" " - - - - - - - - - - - - - -	2	159	872
Main Platte river. - - - - - - - - - - You do not come within two miles of the river, until you arrive at Wood river.	6¾	165¾	865¼
Wood river, 12 feet wide, one foot deep. - - - - - - - - Plenty of timber, and a good place to camp. Banks descending, steep, and some soft–but– but good going out. The road now generally runs from one to two miles distant from the main Platte.	3½	169¼	861¾
Road descends to lower land. - - - - - - - The road now runs near the timber for two miles. The grass is high, and a good chance to camp, without turning off the road.	14	183¼	847¾
Road ascend to higher land. - - - - - - - You will probably have to turn off the road some, for the next camping place.	2	185¼	845 ¾
Deep ravine—steep descent. - - - - - - - -	22¾	208	823
" " - - - - - - - - - - - - - Two and a quarter miles beyond this, is a good place to camp, there being plenty of grass and water, on a low bench, about twenty rods south of the road. There is, however, no timber but willow.	4	208¼	822¾
Deep dry creek. - - - - - - - - - - - - No timber on it.	3½	211¾	819¼

Prominent Points and Remarks	Dist. miles	From W. Qtrs miles	From CofGSL miles
Creek or slough, south side the road. - - - - - - - - - Plenty of willows and grass, but doubtful for water.	1¾	213½	817½
Deep, dry creek. - - - - - - - - - - - - The head of Grand Island is about opposite to this creek, but the road now runs so far from the river, we could not ascertain exactly.	4¼	217¾	813¼
Elm creek. - - - - - - - - - - - - - - Deep banks, plenty of timber, but no water, October 9, 1847.	3½	221	810
Road leaves the river near timber. - - - - - - - - This is a pretty good camping place.	6¾	227¾	803¼
Buffalo creek, south side the road. - - - - - - - - A wide creek, with deep banks, but no timber except a few willow bushes. The road runs alongside this creek for three and a half miles.	2	228¼	802¾
Crossing of Buffalo creek. - - - - - - - -	3	231¾	799¼
R. and R., road runs near the river. - - - - - - - - Pretty good chance to camp.	7	239¼	791¾
R. and R., road runs near the river. - - - - - - - - Plenty of buffalo-grass, and short prairie-grass. Plenty of timber on an island, close by.	5¼	244½	786½
Willow Lake, south of the road. - - - - - - - - Good place to water teams, but no timber for camping purposes.	7	251½	779½
Ptah Lake, south of the road. - - - - - - - - The lake is long and very crooked. About a mile before you arrive at it, the road runs near the river a little piece, then leaves it again.	7¼	259¼	771¾
Deep, dry creek. - - - - - - - - - - - -	2½	261¾	769¼
Low, sandy bluffs, extending to the river. - - - - - - - -	14	275¾	755¼
R. and R. near the Sandy Bluffs: Latitude 41° 0′ 47″. - - - - After leaving this place, the road leaves the river, and runs near the foot of the bluffs, to avoid a bad swamp. You will not strike the river for sixteen miles, but will have no difficulty in finding feed and water.	3	278¾	752¼
Skunk creek, six feet wide. - - - - - - - -	2	280¾	750¼
Crossing of Skunk creek. - - - - - - - - Banks some soft, not difficult. No timber.	5	286¼	744¾
Lake or marsh, south of the road. - - - - - - - -	1	287¼	743¾
Lake, south of the road. - - - - - - - - Plenty of grass and water, but no timber nearer than five or six miles.	1	288¾	742¼
Good spring of cold water. - - - - - - - - At the foot of the bluffs, north of the road, and at the head of the Pawnee swamps.	4¼	293	738
Low, sandy bluffs. - - - - - - - - - - This is opposite to the junction of the north and south forks of Platte river. Lat. 41° 7′ 44″; Long. 100° 47′ 15′; Altitude, 2,685 feet.	1¼	294¼	736¾
Carrion creek, 10 feet wide, one foot deep. - - - - - - - - Good place for grass, but no timber near.	3½	297¾	733¼

Prominent Points and Remarks	Dist. miles	From W. Qtrs miles	From CofGSL miles
R. R. and T., road, river and timber. -------- Good place to camp.	4¾	302½	728½
Last timber on north side the river. -------- You will find no more timber on the north side the river for two hundred miles, except one lone tree. Your only dependence for fuel will be buffalo chips and drift wood.	3¾	306¼	724¾
Wide, deep creek. ---------- Plenty of water, October 4, 1847. The banks are high, but not bad to cross.	2¼	308½	722½
R. R. and lake, road and river near a bayou. ---------- Opposite to this place are several islands covered with willow bushes, which will answer for fuel, and there is little difficulty in getting to it.	1¼	309¾	721¼
Black mud creek. ---------- Plenty of water, October 3, 1847, but little feed for teams.	2	311¾	719¼
R. and R., road joins the river. - -------- After this, the road again leaves the river, until you arrive at the north Bluff Fork. Road good, but poor feed.	2	313¾	717¼
Small creek. ------------- Steep banks but very Little water.	3½	317¼	710¼
North Bluff Fork, 6 rods wide, 2 feet deep. ----------- Swift current, muddy water, low banks, quick-sand bottom, but not bad to cross. Poor place for grass.	3½	320¾	710¼
Sandy Bluffs, east foot. -------- The road over these bluffs is very crooked, but not bad. If a road can be made up the bed of the river, it would save at least two miles travel.	1½	322¼	708¾
Sandy Bluffs, west foot. -------- By following the foot of the bluffs, after this, the road may be shortened at least a mile, and be equally as good a road as to follow the river.	4½	326¾	704¼
2d. Sandy Bluffs, east foot. -------- These bluffs are hard on teams, being mostly soft sand.	4	330¾	700¼
2nd. Sandy Bluffs, west foot. --------	1¼	332	699
Bluff Creek, 4 feet wide, 1 foot deep. -------- After this, the road may be made considerably shorter, by following the foot of the bluffs.	4	332¼	698¾
3rd. Sandy Bluffs, east foot. -------- These bluffs are sandy, and heavy on teams. Near the west side you will find several steep places to descend, but not difficult, the sand being soft.	6¼	338½	692½
Small creek, running between the bluffs. -------- Many small Lizards on the sandy places, but they appear to be perfectly harmless.	4	338¾	692¼
Sandy Bluffs, west foot. --------	2	340¾	690¼
Bluff Spring and small creek 200 yards, and one a quarter of a mile. In the neighborhood of these creeks the land is swampy and soft. The road was made close to the bluffs, to avoid the swamps.	4	341	690

Prominent Points and Remarks	Dist. miles	From W. Qtrs miles	From CofGSL miles
Petite creek, 4 feet wide, 9 inches deep. -------- Plenty of water, some muddy, October 1, 1847. Latitude 41° 12' 50".	1	342	689
Picanninni creek, 3 feet wide. -------- Good spring water, and plentiful, October 1, 1847.	1¼	343¼	687¾
Goose creek, 30 feet wide, 3 inches deep. -------- After crossing this, you pass over a low range of bluffs, very sandy, but only a quarter of a mile wide; then you descend on the bottom land again, but will find it soft and springy.	¾	344	687
Small spring creek. --------- Many springs of cold water at the foot of the bluffs.	1¼	345¼	685¾
Small creek, 4 feet wide. -------- Plenty of clear cold water, October 1 1847.	1¼	346½	684½
Duck-weed creek, 10 feet wide. -------- Abundance of good, cold spring water October 1 1847.	4	364¾	684¼
Shoal stream, 3 feet wide. -------- Dry, October 1, 1847..	2	348¾	682¼
Rattlesnake creek, 20 feet wide, 1 ½ ft. deep. --------- Swift current, sandy bottom, but not bad to cross.	3¾	352½	678½
Cedar Bluffs. -------------- On the south side the river. Lat 41° 13' 44". Long. 101° 52'.	1½	354	677
Creek, six feet wide. -------- Water plenty, September 30,1847. Land, in this neighborhood, sandy.	5	359	672
Creek, four feet wide. ------- Plenty of water, September 30, 1847.	2	359½	671½
Crooked Creek, five feet wide. -------- Plenty of water, September 30, 1847.	4	359¾	671¼
Camp Creek, eight; feet wide. --------- Two creeks here, about the same size, but a few rods apart—water cold and plenty, September 30, 1847. No doubt they rise from springs.	4	363¾	667¼
Creek, three feet wide. ------- Plenty of water, Hay 20, but dry, September 30, 1847.	4	367¾	663¼
Pond Creek, four feet wide. -------- Dry, September 30, near the river, but further north many ponds and tall grass.	4	368	663
Wolf Creek, 20 feet wide. -------- At the east foot of Sandy Bluffs, which are bad to cross, you will probably have to double teams, if heavy loaded.	1½	369½	661½
Sandy Bluffs, west foot. ------- Two hundred yard further, is a creek five feet wide.	¾	370¼	660¾
Watch Creek, 8 feet wide, and 2 feet deep. --------- After this, the road runs pretty near the river banks, to avoid some swamps near the bluffs.	3½	373¾	657¼
"Lone Tree," north side the river. -------- About three hundred yards south from the road.	4¼	378	653
Ash Hollow, south side the river. -------- So named from a grove of Ash timber growing on it. It occupies a space of about fifteen or twenty acres, and is surrounded by high bluffs.	2¾	380¾	650¼

Appendix G: The Emigrant's Guide

Prominent Points and Remarks	Dist. miles	From W. Qtrs miles	From CofGSL miles
Castle Creek, 6 rods wide, 2 feet deep. -------- Swift current, quick-sand bottom, water muddy. Low banks, but not good to cross, on account of quick-sands.	3	383¾	647¼
Castle Bluffs, south side the river. -------- You cross no more creeks of water, untill till you arirve at Crab creek, twenty-five and a half miles from here. The road good, except in one place, where you travel three-fourths of a mile over sand.	4¼	388	643
Sand Hill creek, 12 feet wide, south side the road. ------ Near some sandy mounds, on the north side the road.	¾	388¾	642¼
Creek or slough. ---------- Dry.	1½	390¼	640¾
Creek or slough. ---------- Dry.	7½	397¾	633¼
Sandy Bluffs, east foot. ------	3	400¾	630¼
Sandy Bluffs, west foot. ------	2	401¼	629¾
Dry creek. ---------	4	401½	629½
Dry do. -----------	¾	402¼	628¾
Dry creek, 30 feet wide. ------ The road runs near the river, from here to Crab creek.	4	406¼	624¾
Crab Creek, 20 feet wide, very shoal. -------- Two miles further you will see some high bluffs on the right. By ascending one of the highest you will see Chimney Rock, to the west	3	409¼	621¾
Small lake, south of the road. -------- Good chance to camp, without turning from the road.	1¼	410½	620½
Cobble Hills, east foot. ------ You cross three dry creeks before you arrive here and then you travel over another range of sandy bluffs–ascent pretty steep, but not very sandy.	5	415½	615½
Cooble Hills, west foot. ------ After you descend on the low land, you will find it mostly sandy for ten miles, and in some places very heavy drawing.	2¼	417¾	613¼
"Ancient Bluff Ruins," north side the road. Latitude 41° 33' 3". Resembling the ruins of ancient castles, fortifications, &c.; but visitors must be cautious, on account of the many rattlesnakes lurking round, and concealed in the clefts of the bluffs.	1¼	419	612
R. and R., road joins the river. -------- Good place to camp. After this, the road runs near the river, until you arrive at the next low sandy ridges.	10½	429½	601½
Low sandy bluffs, east foot. ---------	7½	437	594
Low sandy bluffs, west foot. --------- After this, the land for several miles, is soft in wet weather, but good traveling in dry weather.	1	438	593
"Chimney Rock," (meridian) south side the river. ------ The higher land now begins to be sandy and barren. Many Prickly-pears and Wild Sage, which continue mostly through the remainderof the journey.	14½	452½	578½

Prominent Points and Remarks	Dist. miles	From W. Qtrs miles	From CofGSL miles
Scott's Bluffs, (mer.) south side the river. -------- The road here is near enough to the river to camp Lat. of meridian 41° 50′ 52″.; Long. 108° 20′.	19½	472	559
Spring Creek, 10 feet wide, 8 inches deep. -------- South of the road. You do not cross it, but travel half a mile alongside. Good water, and many trout in it.	4	476	555
R. and R. road runs near the river. Good chance to camp.	12½	488½	542½
Low sandy bluffs, north side the road. -------- You travel at the foot of these bluffs. but will find the road sandy and heavy on teams.	2¾	491¼	539¾
Creek, about 200 yards south of road. -------- By ascending one of the highest bluffs near, you have a view of "Laramie Peak" in the Black Hills.	2	493¼	537¾
Timber, north side the river. -------- Road here about a quarter of a mile from the river—after this, generally from one to two miles distant. The road to Laramie, very sandy.	11½	504¾	526¼
"Raw Hide" creek, 1 rod wide. -------- Plenty of water June 1st, but dry, Sept. 15, 1847.	5¼	510	521
"Fort John" or Laramie ford. -------- The fort lays about one and a half miles west from the river. The ford is good in low water. River 108 yards wide (See Note 3.)	12	522	509
Steep hill to descend. ------- The descent being over rock, and very steep, makes it dangerous to wagons, but it is not lengthy.	7¼	529¼	501¾
Steep hill to ascend and descend. -------- In travelling over this hill, you will find the road rocky in places, and about half way over there is a sudden turn in the road over rough rocks, which is dangerous to waggons, if care is not taken.	4½	533¾	497¼
Road leaves the river. ------- At this point, the road bends to the southwest, leaving the river. You will not come to the river banks again for eighty miles.	¾	534½	496½
"Warm Springs," Lat. 42° 15′ 6″. -------- This is a very strong spring of clear water, but it is warmer than river water, at all seasons of the year.	1 ¾	536¼	494¾
Very steep bluff, half a mile up. -------- Before arriving at this, you pass through a narrow ravine, between bluffs. The ascent is unpleasant, on account of cobble stones.	1¼	537½	493½
"Porter's Rock," left of the road -------- A mile beyond this, you descend to the lower land again. The descent is steep, lengthy and sandy.	4¾	542¼	488¾
Bitter Creek and Cold Spring. -------- This was dry, September 13. Here is plenty of timber, and if there is no water, you will find plenty three and a half miles further.	4¼	546½	484½
Bitter Creek—second crossing. ---------	¾	547¼	483¾
Bend in the road. ---------- Road turns south about two hundred yards, to avoid a deep ravine, then back again the same distance.	2	549¼	481¾

Appendix G: The Emigrant's Guide

Prominent Points and Remarks	Dist. miles	From W. Qtrs miles	From CofGSL miles
Dead Timber creek, 10 feet wide. -------- Plenty of timber, grass and water.	¾	550	481
Creek, south side the road. -------- You don't cross this creek, but go just above it. It is a good chance to camp.	1½	551½	479½
Small creek and spring: Lat. 42° 21′ 51″ -------- Not safe to depend on for a camping place. Little grass and not much water–dry, September 13, 1847.	7¾	559¼	471¾
Steep hill' quarter mile up. -------- Pleasant view of the surrounding country from the summit. The descent steep in several places, and many cobble stones in the road.	4	559½	471½
"Horse Creek" and Heber's Spring. -------- The spring lays a little to the right of the road, at the edge of timber. If it is dry, there is water in the creek, about one hundred yards north from this spring.	5½	565	466
Bluff ¾ths of a mile to the summit. ----------- Difficult to ascend on account of six or seven steep places, where you will probably have to double teams.	2½	567½	463½
Small creek: Lat. 42° 29′ 58″. -------- After crossing this, you cross five others, about a mile apart, but none of them safe to depend on for a camping place, being little grass, and less (if any) water.	2¼	569¾	461¼
5th small creek from the last. -------- After crossing this, you ascend a high bluff, the top of which is asuccession of hills and hollows for five miles. The road is good, but crooked.	4¾	574½	456½
"La Bonte" river, 30 feet wide, 2 ft. deep. -------- Good place to camp—plenty of timber, grass, and water. There is also a good chance, a mile further. Plenty of wild mint on the creek.	8¼	582¾	448¼
Branch of La Bonte, 10 feet wide, 18 inches deep. --------- Doubtful about water. Steep banks. You have now travelled near a mile over this dark, red sand, and will find it continue three and a half miles further.	5	587¾	443¼
Very small creek. ----------- Little chance for grass, and less for water. One mile beyond this, you ascend another bluff, but the road is tolerably straight and good. Look out for toads with horns and tails.	6¼	594	437
Very small creek. ----------- Very poor chance for camping.	6¼	600¼	430¾
Very small creek. ----------- The road runs down the channel of this creek, near two hundred yards but there is little grass on it.	2	600¾	430¼
A La Prele river, one rod wide, 2 ft. deep. -------------- Current rapid—good place to camp. Land between creeks mostly sandy and barren. Road from here to the Platte very uneven, being a succession of hills and hollows	1½	602¼	428¾
Small creek. -------------- No place to camp—doubtful for water.	4¼	606½	424½

Prominent Points and Remarks	Dist. miles	From W. Qtrs miles	From CofGSL miles
Box Elder creek, 5 feet wide. - - - - - - - - Clear water, and plenty—but not much grass. Not very good to cross, banks being steep. Some timber on it.	1	607½	423½
Fourche Boise river, 30 feet wide, 2 feet deep: Lat. 42° °51′ 5″. - Current rapid. Plenty of good grass and timber.	3¼	610¾	420¼
North fork of Platte river. - - - - - - - - Not much grass here. You will now find a sandy road and heavy traveling.	4	614¾	416¼
"Deep Creek," 30 feet wide, two feet deep: Lat. 42° 52′ 50″: Altitude, 4,864 feet. - - - - - - - - Lovely place to camp. Swift current, clear water, and abundance of fish. Nice grove of timber on the banks, and a coal mine about a quarter of a mile up, on the east side. After this, you will find sandy roads for nine miles, but not much grass.	5	619¾	411¼
Deep hollow, or ravine— steep banks. - - - - - - - -	2½	622¼	408¾
Sudden bend in the road. - - - - - - To avoid a deep ravine.	5 ¾	628	403
Grove of timber on the banks of the river. - - - - - - - - Good chance to camp. Lat 42° 51′ 47″.	1	629	402
Crooked, muddy creek, 12 ft. wide, 1 deep. - - - - - - - - - - - Not good to cross—steep banks. Plenty of grass, but no wood.	1	630	401
Muddy creek, 3 feet wide. - - - - - - - - Soft banks and bad to cross. Considerable small timber. but little grass. After this, good but crooked road.	5¾	635¾	395¼
Deep gulf. - - - - - - - - - - - - - - -	2¾	638½	392½
Creek, two feet wide. - - - - - - - - No place to camp.	1½	640	391
Muddy creek, 5 feet wide, 1½ feet deep. - - - - - - - - No chance to camp.	1	641	390
2 ravines, near together: Lat. 42° 51′ 44″. - - - - - - - - Opposite here there is a fording place, where companies generally have forded the river.	3	644	387
Creek five feet wide. - - - - - - - - Abundance of fish, early in the season, but little grass and no timber.	3	647	384
Upper Platte ferry and ford. - - - - - - - - Plenty of feed and some timber on both sides the river (See Note 4.) Lat 42° 50′ 18″. Altitude 4,875 feet.	1½	648½	382½
Road turns south, and rises a long hill. - - - - - - - - Ascent gradual. Many singular looking rocks on the south side. Descent rough and crooked. Towards the foot, road very uneven.	7	655½	375½
Mineral spring and lake. - - - - - - - - Considered poisonous. No bad taste to the water, unless the cattle trample in it. In that case it becomes black, and is doubtless poisonous. No timber near.	5½	661	370
Rock avenue and steep descent. - - - - - - - - The road here passes between high rocks, forming a kind of avenue or gateway, for a quarter of a mile.	7½	668½	362½

APPENDIX G: THE EMIGRANT'S GUIDE 175

Prominent Points and Remarks	Dist. miles	From W. Qtrs miles	From CofGSL miles
Alkali swamps amd springs. -------- This ought to be avoided as a camping ground—it is a small valley, surrounded by high bluffs. The land exceeding miry and smells bad. There is a creek of good water northwest. No timber and little grass. Next mile rough road.	2	670½	360½
Small stream of clear spring water. -------- Good camping place. Plenty of grass, but no wood.	4	674½	356½
"Willow Spring." ---------- About three rods west of the road, at the foot of willow bushes. Water cold and good—grass plenty, but creek some miry.	2 ¾	677¼	353 ¾
"Prospect Hill," (summit.) -------- Pleasant view of the surrounding country, to the Sweet Water mountains.	1	678¼	352 ¾
Bad slough. --------------- Plenty of grass, but little water. A mile further is a hill, both steep ascending and descending.	3¼	681½	349½
Creek, 300 yards south of road. -------- Plenty of grass, but no wood.	1 ¾	683¼	347 ¾
Small creek, left of the road. -------- Grass plentiful, but doubtful for water, and no wood. The road runs alongside this creek for half a mile.	2½	685 ¾	345¼
Grease-wood creek, 6 feet wide 1 ft. deep. -------- Very little grass, and no fuel but wild sage. Road from here to the Sweet Water sandy, and very heavy.	1 ¾	687½	343½
Alkali springs and lakes. -------- Here Father your Saleraetus from a lake, west of the road. Land swampy, and smells bad. Water poisonous.	6¼	693 ¾	337¼
"Sweet-water river," 8 rods wide, 2 ft. deep. ------------- Swift current—good water. Grass plentiful, but little timber. (See Note 5.)	4¼	698	333
Independence Rock and ford. ---- On the north side of the river—about six hundred yards long, and a hundred and twenty wide, composed of hard Granite. (See Note 5.)	5¼	704	327
Devil's Gate. -------------- A little west from the road. The river here passes between perpendicular rocks four hundred feet high.—This is a curiosity worthy of a traveler's notice.	5¼	704	327
Creek two feet wide. -------- Not good to cross. The road runs near the river banks for ten miles after this.	2	704½	326½
Creek, 6 feet wide. --------- Good to cross. Water and grass plenty, but lacks timber. You will find grass all along on the banks of the river, but very little wood.	2	705	326
Deep ravine and creek. ------- Plenty of grass and water, but no wood.	6¼	711¼	319¾
Deep ravine and creek. -------- Doubtful for water.	¾	715	319

Prominent Points and Remarks	Dist. miles	From W. Qtrs miles	From CofGSL miles
Road leaves the river: Lat. 42° 28′ 25″. --------- Road after this, sandy and heavy, and passes over a high bluff. Land barren for seven and a half miles. (See Note 6.)	3	715	316
Alkali Lake. --------- On the left of the road.	2	715½	315½
Sage creek. ---------- No grass. High banks. Doubtful for water, but Wild Sage plentiful. One and three-quarter miles further you arrive on the river banks again.	4¾	720¼	310¾
Creek, three feet wide. ------- Doubtful for water, but the road runs close to the river.	4	724¼	306¾
High gravelly bluff. -------- Left of the road, and a very good place to camp.	1¼	725½	305½
Bitter-cotton-wood creek. ------- Doubtful for water and grass. Some timber on it. After this, the road leaves the river for six miles.	1½	727	304
Road arrives at the river. --------- 	6¼	733¼	297¾
Leave the old road and ford the river. --------- By fording here, the road is shorter, and you avoid much very heavy, sandy road. Lat. 42° 31′20″.	4	733½	297½
Road turns between the rocky ridges. --------- After this, you ford the river twice—but it is easily forded. Then the road leaves the river again.	1½	735	296
Ford No. 4—good camping place. --------- After this, the road leaves the river again, and you will probably find no water fit to drink for sixteen and a half miles.	8	743	288
Ice Spring. --------------- This is on a low, swampy spot of land on the right of the road. Ice may generally be found, by digging down about two feet. There are two alkali lakes a little further.	5¾	748¾	282¼
Alkali springs. ------------ On the left of the road.	4	749	282
Steep descent from the bluffs. -------- 	9½	758½	272½
Ford of Sweet-water, No. 5. -------- Plenty of good grass and willow bushes. River about three rods wide, and two feet deep.	1	759½	271½
Creek a rod wide. ----------- Doubtful for water.	4	759¾	271¼
Bluff or hill, 1½ miles to summit. -------- The ascent gradual, though steep in some places.	4	760	271
Road joins the river, and fords it. -------- The river is forded here, to avoid crossing the next big, sandy ridge, making the road much better, and some shorter.	3½	763½	267½
Ford back. -------------- 	2	764	267
River banks and stream, 25 feet wide. -------- This appears to be a branch of the river, running round a piece of land, about a quarter of a mile wide.	2	764½	266½

Prominent Points and Remarks	Dist. miles	From W. Qtrs miles	From CofGSL miles
Creek, two feet wide: Lat. 42° 28′ 36″. - - - - - - - - - A good cold spring, a little to the right of the road and a soft swamp just below, but it is a good place to camp.	3	767½	263½
Road leaves the river. - - - - - - - Good camping place. After this, the road winds around and over a succession of hills and hollows, for three miles.	2	769½	261½
Rough, rocky ridges. - - - - - - - - Dangerous to wagons, and ought to be crossed with care.	2½	772	259
Soft swamp and very small creek. - - - - - - - - No place to camp.	3	775	256
Creek, a foot wide. - - - - - - - - -	1¼	776¾	254¼
Creek, two feet wide. - - - - - - - -	4	777	254
Strawberry creek, five feet wide. - - - - - - - - Plenty of grass and water, and some willows. Good place to camp. There is a popular grove about a mile below.	2	779	252
Quaking-aspen creek. - - - - - - - - This rises in a small grove of timber on the south side the road, but is not safe to depend on for water.	1	780	251
Branch of Sweet-water, 2 rods wide, two feet deep. - - - - - - - Good place to camp. Water good and cold. Grass and willows, plenty.	2¼	782¾	248¼
Willow creek, 8 feet wide, 2 feet deep. - - - - - - - - Good camping place for grass, water and willows. The ford is near three rods wide.	2¼	785	246
Sweet-water, 3 rods wide, 3 feet deep. - - - - - - - - Good place to camp. After travelling seven miles beyond this, and passing between the Twin mounds, you will find a good camping place a quarter of a mile north of the road.	4¾	789¾	241¼
SOUTH PASS, or summit of dividing ridge. - - - - - - - - - This is the dividing rifge between the waters of the Atlantic and Pacific. Altitude, 7,085 feet.	9¾	799½	231½
Pacific creek and springs. - - - - - - - - Abundance of grass any where for a mile. Good water and plenty of Wild Sage for fuel.	3	802½	228 ½
Pacific creek (crossing) three feet wide: Lat. 42° 18′ 58″: **Long. 108° 40′ 0″.** - - - - - - - - Not good to cross. Pretty good place to camp, except for wood. After you leave here you will find a good road, but very little water	1½	804	227
Dry Sandy. - - - - - - - - - - - - - - The water brackish, and not good for cattle. Very little grass, but no wood.	9	813	218
Junction of California and Oregon roads. - - - - - - - - Take the left hand road. Good road a few miles, afterwards sandy and heavy.	6	819	212
Little Sandy, 20 feet wide, 2½ feet deep. - - - - - - - - Muddy water—swift current. Plenty of willows and wild sage. Abundance of grass down the stream. After this, barren and sandy land	7¾	826¾	204¼

Prominent Points and Remarks	Dist. miles	From W. Qtrs miles	From CofGSL miles
Big Sandy, 7 rods wide, 2 feet deep: Lat. 42° 6' 42". - - - - - - - - - Good chance to camp. A few miles further, you wild find a short piece of rough road, over rocks and cobble stones. No grass or water after this for 17 miles.	8¼	835	196
Big Sandy. - - - - - - - - - Good chance to camp. After this, barren, sandy land and heavy road till you arrive at Green river.	17	852	179
Green river ford, 16 rods wide. - - - - - - - - Good camping any where on the banks, and plenty of timber. It is notdifficult fording in low water, but if too high to ford, the best crossing place is up stream. Latitude—2 miles above—41° 52' 3"; Long. 109° 30'. Alt. 6,000 feet.	10	862	169
Good camping place on Green river. - - - - - - - - Plenty of grass here. But no other very good chance to camp on this side the river.	1½	863½	167½
Road leaves Green river. - - - - - - - - No grass nor water after this for fifteen and a half miles. Land rolling,barren—mostly sandy, and several steep places to pass	3½	867	164
Black's fork, 6 rods wide, 2 feet deep. - - - - - - - - Good chance to camp, and a nice place, though not much timber.	15½	882½	148½ 144¾
Ham's fork, 3 rods wide, 2 feet deep. - - - - - - - - Rapid current, cold water, plenty of bunch grass and willows, and is a good campground.	3¾	886¼	
Black's fork again. - - - - - - - - Not much grass, but plenty of willows. You will now have some uneven road, with many ravines.	1¾	888	143
Small creek, 2 feet wide. - - - - - No grass, and probably no water.	10¾	898¾	132¼
Black's fork, third time. - - - - - - After crossing you will find a good camping place. Plenty of bunch grass; also, wild flax.	2	900 ¾	130¼
Black's fork, fourth time. - - - - - You ford again at a good camping place.	2¼	903	128
Stream 2 rods wide, 2 feet deep. - Very swift current, and plenty of bunch grass. Road pretty rough after this.	2¾	905¾	125¼
Stream—good camping place at a bend. - - - - - - - - You do not cross the stream, but there is a good camping place, where the road passes a bend of the creek.	3½	909¼	121¾
"Fort Bridger:" Lat. 41° 19' 13"; Long. 110° 5'; Altitude, 6,665 feet.- - - - - - - - You cross four rushing creeks, within half a mile, before you reach the Fort, and by traveling half a mile beyond the Fort, you will cross three others, and then find a good place to camp. The Fort is composed of four long houses and a small enclosure for horses. Land exceeding rich—water cold and good, and considerable timber. (See Note No. 1 after Great Salt Lake)	8¼	917½	113½

Appendix G: The Emigrant's Guide

Prominent Points and Remarks	Dist. miles	From W. Qtrs miles	From CofGSL miles
Cold Springs, on the right side the road. - - - - - - - - There is timber here, and it is a pretty good camping place.	6¼	923 ¾	107¼
Small creek and springs. - - - - - - - - No feed here, and no place to camp.	1¼	925	106
Summit of High Ridge: Lat. 41° 16' 11". - - - - - - - - After this, you travel several miles on tolerably level land, then you descend to lower land by a steep, tedious route.	1	926	105
Muddy Fork, 12 feet wide. - - - - - - - - Plenty of bunch grass and willows. Water clear, and not bad tasted. After this, you will probably find no good water for eleven miles.	4½	930½	100½
Copperas, or Soda Spring. - - - - - - - - Left of the road at the foot of a hill. The rod now begins to ascend another high ridge.	3¾	934¼	96¾
Summit of Ridge: Altitude 7,315 feet. - - - - - - - - The descent is lengthy, and some tedious. About half way down you pass over rough rocks, and the pass being narrow, makes it dangerous to wagons.	1¾	936	95
Copperas, or Soda Spring. - - - - - - - - Cattle will drink this water, and there is plenty of grass around it. A little further the road turns to the left and passes down a narrow ravine.	1	937	94
Spring of good water, south side the road. - - - - - - - - - - - - This is surrounded by high grass, close to the creek side. There is another spring a little further on the north side the road, which will probably be the last water you will find till you arrive at Sulphur creek.	4½	941½	89½
East foot of dividing ridge. - - - - - - - - Dividing ridge between the waters of the Colorado and Great Basin. Ascent very steep and crooked—narrow summit and steep descending. After this, crooked road between mountains. Altitude of ridge, 7,700 feet.	1	942½	88½
Sulphur creek, 10 feet wide. - - - - - - - - Plenty of grass and some willows; also, small cedar at the foot of the mountain. (See Note 7).	6	948½	82½
Bear river, 6 rods wide, 2 feet deep. - - - - - - - - Swift current—clear cold water; plenty of timber and grass. Altitude at ford, 6,836 feet.	1¾	950¼	80¾
Summit of Ridge. - - - - - - - - - - Half a mile further you cross a small ridge, then descend into, and travel down a nice narrow bottom, where is plenty of grass. (See Note No. 2 after Great Salt Lake)	2¾	953	78
Spring of clear, cold water. - - - - - - - - On the south side the creek, about two rods from the road. The spring is deep—water clear, cold and good. Perhaps it will not be easy to find, being surrounded by high grass.	1¾	954¾	76¼
Yellow creek, cross at foot of rocky bluffs. - - - - - - - - You will soon cross this again, and about a mile further, you ascend another long ridge, the ascent being pretty steep and tedious.	4¾	959½	71½
Summit of Ridge. - - - - - - - - - - Descent pretty steep. About three–fourths of a mile down from the summit, is a spring of good cold water, on the left of the road.	1 ¾	961¼	69¾

Prominent Points and Remarks	Dist. miles	From W. Qtrs miles	From CofGSL miles
Cache Cave and head of Echo creek: Altitude, 6,070 feet. ---- Cave in the bluffs north. Several springs along the road before you arrive here, and one, a quarter of a mile south from the Cave. Plenty of grass, and a good place to camp.	3¾	965	66
Cold spring, on the right of the road. -------- This also is a good place to camp, being plenty of grass.	2	967	64
Cold spring, south side the road. -------- At the foot of a high hill. Good place to camp. After this, you travel down a narrow ravine, between high mountains, till you arrive at Weber river. Not much difficulty for camping down it.	2¼	969¼	61¾
Deep ravine. ---------- Steep on both banks. After this, you will cross Echo creek a number of times, but in no place very difficult.	1¼	970½	60½
Red fork of Weber river: Alt. 5,301 feet. -------- There is a good camping place a mile before you arrive here. Also, almost any where on the banks of the river. Plenty of timber. The stream abounds with spotted trout.	16	986½	44½
Weber river ford, 4 rods wide, 2 ft. deep. -------- Good to ford. Plenty of grass and timber on both sides the river.	4	990½	40½
Pratt's Pass, to avoid the Kanyon. -------- The Kanyon is a few miles below, where the river runs between high mountains of rocks. Some emigrants have passed through, but it is dangerous.	2	991	40
East foot of Long hill. ------- There is a small creek descends down the hollow up which the road is made. There are several springs near the road.	1	992	39
Bridge (over the creek.) -------- Not a bad place to camp.	2¼	994¼	36¾
Summit of Ridge. ---------- The country west looks rough and mountainous. The descent is not pleasant, being mostly on the side hill.	2½	996¾	34¼
Small creek, left of the road. -------- Good place to camp. Plenty of grass, water and willows. The road here turns north a quarter of a mile, then west and ascends a steep hill.	1¾	998½	32½
Kanyon creek, 1 rod wide, 1 foot deep: Lat. 40° 54' 7". ------ You have to cross this creek thirteen times, besides two bad swamps. The road is dangerous to wagons, on account of dense, high bushes, trees, and short turns in the road. Good place to camp. (See Note 9.)	2 ¾	1001¼	29¾

Prominent Points and Remarks	Dist. miles	From W. Qtrs miles	From CofGSL miles
Leave Kanyon creek. -------- Here you turn to the right and begin to ascend the highest mountain you cross in the whole journey. You travel through timber, some on side bills, and cross the creek a number of times.	8	1009¼	21¾
Small spring, left of the road. -------- You will probably find water in several places, but it is uncertain where, as it runs but a little way in a place, and then sinks in the earth.	3	1012¼	18¾
Summit of mountain. Altitude, 7,245 feet. --------- You have now a view of the south part of the Valley of the Great Salt Lake. The descent is steep, lengthy and tedious on account of stumps in the road.	1	1013¼	17 ¾
Bridge over a deep ravine. -------- This is dangerous to cross, and a wagon may be easily upset. The road lays throug a forest of small timber, and is unpleasant traveling.	4	1014	17
Brown's creek and spring. -------- Not a bad place to camp, but there is a much better one, half a mile lower down.	¾	1014¾	16¼
Cold spring on Brown's creek. -------- Within a rod of the road, on the east side, under a grove of Black Birch bushes. Good place to camp, but some miry. Good camping any where for two miles lower.	2¾	1017½	13½
Leave Brown's creek. -------- You now ascend another high mountain, by a steep and crooked road. On both sides this mountain, there are many Serviceberry bushes.	1¾	1019¼	11¾
Summit of last ridge. ------- The descent is very steep, all the way, till you arrive on the banks of Last Creek	1	1020¼	10
Last creek. ---------- You cross this creek nineteen times. Several of the crossings are difficult. There are several side hills which require care in teamsters. Three camping places on it but the road is rough.	¾	1021	10¾
Mouth of the Kanyon. ------- You now enter the Valley of the Salt Lake. The road at the mouth of the Kanyon bad, and rough with stumps. Afterwards, descending and good.	5	1026	5
CITY OF THE GREAT SALT LAKE.	5	1031	—

 The city is located within three miles of the mountains, which enclose the east side of the valley—within three miles of the Utah outlet, and twenty-two miles of Salt Lake. The land is gradually sloping, from the mountain to within a mile of the Outlet, and is of a black, loose, sandy nature. A stream of water rushes from the mountains east of the city, and, at the upper part, it divides in two branches, both of which pass through the city to the Outlet. The water is good, and very cold, and abundance for mill purposes, or for irrigation. The air is good and pure, sweetened by the healthy breezes from the Salt Lake. The grass is rich and plentiful, and well filed with rushes, and the passes in the mountains afford abundance of good timber, mostly *balsam* Fir.
 The valley is about forty miles long, and from twenty to twenty-five miles wide. It is beautifully surrounded on the west, south, and east by high mountains. Salt Lake extends from a point a little south of west, from the city, to about eighty miles north, forming the north-western boundary of the valley. There are two sulphur springs a mile and a half north from the *TEMPLE BLOCK; the water is salt, and a little warmer than blood:

two miles further north there is a sulphur spring of boiling water. There is not much land on the north part of the valley fit for cultivation; but the east side is well adapted for farming, being well watered by several large creeks, and the soil beautiful. The land on the west of the Utah Outlet, is also good for farming, and easily irrigated from the south end of the Outlet.

The latitudes, longitudes, and altitudes are copied from the observations and calculations made by Elder O PRATT.

BIRMINGHAM JOURNAL

The variation of the magnetic needle, at the City of the Great Salt Lake, 15° 47' 23" east, as determined on the 30th July, A. D. 1847, by the mean of several observations, and calculations of the Sun's Azimuths and Altitudes.

*Latitude of northern boundary of Temple Block, 40° 45' 44".

Longitude of do.　　do.　　do.　　11° 26' 34".

Altitude of　do.　　do.　　do.　　1,300 feet.

Note 1. Travelers at present reaching Fort Bridger from the east over the Lincoln Highway will not "cross four rushing streams, within half a mile" of the Fort. Mr. William A. Carter, son of Colonel William A. Carter, successor of Bridger, is of the opinion that the site of the old Fort was along the highway; others have presumed it to be a little west of that point and close to the "east" divided stream of Black's Fork. Alter, in his "James Bridger", shows an "Original Fort Bridger Survey", made by Hockaday for Bridger in 1853. This sketch shows four divisions of Black's Creek (Black's Fork). To reach the Fort from the east you would cross two divisions of Black's Fork; the fort was located on the right hand bank of a third division. The present highway from the east crosses two canals before reaching the monument and Fort Bridger. Mr. Carter states that these "canals" were originally branches of Black's Fork and in use before the water was appropriated. [Ed.]

Note 2. "Note 8" does not appear in the itinerary of the Emigrants' Guide. The original Mormon Pioneers of 1847 traveled on a route south of the present city of Evanston, Wyoming, and crossed the Bear River near "Myers' Crossing". There are three summits between notes 7 and 9 in the itinerary; the Mormons reached the first summit two and three quarter's miles after crossing the Bear River. Note VIII in the Emigrants' Guide and Clayton's journal both emphasize high rocks to the right at this point, now called the "Needles". After crossing the summit, a spring of clear cold water was reached and Yellow Creek was crossed four and three quarter's miles beyond the spring. In his Journal, Clayton states that they camped at noon in a "Narrow Bottom", eight milels from the Bear River. The next summit mentioned in the itinerary is eleven miles from Bear River, and the third summit is forty-six and one-half miles from Bear River. I have concluded, therefore, that Note 8 should have appeared under the "First summit". [Ed.]

EMIGRANTS' GUIDE
NOTES

NOTE, I. If the Elk Horn river is fordable, you leave the main road a mile before you strike the river, and turn north. After leaving the road *three-fourths* of a mile, you will cross a very bad creek or slough, being soft and miry; but, by throwing in long grass, it will be good crossing. You then travel three-fourths of a mile further, and arrive at the ford. You will go up stream when fording, and gradually come nearer to the opposite shore, till you strike a piece of low land on the west side; you then pass by a narrow, crooked road, through the timber, till you arrive on the open prairie. You will then see a *post* erected in near a south direction, about a mile distant. Go straight to that post, and you will find a good bridge over the creek—and there, again strike the main road. From here, you have before you near, five hundred miles travel over a flat, level country, and a good road, with the ereeption of several sandy bluffs mentioned herein. The road generally runs from one to two miles from the Platte river, but not too far to turn off to camp in case of necessity. All camping places, which lay near the road, are mentioned in this work. You will find near two hundred miles without timber, but in that region you will find plenty of buffalo chips, which are a good substitute for fuel. Buffalo are numerous after you arrive at the head of Grand Island, and continue two hundred miles.

NOTE II. The descent to the ford is steep, and at the bottom very sandy. Your best chance to ford will, probably, be to enter the river opposite to where you descend from the bluff; then go near a straight course, but inclining a little down stream, till more than half way over, when you will find a sand-bar. Follow this, down stream near half a mile, and you will then see a good place to go out on the south side. In this river the channels often change-the old ones flill up and new ones are made hence, the wisdom and necessity of having several men go across on on horses, to find the best route, before you attempt to take wagons over. If this precaution is not taken, you may plunge your wagons from a sand-bar into a deep hole, and do much damage. If you ford up stream, and come out higher than where you enter, after crossing, strike for the bluffs, in a direction a very little west of south, till you arrive on the old road.

On arriving at Prairie creek, if you take a south-west course, a short day's drive will bring you to Wood river? six or eight miles above where the old road crosses; and by keeping the same course after crossing Wood river you will strike the Platte ten or twelve miles above where Wood river empties into it. By this means the road would be shortened at least five miles, and probably much more.

NOTE III. Fort "John, or Laramie," lays about one and a half miles from the river, in near a south-west course, and is composed of a trading establishment, and about twelve houses, enclosed by a wall eleven feet high. The wall and houses are built of *abode,* or Spanish brick. It is situated on the Laramie Fork, and is a pleasant location: the latitude of the Fort is 42° 12' 13"; longitude 104° 11' 53", and altitude above the sea, 4,090 feet. After leaving here you begin to cross the "Black Hills," and will find rough roads, high ridges, and mostly barren country. There is, however, not much difficulty in finding good camping places, each day's travel, by observng the annexed table.

There is a road follows the river, instead of crossing the Black Hills, and it is represented as being as near, and much better traveling if the river is fordable. By following this road you have to cross the rrver three times extra, but will find plenty of grass, wood, and water. If the river is fordable at Laramie, it is fordable at those three places, and you can go that route safely.

NOTE IV. The best place to ford will probably be a little below the bend in the river. After this you have fifty miles to travel, which is dangerous to teams, on account of Alkali springs. Great care should be taken to avoid them, by selecting a camping place where none of these springs are near.

NOTE V. In low water the river is easily forded opposite to the Rock Independence; but, if not fordable here, a good place can be found a mile higher up the river.

Independence Rock is one of the curiosities to be seen on the road, mostly on account of its peculiar shape and magnitude. There are many names of visitors painted in various places, on the south-east corner. At this corner most travelers appear to have gone up to view the top; but there is a much better place on the north side, about half way from end to end. Latitude 1½ miles below 42° 30' 16".

The road along the Sweet Water is mostly sandy and heavy traveling. You will find many steep places, and as you approach the Rocky Mountains, you will find some high hills to travel over.

After crossing the mountains the country is level, but still barren, and, if possible, more sandy. You will have to make some long drives to obtain water for camping. There is great lack of timber, from the Upper Platte ferry to Fort Bridger, and in feet scarcely any kind but willows. In all this region the willows and wild sage form your chief ingredient for fuel.

NOTE VI It is supposed that a good road can be made here by following the banks of the river. If so, these high bluffs, and much sandy road, would be avoided.

NOTE VII. At the foot of the mountain, on the south side the road, and at the edge of the creek, there is a strong sulphur spring. A little above the spring, on the side of the mountain, is a bed of stone coal. At the foot of the bluff, west of where you cross the creek, is a noble spring of pure, cold water; and about a mile from this place, in a south-west course, is a "Tar," or "Oil Spring," covering a surface of several rods of ground. There is a wagon trail runs within a short distance of it. It is situated in a small hollow, on the left of the wagon trail, at a point where the trail rises a higher bench of land.

When the oil can be obtained free from sand, it is useful to oil wagons. It gives a nice polish to gun-stocks, and has been proved to be highly beneficial when applied to sores on horses, cattle, &c.

NOTE VIII. From the summit of this ridge, you will see to the west, a ridge of high, rough, peaked rocks. The road runs at the south foot of that ridge, and there crosses Yellow creek. From the place where you now stand, the road runs through a beautiful narrow valley, surrounded by gently rolling hills, and is pretty straight and pleasant traveling, till you arrive at that ridge of rocks. There is little difficulty in finding a good camping place, between here and the ridge in view, except for fuel, which is scarce. There are several springs of good water the creek.

NOTE IX. On this creek is a very rough piece of road; the bushes are high, and road narrow, in consequence of which wagon covers are liable to be torn, and bows broke. There are many short turns in it, where wagon tongues are liable to be broke. Some of the crossing places are bad. There is a good camping place where first you strike the creek—one about half way up, and one a quarter of a mile before you leave the creek.

The ascent up the next mountain is both lengthy and tedious, mostly through high tumber, and there are many stumps in the road. It is a chance whether you will find any water till you descend on the west side.

From this creek to the valley is decidedly the worst piece of road on the whole journey, but the distance is short, and by using care and patience, it is easily accomplished.

Please Note! The commentary and notes on pages 184-186 are taken from the *Emigrant's Guide...* published as a part of the book *A Journal of the Birmingham Emigrating Company...* by Leander V. Loomis, Edited by Edgar M. Ledyard, published in Salt Lake City Utah by Legal Printing Company, Exchange Place, 1928, pages 172-176.

APPENDIX H

Handcart Logbook for 20 March – 6 June 1856
LIVERPOOL, ENGLAND TO IOWA CITY, IOWA

A day-by-day timeline of the Enoch Train Pioneers

20 March 1856 - Thursday
"went to the Enoch Train and received a Berth. visited the Saints in the "Emigrants Home" bought some things for the voyage. Visited Bro. Perks P.M. accompanied Bro. Ferguson to the Ship. E. Train. Spent the afternoon with him, we Took tea at Bro. Perks. Evening we visited at the Conference House, and finished Packing up. Met Bro. Joseph A. Young, Wm G. Young, Edwd Martin, Jesse Haven, F. O. Leonard, Wm C Dunbar, Johns Kay, Samuel A. Little and Daniel D. McArthur all from the baley. we Spent a good time together about ½ past 2 o'clock we retired to rest." [McAllister, p. 103]

Archer Walters booked his families passage at the office, 36 Islington. [Walters]

½ past 9 P.M. Sister Thomas Lyon delivered of a baby daughter on board ship named Christina Enoch, delivered by Sister Janett Hardie from Edinburgh. [McAllister p. 104]

21 March 1856 - Friday
"The ship was towed out about 8 o'clock. Rations served out on the river. All went on very well. ...A band of music abroad ..." [Walters]

"went on board and assisted in serving out provisions. P. M. went to Bro. Perks along with Bro. McArthur Took tea. Evening attended meeting at 26 Idlington. Bro. Franklin Presided. present of brethren from Zion, James Ferguson, C ... Wheelock, W. C. Dunbar, Jim Haven, E. L. Ellsworth, L. D. Rudd, I. A. Hunt, J. O. Lenard, E. Martin Sfrien[?], W. Crandall, N. T. Posty[?].

James Ferguson was unanimously chosen to Preside over the Saints on the Enoch Train. Edmund Ellsworth and Daniel D. McArthur his Counselors. The Brethren felt well and spoke their feelings which were good. Bro. Franklin and Wheelock Blessed us in the name of the Lord....Seperated at Midnight. Bro. McArthur and I slept at Bro. Perks. C on board the Ship at ½ past 9 o'clock. Sister Thomas Lyon was delivered of a Daughter named Christina Enoch. She was waited upon by Sister Janett Hardie from Edinburgh." [McAllister, p. 104]

"While lying at anchor during the night of Friday March 21, a sister Mary Lyon, wife of Elder Thomas Lyon, was delivered of a daughter, which was named Christina Enoch." [*Millenial Star*]

22 March - Saturday
"A. M. went to the office and received £5.0.0 from President Richards. Signed a Promisory note for the Same. At 10 o'clock went on board the ship with President Richards, Bro Wheelock, Ferguson, Ellsworth, McArthur, Hunts, Dunbar, Rudd, Porter and many others of the Brethren. The Ship's Company of Emigrating Saints was assembled on the quarter deck and received us with cheers, all passed the Doctor and Government officers, after which Bro. Franklin ... Ferguson and several other Brethren left the Ship while the band under Ellsworth direction played "Auld Langsyn" and we gave them ...three cheers at a quarter to 3 P. M. Bro. Ellsworth Called us together and after a short address I was Chosen Clerk of the Company. on motion of Elder E. Ellsworth, seconded by Elder D. D. McArthur that the Ships Company be divided into 5 wards and that Elder John A. Hunt Preside over No. 1 ward and that Elder N. L. Porter over No. 2. Elder A. Galloway over No. 3, Elder S. W. Crandall over no. 4 and Elder T. Leonard over no. 5 also was Chosen Captain

of the Guard, the fore going motion was carried unamiously after a few remarks by Elder Ellsworth, we numbered off the wards prepared the guard List and posted the Guard at 8 o'clock. Prayers were attended to by the Presidents of the wards and all retired to rest. I was called upon to accompany Bro. Wheelock and Ferguson ashore, returned between 9 and 10, and 1 I retired to Rest." [McAllister, p. 105]

23 March - Sunday *1

Departed Liverpool on 23 March 1856. [Hafen, p.56]

"A. M. at 6 o'clock the horn was blown. The Decks were Cleaned and at ½ past 7. the different wards assembled for prayers. about 8 we weighed anchor, wind N.N.E. weather fair, was towed down the river by the Steam tug "Independence" at ½ past 9 o'clock all the Comp. was mustered to see if there was any stoway's, found none, while the inspection was going on a Steamer came along side with a McHodgetts and Some additional officers to search the Ship for the former's family. Mrs. McHodgett did not wish to go back, although Mr. H. promised to sell his property and go to Zion with them, but by the persuasion of Elder Wheelock, Ferguson and others She consented to do so. Took three of her Children with her and left two behind age 17 and 15. at midday water was served to all the Company about 5 P.M. Bro. Wheelock and Dunbar left us in the tug that had been towing all day. They gave us three Cheers, we all returned it and the Band played a lively air. at 8 o'clock the guard was posted. ½ past 8 prayers were attended to. all went to rest. a fresh Breeze filled our Sails and we glided ..." [McAllister, p. 106-107]

"At mid-day, water was served to all the company. About five p.m., brothers Wheelock and Dunbar left in the tug that had been towing us during the day. Towards evening a fresh breeze filled our sails, and we glided along nicely. A few were sea sick." [*Millenial Star*]

24 March - Monday *2

"Trumpet blowed at 6 o'clock. All got up as could. My wife and children all sick but I got them on deck and at 12 o'clock was all better. Towards night, all sick more or less besides myself." [Walters]

"A. M. at 10 minutes to 2 o'Clock Sister Agness, Wife of Samuel Hargraves was delivered of a <u>Son</u> named Enoch Train waited upon by Sister Janet Hardie. 8 o'clock wind S.E. weather fair going at the rate of 5 knots an hour. Several of the Company very sick. P. M. all feeling Better. Served water to all the Company. Posted the guard at 7 o'clock, prayers were offered near 9. at 15 minutes past 10 Sister Elizabeth, wife of Wm Johnston was delivered of a Son named <u>Hamilton</u>. waited upon by Sister Janet Hardie. about Midnight the Ship rolled heavy, going at the rate of 11 Knots." [McAllister]

25 March - Tuesday *3

"A good strong wind. The ship heaved and worked and nearly all sick. Very queerly myself. Got out of the Irish Channel about 6 o'clock. Got still on board." [Walters]

"A. M. 6 o'clock the horn was sounded, a great many so sick they could not rise. at 7 prayers were called very few attended. Ship still sailing, going 10 Knots wind E.S.E. weather [p. 107] Cloudy. Ship making 10 Knots. 8 o'clock raining very fast and Squally .... I was very sick but kept about. Many of the sick were administered to by the Elders. Some of them got better ..... Posted the guard at 7. ¼ past prayers were attended to. About this time we Cleared the Chanel and Sailed on the broad Atlantic." [McAllister]

26 March - Wednesday *4

"Sickness not so bad. I am better and am thankful. My wife, Henry and Harriet and Lydia and Sarah still sick. Ship going at good speed; wind nearly south. Harriet very sick. Rained hard towards night. All went to bed. Could eat nothing for we had no salt nor vinegar and we could not eat pork. The ship rocked all night. Was very poorly; no appetite. Rough breakers; sea wind blowing southeast, east." [Walters]

"The next day we spoke the barque "Emily Flyn" of Belfast. The boat was lowered and manned for the purpose of putting off our Channel pilot. ...it was found that she was bound for Hamburgh. The pilot... returned to us again." [*Millenial Star*, p. 354]

27 March - Thursday *5

"All better except Harriet, for which I thank my Heavenly Father. Wind blowing briskly after a wet night. Now 12 o'clock and all well and merry. Most are getting over their sea sickness. A ship in sight bound for

England. Trumpet sounded for prayers and we laid down in peace, committing our souls to the care of our Heavenly Father." [Walters]

"Nearly all the sick were on deck, chatting, singing, and running about. We had a splendid run for a few days, and expected to be in Boston in four weeks, but it was ordered otherwise by a kind Providence. The captain steered south to escape the ice." [*Millenial Star*, p. 354]

"A. M. Ship making 6 knots wind East weather fair at 1/2 past 5 o'clock the horn Sounded the rise. The Brethren turned out, and Scrubed decks. ...The day passed off very pleasant. P. M. posted the guard at ½ past 7 o'clock, at ½ past 8 attended prayers...." [McAllister, p. 108]

28 March - Friday *6

"A fine morning and many better of sea sickness and our rations served out. Salt and vinegar; beef, as we have had none before. Many on deck and not many in bed. Band played on deck; all rejoicing, etc. Songs, etc." [Walters]

"A. M. ½ past 5 the Horn was Sounded. Ships nearly .... wind becalming, weather Cloudy with rain. at ½ past 7 o'clock attend prayers. The Brethren prayed for favorable wind, which came imediately[?] from the N.E. Ship Sailed at the rate of 8 Knots. the weather faired So that the Saints could enjoy themselves on deck. P. M. Potatoes were served to the Company, and water as usual. Posted the guard at ½ past 7 o'clock attended prayers at ¼ past 8." [McAllister, p.109]

29 March - Saturday *7

"A. M. the rise was sounded at ½ past 5 o'clock. Wind N.N.E. weather fair. Ship Sailing 10 Knots at ½ past 8 attended prayers. The Band favored us with Several lively airs. P. M. attended to the Serving of Provisions to all the Company. The Ship was becalmed about 5 hours. Posted the guard at ½ past 7 o'clock attended prayers at ½ past 8." [McAllister]

30 March - Sunday *8

"A fine morning, wind blowing west and the ship not making three miles an hour. We hope the wind will change. A few sick but all busy cooking and many on deck in the afternoon. Some of the brethren spoke. We retired to rest, commiting our cares into the hands of the Heavenly Father." [Walters]

"A. M. the Horn was Sounded at ½ past 5 o'clock. Wind S.W. Cloudy and raining very fast. Making about 5 Knots. attended prayers as usual. The day was so very wet could have no meeting on deck. P. M. water was Served. Posted the guard at ½ past 7. attended Prayers at ½ past 8." [McAllister]

31 March - Monday *9

"At night, Sister Esther Devereux, aged sixty-nine years, wife of John Devereux died of consumption...a native of Dymock, Gloucestershire, England, late of the Herefordshire Conference. The next day it was so very rough that we could not attend to the burial." [*Millenial Star*, p. 354]

"...Ship nearly becalmed. Drew out a list to Serve Provisions by Lot[?]. 2 o'Clock attended meeting on deck....Ship about 3 points off her Course....during the night Sister Ester, wife of John Devereux of the Hareford Shire Conference died of Consumption of the Lungs." [McAllister, p. 110]

1 April - Tuesday *10

"A sister died during the night named Esther Devereux, from Hereforshire Conference; age 60 years. A rough day. Ship rolled and boxes rattled. Bottles upset. Bedsteads broke down and cooking did not please all, for the saucepans upset in the jelly. Some scolded and some fell and hurt themselves. A thing to try the patience of some. Went to bed ship-rocked and rolled about; did not sleep well but all night the President and Captains of the different wards do their best for all and all good Saints feel well." [Walters]

"A. M. Blowing a gale Ship about four points off her course ...So rough no water could be served at 5 o'Clock the body of our Sister Devereux was carried up on deck fresh in the Hospital..." [McAllister]

2 April - Wednesday *11

"The dead sister's body committed to the deep. It was the first I ever saw buried in the sea and I never want to see another. A rough day all day." [Walters]

"At six a.m., Sister Devereux was committed to the deep, in lat. 41" 32' N, long. 24' 42' W...." [*Millenial Star*, p. 354]

"...Body of our Sister was committed to the deep...Lat 41-32 North. Long 29-41 West." [McAllister, p. 111]

3 April - Thursday *12

"A fine morning; almost all on deck. Some few below sick...The band from Birmingham is playing and merrily; the ship rocking now and then sends them sprawling and make them laugh if one fell on top of another or 4 or 5 together. 11 o'clock and then we are out of a day's water and no extra water for cooking at all but all night we are happy. Several songs during the afternoon by Messrs. McAllison, Frost, Walters, etc. Band playing and dancing until dark when all went below...Sister Leasly fell and hurt herself during the night but is better this morning." [Walters]

4 April - Friday *13

"All well. Some good boiled rice for breakfast but cried for gruel and mother did not like it and Sarah grumbled, but if the grumble now what will they do before they get to the Valley. Nearly 12 o'clock. The wind blowing nearly west and not going very fast. Waves kept splashing on deck. Wind blowing against us... All merry on board. Henry sick and mother and Harriet crying because there is no sugar, and Sarah not well pleased and mother scolding. Henry got some preserves given him. He went to bed but was very sick. Sons up and down stairs...We went to bed, committing our souls into the care of our Heavenly Father and bid each other good night." [Walters]

"A. M. the horn was Sounded at 5 o'Clock, Prayers at 7 ½. the day being fine the Saints got upon deck. two Ships passed us yesterday. Homeward Bound. P. M. potatoes was Served to the Company." [McAllister]

5 April - Saturday *14

"All arose at 6 o'clock. A beautiful morning. Many on deck with cheerful countenances. Henry better. Some potatoes for breakfast and gruel. Double working, tomorrow being the 6th of April. Rations served out, both beef and pork. Henry well. Saw two ships sailing slowly. The finest we have had since we left Liverpool. All the sick on deck. Band playing, dancing and singing until a late hour. Cooking until 12 o'clock at night, tomorrow being the anniversary of the 6th of April." [Walters]

6 April - Sunday *15

"A beautiful morning. No cooking only tea kettles boiled. Most all up 7 o'clock washing and preparing for a good time today...Two porpoises were seen but they were thought to be whales. Soon a whale made its appearance and threw the water into the air a great height, all eyes looking at it and my children all astonished and asking a thousand and one questions to which I could not answer. The sea is very calm and the ship almost standing still and the sun shines with a beautiful clear sky. ..Meeting called to order by Pres. Ferguson and he said we might as well hold it as a Conference as it is the 6th of April, as it is held this day in Zion." [Walters]

"The morning was nearly calm, and sea smooth. The horn was blown as usual. Prayers at a quarter-past eight o'clock. At two p.m., according to appointment, the company assembled in a Conference capacity. Elder James Ferguson presided. The hymn commencing, 'O Lord, thy people bless' was sung. Prayer by Elder McAllister. 'Now let us rejoice in the day of salvation' was then sung. The blessing of the children who were born on board, and several others, was then attended to. The usual Conference business then commenced, by motions being made to sustain the general authorities of the Church in Zion, and also to sustain President F. D. Richards and his Counsellors, and the authorities of the company as it was then organized. These motions were adopted by a unanimous vote. Elder McArthur was then called upon to address the Conference.

"He spoke upon the first principles of the Gospel, and practical 'Mormonism,' and bore his testimony to the truth of the same. Elder Ferguson bore his testimony to what had been said, and spoke upon the principle of marriage; and advised the Saints, those that had come on board with the intention of getting married, to wait until they got home to Zion. He also made some remarks upon the death of sister Devereux, and her burial at sea, and gave instructions calculated to do good to the company. Elder Ellsworth gave some very good instructions, and bore his testimony to the truth of 'Mormonism.' A committee of cleanliness, and one to keep order around the galley, were then appointed.

"The Conference closed by Elder McAllister singing the 'Merry Mormons.' Benediction by Elder Spicer

W. Crandall. The Captain then presented Enoch Train Hargraves with a sovereign. The day was lovely, and the sperm whales played about us for some time. The weather was warm and everybody rejoiced exceedingly." [*Millenial Star*, p. 354]

7 April - Monday *16
"Wind blowing contrary. Rather cold and windy. Saw no ships. Quite dull and wet at times. Much grumbling about cooking. One man said if he had his money and could get to Liverpool, he would go to Hell if he would not, but it takes very little to prove some; the spirits soon show what they are." [Walters]

8 April - Tuesday *17
"Rather wet morning; wind ahead and has been for a week past. Still some grumbling about cooking. 10 gallons of water for every 100 persons but none did we get. My children dissatisfied about the victuals; some could eat one thing and some another; could not please all but expect they will get better as they get used to it. But a biscuit and water with health is a blessing for which I feel thankful. Dancing at night on deck." [Walters]

"...Bro. Ellsworth assisted me in drafting and Cutting Tents the Saints Commenced their tent making for the Plains. Evening all assembled at the main Hatch when Bro. Ferguson addressed us gave Some Council and instruction necessary for our Circumstances." [McAllister]

9 April - Wednesday *18
"A. M. the usual duties of the Ship were attended to. water and Potatoes Served to the Company. wind unfavorable. Posted the guard at 7 ½ o'Clock, attended prayers at 9. administered to Several of the Sick who were relieved imeaditly." [McAllister]

10 April - Thursday *19
"Windy and wind more favorable. Grumblers about cooking. Lost my Tomiliner hat. Henry very poorly and he says that he will never come on the sea again. Feel not very well myself but am thankful. All things will work right and will be for our good. The wind still in the west. Ship rolling and the sea rough; a deal of tacking about which makes plenty of work for the sailors. [Walters]

11 April - Friday *20
"A. M. the Horn Sounded at 5 o'Clock prayers 7½. water Served to the Company. wind N.W. Ship making 6 Knots weather fine. P. M. the wind haul'd more favorable. Evening attended meeting and in connexion with others addressed the Saints." [McAllister]

12 April - Saturday *21
"Provisions served out today. The change of diet is worse for all of us than the sickness of the sea. Henry almost sick if you mention rice. Little Lydia the best amongst us all. A calm day up to 3 o'clock. The children glad to have some sugar. No sooner than we got out pork than Harriet wanted the frying pan. Busy on deck making and sewing tents; dancing commenced at 6 o'clock, prayers at 8 o'clock and then, it being a moonlight night, another half hour was given on deck; drop hankerchiefs; songs; and went to bed. Ship sailed fast all night." [Walters]

13 April - Sunday *22
"A. M. wind S.W. Ship making 9 Knots weather rainy. the Saints arose and attended prayers as usual. Served water. P.M. passed the English Barque Architect of Windsor. 21 days from Aberdeen bound for Halifax. 3 o'Clock attended meeting and addressed the Saints. Posted the guard as usual prayers at 9 o'Clock. wind N.E. Ship Sailing fine on her right course." [McAllister, p. 115]

14 April - Monday *23
"Ship run well all night and is going well this morning. Rather a dull day. We hope to be in Boston next Monday if all's well. The Bros. want me to shave. I do not know what to my top lip is so tender and I have shaved myself for this 16 years passed, and I have determined in my own mind long since as soon as I got aboard a ship I never would shave again until I reached the Valley, and not then until I was told. Band played; trumpet for prayers. The moon shined and the lads and lasses were playing on deck until nearly 11 o'clock." [Walters]

15 April - Tuesday *24

"Ship rocked all night. Quite a calm. Some grumbling by a Bro. Many spirits. The body of a man seen floating past the ship. A many very poorly, principally old folks. some council and instructions given by the Elders about Tobacco smoking, obedience, etc." [Walters]

"...Ship becalmed the Saints worked at tents. Served water and Potatoes. P. M. Posted the guard as usual 9 o'Clock assembled for meeting was addressed by the President and Council." [McAllister]

16 April - Wednesday *25

"...not much wind. Sea Smooth. Served water. P. M. the wind blew Strong and fair. Ship making 9 Knots ..." [McAllister]

17 April - Thursday *26

The sailing ship Samuel S. Curling departed Liverpool 17 April 1856.[DUP *Stories of*, p. 354] *An Enduring Legacy* shows the departure date of 19 April 1856.[Crandal, *Legacy*, p. 145]

"...My wife very poorly and we all feel no great shakes, the diet being so different and cooking so badly managed, having only the ship allowance, - no preserves, butter, cheese, ham, as a many have, but thank God we shall by his blessing get through." [Walters]

"Sister Mary, wife of James Sheen, junior, was delivered of a son. All the sisters in their confinement, were attended by sister Hardie of Edinburgh. Our passage has been a pleasure trip. All have been happy and contented. Those that were not were soon made so. Our steward and cooks have done well. God bless them. In fact we can say God bless all, for they have done nobly." [*Millenial Star*, p. 354]

"...at Noon today about 13 hundred miles from Boston by the Chart. ...Ship making 6 Knots." [McAllister]

[6 knots = 6.9 m.p.h. — if maintained for 24 hrs. a day = 165.6 miles per day.]

18 April - Friday *27

"Sailing very slowly. Rations served out. A better allowance of sugar....From 1200 to 1300 miles from Boston. The ship has rocked since 1 o'clock this morning-upset water bottles-..Have as much bone as beef today. Hope to be at Boston next week at this time. Meeting below deck and some council and instructions by the Elders. Ship sailing very fast." [Walters]

"P. M. the Saints worked at the Tents..." [McAllister]

19 April - Saturday *28

"Sleep well all night. The ship still sailing very fast. Wind changed about 10 o'clock and not sailing so fast. Some hard feelings with Sister Parker and my wife about the children. Better suffer wrong is my council to my wife. We are all well and I feel truly thankful to my Heavenly Father." [Walters]

"...we Sailed Since yesterday noon until 7 o'Clock this Morning 123 miles. water was Served to the Company. was waiting for the Capt. all day Dined with him." [McAllister, p. 117]

• [Excerpt from Diary on S.S. Curling, 19th April 1856] "The resolutions passed were, that the President of each ward have a sufficient number of men up every morning to wash and clean under and before each berth in his ward, and to have it finished and prayers over at 6 o'clock. Any neglect of the rules passed by the council or presiding, the President of the ward will be held responsible and will be liable to be tried by a council of his brethren.

"The cook house to be open to receive the 1st and 2d wards at 6 o'clock for cooking breakfast. 3d and 5th ward to cook from 6½ to 7, 4th and 6th 7 to 7½, 7th and 8th 7½ to 8, 9th and 10 and 11th 8 to 0.

"Dinner to follow the same rotation, commencing at 11 o'clock and ending at 3. Supper or Tea, same rotation commencing at 4½ and ending at 7½, when the galley fires are to be put out.

"Prayers are to be over in each ward at 8 o'clock p.m., and the President of each ward to have a teachers' meeting within this time, say to commence at 1/48.

"In order to prevent disease, the Presidents are to have the Saints go on deck as much as possible.

"There were many other resolutions passed with regard to the regulation ...in the different wards, one of which was that the Hospital be allotted to Brother Jones and the Clerks for an Office, and that we keep all sickness out of the ship." [Wakefield]

20 April - Sunday *29
"Beautiful morning. Ship going slowly. Sister Leasly was talking and I asked her if she was not restored to health by the power of God and she said she was for she went on deck very sick and fell back on her head and was brought to her bed, but was soon better after the Elders had laid their hands on her. About 950 miles from Boston, 12 o'clock. The Saints are more united and a better spirit is amongst the whole of us...Meeting held on deck. Brother Galaway spoke on Obedience ..., Brother Leonard...a short history of his mission and Pres. Ferguson...upon Cleanliness, and...appointed...the 'Louse Committee.' Singing until 11 o'clock by Mrs. MacAllison, - Co. Ship sailing fast." [Walters]

"...our Lat. was 39-26 Long 51-02. 940 miles from Boston by the Chart."[McAllister]

21 April - Monday *30
"Cloudy morn...Some lice found on several....798 miles from Boston 12 o'clock." [Walters]

"Spoke to Typhoon (iron ship) bound for Liverpool. We wanted her captain to take our pilot, and some letters to England, but he would not." [*Millenial Star*, p. 354]

22 April - Tuesday *31
"Wet day. Sewing and making tents...Ship rocked. The sailors all cleaning the ship. Expect to be in on Saturday." [Walters]

"...Today noon 650 miles from Boston." [McAllister, p. 118]

23 April - Wednesday *32
"Wet morning. Ship sailing about 6 knots...Last night went on watch ½ past 7 o'clock. Very cold night and the coldest day that has been since on board the ship." [Walters]

"A. M....at 8 o'Clock. wind .... but very light. Ship nearly becalmed. water and Potatoes Served to the Company. the Saints worked on the Tents. wind ahead all day." [McAllister]

24 April - Thursday *33
"Very cold morning. A child died at 4 o'clock the son of Sister ____ from ____ Conference. 12 o'clock the ship still. Quite a calm. The little boy committed to the deep. Bro. Ferguson spoke before the plan was drawn. Quite a solemn time to the children and parents as well; indeed all sailors looked straight down their noses." [Walters]

"Between two and three o'clock a.m., Jane, daughter of Hugh and Jane Clotworthy, aged two years, died of consumption of the bowels. She was buried at two o'clock p.m. " [*Millenial Star*, p. 354]

"A. M. between 2 and 3 o'Clock Jane, Daughter of Hugh and Jane Clotworthy died of Consumption of the Bowels. Aged 2 years, 1 month and 24 days...Saints assembled on the Main deck to witness the Burial ...hymn on page 183 was Sung, prayer by Elder Ellsworth, Elder Ferguson Made Some very appropriate remarks. the Body was then launched into the deep. Latitude 42-52 Longitude 59-32. Distance from Boston 513 miles. " [McAllister]

25 April - Friday *34
"Last night, at half-past nine o'clock, we cast anchor. The Saints assembled for meeting between decks. Elder Ferguson and Council addressed them. After the instruction, Hosannah was shouted three times. A heavenly time we had, and one never to be forgotten. The five Presidents were instructed to look after their wards while journeying to the frontiers, and to select two Counsellors each. The Saints were instructed to remain on the ship until all should leave it. If they needed anything from Boston they were counselled to inform their Presidents. All agreed to do so. By a unanimous vote ...a resolution was passed, instructing brother Ferguson to tender ...sincere thanks for the provisions and medical stores...kindly provided... We have just passed the doctor. The inspection - from the time he jumped on deck until he got on his own craft again - occupied about fifteen minutes." [*Millenial Star*, p. 354-55]

"...wind fair. Ship making 11 Knots weather Cold and rainy." [McAllister]

26 April - Saturday *35
"A. M. at ½ past 4 o'Clock we Struck a for and aft Schooner, her main Topmast caught in our crockir[?] yard, and was carried away...Distance from Boston today noon 185 miles. weather very cold, wind fair. Ship making about 5 Knots." [McAllister]

27 April - Sunday *36
"Ship nearly becalmed, scarcely made any head way all night. weather fair... engaged most of the day with the Saints...for their passage to Boston...attended meeting between decks Elder Ferguson and Ellsworth, McArthur and Several others addressed us. a note of thanks was tendered to Capt. Rich through Ferguson." [McAllister]

28 April - Monday *37
"Captain Rich is a man in every sense of the word, and has been very kind to us. At a previous meeting a vote of thanks was tendered to him through President Ferguson...When...present to the Captain, he presented ...letter for President Ferguson, written ten days previously, in order to be ready when he came in sight of Boston lights...to tender to you our thanks for the spirit of kindness manifested by you all during the present voyage, tending to the health, and comfort of our passengers under your charge. If such rules and regulations could be followed by all emigrant ships, we should have less, far less of sickness and distress at sea. Cleanliness is part of your religion, and nobly you have carried it out. May your trip across our states be one of pleasure, and when this is passed, and you are encamped upon our western prairies, may your thoughts wander back with pleasure to your ocean voyage."[*Millenial Star*, p. 355]

"We have no grumblers and no murmurers, everybody is contented and happy. Yesterday our pilot was received by three cheers from the company, and 'Yankee Doodle' by the band." *Millenial Star*, p. 355]

29 April - Tuesday *38
"A very fine morning and the Captain and crew rather troubled about a buoy being in a place they never saw before and he hoists a flag for a pilot. Spoke to a fisherman and found plenty of water and only 15 miles from Boston. A pilot soon came on board. We soon anchored on Quarantine, 9 o'clock in the evening, 3 or 4 miles from Boston. A general meeting below deck and thanksgiving to our Heavenly Father for his protecting care over us while many perish on the sea at the same time." [Walters]

"the horn Sounded Prayers attended to as usual about 6 o'Clock. a Buoy was discussed on the Larboard Side it was not noticed on the .... and bothered the Capt a little. he Stood off and on until Noon. P. M. Spoke the Schooner "Flag of Truce" of Gloucester who informed us we were 24 miles from Opa[?] Ann and 12 from Boston. 4 o'Clock the Pilot Boat "Jane" of Boston came along Side and put a Pilot on Board of us. the Band and all the Company of Saints were on deck and gave them heardy cheers. the Band played "Yanke Doodle. land in Sight water served to day as usual. Posted the guard at 7½ o'Clock. at 9½ we cast anchor. the Company assembled between decks for Meeting Elder Ferguson and Council addressed us...the Presidents were instructed to look after the Saints of their Several wards [p. 122] while journing to Frontier,...letter was then read by Bro Ferguson which had been handed him by the Capt." [McAllister, p. 123]

30 April - Wednesday *39
"A. M. was visited by the owners of the Ship . Quarantine, and other officers they considered us the best passengers that ever arrived in Boston. the Doctor passed us all in about 15 minutes. P. M. I accompanied Bro Ferguson ashore Met Elder N. H. Felt in Train ... office. he returned to the Ship with us in a Small boat, ...Spent the night on board."[McAllister]

1 May - Thursday *40
Constitution Wharf, Boston, was its port of entry 1 May 1856. Passage time was 39 days. 534 passengers: 19 converts from Switzerland; 4 converts from Cape of Good Hope, South Africa; 2 converts from Denmark; 2 converts from East India Missions; 507 converts from British Isles and returning missionaries. 431 passengers were financed by the Perpetual Emigration Fund.[Hafen, p.56]

"Landed at Boston Constitution Wharf. Ladies came to visit us and sent oranges for the children, New Testament to all heads of families and many little cards and books for children." [Walters]

2 May 1856 - Friday *41
"Band played, songs, etc. Left Boston for New York and arrived at New York May 2nd. Went to see George Mayland and he was very kind to us." [Walters]

"A. M. very early arose and attended Prayers. all Bustle preparing to leave . Served Half ration of Provisions. P. M. at 4 o'Clock left by Omnibus for the Railway Station the American flag waved from the top of the leading Bus we left Boston by the 5½ train arrived in ? at 9. Took Steamer Plymouth Rock to New York arrived at 6 P. M..." [McAllister, p. 124]

"...Chicago, arrived at the evening of the 8th stopped in the [?] all night." [McAllister, p. 126]

3 May 1856 - Saturday *42
[No exact dates are given] "All emigrants from the "Enoch Train" now traveled in a body to New York, they went by rail and water. At New York Apostle John Taylor came to the boat to talk to the Saints. He ...turned to our captain and said, "How long since these folks have had any refreshment?" "Two days," was the answer. "Brothers and Sisters," said John Taylor, "I should like to see you eat before I speak to you." In less than half an hour bakers bread, steak and coffee were brought onto the ship. I had not thought about being so hungry until then. How nice this food tasted." [Sabin]

"...Again we continued traveling, this time by rail to Rock Island, Illinois. Our train was scheduled to cross the Mississippi River on a bridge at eight o'clock. We were fifteen minutes late. The bridge had broken with the train just ahead of us and a great wreck occured. We had to stay at Rock Island from Saturday morning until Monday morning. On Monday morning we crossed the Mississippi River in a boat, it was a mile wide. On the other side of the river from Rock Island we entered a train of box cars. We reached Iowa City late at night." [Sabin]?

4 May - Sunday *43
"...left New York 5 o'clock for Iowa. Travelled by rails and was very short of bread for children and they cried for something to eat from May 4th until Friday 9th of May, and then my wife went into town and she had 2 cents and two slices of bread for meat, and bread was plentiful and Bro. Frost gave us 15 cents. Left Chicago 11 o'clock at night; arrived at Rock Island 9 o'clock morning May 10th. [Walters]

9 May - Friday *44
" A. M. Brother Daniel Spencer overtook us on way to Saint Louis. P. M. At 2 o'Clock we took the express train to Rock Island, arrived at 10. Stopped in the back[?] all night." [McAllister]

10 May - Saturday *45
"Had more bread allowed us and got some rice from our box that we left from our ship allowance and the children were more satisfied. Slept in a store house Saturday night and Sunday night went on watch 8 o'clock until 12." [Walters]

"A. M. Due to the extra large [?] perishin[?] house kindly loaned by the railway company. Commenced receipting for passage to Iowa City. At 9 o'Clock P. M. the horn sounded for Prayers." [McAllister]

11 May - Sunday *46
"A. M. Finished receipting the company to Iowa." [McAllister]

12 May - Monday *47
"Crossed the River Missouri 8 o'clock Monday 12th of May; arrived at Iowa 3 o'clock. Drawed our luggage about 2 miles to camp ground. Fixed some tents that was made aboard a-ship. It rained and it was cold. My wife and daughters got into a tent. Henry and me slept in a tent but was very cold and should of been worse if Bro. Webb had not covered us up." [Walters]

"A. M. Brother Ferguson and Ellsworth with half of the company by tug boat to Davenport and by rail to Iowa, I was detained to accompany the balance. We left at 2 P. M. and arrived in Iowa at 10 o'Clock. We were all housed in the depot and remained there until the 14th." [McAllister]

"We reached Iowa City late at night. We walked four miles from Iowa City out to the camping place of the Saints. Mother rode, not being strong enough to walk...." [Sabin]

When they arrived 12 May the contracted handcarts were not ready yet and they had to wait 4 weeks. Some of the pioneers like Archer Walters, a carpenter, was put to work building handcarts. [Hafen, p. 56]

13 May - Tuesday *48
"Got up. Very cold; still raining and very uncomfortable." [Walters]

14 May 1856 - Wednesday *49
"A fine day. Helped Bro. Webb spice some tent poles. Slept in tent with Bro. Lee. His children down with fever." [Walters]

"A. M. Commenced hauling our luggage to camp on wagon and handcart. All were safely lodged in camp by 11 o'Clock. Many wet to the skin, for it rained very fast. Brother Ferguson and I overtook a family and carried two of their little fellows into camp. It was located on a beautiful hill about 3 miles from the center of the city. Plenty of food and water." [McAllister]

15 May - Thursday *50
"Went to the same tent. A fine day. Stil slept with the children that had the fever and could not be removed and I thought it hard but took it patiently." [Walters]

"Due to camp life[?] and camp duty[?], the company generally helped. The balance of our luggage came today." [McAllister]

16 May - Friday *51
"Went to Iowa to seek work. The bosses was short of lumber and got no work. Come back to camp. Tent was down and we was moved to another tent. The children bad with fever still with us and another family of healthy put with us." [Walters]

"A. M. 4 o'Clock Sister Catherine, wife of Walter Granger, was delivered of a daughter. [?] was alive the day previously, named Elizabeth [?]. Adopted daughter of John Taylor died of croupe, age five months. The two were buried in the camps graveyard about a quarter of a mile from camp. Served provisions as usual." [McAllister]

17 May - Saturday *52
"Bro. Godsall was sent to look at the children bad with fever and he agreed with me that we ought to be separated, and I still loved Bro. Lee the same and we was separated. Bro. Lee made a tent to himself and it was better for both of us and all was right." [Walters]

"A. M. Camp was regulated. P. M. President Daniel Spencer arrived, all were very glad to see him." [McAllister]

18 May - Sunday *53
"Beautiful morning. Very warm. Camp meeting ½ past 10. Opened by singing. Prayer by Elder Ellsworth. Bro. Van Cott introduced Bro. Spencer. He spoke short. Elder Ferguson was called to address the meeting. He spoke some length upon polygamy. Bro. McAllister sung a song, 'The Good Honest Heart'; singing by the Saints, Upper California. Benediction by Elder Godsall. Adjourned until ½ past 1 o'clock. Very attentive. Bro. Bunker addressed the meeting." [Walters]

"A. M. Very many visitors in camp. 2 o'Clock had meeting, Brother Spencer spoke a short time. Brother Ferguson then preached on the plurality of wives. Adjourned for one hour. ½ past one assembled again. Brother Ellsworth, Bunker and I addressed the multitude. Evening took a walk with Claude. E. G. Webb, the sisters Hardie, Burdett and Godsell. Slept until [?] in the office. Tent[?] as usual." [McAllister]

19 May - Monday *54
"Went into the city of Iowa. Short of lumber. Saw a chapel or church burnt down. They say they were preaching against us yesterday but perhaps they will learn better by this purifying by fire. Had some whiskey and water which took all my strength for it was so hot. Got to camp about ½ past 8 o'clock." [Walters]

"A. M. 10 o'Clock, Sister Maria, wife of James Shinn, died of consumption. Age 60 years. Stayed busy all day, served provisions as usual. Was very hot during the day and cold at night. Evening a meeting was called, Brother Spencer presides. The company was divided into two handcart companies, Brother Edmund Ellsworth was chosen captain of one and I captain of the other. Several of the brothern spoke, all felt well and happy." [McAllister]

"On the 19th of May, 1856, our company, which had crossed the sea with us, were divided, by President Daniel Spencer, into two handcart companies, Brother Edmond Ellsworth to take charge of the first and I, Daniel D. McArthur, to take charge of the second company. Then every move was made to get our carts ready, which job was a tedious one, but by using all our efforts, the first company was enabled to start on the 9th of June, and the second on the 11th, about 11 o'clock. This second company numbered 222 souls, and were bound for Florence, and from thence to the Valley, at which place (Florence) we arrived on the 8th day of July, distance, 300 miles, or there abouts. We had the very best of good luck all the way, although the weather was very hot and sweltering, but let me tell you, the saints were not to be overcome. Our carts, when we started, were in an awful fix. They moaned and growled, screeched and squealed, so that a person could hear them for miles. You may think this is stretching things a little too much, but it is a fact, and we had them to eternally patch, morning, noons and nights. But by our industry we got them all along to Florence, and being obliged to stop at Florence some two weeks to get our outfit for the plains, I and my council, namely, Truman Leonard and Spencer Crandall, went to work and gave our carts a thorough repair throughout, and on the 24th of July, at 12 o'clock, we struck our tents and started for the plains, all in the best of spirits. Nothing but the very best of luck attended us continually. Our train consisted of 12 yoke of oxen, 4 wagons, and 48 carts; we also had 5 beef and 12 cows; flour, 55 lbs. per head, 100 lbs. rice, 550 lbs. sugar, 400 lbs. dried apples, 125 labs. tea, and 200 lbs. salt for the company.[McArthurs Report to Wilford Woodruff]

20 May - Tuesday *55
"Went to work to make hand carts. Was not very well. Worked 10 hours. Harriet very poorly." [Walters] (1st Company)

"A. M. Called my company together and appointed Captain of the Guard and a clerk of the company, Henry Borin to the former office and William Wright to the latter. P. M. Brother G. D. Grant and William W. Kimballs arrived with cattle for our company. Sister Shinn was buried at 7 o'Clock." [McAllister] (2nd Company)

21 May - Wednesday *56
"Went work. Harriet not so well. Very hot. All very well considering the heat and change of diet." [Walters] (1st Company)

"A. M. Commenced weighing the handcart luggage. Evening held a meeting of the company, spoke to the saints. Brother J. [?] Hunt, Mr. Heaten[?], and T. Leonard made some very good remarks." [McAllister] (2nd Company)

22 May - Thursday *57
"Harriet worse with what we are told is the American Fever. Sometimes like the Ague. Sarah went to Lindley's Farm to work and sent poor Harriet some milk and crust of bread." [Walters] (1st Company)

"Busy with the company nearly all day. [?] to my wife." [McAllister] (2nd Company)

23 May - Friday *58
Sailing Ship Samuel S. Curling reached Boston, its point of entry, 23 May 1856.[*Millenial Star*, 2 Aug 1856] They had a one day quarantine. Passenger Total was 770.[Crandal, *Legacy*, p. 145]

"Harriet still very ill. I went to work. Still very hot to me. All the rest very well and I thank my Heavenly Father." [Walters] (1st Company)

"Was appointed commisary. Brother Truman Leonard was chosen to assist me with my company and get us ready for the plains." [McAllister] (2nd Company)

•"Priscilla Merriman Evans..."S. S. Curling." Landed in Boston on May 23rd and traveled in cattle cars 300 miles to Iowa City where they waited three weeks for the handcarts to be made..."[D.U.P. *Stories*, p. 354]

24 May - Saturday *59
"Harriet still very ill. Still at work at the carts. Rations served out and got more sugar." [Walters] (1st Company)

"A. M. Brother Ferguson and [?] left us, the former to Boston, the latter to Saint Louis. A company called the Independent was organized by Brother D. Spencer and [?] Hodgett and chosen captain, John Cooper Clark, Davis captain of the guard. Brother Spencer addressed the company. Brother French[?] Hodgess[?] and myself made some remarks. All felt to rejoice in Mormonism. I was busy in the storehouse most of the day. Wrote an introductory letter to my parents and relatives for Brother Ferguson." [McAllister] (2nd Company)

25 May - Sunday *60
"Morning meeting. Bro. Godsall, from Birmingham, addressed the meeting. Meeting ½ past 2. Brother Webb spoke and someone had been speaking against us. He roared out like a lion and would of slain them with a look of his eyes and if any was honest in heart and had been guilty they must have trembled for he spared none." [Walters] (1st Company)

"A. M. By appointment from President Spencer, I presided over the meeting. Elder John Dogett[?] preached the Gospel. P. M. Johnson T. Webb, very many strangers present, even had a meeting of the Saints, Brother Spencer addressed them. Ellsworth, Leonard and I made some remarks. Bore testimony, the same as Brother Spencer, the Spirit rejoiced exceedingly." [McAllister] (2nd Company)

26 May - Monday *61
"Went to work. Harriet still very bad. Lightened very bad; began about 8 o'clock until 11 o'clock. Never saw it so in my life and it rained hard and our beds began to swim. I was wet on my side as I laid until I found it out." [Walters] (1st Company)

"Went to be in the store all day. Brother Leondard [?], Brother Spicer W. Crandall arrived. Evening we experienced a dreadful storm from the N.W." [McAllister] (2nd Company)

27 May - Tuesday *62
"Went to work at hand carts. Shift tent on a hill and was scolded for it." [Walters] (1st Company)

"A. M. Went to store as usual. P. M. Received a letter from Claude. In the evening Sister Jane, wife of John Fruge[?], was delivered of a son about 10 ½ o'Clock. He named him William McAllister Fruge[?], Sister Hardie waited on her." [McAllister] (2nd Company)

28 May - Wednesday *63
"At work." [Walters] (1st Company)

"A. M. At 8 ½ o'Clock a horn sounded for Prayers as usual. I was busy in the store all day." [McAllister] (2nd Company)

29 May - Thursday *64
"Thursday at work. Harriet still very bad." [Walters] (1st Company)

"A. M. All things moving within camp, things getting better. Busy as usual in the store. Brother Ferguson arrived today noon and brought a good report from Captain Dan Jones company, which he met at Albany." [McAllister] (2nd Company)

30 May - Friday *65
"A child born in our tent ½ past one a.m." [Walters] (1st Company)

"A. M. At 2 ½ o'Clock Sister Elizabeth, wife of John Lloyd, was delivered of a daughter named Martha. Waited upon by Sister Hardie." [McAllister] (2nd Company)

31 May - Saturday *66
"Martha began to be ill. Still at work at the hand carts. A meeting at night and we are to prepare for off." [Walters] (1st Company) (2nd Company)

"Very busy all day. Suffered very much with boils which gave me great pain. Brother Spencer arrived at noon. Had a meeting in the evening. [?] Elizabeth, wife of Ralph Ramsey, was delivered of a daughter and [?] something in the morning." [McAllister] (2nd Company)

1 June - Sunday *67
"Meeting ½ past 10. Bro. ___ spoke and Bro. Webb. Sarah still at the farm, Mr. Linley's. Henry went on watch to the cattle. The band played several tunes after the meeting." [Walters] (1st Company)

"A. M. My hands are so painful I cannot do meetings. Brother Ellsworth presided all day. Brother Daniel Tyler and E. G. Webb addressed the assembly. P. M. Brother J. Ferguson address, Saints and strangers felt well. Evening Elizabeth daughter of Constant and Ann H. Schroder and wife of Elizabeth White, born 26 March 1832, Kentucky, U.S.A., baptized by Elder James Holly, confirmed by Elder John Cooper. Alice Ellen Daughter[?] of Elias and Elizabeth White, born August 2, 1855 blessed by James Holly and John Cooper. [?] baptized by John Edward Frost, confirmed by Elder John A. Hunt. George [?] and Ellen Bowing were re-baptized by Elder [?]. After the baptism we had a meeting and President Spencer addressed the Saints. I was released from the Presidency of the handcart company to take charge of the Commesary Department. Brother Daniel D. McArthur succeeded me in the presiding of the company. Brother Daniel Tyler was unanimously chosen as bishop of the stake or campgrounds, Brother Daniel Spencer as first and James Ferguson second counselor. Several of the brethren addressed the Saints, all felt well. By order of President Spencer I married Arthur Maxwell and Elizabeth McArtland[?]." [McAllister] (2nd Company)

S. S. Curling Passengers arrived in Iowa City 1 June 1856 [Crandal, *Legacy*, p. 145]

• "We traveled night and day by rail, buying our victuals at the stations, never undressing for more than a week. We stopped about two hours at the beautiful city of Chicago. I traversed its broad streets, buoyant and glad to think I could still further pursue my journey to Zion. We arrived in Iowa about the 1st of June." [Crandel, *Y.W. Journal*, p. 318] (2nd Company)

Companies 1 & 2 were organized in early June: [Hafen, p. 58] 37 year old returning missionary Edmund Ellsworth was made captain of company 1 and 36 year old returning missionary Daniel D. McArthur was made captain of company 2.

When Saints from "Samuel S. Curling" arrived in Iowa City 1 June, Mary Brannigan Crandal states: "We found tents pitched, men making handcarts, and women cooking out of doors. While waiting for the handcarts to be finished, three or four of us went to Florence and got sewing to do at five dollars a week and board." [Crandal, *Legacy*, p. 145]

2 June - Monday *68

"Harriet very ill. Still working at the hand carts." [Walters] (1st Company)

"Busy all day. P. M. Captain Daniel Jones company which left Liverpool by the "S. Curling" arrived about 6 o'Clock. The following returning missionaries were with him [J] L. Woodward and William Butler. The company generally healthy and excellent spirits, Brother David Grant came also." [McAllister]

3 June - Tuesday *69

"All well but Harriet." [Walters] (1st Company)

"A. M. Captain Ellsworth and McArthur [?] very pressing to leave for the bluff on their way to the valley. Brother Olsey[?] and Butler were appointed to go with Brother Ellsworth. Brother Leonard and Crandall with Brother McArthur. Brother Joseph France was appointed to go ahead and make all necessary arrangements between Iowa and the bluffs for provisions. [?]" [McAllister]

4 June - Wednesday *70

"Martha poorly. Made a coffin for a child dead in camp." [Walters] (1st Company)

5 June - Thursday *71

"All expect to go with our hand carts. I was liberated from working and my tools to go with us to do repairs on the road." [Walters] (1st Company)

6 June - Friday *72

"Made another child's coffin and a rough table for the Elders to eat upon. Bro. Spencer said as I had been working my extra luggage should go through." [Walters] (1st Company)

APPENDIX I

HANDCART LOGBOOK
THE ENOCH TRAIN PIONEERS – 9 JUNE TO 8 JULY 1856
IOWA CITY, IOWA TO FLORENCE, NEBRASKA

The First Handcart Company Log:

7 June 1856 - Saturday
"Started abut 60 yards. Camped for the night and remained Sunday, June the 8th, and meetings held as usual. Harriet dreamed about eating fish and Henry went and catched one and she eat it all. I rode Harriet in the hand cart round the camp. Very bad night owing to camping so late, the dew being on the grass. [Walters]

8 June - Sunday
"Meetings as usual. Went to bid Mr. Lindley good-bye. We journeyed 3 miles. Lost the cattle at night. Camped amongst bush and did not rest well. Harriet very ill. Found cattle Tuesday night at the old camp ground." [Walters]

9 June - Monday
"Left on 9 June 1856 with 274 souls." [*Millennial Star*, 2 Aug 1856]
"At 5 p.m. the handcarts were in motion, proceeding Zionward (from the camp ground west of Iowa City). The Saints were in excellent spirits. The camp traveled about 4 miles and pitched their tents for the night." [Galloway, p. 444]
"At 5 p.m., the carts were in motion proceeding Zionwards. The Saints were in excellent spirits. The camp traveled about four miles and pitched their tents. All well." [Ellsworth, p. 96]

10 June - Tuesday
"The emigrants remained in camp all day, owing to the fact that three yoke of oxen had strayed away from the her. While some of the brethren went out in search of the animals, the Saints in camp engaged in various duties." [Galloway, p. 444]
"We remained in camp all day, owing to three yoke of oxen having strayed from the herd. The brethren went out in search of them. The camp was engaged in various duties." [Ellsworth, p. 96]

FIRST HANDCART COMPANY LOG

11 June - Wednesday
"Journeyed 7 miles. Very dusty. All tired and smothered with dust and camped in the dust or where the dust blowed. Was Captain over my tent of 18 in number but they were a family of Welch and our spirits were not united. Had a tent but Elder Ellsworth would not let me use it and have to leave my tent poles behind me." [Walters]

SECOND HANDCART COMPANY LOG

11 June 1856
"Captain D. D. McArthur left on the 11th with 221 souls, accompanied by Elders Crandall and Leonard as assistants. These numbered in all 497 souls, embraced 104 of the 'Curling's Company', and their fit out was, together, 100 handcarts, 5 wagons, 24 oxen, 4 mules, 25 tents, and provisions to Florence. Brother Ferguson visited their camp 35 miles out, and accompanied them during a portion of a morning's

FIRST HANDCART COMPANY LOG

"Early in the morning, the strayed cattle were brought to camp, and about 8 a.m. the company started forward. After traveling 5 miles, encampment was made for the night. The carts of Brothers Robinson and James broke down." [Galloway, p. 444]

"Early this morning the stayed cattle were brought back. About 8 a.m. the camp started forward and traveled five miles. Pitched tents. Brothers ROBINSON'S and JONES' carts broke down."[Ellsworth. p. 96]

SECOND HANDCART COMPANY LOG

march. He reports that though their first two days travel were good marches for men, considering the sandy roads, he never visited a camp of traveling Saints so cheerful and universally happy." [*Millennial Star*, 2 Aug 1856]

"On the 11th of June we commenced our journey westward, with D. D. McArthur as captain. The day we started the dust flew into our eyes until we could hardly see. I went to the captain and told him if he would let me have a handcart I would haul it myself. He said he would let me try, so I started with my bedclothes, provisions, cooking utensils and clothes strapped on the cart. Soon two other girls were with me. The buffalo were very plentiful, and we had meat every day while we were in that section. In one place where we camped the Indians danced all night. One day an old man named McLane died. It was a solemn sight to see him buried on the plains with nothing to mark his resting place. There was an old Scottish sister who had worked in the coal pits for years. She would travel ahead and swing her cane and shout, 'Huree for the handkerts.' One day she was bitten by a rattlesnake. The elders ran with oil and administered to her and she was healed." [Crandal, *Legacy*, p. 145]

"There was an old sister named Bathgate. We all called her Mother Bathgate, for she must have been upwards of sixty. She told me she had been in the coal-pits for forty years. She would travel on ahead and swing her cane and shout, 'Hurree for the handkerts.' She was a native of Scotland. One day as she sat down to rest, a rattlesnake bit her on the leg. The word came 'Stop the train!' All stopped instantly. The Elders ran with the oil and administered to her and she was instantly healed. Rode in the wagon that afternoon, but was able to cheer the company next day. I know she was bitten, for I saw her leg myself, and held the bottle of oil while Brothers Leonard and McAllister administered to her. She lived to reach her destination, and many years after." [Crandal, *Y.W. Journal*, p. 322]

"This day started from Camp D. D. McArthur, T. Leonard and Spicer W. Crandle as his Counsellors, Walter Granger as one of the Comisaries & Wm. Heaton the other, as those at the head of each hundred too under us. 117 persons in my hundred and 100 in Bro. Cradles. It being put upon me to take charge of the Oxen or teams at present I done so; yoked them and was ready for a start at 12 o'clock. When we started out under heavy shouts from those who remained Bro. Spencer at their head. Brothers Ferguson & McAllister

FIRST HANDCART COMPANY LOG | SECOND HANDCART COMPANY LOG

went a mile or to and comforted our hearts by singing the hand cart song and 3 cheers for all who aided in this operation.

"Traveled about 2 miles when our head cart was broken which for a moment put a damper on many but Bro. Dan and myself had it fixed in 25 minutes by putting in a new Axle in place of the one that had broken.

"It was quite warm and dusty but still traveled 8 miles and camped after Breaking an ox yoke which was replaced by the next morning in time to start I had bot. a stick from one Holler by Name who was kind to me also listened to my testimony in favor to Mormonism etc & lent me an orger to use for the purpose of making the yoke. Got into camp with the 1st company at sundown; the sick improving. All tired yet in good spirits." [Leonard, p. 1]

12 June - Thursday

"Journeyed 12 miles. Went very fast with our hand carts. Harriet still ill." [Walters]

"The journey was resumed at 6 a.m., and the company traveled 12 miles, over a very dusty road. Tents were pitched about 2 p.m., the Saints were in good spirits." [Galloway, p. 444]

"The camp started this morning at 6 a.m.

12 June - Thursday

"Day a dreadful one, dust beyond anything I think I ever saw. Traveled 12 miles & camped with Bro Edond again. Many were very tired but most took it without murmuring. one family however were dissatisfied. they had broke the order by taking to shun the dust and lost the Spirit of the Camp & one lad took plenty of the spirit of liquor Had my hands full in driving the carts teams and taking care of

Traveled twelve miles. The road was very dusty. Pitched tents about 2 p.m. All in good spirits." [Ellsworth, p. 96]

"the sick never was more worried more in my life....This day 10 persons with Birmingham & List as at their head left or refused to go further with us so we took their carts and left them on the ground" [Leonard, p. 1]

13 June - Friday

"Journeyed 7 miles. A pleasant road but journeyed so fast." [Walters]

"The journey was continued about 8 a.m., over good roads, and all went well. During the day a number of strangers visited with the Saints, who traveled that day 7 miles." [Galloway, p. 445]

"The camp started about 8 a.m. Traveled seven miles. Good roads. All went off well. Visited by a good (many) strangers." [Ellsworth, p. 96]

13 June - Friday

"Traveled about 7 miles and stoped at 2 o clock. Marked the cattle on the right hip with tar the figure was No 1; then fixed a lot of hand carts in connection with Capt. McArthur, found many arms much worn which we remedied by putting double boxing of tin. In the evening had meeting, and had sanctioned by the company by vote Mc Arthur myself and Bro. Crandel also the Presidents of each 20, who were stand as head to look after the interests of each tent, I was called upon to open by prayer and after much was said by Elders Dan & Spicer I spoke upon the propriety of going on foot instead of riding in the wagons as it would be no honor so to do, and again it was the salvation of the Camp to preserve the teams, also for the weakly ones when they were traveling

APPENDIX I: HANDCART Logbook for 9 June to July 8, 1856   201

FIRST HANDCART COMPANY LOG	SECOND HANDCART COMPANY LOG

SECOND HANDCART COMPANY LOG (continued): among the gentiles not to complain or murmur but to preach Mormonism and bear a faithful testimony of the truth for the sake of the cause and others who were destined to follow us.

"I also advised the sisters to take of their extra baggage and trade it off for provisions as I had done getting more than the things were worth.

"I also had the privelege of preaching Mormonism to several who listened attentively." [Leonard, p. 1-2]

14 June - Saturday (First Company)
"Journeyed 7 miles. Pleasant." [Walters]

"The company resumed the journey at 6 a.m. in good spirits, and traveled 7 miles over good roads. Tents were pitched at 9 a.m. Toward evening, James Ferguson arrived from the general camp. About 6 p.m. William Lee, the 12-year-old son of John Lee, died of consumption." [Galloway, p. 445]

"The camp started this morning at 6 a.m. In good spirits. Traveled seven miles. Pitched tents about 9 a.m. The roads good. The camp in good spirits. Towards evening Elder JAMES _____

14 June - Saturday (Second Company)
"Started early went 7 miles and camped again with Bro. Elsworths Company But about 12 o Clock Broke a yoke and false tongue and bearly escaped great danger from wild cattle etc; got into camp procured a stick for a ox yoke and made it before night; Just as James Ferguson an Birminhams and Lucus's folks came into camp who had been persuaded so to do by the former, we gave them 3 cheers each although they did not deserve it by any means.

"Bro Lee's Wellings boy in Bro Elsworth camp died about the time Bro James came into camp." [Leonard, p. 2]

FERGUSON came to us from the General Camp. About 6 p.m. WILLIAM LEE, son of JOHN LEE, died of consumption, age 12 years." [Ellsworth, p. 96]

15 June - Sunday (First Company)
"Got up about 4 o'clock to make a coffin for my brother, john Lee's son named William Lee, aged 12 years. Meetings as usual, and at the same time had to make another coffin for Sister Prator's child. Was tired with repairing hand carts the last week. Went and buried them by moonlight at Bear Creek." [Walters]

"The Saints remained in camp and held two meetings. The morning meeting which was commenced at 10:30 a.m. was addressed by Elder Joseph France, and the afternoon meeting, commencing at 1:30 p.m., by Edward Frost. A great number of strangers attended the meetings and they all paid good attention. At 9 o'clock in the morning, Lora Praeter, daughter of Richard Praeter, died of whooping cough; she was 3 years old. At 7:30 p.m. the sacrament was administered to the two companies. It was a time of rejoicing for all. Elder Ferguson addressed the Saints about 9 p.m. the remains of two children who had died were interred on the banks of Little Bear Creek. [In Iowa County, 35 miles from Iowa City.] [Galloway, p. 445]

"Today is Sunday. The Saints remained in camp and held two meetings. The morning meeting commenced

15 June - Sunday (Second Company)
"35 miles from cart camp at Iowa City. Had meeting Bro. France preached to the gentiles who had assembled to the Nos of I think 150. At half past one had another meeting which was opened by me when Bro. Frost preached upon the first principles. A good spirit prevailed. In the evening had meeting partook of theSacrament. J. Ferguson too gave us much good instruction. Two deaths in Bro Edmonds com." [Leonard, p. 2]

FIRST HANDCART COMPANY LOG

at half past ten. Singing. A prayer by Elder HEATON. Elder JOSEPH FRANCE addressed the meeting. Afternoon meeting commenced at half past one o'clock. Singing with prayer by Elder LEONARD. Elder EDWARD FROST addressed the meeting. A great many strangers attended the meetings. Good attention by all present. At nine o'clock this morning LORA PRATTER, daughter of RICHARD PRATTER, died of whooping cough, age 3 years. At half past seven the sacrament was administered to the two companies. It was a time or rejoicing for all. Elder FERGUSON addressed the Saints. About 9 p.m. the above named two children were interred at Little Bear Creek." [Ellsworth, p. 97]

16 June - Monday

Travelled 19 miles...pitch tent...mended carts. [Walters]

"At 6:30 a.m. the company resumed the journey in good spirits. After traveling 13 miles the company rested from 11:30 a.m. until 4 p.m. on Big Bear Creek. After traveling 2 miles further in the afternoon, encampment was formed for the night. About 9 p.m. the camp was visited by a rainstorm." [Galloway, p. 445]

"At half past six a.m. the camp moved off in good spirits. Traveled thirteen miles and rested from half past eleven a.m. until four p.m. at Big Bear Creek. The camp moved two miles and camped for the night. About nine we had a storm of rain.": [Ellsworth, p. 97]

17 June - Tuesday

Travelled 17 miles...pitched tent. "Made a little coffin for Bro. Job Welling's son and mended a hand cart wheel." [Walters]

"The bugle was blown at 4 a.m. for all hands to turn out. The company moved at 6:45 a.m., traveled 10 miles, then rested 2 hours, and at 2:20 p.m. tents were pitched for the night at a place where there was no wood, but plenty of water. About 3 p.m. Job Welling, son of Job Welling Sr., age 1 year and 7 months, died of canker or inflammation of the bowels." [Galloway, p. 445]

"At four a.m. the bugle was blown for all to turn out, and at quarter to seven the camp moved off. Traveled ten miles and rested two hours. At twenty past two we pitched our tents. The journey was performed without an accident. No wood, plenty of water. About twenty minutes past three, JOB WELLING, son of JOB WELLING, died, age one year and seven months. Died of canker or inflammation of the bowels." [Ellsworth, p. 97]

SECOND HANDCART COMPANY LOG

16 June - Monday

"Traveled 15 miles, tolerable good road; but the day was warm and many were very tired, sick improveing fast. Bro James after going about 2 miles with us took his leave for camp 45 miles, bought about 60 lbs lard for cart us and other purposes, Good Spirit in Camp Camped on Rear Creek." [Leonard, p. 2]

17 June - Tuesday

"Day fine and roads good. Went 15 miles further and camped on the Prarie, had much the appearance of rain. A goodly No of strangers present for whom the band plaid for them and received some pay." [Leonard, p. 3]

First Handcart Company Log	Second Handcart Company Log
18 June - Wednesday "Rose before sun rise; travelled about 10 miles. Very hot; and camped for the day. Harriet still very ill but hope she will soon be better if it please my Heavenly Father." [Walters]	**18 June - Wednesday** "Wednesday went 10 miles starting early, the day was warm & many gave out for want of food and water, Arrived at Dixons about 10 O clock and his well supplied all our 2 companies, the woman did not like it but the man was a gentle- "At 4 a.m. the bugle sounded for all to rise and at 5:20 the company resumed the journey, traveled 10 miles without accident, and pitched tents at 8:35 a.m., in order to give the sisters an opportunity of washing their clothes. During the day, the remains of Job Welling's little son were interred at a point 3 feet from the north-east corner of Mr. Watson's farm, in Section 25, Township 80, Range 17 West." [Galloway, p. 445] "At four a.m. the bugle sounded for all to turn out. At twenty minutes past five the camp rolled out, and traveled ten miles without an accident. Pitched tents at thirty-five past eight a.m. to give the sisters an opportunity of washing the clothes. Today the body of JOB WELLING was interred three feet from the Northeast corner of Mr. WATROUS' Farm, township 80, Range 17, Section 25. [Ellsworth, p. 97] man I told him he was doing the greatest favor he ever done in his life and I said God bless all who feel well towards this people Arrived in camp about 11 and fixed hand carts till dark. put a tin and iron on nearly all the arms to our carts. "Mr Gideon Gardner heard of me and came 4 miles with his Wife and 3 others to see me. we had a long talk and parted with the best of feelings. He plead hard for me to go home with him but I could not In the evening had meeting" [Leonard, p. 3]
19 June - Thursday Travelled about 13 miles. Camped Bear Creek [Walters] "The camp rolled out at 7:45 a.m. and traveled 15 miles without accident. Encampment for the night was made about noon at a place where wood and water was plentiful. Several of the Saints were rebaptized for their health by Elder John Oakley." [Galloway, p. 445] "The camp rolled out today at quarter to seven a.m. and traveled fifteen miles. The journey was accomplished without an accident. We camped at ten minutes to twelve noon. Plenty of wood and water. Several were baptized by Elder JOHN OAKLEY of their health. Three miles from Greenhustle." [Ellsworth, p. 97]	**19 June - Thursday** "Day warm at noon passed over North Skunk a beautiful stream. stoped to rest an hour or two; then had to rise a tremendous hill before which however I had to with 3 yokes cattle drove a balky team up loaded with 2 That for which the drive gave me 50 cnts. Traveled in all through the day 15 miles which caused us to be very tired at night. Camped on Elk Creek in a beautiful grove at 3 O Clock, when I fixed up my rifle with some balls went out and the first shot I ever made with her I cut a gray squirrel nearly in two the 2nd I centered a single pigeon and then tried it at a mark with success and satisfaction The little game I got was made good use of by the sick and feeble who are all improving." [Leonard, p. 3]

First Handcart Company Log	Second Handcart Company Log

20 June - Friday
  Travelled about 14 miles. [Walters]
  "The camp moved at 6:45 a.m., traveled 16 miles over a very hilly and rather rough country, making the day's journey very hard. In the morning, John Lloyd, wife and family 'backed out.' He was very much given to drinking whisky along the road. The company passed through the town of Newton in the morning about 9 o'clock. A halt was made from 10 to 12 o'clock, and tents were pitched for the night ___
	20 June - Friday
	  "again went about 15 miles and camped on Indian creek on our way we passed through the town of Newton where several hard customers were found, one man Uvel by name said he should hurry home and stop every damned Mormon from stopping on his primeses. another (while I was talking with a man by the Name of Wilson who said he was going along 2 1/2 miles to enquire of our principles) highly Insulted me by burlesqueing the company, Joseph Smith and finally our whole people and
	  4 p.m. on the banks of a beautiful stream of water, where there was plenty of wood. Several of the Saints were baptized for their health by Elder Oakley." [Galloway, p. 445-46]
	  "The camp moved off at quarter to seven a.m. Traveled sixteen miles. The road was very hilly and rather rough. It was rather a hard day's travel. About a quarter of eight this morning JOHN LLOYD, wife and family, backed out. He was very much given to drinking whiskey along the road. We passed through the city of Newton this morning about nine a.m. We rested by a stream from ten until twelve. Pitched our tents at four p.m. along side a beautiful stream of water. Plenty of wood Several were baptized for their health by Elder Oakley." [Ellsworth, p. 97-8]___ principles; I told him 3 times at different times in the hight of excitement that he was a liar, and came very near strikeing him, he was scared and begged pardon for Insulting me as he said I told him I cared not what he said to me but to hear Joseph Smith and this people abused I would not stand it he said the company had been duped because of their Ignorance and not a half dozen of them could read or write; he also had a good deal to say about our doings at Utah and as to becoming a state we never should, and also that we were a disloyal people, this made me more like cusing him than ever and preached fast I do say till he was confounded and the others said he had said enough and better hold on for the Mormon was to much for him.
	  "Bro Elsworth run against one of two other mean curses who harped upon the same things that the one did who talked to me. I saw another man Hammer by Name and a Mason who told me not to mind anything about what that fellow had said as he was a mean fellow at Noon we stoped at a creek where we stoped about 2 hours rested ourselves caught some fish then went on and in crossing a prarie in the heat many gave out with fatigue and want of water. I had I think high as 25 in my wagons at a time Mathew Hardy for the first time give out" [Leonard, p. 3-4]

First Handcart Company Log	Second Handcart Company Log
21 June - Saturday "Travelled about 13 miles. Camped at Indian Creek. Bro. Jas. Bower died about 6 o'clock; from Birmingham Conference. Went to buy wood to make the coffin but the kind farmer gave me the wood and nails. It had been a very hot day and I was never more tired, but God has said as my day my strength shall be. For this I rejoice that I have good health and strength according to my day." [Walters] "At 6:30 a.m. the camp moved on, traveled 13 miles, rested 30 minutes by the side of a stream, and later an hour on the top of a hill. About 1 p.m. tents were pitched for the night in a grove where there was plenty of wood and water. At 4:45 p.m. James Bowers died of quick consumption, aged 44 years." [Galloway, p. 446] "At ten minutes to seven the camp moved off and traveled thirteen miles. Rested thirty _____	**21 June - Saturday** "Hard roads traveled 13 or 14 miles, and on the way broke 2 axeltrees out of Frews and Kennsington sustained the loss, we had one whole one and splised the 2nd & all was fixed up without delaying the company above what was necessary for their good. At 2 O Clock we crossed over South Skunk bridge at which we rested and I changed our cattle by putting a raw pair of steers on the lead to get from the tongue an ox that would hold back and stop the wagon and team Got into camp at 3 O Clock and at 5 Bro. Bowers died by whose side I had sat from nearly the time I had come into camp I closed his eyes amid great mourning among his family and friends, In the evening Capt Dan and myself went back to the Tavern and bought 3 rails which Mr. Reith gave us turned to axeltrees 8 in No of the best kind of Hickory. He said we had helped him to raise a bent to his barn and he would not charge us anything." minutes by the side of a stream, and an hour on the top of a hill. No accident happened to the camp. All was well. At ten minutes to one p.m. we pitched our tents in a grove. Plenty of wood and water. At a quarter to five p.m. JAMES BOWERS DIED of quick consumption. Age 44, 24th of January 1856." [Ellsworth, p. 98] [Leonard, p. 4]
22 June - Sunday "Got up at day break and made the coffin for Bro. James Bowers by 9 o'clock and he was buried at 11 o'clock. Ages 44 years, 5 months, 2 days. His relatives cried very much after I liften him in the coffin and waiting to screw him down. 11 o'clock, washed in the creek and felt very much refreshed. Meeting 2 o'clock until seven. Bro. MacCarter spoke about being driven and he did walk into the Gentiles first rate and told them that they did not mean to be driven again and not to be excited by the priests to come against us as a people again for they would fine them a terrible people." [Walters] "The remains of James Bowers were buried near two other graves, a quarter of a mile east of the main line for Fort Des Moines, in Section 26, Township 79, Range 22. The camp was called together for meeting at 4:20 p.m. Elders Wm. Heaton, Daniel D. McArthur and Edmund Ellsworth preached and gave good instructions." [Galloway, p. 446] "Brother JAMES BOWERS was buried near two other graves a quarter of a mile east of the main line of Fort Des Moines, Section 76, Township 29, Range 72. The camp was called together for meeting at twenty	**22 June - Sunday** "This morning James Bowers was burried. The day was very warm; had one meeting in the afternoon, I was called upon to pray and was nearly overcome by foul Air etc. Bro. Heaton preached a noble sermon, the Gentiles of a [?] a goodly No. were present paid good attention After this Elders Elsworth & McArthur spoke to the saints as dictated by the spirit of God. We then administered to several who were sick indeed." [Leonard, p. 4]

FIRST HANDCART COMPANY LOG

minutes past four p.m. Singing. Prayer by Elder LEONARD. The meeting was addressed by Elders, HEATON, McARTHUR, and ELLSWORTH. Much good instruction was given." [Ellsworth, p. 98]

23 June - Monday

"Rose early and travelled 10 miles; then repaired the hand carts. Harriet a little better." [Walters]

"The camp resumed the journey at 7:25, traveled 10 miles and pitched tents at 10 a.m. The roads were rather rough and dusty part of _____

24 June - Tuesday

"Travelled 18 miles. Very hot. Bro. Ellsworth being always with a family from Birmingham named Brown and always that tent going first and walking so fast and some fainted by the way. Bro. Frost worn out by going so fast and not resting and many more." [Walters]

"The camp rolled out at 6:30 a.m., traveled 11 miles over a somewhat rough and dusty road. The day was exceedingly warm, and it was rather hard pulling for the handcart boys. Tents were pitched at 1:30 p.m. at a place where wood and water was plentiful. About half a mile from the camp, on the left side of the road, an old mobocrat came into camp and tried to make a fuss with Capt. Ellsworth. Sydney Shinn, son of James and Mary Shinn, died in the morning. He was buried

SECOND HANDCART COMPANY LOG

23 June - Monday

"Rose early hewed out 8 axiltrees; at half past 7 started went 10 miles so staid and camped on 4 mile Creek. On the way saw a Mr. Clafton a Mason and County Surveyor; also a friend to Mormons. He employed many of them at the drive from Nauvoo; one Barker in particular and family. I bought 13 lbs of lard the way and led through a hilly country. During the day,, the company crossed two good sized streams. Encampment was made for the night, 4 miles from Fort Des Moines, where wood and water was plentiful. In the morning the company passed through a small town 7 miles from the Fort." [Galloway, p. 446]

"The camp moved out at twenty-five past seven a.m. Traveled ten miles. Pitched tents by 10 a.m. The roads were rather rough in some parts and a little hilly and somewhat dusty. We passed two middling good streams of water, a good camping ground, plenty of wood and water, four miles from Fort Des Moines. Passed a small town this morning seven miles from the Fort." [Ellsworth, p. 98]

for 105 cts for cart grease, In arriving in camp a man was stalled & I hitched on 4 yoke of cattle broke 2 chain hooks but hauled the load of 5000 out his Name was Smith. I also went to the saw mill near by bought a piece of stuff to make false tongue and put in in. I also preached Mormonism to several men who listened attentively and acknowledged our doctrine. We are now within 4 miles of Fort Demoin and have flour and Bakon to buy." [Leonard, p. 4-5]

24 June - Tuesday

"Traveled 13 miles amid a dreadful hot day, passed fort Demoin on the ferry Bridge where they tried to pick up a row with me as I was the last to pass, they demanded 20 cts more than had been agreed upon and I paid it rather than have a fuss. there were 20 or 30 together asking for a fuss but we outwitted the Devil & his imps; One ton of flour was bot. today at 6 Dollars per hund. In the evening many strangers were present 1 by the Name of Hedge a Mason, they std still 10 O Clock to hear us talk and preach Mr. Bennett the owner of the land on which we camped got mad & ordered us off, but Bro. Elsworth we would not go till morning." [Leonard, p. 5]

under an elm tree." [Ellsworth, p. 98]

FIRST HANDCART COMPANY LOG

30 yards south of the bridge on the bank of Four Mile Creek, under an elm tree." [Galloway, p. 446]

"The camp rolled out at thirty past six a.m. Traveled eleven miles. The roads were a little rough and somewhat dusty. The day was exceedingly warm, through which it was rather hard for the handcart boys. Pitched tents at thirty past one p.m. Plenty of wood, water, about a half mile from the camp on the left side of the road. An old mobocrat came and tried to make a fuss with our captain. SIDNEY SHINN, son of JAMES and MARY SHINN Jr., died this morning. Buried thirty yards south of the bridge on Four Mile Creek, on the east bank,

25 June - Wednesday

"Travelled about 13 miles. Sold some files to a carpenter; repaired some hand carts." [Walters]

"The camp resumed the journey at 6:25 a.m. and traveled 19 miles. A gentle, refreshing breeze blew nearly all day. The roads were good. There was plenty of water at Six Mile Creek and at Nine Mile Creek. Tents wer pitched at 1:45 on the bank of a river, where there was plenty of wood." [Galloway, p. 446]

"The camp rolled out this morning at twenty-five past six a.m. Traveled nineteen miles. A gentle breeze blew all the way. It was quite refreshing. The roads good; supplied water at six miles and at nine. Pitched tents at forty-five past one p.m. along side of a river bank. Plenty of wood." [Ellsworth, p. 98]

26 June - Thursday

"Travelled about 1 mile. Very faint for the (lack) of food. We are only allowed about 3/4 of lb. of flour a head each day and about 3 oz. of sugar each week. Tea good and plenty; about a 1/4 of lb. of bacon each a week; which makes those that have no money very weak. Made a child's coffin for Sister Sheen - Emma Sheen ages 2 1/2 years." [Walters]

"The camp moved off this morning at 6:30 a.m., traveled 10 miles, forded the river Raccoon, about 1 mile from the camping ground, passed the town of BA_____ at 12 o'clock noon. The camp again forded the river and camped on the west bank where there was plenty of wood and water. The road was good, with the exception of passing over two or three hills. Emma Sheen (2 years and 8 months old) daughter of Robert and Eliza Sheen, died of whooping cough." [Galloway, p. 446-47]

"The camp moved off this morning at thirty past six a.m. Traveled ten miles. Forded the River Racoon about one mile from the camping ground. Passed the town of Balley. At 12 noon we again forded the

SECOND HANDCART COMPANY LOG

25 June - Wednesday

"In the morning made an axeltree; & started about 7 O Clock went 18 or 19 miles; many gave out & we had all we could draw without using up the cattle. Camped at 4 on Coon River and took a bathe. In the evening had a meeting and heard from several of the Brethren who bore testimony of the power of God in strengthening them thus far. Some are ready to apostasize or stop among the Gentiles Sister Ludert & Reed are among the No. Sister Hannah Forres fainted and fell while pulling the cart Bro Ramseys child is very sick and by some not expected to live. at even a goodly No of Gentiles came in to the camp so I preached Mormonism to several of them for some time." [Leonard, p. 5]

26 June - Thursday

"In the morning made another axile had prayers and started at 7 O, Clock went half a mile forded the Coon river the water one foot deep and 60 feet wide about the women walked over boldly. Went 12 miles and camped at 4. Just in time to escape a shower. During the day Bro Cunningham from the Bluffs came to meet and give us much good news especially some from my family as he had seen them in Sept last." [Leonard, p. 5]

EMMA SHINN, daughter of ROBERT and ELIZA SHINN, died this morning of whooping cough, age two years and eight months." [Ellsworth, p. 99]

First Handcart Company Log

Racoon and camped on the west bank. Plenty of wood and water; the road good with the exception of two or three hills.

27 June - Friday

"Got up before sun rise. Cut a tomb stone on wood and bury the child before starting from camp. Travelled about 10 miles. Repaired hand carts and quite tired and slept without rocking." [Walters]

"The body of Emma Sheen was buried in the morning. 12 feet south of a walnut tree, on the west bank of the Raccoon River, opposite the saw mill. At 7 a.m., the camp rolled out, traveled 10 miles over good roads and camped at 10:30 a.m. in a beautiful valley on the banks of a good sized steam. On the west bank of the stream is a beautiful spring of water." [Galloway, p. 447]

"EMMA SHINN was buried this morning twelve feet southeast of a walnut tree on the west bank of the Racoon, nearly opposite the sawmill. At seven a.m. the camp rolled out and traveled ten miles. Good roads. Camped at thirty past ten a.m. in a beautiful valley alongside of a good stream. On the right side of the road on the west bank of the stream there is a beautiful spring of water." [Ellsworth, p. 99]

28 June - Saturday

"We think Harriet a little better. Rose soon after 4 o'clock. Started with high wind. Short of water and I was never more tired. Rested a bit after we camped then came on a thunder storm, and rain blowed our tent down. Split the canvas and wet our clothes and we had to lay on the wet clothes and ground. I thought of going through needful tribulation but it made me cross. I took poor Harriet into a tent and fixed the tent up again as well at Bear Creek Station." [Walters]

"The camp moved at 5:40 a.m. and traveled 16 miles over good roads except certain parts of it, which led through a hilly country. For a distance of about 13 miles, the water was scarce, but the emigrants were supplied with water at Bear Station. Tents were pitched at 1 p.m., and near the camping ground there was plenty of ___

water while wood was rather scarce. During a heavy thunder storm, about 6 p.m., one of the tents was blown down, while other tents were rent from top to bottom." [Galloway, p. 447]

"The camp moved off at forty past five and traveled sixteen miles. The road was good with the exception of some parts of it being rather hilly. The water rather scarce for about thirteen miles. We got supplied with

Second Handcart Company Log

27 June - Friday

"Traveled 9 miles and after getting in at 12 O Clock on South Coon whare I mad a [?] and then was oblizeged to do the painful necessity of getting some lumber from a Mr France for 10 cents worth 15 cents to make a coffin for John Ransay aged 19 months who died at 6 O'Clock. I made the coffin and finished it at dark and put the body into it." [Leonard, p. 5-6]

First Handcart Company Log	Second Handcart Company Log

water at Bear Station. Pitched tents at 1 p.m. Pretty good camping ground; plenty of water; wood rather scarce. We had heavy thunder storm about six p.m. One of the tents was blown down and another rent from top to bottom." [Ellsworth, p. 99]

29 June - Sunday

"Rather stiff in joints when we rose and thought, as thy day thy strength shall be, was fulfilled upon us for which I feel thankful to my Heavenly Father. Busy all day. My wife and Sarah mending. Short of provisions. Children crying for their dinner. Got the tent up and slept comfortable." [Walters]

"The company remained in camp all day to rest. The weather was fine. Several strangers visited the camp. About 4:21 p.m. the Saints met together for worship, and the meeting was addressed by Elders Samuel Hargreave, Edmund Ellsworth, Daniel D. McArthur and Spicer W. Crandall." [Galloway, p. 447]

"We remained in camp all day and rested our bodies. The day was fine. Several strangers were in the camp. At twenty past four p.m. the saints met together for meeting, singing, and prayer by Elder CRANDALL. The meeting was addressed by Elders HARGREAVE, ELLSWORTH, McARTHUR, LEONARD, and CRANDALL on a variety of subjects for the benefit of the Saints." [Ellsworth, p. 99]

30 June - Monday

"Rose in good health, except Harriet, and started with out hand carts with but a little break-fast as only 3 1/2 lbs. of flour was served out over night, but never travelled 17 miles more easily. Got 5 lbs. of flour and bacon about 1 1/4 lb., 3/4 rice, sugar 3/4 lb. and was refreshed after satisfying nature. Sleep very well after prayers in tent." [Walters]

29 June - Sunday

"Day most beautiful some strangers came to our tent to whom we preached to for an hour or two. Meeting at 4 O'Clock I was called upon to take the charge of the same, prayer by Bro. Elsworth & then after singing again called upon Elder Hargeaves to come forward & address the congregation which he done to great satisfaction the gentiles to a considerable number paid good attention. I also bore a strong testimony to what had been said and added a few ideas upon the gathering. The strangers were then released and the Saints requested to remain where they were instructed by Elders Crandle Elsworth Mc Arthur and myself as dictated by the spirit of God and surely there was some most cutting instructions unto murmurers disobeyers of counsel and women who were dictating & finding fault with their husbands all of which had a good affect we also told them what they might depend upon when they got upon the other side of the River about riding in those Wagons, etc. The Saints felt first rate." [Leonard, p. 6]

30 June - Monday

"Made an axile in the morning and started out at half past six; traveled 16 miles over a fine road with great ease very few in the wagons nearly off hill the walk after the severe lecture they had received. In the afternoon Bro. Crandle drove the teams. while I conversed for miles on Mormonism with Mr Lockwood a reasonable man. We camped on the

"The camp moved out at 6:55 a.m., traveled 16 miles, during the day, and 12 miles without resting. Part of the day, the road led through a hilly country, and there was no water for 12 miles. Tents were pitched at 1:10 p.m. at a place where there was plenty of wood and water. A good spirit prevailed in camp." [Galloway, p. 447]

"The camp moved out at fifty-five past six a.m. Traveled sixteen miles. We traveled twelve miles without resting. The roads were but middling; part of the way somewhat hilly. No water for twelve miles. Pitched tents at ten past one p.m. All in good spirits. Plenty of wood and water." [Ellsworth, p. 99]

head waters of Turkey Creek. by ourselves." [Leonard, p. 6]

First Handcart Company Log

1 July - Tuesday

"Rose soon. It looked very cloudy and began to rain. Travelled about 15 miles. Walked very fast - nearly 4 miles an hour. Brother Brown's family and some young sisters with Bro. Ellsworth always going first which causes many of the brothers to have hard feelings. I have heard them call them Bro. Ellsworth as well, as he always walks with them and looks after them, being in the same tent. 1/2 lb. of flour each; 2 oz. of rice; which is very little and my children cry with hunger and it grieves me and makes me cross. I can live upon green herbs or anything and do go nearly all day without any and am strengthened with a morsel. Repaired hand carts. A storm came on about 11 o'clock and lasted 1 hour 1/2. Split the tent and not a dry thread on us." [Walters]

"The camp moved out at 7:10 a.m., traveled 15 miles over a rather rough road, passed a creek and camped for the night on the bank of a creek; wood was plentiful about half a mile from camp. About 10:30 p.m. a thunder storm visited the camp, during which one tent was blown down and another one rent." [Galloway, p. 447]

The camp moved out at ten past seven a.m. and traveled fifteen miles. The road was rather rough. Passed one creek of water. Camped on the side of the creek. Plenty of water. Wood plentiful; about a half a mile from the camp. About half past ten p.m. we had a severe thunder storm. One tent was blown down and another rent." [Ellsworth, p. 99-100]

2 July - Wednesday

"Rose about 5 o'clock after sleeping in wet clothes, and made a coffin for Bro. Card belonging to the Independent Company but travels with us, for his daughter named ____ Card, aged ____. 5 miles from Indian town. Brother Parker's boy, from Preston, England, aged 6 years, lost. 2 miles gone after him which make us stop today and we hope the brothers will find him. No found; traveled about 14 or 15 miles." [Walters]

"The company remained encamped until 3:50 p.m., owing to Brother McArthur's company having lost a boy on the way. After starting, the company traveled 10 miles, camped about an hour on the banks of the Nishnabotna River, a short distance northwest of an Indian town situated on the banks of a river. The camping ground was a most delightful one." [Galloway, p. 447]

"We remained in camp till fifty past three p.m.

Second Handcart Company Log

1 July - Tuesday

"Left camp at 7.30 traveled 14 miles, and camped on the Prairie But during the day lost Arthur Parker. He was not mired over 30 minutes before one of the drivers was dispatched after him but without success. he arrived in camp and another man was sent on a mule he staid out till after midnight and through the most dreadful storm I ever witnessed on the plains. The rain poured in torrents and the wind blew almost a gale, one of our tents was riven to tatters and all in it drenched we got them into the wagon and our tent till morning. Our team that we sent for provisions came with 700 pounds of meat one death in Eds camp." [Leonard, p. 6-7]

2 July - Wednesday

"Capt Dan and myself started early on mule and horse in pursuit of the boy went 14 miles back enquiring of all we saw but not a word could be hear from him We then traversed the Creek for miles looking for some sign of the wanderer but not a single trace could be found. We were as well as our animals very tired, so we stoped at Peter Conhauwers took something too eat for which we paid 50 cts. We then went to Lockwoods who was quite stiff thinking we ought to stop & hunt till the boy was found dead or alive Brother Parker staid to get help and search still longer but we were obliged to abandon it or hasard the lives of hundreds who might be without provisions in a country where it could not be had" [Leonard, p. 7]

FIRST HANDCART COMPANY LOG

owing to Brother McARTHUR'S company having lost a boy by the way. At the above hour we started and traveled ten miles. Rested about half an hour on the bank of the river Nishnabotna. Camped two and one half miles west northwest of an Indian town on the banks of a river. Plenty of wood. A most delightful camping ground." [Ellsworth, p. 100]

3 July - Thursday

"Ever to be remembered. Bro. Card gave me 1/2 dollar for making his daughter's coffin. Start with my cart before the camp as others had done but was told not and had to suffer for it. Went the wrong way; about 30 of the brothers and sisters and went 10 1/2 miles wrong way. We put our three hand carts together and made beds with all the clothes we had and all layed down about 1/2 past 10 o'clock. 11 o'clock Bro. Butler, who had charge of the mule teams, came with the mules and wagon to fetch us. Got to camp when they were getting up. Laid down about an hour and started with the camp." [Walters]

"The company resumed the journey at 9:45 a.m. and traveled 14 miles. After traveling 6 miles a halt was made on the bank of a creek, with but very little water. After traveling 12 _____

4 July - Friday

"About 20 miles. Tired out. Tied my cart behind the wagon and we got in after 3 nights. 1st night, thunder, lightning and rain and our tent splitting and blowing over. All wet to the skin. 2nd night; wind blowing; had hard work to hold the tent up and this last night no sleep. Went to bed; slept never better and rose refreshed." [Walters]

"The company moved out at 7:10 a.m. and traveled 20 miles. During the day, they crossed two creeks. The first ten miles they had plenty of water, but the last ten there was none. The roads were good. At 3:15 p.m. encampment was made by the side of a good creek where there was plenty of wood. This place was 14 miles from Council Bluffs. All the emigrants were in good spirits." [Galloway, p. 448]

SECOND HANDCART COMPANY LOG

3 July - Thursday

"Started early to overtake Bro Elsworth who had started out the day before. Traveled 12 miles by Indian town and stoped to noon and soon after came to where B E. Camped, here we found several of our crowd whom Bro Butler had taken in the muleteam here Sister Parker was determined to stop but we prevailed on her finally to come on with us; while her husband was still back in pursuit of his son which was truly a lamentable case. We then went 12 miles further (and after stoping at 5 O'Clock taking tea) camped on Prairie Creek with Bro Edmonds company mid loud cheers. But some of this crowd was out all night some of them on another road." [Leonard, p. 7]

miles, the company turned down a road leading to the right, and after traveling 2 miles down that road, an encampment was made by the side of a creek with plenty of water, but only a little wood. About 20 of the camp people lost their way, but found their way to camp about midnight." [Galloway, p. 447-48]

"The camp moved out at forty-five past nine a.m. and traveled fourteen miles. Rested at the side of a creek six miles from where we started. Very little water as we came along. After traveling twelve miles, we turned down a road to the right two miles and camped by the side of a creek with plenty of water. Little wood. About twenty of the camp lost the road, but returned about midnight." [Ellsworth, p. 100]

4 July - Friday

"Struck our tents at 7, & was soon upon our way, traveled 17 miles, passing the Mishenebotany. - after stoping 2 hours and taking some refreshments at half past 2, came into camp at 6, on Silver Creek There Bro. Arguyle shot a tame elk for which had to be paid twelve Dollars we had the half of it." [Leonard, p. 7]

FIRST HANDCART COMPANY LOG

"The camp moved out at ten past seven a.m. and traveled twenty miles. We passed two creeks the first ten miles, the other ten, no water. The roads good. Camped at fifteen past three p.m. alongside of a good creek of water. Plenty of wood. Fourteen miles from Council Bluffs. All in good spirits." [Ellsworth, p. 100]

5 July - Saturday

"A deer or elk served out to camp. Brother Parker brings into the camp his little boy that had been lost. Great joy right through the camp. The mother's joy I cannot describe."

6 July - Sunday

"Made 2 doors for the farmer, 3 dollars and boarded with the farmer." [Walters]

"The company remained in camp. A meeting was held at 4:20 p.m., which was addressed by Elders Andrew Galloway, John Oakley, Edmund Ellsworth, and Daniel D. McArthur. The meeting was attended by quite a number of strangers, some of whom paid good attention, while others, who did not care to hear the doctrines advocated, walked off grumbling." [Galloway, p. 448]

"Today is Sunday. We remained in camp. Had meeting at twenty past four p.m. Singing and prayer by Brother CRANDALL. The meeting was addressed by Elders GALLOWAY, OAKLEY, ELLSWORTH and McARTHUR. A good many strangers present. Some were attentive, others could not bear the doctrine and walked off grumbling." [Ellsworth, p. 100]

7 July - Monday

"Harriet better. Lydia poorly. Travelled about 20 miles." [Walters]

"The camp rolled out at 7 a.m. and traveled 15 miles through a hilly country; rested 30 minutes on the bank of a good creek. For a distance of about 8 miles, there was little of no water. A few houses were passed about

SECOND HANDCART COMPANY LOG

5 July - Saturday

"Laid in camp all day done a good deal of washing, and at 5 O Clock went out on a hunt and after a good deal of tramping started 2 deer, one of which I had as fair a chance as ever

Expect we are going to rest. Washing, etc. today, Jordan Creek. Make a pair of sashes for the old farmer. Indian meal; no flour. Slept well." [Walters]

"The company remained in camp all day to rest, wash clothes, etc." [Galloway, p. 448]

"The company remained in camp today to rest and get their clothes washed." [Ellsworth, p. 100]

I had in my life but in cocking my rifle it drew off the camp and when I pulled on the [?] bellow of course it was without effect although broad side & within a stones throw Taylor killed a hug doe to be dealt out in the morning." [Leonard, p. 7-8]

6 July - Sunday

"Camp Israel on Silver Creek Sunday July 6th 1856. In camp all day rested well, laid hands on Father Holihue and daughter, great faith was exercised At 5 had a meeting, Elders Galloway Oakley Elsworth and Mc Arthur preached to us much instruction was given after which we laid hands on Father Ivins was mouth & pronounced a great blessing upon his head Although of great age I told him he should arrive safe in the Vallie of the Mountains and receive a blessing from the Prophet Brigham." [Leonard, p. 8]

7 July - Monday

"Left at half past 7 Traveled to Musketoe Creek 7 miles on our way saw several old Nauvoo Mormons Charles Alen, Joseph Walker who gave me The Mormon, New York Tribune and the Banner of Liberty. I also saw Mr Morcer from Portage Co Ohio he knew several of my friends in those parts especially in

First Handcart Company Log	Second Handcart Company Log
2 miles from the camping ground, where several old 'Mormons' were staying. Tents were pitched about 5 o'clock p.m." [Galloway, p. 448] "The camp rolled out at 7 a.m. Traveled fifteen miles. The roads were very hilly. Rested thirty minutes alongside of a good creek. For about eight miles there was little or no water. **8 July - Tuesday** "Travelled around-about road about 20 miles. Crossed the river Missouri and camped at the City of Florence. Very tired; glad to rest. Slept well. Lydia better and Harriet. All in good spirits. Expect to stop some time. Old Winter Quarters." [Walters] "The journey was resumed at 7 a.m. and the company traveled 16 miles over a very rough road and up and down hills. One of the handcarts broke down on the way. The company rested on Pigeon Creek about 2 1/2 hours. Here the company cooked their dinner and got well rested. They then crossed the Missouri River on the steam ferryboat, a short distance below Florence. They arrived at the camp ground at Florence, about 5 p.m." [Galloway, p. 448] "The camp moved out at 7 a.m. and traveled sixteen miles over a very rough road up and down hills. One handcart broke down by the way. The camp rested at Pigeon Creek for two and a half hours. Cooked dinner and got nicely rested. Crossed the Missouri by the steam ferry-boat a little below Florence. Got to the camping ground at Florence at fifty past four p.m." [Ellsworth, p. 100-01]	Akron. I preached Mormonism to him and he bid us God speed." [Leonard, p. 8] Passed a few houses about two miles from the camping ground where a good many old Mormons were staying. Pitched tents about 5 p.m." [Ellsworth, p. 100] **8 July - Tuesday** "This morning several of the old mormons came to see us among others was old Hetherington who gave us considerable [?] The day was very warm and the roughest road I ever traveled went 17 miles stoping on or near Pigeon took some dinner then went to the Ferry crossed the River in an hour & a half on the steam Ferry Nebraska arrived in camp at half past 7 O'Clock felt first rate. Saw McGow & F. Wooley." [Leonard, p. 8]

APPENDIX J

Handcart Logbook
The Enoch Train Pioneers – 17 July to 28 September 1856
FLORENCE, NEBRASKA TO SALT LAKE CITY

First Handcart Company Log

17 July - Thursday
"Left Florence City and we travelled about 3 miles. Went to ___ to seek work by buy a pair of shoes for Sarah but got no work for want of tools. Stopped there all night; slept in a stable. Came back to camp Friday morning." [Walters]

"The camp rolled out at 11 a.m. Traveled two and one-half miles to Summer Quarters." [Ellsworth, p. 101]

18 July - Friday
"Harriet very ill. Bought her some little niceties but she could not eat the pickles. Had a piece of buffalo beef given to me." [Walters]

"July 18th and 19th. We remained in camp till Saturday, finishing the carts and getting the balance of our outfit." [Ellsworth, p. 101]

19 July - Saturday
"Repairing carts all day." [Walters]

20 July - Sunday
"Preparing to start; travelled about 7 miles." [Walters]

"The camp rolled out at 6 p.m. and traveled seven miles. Pitched tents half past nine." [Ellsworth, p. 101]

21 July - Monday
"Travelled about 18 miles. Harriet better." [Walters]

Second Handcart Company Log

17 July - Thursday
"Bro. Elsworth Co. rolled [?] to Cutters Park, Capt. Dan and myself helped McGow & Grant to separate and mark as also to turn over to the Church the cattle which George had bought. Made one ox yoke; helped to get Bro. Crandel and Dickman off after some yoke and berie timber. In the evening had a meeting. Bro George Capt Dan myself and Crandl spoke to the people as the spirit dictated & truly we had a time of rejoiceing. A great many of the Brethren and Sisters all out to wash so that we cannot go out to camp in a new place wich would be very agreeable in consequence of a great quantity of dust in this place." [Leonard, p. 10]

18 July - Friday
"In connection with Bro. Dan made 8 pair of Ox Beaux and much other work a part of which was to help to select cows and cattle for our outfit to the Vallie. George Grant Preached to us in the evening." [Leonard, p. 10]

19 July - Saturday
"Fitted up our yokes etc. & Wrote a letter to my Wife. Brother Bunker arrived with the 3rd company of hand Carts. In good spirits etc." [Leonard, p. 10]

20 July - Sunday
"Went out to Capt. Elsworths Company enjoyed ourselves first rate, took dinner with them as also some brandy. They started out and went 3 miles and camped on little Papp. Bro. William Kible The steamer that had [?] bit came in sight." [Leonard, p. 10]

21 July - Monday
"Florence Nebraska This morning the Genoa landed and left 800 sacks of flour with sugar apples

First Handcart Company Log

"The camp rolled out at nine a.m. and traveled eighteen miles. Crossed the Elk Horn by the Ferry Boat and camped about five p.m. Before all the tents were pitched we had quite a thunder storm, and continued more or less all the night." [Ellsworth, p. 101]

22 July - Tuesday
"Passed off the ferry at (H)elk Horn. Travelled about 12 miles. Thunder storm." [Walters]

"The camp rolled out at twelve p.m. and traveled seventeen miles along a good road. Passed five dead oxen. Camped at half past seven p.m. at Liberty Pole camping ground close to the Platte River." [Ellsworth, p. 101]

23 July - Wednesday
"Very hot day. Travelled about 14 miles. Harriet much better." [Walters]

"The camp rolled out at half past seven a.m. and traveled fourteen and one half miles. Camped at Loop Fork at four p.m. An excellent camping place. Good feed for cattle. The roads were rather heavy and the day very warm. Water scarce." [Ellsworth, p. 101]

24 July - Thursday
"Very hot. Went about 18 miles. Harriet still better." [Walters]

"The camp rolled out at half past seven a.m. Traveled nine miles. The roads pretty good. Camped at twelve p.m. at Shell Creek." [Ellsworth, p. 101]

Second Handcart Company Log

etc etc. We onloaded 3 wagons and yoked 6 yokes of oxen and Capt. Dan

Crandel and myself took charge of them and drove 4 loads apiece, or at least 2 of us. Bunkers teams also helped. In the evening had another tin— with the cows. In the afternoon Baptised a Prusian by the name of Heffing also rebaptised Ludert and Mother Lourermore Brother Crandel went with me." [Leonard, p. 10]

22 July - Tuesday
"Capt Dan and myself made some ship lashes, I also bought some pant stuff, and some hickory for shirts paid 1.70 Elizabeth [?]ooddle made the pants and Sister Wanless the shirts of Hickory busy in getting ready as also waiting for McGowe, got Haples and sings" [Leonard, p. 10]

23 July - Wednesday
"This morning had a wagon bought for us at 75 dollars, which we had to make beaux for we also got our out fit on the wagons and guns [?]lected with a limited portion of amunition, I also had the mule shod and staples furnished and fret in In the evening had a meeting Capt Dan put it upon Bro. Crandle and myself to talk to the people. much good and powerful instruction was given. after which Bro James Reed by his own carlessness was shot by some scoundrel through the thigh; he cannot go on the would is so serious." [Leonard, p. 10-11]

24 July - Thursday
"This day made a start, at 11 O Clock went 7 miles & camped on little Pappose our teams were tremendously heavily loaded it took from 5 to 7 yoke to draw each of our wagons up the hill from Florence on the start, we had 13 yoke of cattle 3 on each of Brothers Crandels, Marriott, and Dickmans team, and 4 on mine [?] axel-trees; our cattle are good ones but some are quite wild. I had the manageing and dividing of their strength, which was done to satisfaction. The Saints felt first rate and strong, but 3 which we had to bant 2 germans and mother Burdett." [Leonard, p. 11]

"Left Florence. Travelled 7 miles." [Wakefield, "Birmingham Dairy," & Hafen, *Handcarts*, p. 72]

"...on the 24th of July, at 12 o'clock, we struck our tents and started for the plains, all in the best of spirits. Nothing but the very best of luck attended us continually. Our train consisted of 12 yoke of oxen, 4 wagons, and 48 carts; we also had 5 beef and 12 cows; flour, 55 lbs. per head, 100 lbs. rice, 550 lbs.

First Handcart Company Log

25 July - Friday

"Travelled about 18 1/2 miles." [Walters]

"The camp rolled out at seven a.m. and traveled nineteen miles. The roads were pretty good with the exception of about five miles. Rather sandy. Camped at six p.m. two miles from Loop Ferry Fork." [Ellsworth, p. 101]

26 July - Saturday

"Passed over the Ferry -Luke Fort. Travelled about 6 miles. (H)as soon (h)as we crossed it looked very heavy and black. We had (not) got far and it began to lightning and so on the thunders roared and about the middle of the train of hand carts the lightning struck a brother and he fell to rise no more in that body, by the name of Henry Walker, from Carlisle Conference; aged 58 years. Left a wife and children. One boy burnt a little, named James Studard; we thought he would die but he recovered and was able to walk and Brother William Studard, father of the boy was knocked to the ground and a sister, Betsy Taylor, was terribly shook but recovered. All wet through. This

Second Handcart Company Log

sugar, 400 lbs. dried apples, 125 labs. tea, and 200 lbs. salt for the company." [McArthur Report & Hafen, *Handcarts*, p. 214-17]

25 July - Friday

"Bad luck during the night our mule run back with a heavy ox yoke attached to him Capt Dan & Bowering left at day break in pursuit of it We were obliged to do with one yoke of cattle less, but still I proposed we did not wait for dan, but started out puting my load of 4000 hundred with 3 yoke of oxen, went 16 miles and camped at the Horn crossing big papy at half past 10. where we become bog down we also left one at the camp ground When he arrived at 5, o'clock but not in time to get over and to a good camp ground. At 8 Capt Dan came in with the mule but Bowering was down and 2 or 3 miles back having traveld over 40 miles on one meal of vietuals. Quite a number of Omahas upon the ground, and in the night 1 of them was wounded in a [?]" [Leonard, p. 11]

"Traveled 20 miles, to Elkhorn River, where we found a camp of Indians, many of whom came to meet us and were very friendly. The chief took my cart and drew it into camp about 1/4 mile and although a tall strong looking man, it made the perspiration run down his face until it dropped on the ground. Many of the Indians got drunk in the night and commenced fighting among themselves, but not knowing what they were at we were all called out of our beds and ordered to load our guns. After watching for some time, all became quiet and we returned again to the arms of Morpheus. In the morning we heard that one of the Indians had been shot in the arm by one of his fellows, which we soon verified, their sending over to our camp to know if we had a doctor amongst us. Brother Eatkin went and dressed it." [Wakefield, "Birmingham Dairy," & Hafen, *Handcarts*, p. 71-72]

26 July - Saturday

"Elkhorn At half past 7 was at the ferry ready to cross before this I had bot a chain to supply one that we had lost paid 2 dollars for it, we the teams [?] 1/2 dollar each. got all accross safely in little less than 2 hours, I worked very hard; swam our cattle and were ready to start at 10 O'Clock across to the Platte 14 miles without water, heavy sand a part of the way, arrived a 5 O'Clock greatly rejoiceing a getting water, the day was cool or we should suffered severely; arrived just in time to escape a heavy shower of rain." [Leonard, p. 11]

"Crossed Elkhorn River by means of a very roughly constructed ferry. For the conveyance of us over, the

First Handcart Company Log

happened about 2 miles from the Ferry and we then went 2 miles to camp. I put the body, with the help of others, on the hand cart and pulled him to camp and buried him without coffin for there was no boards to be had." [Walters]

"At nine a.m. the camp rolled towards the ferry, where we were detained five hours in crossing. At half past five p.m. the camp again moved on about three miles, where we were overtaken by a most terrific storm of thunder and rain. In the open prairie without tents. Two brothers and two sisters were knocked down by lightening. Brother HENRY WALKER from Carlisle was killed. Age fifty-eight. He was a faithful man to his duty. We again moved on for one and one quarter miles and camped for the night. Traveled six miles. [Ellsworth, p. 101-02]

27 July - Sunday

"The next morning, Sunday 27th, 1856, four miles west of Luke Fort Ferry. Rose about 4 o'clock. Put a new axletree to a cart that was brok yesterday. Travelled about 2 miles to a better camping ground." [Walters]

"Brother H. WALKER was buried this morning four miles west of Loop Fork Ferry on sandy rise, right hand side of the road. At twelve noon the camp rolled out and traveled two and a half miles to a better camping ground, where we remained for the rest of the day. A beef was skilled at night for the camp. About eight p.m. a meeting was called Brothers OAKLEY, FRANCE, and ELLSWORTH addressed the meeting." [Ellsworth, p. 102]

28 July - Monday

"Travelled about 18 miles. Harriet much better; for such we feel thankful." [Walters]

"At fifteen past seven a.m. the camp rolled out and traveled twenty miles. The roads in many parts were heavy. We rested two hours and had dinner. We turned up to the right about half a mile and camped for the night at half past six p.m." [Ellsworth, p. 102]

Second Handcart Company Log

company had to pay $6. Travelled 15 miles without water until we came to the Platte River, where the water was a joyful sight to many, being 6 or 7 hours under the burning sun without a drop to cool our tongues." [Wakefield, "Birmingham Dairy," & Hafen, *Handcarts*, p. 72]

27 July - Sunday

"Fine day took a bathe in the Platte changed our clothes and rested all day. took good care of the cattle salted them and on yoked all the wild steers In the evening had a meeting Capt. Dan Crandel and myself as usual spoke to the people and that too most satisfactorally. In the evening [?] some bullets, there also collected at our tent some girls and sang for us. The people felt first rate and nearly all are well or improveing very fast. one boy however cut his foot." [Leonard, p. 11-12]

"Camped all day on the north bend of the Platte. Took a dose of castor oil which sickened me very much and kept me cantering for a long time." [Wakefield, "Birmingham Dairy," & Hafen, *Handcarts*, p. 72]

28 July - Monday

"Rose early and was ready to start at half past 6 O Clock, traveled on nicely tho, some sand, traveled 12 miles and came to the North bend of the Plat here we were made glad again to get water as we had suffered considerable. Stoped 2 hours became refreshed and went about 5 or 6 miles further, and camped at a settlement whare a man by the Name of McNaughton joined us with family a team 6 cows, he promised to haul some of our people ones that does not belong to the Church." [Leonard, p. 12]

"Rather weak this morning and terribly annoyed by two boils, one on my jaw about as big as a pigeon egg and another on the calf of my leg which torments me very much when drawing the handcart." [Wakefield, "Birmingham Dairy," & Hafen, *Handcarts*, p. 72]

FIRST HANDCART COMPANY LOG

29 July - Tuesday

"Travelled about 15 miles. Met a Company coming from California. A child born in camp. Sister Doney. My birthday." [Walters]

"At nine a.m. camp rolled out and ascended a bluff to the right of the camping ground. Traveled fifteen miles. The roads in some parts a little sandy. Camped at quarter to three p.m. about four miles from the upper crossing. Plenty of wood and water. Two good springs on the west side of the camp ground. One of them dug out by Brother CARD." [Ellsworth, p. 102]

30 July - Wednesday

"Travelled 22 miles." [Walters]

"The camp rolled out at seven and traveled twenty-five miles. A great part of the road very sandy and heavy for handcarts and wagons. No wood, no water till we camped, and that not very plentiful. Still plenty for camping purpose. Camped at fifteen past six p.m." [Ellsworth, p. 102]

31 July - Thursday

"Travelled 18 miles. Heavy thunderstorm." [Walters]

"The camp rolled out at seven a.m. and traveled eighteen miles. The road leading from the camp is a

SECOND HANDCART COMPANY LOG

29 July - Tuesday

"Left our Camp at half past 8 as it rained severly we [s]tarted our wagons and passed Shell creek at 12 O'Clock and then went a long stretch of 13 mi made a grass bridge and crossed by doubling teams, rolled on till dark over a heavy and wet road, camped again on the Platte 18 miles." [Leonard, p. 12]

"Boils very sore this morning but must draw on the cart still. With such sores at home I would lie upon two chairs and never stir until they were healed. Started early this morning and traveled 20 miles." [Wakefield, "Birmingham Dairy," & Hafen, *Handcarts*, p. 72]

30 July - Wednesday

"Started at half past 6, went 7 miles and stoped at Turkey Grove a while, and then went on to the Ferry 2 miles further where we arrived at 3 O'Clock. Birch the Ferryman said we would get accross this evening, because the water was low and we would have to move the Ferry, but Capt. Dan and I went in a canoe with Birch and found where we could ford nearly all the way and push the load and by hard work and about 40 of us wet to the neck nearly we got over and at camp about dark. We with some difficulty swam the cattle I got on the back of one I called Lou my near shirl at and led the band, the water was swimming dirt for a short distance. The Ferryman treated us with the best of Brandy and his charge was nine dollars giving us a bottle of the oratter into the bargain. Camped with a lot of return California Emigrants. Good news in the Vallie the 20th of July they were harvesting rye, Capt Edmond is about 55 mile ahead of us doing his best, had a man killed by [?]" [Leonard, p. 12]

"Started early this morning and travelled 12 miles to Loup-fork ferry, over which we had to ferry the cars and wagons and women and children. It was really funny to see some 50 of the Brethren hauling a large ferry boat over this ferry and when they would come to a deep place in the stream, all make a rush to get on the boat, some succeeding, some tumbling in and others obliged to swim for it. It took 3 1/2 hours to ferry all over. Camped on the other side." [Wakefield, "Birmingham Dairy"]

31 July - Thursday

"This morning the California Gold diggers persuaded McNaughton to go back which we were glad of because he was of no account. Started out and went about 8 miles at a good camp ground, plenty

APPENDIX I: HANDCART *Logbook for 17 July to September, 1856* 219

| FIRST HANDCART COMPANY LOG | SECOND HANDCART COMPANY LOG |

heavy sandy road and continued so for about thirteen miles. It is also very hilly. Camped about fifteen minutes past six p.m. alongside of Prairie Creek. No wood, but plenty of buffalo chips. There is a well about seven miles from where we camped last night on the right hand side of the road." [Ellsworth, p. 102]

of wood etc. 14 or about 15 miles further without water making about 23 in all in good spirits only 2 or 3 gave out. Camped on the Loup Fork in a beautiful place, got in at 7 O'Clock looked much like rain but passed off." [Leonard, p. 12]

"Left Loup-Fork and traveled 20 miles without water. I was so exhausted with my sores and the labour of pulling that I was obliged to lie down for a few hours after arriving in camp before I could do anything. Kate was also so tired and fatigued out that she was glad to get lying down without any supper and I was not able to cook any for ourselves so we were obliged to do with a bit of bread and a pint of milk. This is the quantity of milk we have been allowed morning and evening since we left Florence. Sometimes it is less. Rather little for 5 persons. While traveling this day, often was I near falling on the road for want of water, and with fatigue. Many did fall right down and some had to put into the wagons but many were obliged to wait until they recovered a little and foot it again. 8 o'clock when we got into camp." [Wakefield, "Birmingham Dairy," & Hafen, *Handcarts,* p. 72]

1 August - Friday
"Travelled 16 miles and camped at Prairie Creek." [Walters]

"The camp rolled out at eight a.m. Traveled sixteen miles. The road is in good condition. Crossed Prairie Creek twice. The second crossing, the handcarts had to be carried over by the brethren. There was a little difficulty in getting the wagons over, the banks of the creek were so steep. We also crossed Wood River by means of a good bridge. We came very close to a herd of buffalo. Brother ELLSWORTH went out with his rifle. Wounded two but not sufficient for him to get them. At thirty past six p.m. we camped alongside of Wood River. Plenty of wood and water. A good camping ground. [Ellsworth, p. 102-03]

1 August - Friday
"Left camp at half past 6 traveled 8 miles and came to where the road left the Loup fork, over a heavy sand hill which we raised by doubling teams heavily after going a mile to the river to supply us and our cattle with water. We left at one O'Clock and for some time the roads were sandy traveled about 12 miles & camped on the South fork again about a mile distant and near where the old road came in. It looked much like rain but it again passed off." [Leonard, p. 13]

"We remained in camp all day and attended such duties as we were necessitated to do. Meeting at seven p.m. Brothers OAKLEY, BUTLER and ELLSWORTH addressed the Saints."[Ellsworth, p. 103]

"23 miles over a bad road. No water, only what we carried. Sister Hardy from Scotland fainted on the road today." [Wakefield, "Birmingham Dairy"]

2 August - Saturday
"Crossed over 2 creeks, forded them. Stop dinner. Camped by Wood River. We saw many buffalo. Travelled about 18 miles." [Walters]

2 August - Saturday
"Day cool and beautiful traveled 5 miles & came to a fine spring of water, here Capt Elsworth com. camped and had a child come leaving notice to that effect as also stating it was 25 miles to water, we put in a good supply and traveled till dark over a heavy road & camped without water The day was a very fatiguing one to us" [Leonard, p. 13]

"Started early this morning and travelled 28 miles over a very bad road, having to pull the carts through

FIRST HANDCART COMPANY LOG

3 August - Sunday
"Rested but mended hand carts. Got shell fish out of the creek for we was very hungry. Only 3/4 lb. of flour; 1 1/2 oz. of sugar; a few apples; tea plenty." [Walters]

SECOND HANDCART COMPANY LOG

heavy sand, sometimes for miles. We were obliged to carry water with us today. Camped on the open prairie without either wood or water and consequently had to go to bed supperless." [Wakefield, "Birmingham Dairy"]

3 August - Sunday
"Up early and just as we were ready to start, the mule stumbled threw its rider got away and ran about 16 miles. This gave Capt Dan and me a hard pull. I ran most of the way and finally caught the animal before I knew that McArthur was within 5 miles of me as I had out run him & supposed he had gone back. The mule appeared to be bound for water & determined to make the main Platte 28 miles distant, but coming to a dry slew he stacked up and with some difficulty I got hold of the lasso & then I saw at a distance Capt Dan swinging his hat for joy. We then both got upon the mule & come back to the joy of the camp and I think my legs was as lame as ever I had them, at this time Crandel was getting on 5 or 6 miles after which we went to Prairie Creek in all about 16 miles, though at 10, we found a slew out of which we watered our animals and had some refreshments. In the evening we killed a beef creature, a muley I shot her and it was dressed in less than an hour. At 11 O'Clock at night the cry was made the cattle is gone & the guard are asleep, Ralph Maxwell and John Hardy." [Leonard, p. 13]

"Started at 5 o'clock without any breakfast and had to pull the carts through 6 miles of heavy sand. Some places the wheels were up to the boxes and I was so weak from thirst and hunger and being exhausted with the pain of the boils that I obliged to lie down several times, and many others had to do the same. Some fell down. I was very much grieved today, so much so that I thought my heart would burst–sick–and poor Kate–at the same time–crawling on her hands and knees, and the children crying with hunger and fatigue. I was obliged to take the children and put them on the hand cart and urge them along the road in order to make them keep up. About 12 o'clock a thunder storm came on, and the rain fell in torrents. In our tent we were standing up to our knees in water and every stitch we had was the same as if we were dragged through the river. Rain continued until 8 o'clock the following morning." (There are no diary entries from 4-12 Aug inclusive) [Wakefield, "Birmingham Dairy," & Hafen, *Handcarts*, p. 72-73]

APPENDIX I: HANDCART Logbook for 17 July to September, 1856

FIRST HANDCART COMPANY LOG

4 August - Monday
"Travelled 18 miles. Camped by Platte River." [Walters]

"At quarter to eight a.m. the camp rolled out and traveled eighteen miles. Good roads. Camped at quarter to three p.m. near the Platte." [Ellsworth, p. 103]

5 August - Tuesday
"Travelled 16 miles." [Walters]

"At eight a.m. the camp rolled out and traveled sixteen miles. The road pretty good with the exception of one or two places. Camped about four p.m. Wood rather scarce, still plenty for camping purposes."[Ellsworth, p. 103]

6 August - Wednesday
"Saw thousands of buffalo. 4 was killed. So thick together that they covered 4 miles at once. Camped by Buffalo Creek. Travelled 10 miles." [Walters]

"At nine a.m. the camp rolled out and traveled twelve miles. Roads good. Camped about two p.m. on Buffalo Creek four miles from the crossing of B. Creek. We killed four buffaloes today. The camp got quite a good supply of meat." [Ellsworth, p. 103]

7 August - Thursday
"Thousands of buffalo. Travelled 25 miles. Camped late at night. Had to dig for water and it was very

SECOND HANDCART COMPANY LOG

4 August - Monday
"In the morning heavy rain which detained us till 1 O'Clock. we then hitched up and crossed Prairie Creek 2 rods wide and 2 feet deep, and went 10 miles and camped on the same creek again good feed and water, though heavy road to it" [Leonard, p. 13]

(There are no diary entries from Birmingham August 4th–12th inclusive.) [Wakefield, "Birmingham Dairy," & Hafen, *Handcarts*, p. 72-73]

5 August - Tuesday
"Here we rested or rather stoped til afternoon, let the women wash and repaired carts etc. We also had the painful duty to inter Bro. Aniki Smith who departed this life a few minutes before 12 O'Clock. We buried him upon the ground within 12 feet of where he died. He bore a faithful testimony. said he knew that Brigham was a Prophet and that mormonism was true, and exhorted the Saints to be faithful and all would be well, and although he was cut off by the bond of death all was right for he should come forth in the first resurrection and reign upon the Earth. He wished to be remembered to Brigham and his counsellors as also his friends in the Vallie. He then shook hands and bid us good buy and died shouting Halelujah 15 minutes before 12 O Clock. I got a heavy post, put on a wide board & had Bro. Henry Bowering cut his Name age and date of death etc and to what camp he belonged. The body was then wraped in sheets and after bury by myself according to the request of Capt Dan and some observations by himself the body was deposited and respectfully intered too, and we ready to move off by 3 O'Clock went [?] miles & camped on the same creek." [Leonard, p. 13-14]

6 August - Wednesday
"Traveled 17 miles and camped on Wood river, passed several lots of Emigrants on their return from the gold mines They gave us good news about the Vallie and also told us that Bro. Elsworth was only about 40 miles ahead of us; our road today was rather bad over many deep slews, dry creeks and hollows etc. The day was very warm and fatigueing, several or quite sick too, and our teams are complaining of their loads as they are nearly s heavy as they were when we started. Crossed Wood River Bridge about 5 O Clock and camped about 6 on the same stream" [Leonard, p. 14]

7 August - Thursday
"Opposite to Fort Kearney, crossed a dry Prairie 18 miles and arrived at a Branch of the Platte at 2 O'Clock,

First Handcart Company Log

thick. Our hungry appetites satisfied by the buffalo. Got up soon to repair hand carts. [Walters]

"At fifteen to nine a.m. the camp rolled out, and traveled twenty-five miles. The roads good, with the exception of about two miles which is rather sandy. There is no water after leaving the crossing. Camped at about thirty past eight p.m. No water but by digging for it. No wood. Plenty of chips." [Ellsworth, p. 103]

8 August - Friday

"Rose soon to repair carts. Travelled about 15 miles. Camped by the side of Flat River. Repaired hand carts. Harriet getting round nicely and I feel truly thankful. My wife very ill tempered at times. An old brother lost named Sanderson. Many went in all directions but could not find him." [Walters]

"At fifteen to nine a.m. the camp rolled out from this place of desolation and traveled thirteen miles without water. The roads good. Camped about thirty past two alongside the Platte. By turning off to the left about one half mile you will find a good camping ground but no wood. There is another camping ground about two miles ahead. By some means Father SANDERS got left behind. The brethren have been out on foot and horse. As yet they have not succeeded in finding him." [Ellsworth, p. 103]

9 August - Saturday

"Found the old brother Sanderson on a hill about 6 o'clock. Brought him into camp on a mule. Travelled about 15 miles after repairing hand carts until 12 o'clock." [Walters]

"The camp rolled out at ten past 1 p.m. and traveled thirteen miles. Brother THOMAS FOWLER found Father SANDERS this morning about five miles ahead of the camp. The road for about seven miles is very, very heavy, sandy road; hard pulling for handcarts and ox teams. Camped beside the Platte about two miles from Skunk Creek about fifteen eight p.m." [Ellsworth, p. 103]

10 August - Sunday

"Travelled 14 miles. All, or most of the people bad with diarrhoea or purging, whether it was the buffalo or the muddy river water." [Walters]

"About nine a.m. the camp was called together for meeting. Elders ELLSWORTH, FRANCE, and OAKLEY addressed the Saints. A good meeting. The camp rolled out at ten past eleven a.m. Traveled fourteen miles. For two or three miles the road is sandy and bluffy, but they can be greatly avoided

Second Handcart Company Log

day cool and beautiful, rested 2 hours and went on 6 miles and camped on deep dry creek good feed and buffalo chips with water." [Leonard, p. 14]

8 August - Friday

"drove about 9 miles and came to Elm creek here we were among the buffalo in earnest. Stoped and several of us went in pursuit of them, after a long walk I succeeded in getting several shots but only succeeded in killing one old bull which I shot through the spine of the back which brought him down immediately. Capt Dan shot and wounded one severly but still lost him. We took what we were able to pack and went to the train for It had started on. Peacock had killed an old cow near the road which we saved, by dark and then drove on and camped in the prairie without water. trouble with cattle" [Leonard, p. 14]

9 August - Saturday

"Started at 5 O'Clock and drove to Buffalo creek—here we stoped, and Capt Dan and I with some others went to waylay some buffalo at the watering place & killed a dry fat heifer and a young Bul both first rate beef and weighed about 800 pounds, got it secure on the carts etc and drove on about 6 miles crossing the Buffalo creek in a very bad place. feed good but water very scarce dug for it but got it the next morning. Several buffalo made an attempt to get among the cattle but we kept them at bay by firing at them. Lawson and myself shot at one and he was found dead near in the morning dead." [Leonard, p. 14-15]

10 August - Sunday

"Stoped all day killed one buffalo that is Bro Birmingham shot it the better parts of which was saved hung up our meat to dry all about the camp. Some Californians from the mines gave us some news about the Vallie, good crops, but bad feed [?] about 35 miles ahead of us. In the evening had a meeting Capt Dan, myself and Crandel spoke to the people as we were dictated by the Spirit of the Lord, administered to several who were sick." [Leonard, p. 15]

First Handcart Company Log

by winding them. Camped at Cold Springs camping ground about six p.m. A most excellent place for a camp." [Ellsworth, p. 103-04]

11 August - Monday

"Travelled about 17 miles. 4 men sent to shoot Buffalo. Harriet much better; very weak myself. I expect it is the short rations; 3/4 of a lb. of flour per day. It is but little but is is as much as the oxen teams that we have could draw from St. Florence. Forded over 2 creeks. Met a man coming from California by himself; going to the States. One of our cows died. Buffalo killed." [Walters]

"The camp rolled out at fifty past seven a.m. and traveled seventeen miles. The roads were pretty good with the exception of some that ar sandy, but that can be avoided by turning off a little either to the right or left. Plenty of water every three or four miles. One of our milk cows died near the camping ground. We crossed over a small creek and camped close to the Platte opposite to two or three small islands, where there is wood, but rather difficult to get at. We had two buffaloes brought into camp tonight killed by brethren appointed for that purpose. We camped at four p.m. All well." [Ellsworth, p. 104]

12 August - Tuesday

"Rested while some of the brethren with Captain Ellsworth went and shot 2 more Buffalo and we dried the meat." [Walters]

"We remained at rest today to cut up buffalo to dry for the journey; and repair the hand-carts." [Ellsworth, p. 104]_

13 August - Wednesday

"Travelled 12 miles; forded a large creek." [Walters]

"The camp rolled at thirty past nine a.m. and traveled twelve miles. The roads were rather heavy

Second Handcart Company Log

11 August - Monday

"Left at Six and traveled 13 miles and stoped where we found holes in a slew and got water at the left of the road. Buffalo the most numerous I ever saw went 15 miles & stoped in the dry bed of the Platte; water by digging" [Leonard, p. 15]

"On the 11th of August a man came to camp pretending to be starved nearly to death, and wished me to give him some provisions, for he had had nothing for many days but what he had hunted for. So I gave him bread and meat enough to last him some four or five days and he acted as though he had met with some friends indeed. He said, that he had been robbed by some Californians somewhere near Fort Bridger, with whom he was in company on their way to the States..." [McArthur Report & Hafen, *Handcarts*, p. 214-17]

12 August - Tuesday

"Started early Traveled till noon and I went out to get a calf, shot one through but lost it. I afterwards shot a fat 2 year old Heifer, on the run She ran half mile and being much exhausted for lack of blood for I shot a heavy ball through fore part of her breast breaking the foreleg on the opposite side to where I stood. She was dressed in half an hour or a little and hauled into camp on a couple of [?] Half a mile from the river, started again traveled late over much sand and camped on the Platte. It was dark and the cattle as the left the river started and ran as hard as the could stamped fashion I followed and the men at camp were in time to stop them, they were uneasy and we gathered up the old cattle and chined them to the wagons, and toward morning we had one of the most dreadful rain storms I ever experienced water ran through most of the tents in camp. Travels of about 17 miles." [Leonard, p. 15]

13 August - Wednesday

"Started at 10 O'Clock went 15 miles over heavy sand much of the way with little water and camped on the Prairie with but little water and no wood Killed an old Bull to kick him out of camp" [Leonard, p. 15]

First Handcart Company Log

owing to last night's rain. Camped about five p.m. alongside of Bluff Fork. We forded the river previous to camping." [Ellsworth, p. 104]

14 August - Thursday

"Travelled 18 miles. Crossed three creeks. Last herd of Buffalo seen." [Walters]

"The camp rolled at ten past eight a.m. and traveled eighteen miles. The first twelve miles was nearly all over heavy sandy bluffs. Right from the camp it made heavy pulling. The last six miles the road was pretty good. One of the covered handcarts broke down. Camped about seven p.m. alongside of the Platte." [Ellsworth, p. 104]

15 August - Friday

"Forded over 5 creeks; camped at Snake Creek. Travelled 19 miles; from Florence 352 miles. Harriet much better and walked all the way." [Walters]

"The camp rolled out at one quarter to eight a.m. traveled fourteen miles. For the first six miles the sand was fully as bad, if not worse, than yesterday. We crossed four creeks, took dinner at Goose Creek. For the next eight miles the road was good. We forded Rattle Snake and camped about a half a mile from the old Rattle Snake camping ground. Camped about one quarter past six p.m." [Ellsworth, p. 104]

16 August - Saturday

"Forded over 5 or 6 creeks. Travelled 17 miles. Camped by Wolf Creek." [Walters]

"The camp moved off at quarter to eight a.m. and traveled sixteen and three quarter miles. A good part of it heavy sandy traveling. Other parts of the road was good traveling. We crossed small creeks, had dinner on the banks of Camp Creek. Camp about seven p.m. on the east bank of Wolf Creek. Buffalo chips no so plentiful here. Good feed for the oxen." [Ellsworth, p. 104]

Second Handcart Company Log

"Started out at 10 o'clock and Kate was obliged to travel all day without a shift and nothing on but a shawl and petticoat and those half wet. Had to travel over a great many sand hills and camped on the wet ground in a wet blanket as well as to go to bed supperless. No wood to make a fire and very bad water. Went on to the camp guard from 12 o'clock till 4." [Wakefield, "Birmingham Dairy"]

14 August - Thursday

"traveled 19 miles by starting out at 5 O Clock before breakfast, went 7 miles stoped on the Platte 4 hours I had an Ox and traveled 12 miles breaking a cart ex on the way stoped in the river good feed and shade" [Leonard, p. 15]

"Started at 5 1/2 o'clock without any breakfast. Travelled 8 miles and halted at the River Platte. Got breakfast and dried all our wet clothes and then travelled 14 miles more. A few days previous to this we met a man coming from California. He was deserted on the plains by his companions, who left him 1 with nothing but a shirt and trousers which he had on. He was making his way as fast as he could to Council Bluffs. He was then 200 miles from it. We gave him some bread." [Wakefield, "Birmingham Dairy"]

15 August - Friday

"Traveled 15 miles over heavy sand roads much of the way and camped some ways from the River. We wished to go further but a majority were not willing Buffalo chip in abundences I also tried hard for a buffalo but did not get one althoug I had 3 shots" [Leonard, p. 16]

"Travelled 17 miles — 5 miles sand." [Wakefield, "Birmingham Dairy"]

16 August - Saturday

"Traveled 18 miles over the worst road I ever passed on the plains. Almost everything worked against us to. In the first place Mother Rathgate was bitten by a rattle snake seriously too, she sent back for she was way ahead as usual for the Elders to come immediately we don so in haste, and on arriving I took a knife cut the wound to make it bleed then put on plenty of oil and we laid on hands in faith believing she would be healed. At a stopping soon after Mother Park another of our best women and the oldest in camp I think went to see Sister Rathgate and my wheels run over her, thank god I helped her out as quick as I could but not

APPENDIX I: HANDCART Logbook for 17 July to September, 1856

FIRST HANDCART COMPANY LOG

SECOND HANDCART COMPANY LOG

until the hind wheel had run over both ankles. we supposed her were all smashed to pieces but were not; we administered to her and went on until one or two others that had not rode also were obliged to ride so by at about 2 we were out our wagons which made it the hardest day we had" [Leonard, p. 16]

"Started this morning before breakfast at 4 1/2 o'clock. Stopped at 8 o'clock for breakfast. This morning an old woman belonging to our company was bitten by a rattlesnake in the leg and before half an hour her leg swelled to four times its thickness. She was administered to by the Elders and we started again, but unfortunately as we were starting another old woman was run over by one of the way and the hind wheel passed over her ankles. We all thought that she hind wheel had run over both ankles. we supposed her were all smashed to pieces but were not; we administered to her and went on until one or two others that had not rode also were obliged to ride so by at about 2 we were out our wagons which made it the hardest day we had" [Leonard, p. 16]

"Started this morning before breakfast at 4 1/2 o'clock. Stopped at 8 o'clock for breakfast. This morning an old woman belonging to our company was bitten by a rattlesnake in the leg and before half an hour her leg swelled to four times its thickness. She was administered to by the Elders and we started again, but unfortunately as we were starting another old woman was run over by one of the wagons. The front wheel went over her thighs and the back wheels over her shins, and singular to say, although the wagon was laden with 32 cwt. of flour, not one of her bones was broken. This day we had the most severe day's journey we had since we started and travelled over 20 miles of heavy sand hills or bluffs. Besides having to ford many streams. All seemed to be fully worn out when they got into camp." [Wakefield, "Birmingham Dairy," & Hafen, *Handcarts*, p. 73]

"...on the[August] 16th, while crossing over some sand hills, Sister Mary Bathgate was badly bitten by a large rattlesnake, just above the ankle, on the back part of her leg. She was about a half a mile ahead of the camp at the time it happened, as she was the ring leader of the footmen or those who did not pull the handcarts. She was generally accompanied by Sister Isabella Park. They were both old women, over 60 years of age, and neither of them had ridden one inch, since they had left Iowa camp ground. Sister Bathgate sent a little girl back to me as quickly as possible to have me and Brothers Leonard and Crandall come with all haste, and bring the oil with us, for she

FIRST HANDCART COMPANY LOG	SECOND HANDCART COMPANY LOG
	was bitten badly. As soon as we heard the news, we left all things, and, with the oil, we went post haste. When we got to her she was quite sick, but said that there was power in the Priesthood, and she knew it. So we took a pocket knife and cut the wound larger, squeezed out all the bad blood we could, and there was considerable, for she had forethought enough to tie her garter around her leg above the wound to stop the circulation of the blood. We then took and anointed her leg and head, and laid our hands on her in the name of Jesus and felt to rebuke the influence of the poison, and she felt full of faith. We then told her that she must get into the wagon, so she called witnesses to prove that she did not get into the wagon until she was compelled to by the cursed snake. We started on and traveled about two miles, when we stopped to take some refreshments. Sister Bathgate continued to be quite sick, but was full of faith, and after stopping one and a half hours we hitched up our teams. As the word was given for the teams to start, old Sister Isabella Park ran in before the wagon to see how her companion was. The driver, not seeing her, hallooed at his team and they being quick to mind, Sister Park could not get out of the way, and the fore wheel struck her and threw her down and passed over both her hips. Brother Leonard grabbed hold of her to pull her out of the way. before the hind wheel could catch her. He only got he out part_wagons. The front wheel went over her thighs and the back wheels my wheels run over her, thank god I helped her out as quick as I could but not until the hind wheel had run over both ankles. we supposed her were all smashed to pieces, but were not; we administered to her and went on until one or two others that had not rode also were obliged to ride so by at about 2 were were out our wagons which made it the hardest day we had." [Leonard, p. 16] "Started this morning before breakfast at 4 1/2 o'clock. Stopped at 8 o'clock for breakfast. This morning an old woman belonging to our company was bitten by a rattlesnake in the leg and before half an hour her leg swelled to four times its thickness. She was administered to by the Elders and we started again, but unfortunately as we were starting another old woman was run over by one of the wagons. The front wheel went over her thighs and the back wheels over her shins, and singular to say, although the wagon was laden with 32 cwt. of flour, not one of her bones was broken. This day we had the most severe day's journey we had since we started and travelled over 20 miles of heavy sand hills or bluffs. Besides having to

First Handcart Company Log	Second Handcart Company Log
	ford many streams. All seemed to be fully worn out when they got into camp." [Wakefield, "Birmingham Dairy," & Hafen, *Handcarts,* p. 73]

"...on the[August] 16th, while crossing over some sand hills, Sister Mary Bathgate was badly bitten by a large rattlesnake, just above the ankle, on the back part of her leg. She was about a half a mile ahead of the camp at the time it happened, as she was the ring leader of the footmen or those who did not pull the handcarts. She was generally accompanied by Sister Isabella Park. They were both old women, over 60 years of age, and neither of them had ridden one inch, since they had left Iowa camp ground. Sister Bathgate sent a little girl back to me as quickly as possible to have me and Brothers Leonard and Crandall come with all haste, and bring the oil with us, for she was bitten badly. As soon as we heard the news, we left all things, and, with the oil, we went post haste. When we got to her she was quite sick, but said that there was power in the Priesthood, and she knew it. So we took a pocket knife and cut the wound larger, squeezed out all the bad blood we could, and there was considerable, for she had forethought enough to tie her garter around her leg above the wound to stop the circulation of the blood. We then took and anointed her leg and head, and laid our hands on her in the name of Jesus and felt to rebuke the influence of the poison, and she felt full of faith. We then told her that she must get into the wagon, so she called witnesses to prove that she did not get into the wagon until she was compelled to by the cursed snake. We started on and traveled about two miles, when we stopped to take some refreshments. Sister Bathgate continued to be quite sick, but was full of faith, and after stopping one and a half hours we hitched up our teams. As the word was given for the teams to start, old Sister Isabella Park ran in before the wagon to see how her companion was. The driver, not seeing her, hallooed at his team and they being quick to mind, Sister Park could not get out of the way, and the fore wheel struck her and threw her down and passed over both her hips. Brother Leonard grabbed hold of her to pull her out of the way. before the hind wheel could catch her. He only got he out part way and the hind wheel passed over her ankles. We all thought that she would be all mashed to pieces, but to the joy of us all, there was not a bone broken, although the wagon had something like two tons burden on it, a load for 4 yoke of oxen. We went right to work and applied the same medicine to her that we did to the sister who was bitten by the rattlesnake, and although |

First Handcart Company Log

17 August - Sunday

"Crossed over some creeks. Camped over the Platte River. Travelled 12 miles. Brother Missel Rossin, Italian, found dead by the side of the road." [Walters]

"The camp moved out at a quarter to nine a.m. and traveled twelve miles. We crossed over Wolf Creek and ascended the Sandy Bluff. We crossed the bluff to the left instead of going up the old tract. It is easier for handcarts and for ox teams. The road today was very sandy for several miles. Passed over several creeks. Camped at four p.m. on the side of the Platte opposite to Ash Grove. Brother PETER STALLEY died today. He was from Italy." [Ellsworth, p. 105]

18 August - Monday

"Travelled 20 miles. Camped by the Platte River." [Walters]

"The camp rolled out twenty past seven a.m. and traveled nineteen miles. The road was very good today. Forded Hustle Creek. Passed no other creek during the day. Had dinner alongside of a slough. Passed over a sand ridge. Two dry sloughs on the left hand side of the road about four miles from the Platte. Camped at twenty to seven p.m. on the side of the Platte." [Ellsworth, p. 105]

19 August - Tuesday

"Travelled 19 miles. Camped by the Platte River. A new camping ground. Buffalo chips to burn." [Walters]

"The camp rolled out at a quarter to eight a.m. and traveled twenty miles. The road today in parts was very sandy. Especially crossing the cobble hills it was very sandy. We crossed Crab Creek today. Camped about thirty past (?) p.m. on the Platte opposite ancient Bluff ruins." [Ellsworth, p. 105]

Second Handcart Company Log

quite sore for a few days, Sister Park got better, so that she was on the tramp before we got into this Valley, and Sister Bathgate was right by her side, to cheer her up. Both were as smart as could be long before they got here, and this is what I call good luck, for I know that nothing but the power of God saved the two sisters and they traveled together, they rode together, and suffered together." [McArthur Report & Hafen, *Handcarts*, p. 214-17]

17 August - Sunday

"To us a day of rest surely but seeing two Buffalo near the camp and we nearly out of meat Capt. Dan and myself went in pursuit of them for 4 or 5 miles had several chances at them but our guns would not go off, we saw 9 in all, On my way home I hot a large blowadder. and found lots of ground cherries to take in. We took a bathe and done some writing etc, In the evening had a meeting I was called upon to speak to the people, and among other things spoke upon the necessity of obeying those who were set over us. refering to instances where this company had not done it and that the result was against us curiously. Another of Father Elakers daughters died today." [Leonard, p. 16]

"In camp all day. Spent the day mending my boots, and Kate was washing. This day, a German sister died." [Wakefield, "Birmingham Dairy," & Hafen, *Handcarts*, p. 73]

18 August - Monday

"Traveled about 14 miles over a hard sandy road crosing 5 or 6 beautiful mountain streams some of which were Bluff Creek Watch Creek, Calm creek etc. Camped nearly opposite to Ash Hollow on the Platte." [Leonard, p. 16]

"Buried the girl and started out of camp at 5 1/2 o'clock. Travelled 20 miles. 10 miles of sand today and had to ford 6 streams." [Wakefield, "Birmingham Dairy"]

19 August - Tuesday

"Traveled 18 miles again over a bad road, crossed several streams, at one of which we broke Ox Cart axeltree which I replaced foregoing a bit in the operation belonging to Father Bill. Mother Rathgate and Park are getting better." [Leonard, p. 16]

APPENDIX I: *Handcart Logbook for 17 July to September, 1856*

| FIRST HANDCART COMPANY LOG | SECOND HANDCART COMPANY LOG |

20 August - Wednesday

"Travelled 19 miles. Camped by River Platte." [Walters]

"The camp rolled out at thirty past seven a.m. and traveled twenty miles. The road was tolerable good till we came to the last five miles, when it became very sandy in some parts, especially in crossing over sand bluffs. Camped on the side of the Platte forty-five past six p.m." [Ellsworth, p. 105]

"Traveld 19 miles over tremendous sand double teams. Camped on the Platte near some return strangers [?]

"One Williamson who had been in the Vallie gave good news relative to crops and also about my folks especially John who he said had been very sick." [Leonard, p. 16]

21 August - Thursday

"Travelled 18 miles. Camped 4 miles past Chimney Rock, Platte River. Sandy road the last 3 or 4 days." [Walters]

"The camp rolled out at thirty past seven a.m. and traveled sixteen and one half miles. The road today was tolerably good. No water for fourteen and one half miles. Camped on the Platte two miles beyond Chimney Rock at four p.m. Buffalo chips rather scarce." [Ellsworth, p. 105]

22 August - Friday

"Good road. Travelled 24 miles. Camped by Platte River." [Walters]

"The camp rolled out at twenty past seven a.m. and traveled twenty-one miles. The road today was good. We were detained three hours on the road by a thunder storm. Twelve miles without water. Camped about thirty past seven p.m. on the Platte about half a mile from Spring Creek. Buffalo ships and wood scarce. Poor fee for cattle." [Ellsworth, p. 105]

23 August - Saturday

"Travelled 16 miles. Camped by Platte River. Harriet getting well, thank God, and not been in the wagons to ride. Our allowance of flour tonight was 1 lb. a head. For this I was thankful for I never was so hungry in my life. Captain Ellsworth shot a cow. Very thankfully received." [Walters]

"The camp rolled out at five past eight a.m. and traveled fifteen and a half miles before we struck the Platte, where we camped. Wood plentiful on the south side by fording for it. The river from two to three feet deep. About six miles of the road was rather sandy. Camped about two p.m. on the side

"**19th — 20th — 21st — 22d — 23d — AUGUST:**
These five days we travelled at the rate of about 22 miles per day. Some days starting as early as 5 o'clock and never after 7. Most of those days we had heavy sandy roads. Sometimes for ten miles at a time." [Wakefield, "Birmingham Dairy"]

21 August - Thursday

"Went 20 miles after having an ox and a cow which were overcome; had an occasion to talk very briefly to Bidow Eardley who had been a shirk as the man from Iowa City. Killed 4 Rattle Snakes all in my path as if to bit me they were determined. Gained some of Capt Elsworth Company who were about 35 miles ahead of us." [Leonard, p. 17]

22 August - Friday

"day cool drove 20 miles over rather a hard road. At one O'Clock had a storm and wind storm, nearly all got wet met some immigrants who gave us some good news from the Vallie, teams are coming said Elsworth is only 25 or 30 miles ahead, camped a half mile from the river few chips and wet at that." [Leonard, p. 17]

23 August - Saturday

"Drove 23 miles and camped apposite of Chimney Rock, killed a beef which the people were greatly in need of. road pretty good mostly through the day" [Leonard, p. 17]

First Handcart Company Log	Second Handcart Company Log
of the Platte near..... Killed a buffalo tonight." [Ellsworth, p. 105-06]	

First Handcart Company

24 August - Sunday

"Rested from travels but had to repair hand carts. Meeting at night. Received the Sacrament. Spoke at the meeting. Bro. Ellsworth spoke some time and said we had made great improvement; that the last week there had been less quarreling and those that had robbed the hand carts, or wagons, unless they repent their flesh would rot from their bones and go to Hell." [Walters]

"The camp did not travel any today. We were busy with the handcarts. At six p.m. we had a Sacramental and Saints' meeting. A good time of it." [Ellsworth, p. 106]

25 August - Monday

"Travelled about 19 miles. Saw many Indians. Camped about 19 miles from Fort Laramie. Hand cart axle tree broke on the road. Plenty of wood. Quite a treat after burning so many buffalo chips." [Walters]

"At half past seven a.m. the camp rolled out and traveled nineteen miles. For six or seven miles the road was rather sandy. At a quarter to five p.m. we camped not far from the Platte. Good feed. Plenty of wood." [Ellsworth, p. 106]

26 August - Tuesday

"Travelled about 19 miles. Camped 3 miles from Fort Laramie. Tucked away a dagger for a piece of bacon and salt and sold one for 1 dollar 1/4. Bought bacon and meal and Henry and me began to eat it raw we was so hungry. Forded the river. Sister Watts got hurt by the wagon. My wife thinks she would of fell when half way over the river. Bro. John Lee came to her assistance." [Walters]

"The camp rolled out twenty past seven a.m. and traveled seventeen miles. For about fourteen miles the road was very sandy. Heavy drawing. Forded the Platte opposite to Laramie. Camped at thirty-five past five p.m. on the side of the Platte four miles from Laramie. Good feed, plenty of wood." [Ellsworth, p. 106]

Second Handcart Company

24 August - Sunday

"In camp all day shod 2 oxen; helped to dish out the beef and in the evening had a meeting I was called upon to pray and Capt Dan and Crandel spoke to the people had a good time after which [?]" [Leonard, p. 17]

"Camped all day at Chimney Rock. Spent the day mending my clothes and baking and cooking while Kate was washing and mending the children's clothes. On the 22nd while we were on the road travelling, we were overtaken by a very heavy thunderstorm which wet us all to the skin, but as soon as it was over we went at it again and made a journey of 7 or 8 miles before we camped and then we had to lie on the wet grass all night, and go to bed supperless, there being no firewood to cook, the Buffalo chips being wet. We had to ford 20 streams this week." [Wakefield, "Birmingham Dairy," & Hafen, *Handcarts*, p. 74]

25 August - Monday

"Started early and traveled 26 miles road good, and plenty of water Camped near Scotts Bluff where one of the girls got lost and lay out all night Catherine Granger was her Name." [Leonard, p. 17]

"25th — 26th — 27th AUGUST
Very heavy travelling through sand all the time at about 19 miles per day." [Wakefield, "Birmingham Dairy"]

APPENDIX I: HANDCART *Logbook for 17 July to September, 1856*

FIRST HANDCART COMPANY LOG

26 August - Tuesday
"left at 7 O'Clock and traveled 16 miles and camped again on the Platte, during the day had a real storm of rain." [Leonard, p. 17]

27 August - Wednesday
"Travelled about 18 miles. Had bacon and meal porridge for supper; the best supper for many weeks. A camp of Indians passed us." [Walters]

"The camp rolled out at quarter past seven a.m. and traveled twenty-one miles. The roads good with the exception of about four miles, rather rough and rocky. At a quarter to five p.m. we camped at Bitter Cottonwood. Wood and water plenty. Feed scarce." [Ellsworth, p. 106]

28 August - Thursday
"Travelled about 15 miles. Mended hand carts good and had road hilley. Camped at a nice place called Horse Shoe Creek. Mother and Sarah washed clothes." [Walters]

"The camp rolled out this morning at thirty past eight a.m. and traveled fifteen miles. Eight miles from Bitter Cottonwood Creek to the Platte, three miles from that to a good spring, and pretty good feed on the right side of the road. Four miles from that to the Horseshoe Creek. Good feed and plenty of wood and water. Camped about thirty past four p.m." [Ellsworth, p. 106]

29 August - Friday
"Travelled 25 miles. Camped Platte River. Met some Californians." [Walters]

"The camp rolled out at fifteen past seven a.m. and traveled twenty-five miles. The road was pretty good. Sixteen miles to the Platte where we took dinner. Traveled two miles and forded the Platte. Camped about thirty past six p.m. on the Platte. Plenty of wood; feed pretty fair." [Ellsworth, p. 106]

30 August - Saturday
"Travelled 22 miles. Met some Californians and they told us the wagons was waiting at Deer Creek for us." [Walters]

"The camp rolled out at twenty-five past seven a.m. and traveled nineteen miles. The road pretty fair. Forded the Platte again. Traveled about six miles and camped by the side of a creek. Plenty of wood, water, and feed. We passed two emigrants from California. By them we were informed that five wagons were

SECOND HANDCART COMPANY LOG

27 August - Wednesday
"Traveled 20 miles day very warm water not very plenty; land very heavy indeed" [Leonard, p. 17]

28 August - Thursday
"traveled 11 miles and arrived at Laramy crossed the River; went to the Fort in com with Capt. Dan to get some nails &c Ox nails were 2 dollars per pound I bot .50 cents worth. Quite a No of our people bot. flour Bacon etc. Came a mile and a half and camped with but little feed." [Leonard, p. 17]

"After travelling 12 miles through sand, came to Fort Laramie where after crossing the river and getting some wet trousers and petticoats we remained all night. Passed many camps of Indians, all peaceable..." [Wakefield, "Birmingham Dairy," & Hafen, *Handcarts*, p. 74]

"On the 28th of August, we arrived at Laramie..." [McArthur Report & Hafen, *Handcarts*, p. 214-17]

29 August - Friday
"travelled 21 miles and camped on the creek almost without feed except brush, one of our oxen sick came 12 miles in the afternoon, some of our camp did not get on till near 8 O clock" [Leonard, p. 18]

"29th —30th August
These two days we travelled 50 miles. The 30th we crossed the Platte again to the north side. Remained in camp all day." [Wakefield, "Birmingham Dairy"]

30 August - Saturday
"Started early and traveled 25 miles and struck [?] the catle, passing two small lots of water, one at 4 miles the other [?]" [Leonard, p. 18]

First Handcart Company Log

waiting on us at Deer Creek. Camped at about thirty past six p.m." [Ellsworth, p. 106]

31 August - Sunday

"Very poorly, faint and hungry. Travelled to Deer Creek, 22 miles. Brother R. Stoddard from Carlisle Conference, about 54 years old, died in the wagon on road. More provisions given out." [Walters]

"The camp rolled out at quarter to seven a.m. and traveled twenty-four miles. The roads were very good. Camped at Deer Creek about thirty past five p.m. Found the wagons waiting on us. A most excellent camping ground. Plenty of wood, water, and feed for the cattle. ROBERT STODDARD died of consumption, age 51. Buried about four hundred yards from the left hand side of the road." [Ellsworth, p. 106-07]

1 September - Monday

"Rested from travels. I mended carts. Meeting about flour and paying for extra that was brought in the wagons. Harriet getting quite well and walks all the way. 18 cents per lb." [Walters]

"We remained at Deer Creek today to rest ourselves and the cattle. Busy repairing the handcarts. Killed a cow. Had a good meeting at night. Addressed by Brother ELLSWORTH, and the brethren from the Valley. We spent a first rate day of it." [Ellsworth, p. 107]

2 September - Tuesday

"Platte River. Travelled 19 miles. Walter Sanderson, aged 56, died." [Walters]

"The camp rolled out at a quarter to seven a.m. and traveled twenty miles. The road tolerably good, but very dusty owing to a heavy wind. Camped beside the Platte. Plenty of wood. Feed scarce. Crossed a creek eleven miles from where we started. WALTER SANDERS died last night. Buried this morning about three hundred yards from the south side of the road. Age sixty-five." [Ellsworth, p. 107]

3 September - Wednesday

"Met 4 wagons; Henshaw from Nottingham; John Barns from Sheffield. Travelled 15 miles." [Walters]

"The camp rolled this morning at thirty past eight a.m. and traveled eleven miles. It was very heavy pulling owing to the dust and a heavy wind. Crossed the Platte a mile and a half below the upper cross-

Second Handcart Company Log

31 August - Sunday

"Rainy day had 4 cows and 2 oxen killed [?] which to [?] I had to shoot it [?], cattle had a good place to feed, expected to have a meeting but were to busy, had a sick steer and after consecrating some pain killer drenched him with it, and in doing so hurt my hand severly." [Leonard, p. 18]

"Travelled 29 miles and crossed the Platte over to the south side." [Wakefield, "Birmingham Dairy"]

1 September - Monday

"Traveled 25 miles, crossing the River to the North side at 11 O'Clock, done very well for water but feed none as it was after dark before we got into [?] Met Cushombo a Mt-eer who gave us some beef." [Leonard, p. 18]

"1st — 2ns — 3rd SEPTEMBER

Travelled at about 25 miles a day. On the 2d lost a German boy." [Wakefield, "Birmingham Dairy"]

2 September - Tuesday

"Rose early drove our cattle accross the river and staid by them and the mule till near 7 O Clock when we drove them in, again drove 25 miles crossing the River to the South at one O'Clock In the afternoon had no water for 12 miles, after dark when we got into camp again on a large creek wood plenty but feed poor; about 45 sick and lame in the wagons." [Leonard, p. 18]

"...on the 2nd of September we met the first provision wagons from the Valley. On Deer Creek we got 1000 lbs. of flour, which caused the hearts of the saints to be cheered up greatly." [McArthur Report & Hafen, *Handcarts*, p. 214-17]

3 September - Wednesday

"Rose early greased the wagons, which we made an every two days job, at noon to our joy met with the Vallie boys with flour from the Mountains, they were at deer creek. at 2 O Clock started out went 11 miles the Brethren going with us, & in the evening we held a meeting to learn if the companys were willing

First Handcart Company Log

ings. A good place to ford. Camped beside of the Platte at thirty past four p.m. Plenty of wood. Feed middling." [Ellsworth, p. 107]

4 September - Thursday
"Travelled 10 miles." [Walters]

"The camp rolled out this morning and traveled twenty-six miles. The roads were very good for traveling. Had dinner by the side of Mineral Spring Creek. Camped at Little Stream Creek at thirty past five p.m. About a half an hour after getting to camp it got very cold and rained for several hours so that we could not light a fire." [Ellsworth, p. 107]

5 September - Friday
"Rested. Rained all day." [Walters]

"We remained in camp today owing to the inclement state of the weather. It rained and snowed alternately for the whole of the day so that we could not cook hardly anything." [Ellsworth, p. 107]

6 September - Saturday
"Lost cattle." [Walters]

"About four a.m. this morning the weather became more settled, but we found to our sorrow that twenty-four head of our cattle were missing, owing to the negligence of ROBERT SHINN AND JAMES SHINN Jr., who were on guard. We had to remain in camp again today as the cattle were not found till about three p.m." [Ellsworth, p. 107]

7 September - Sunday
"Travelled 26 miles. Bro. Nipras died. Left on road." [Walters]

"The camp rolled out this morning at thirty past seven a.m. and traveled twenty-two miles. The road

Second Handcart Company Log

to pay 18 dollars per hund for flour they said sis. Bro. Nealy had the charge of the flour" [Leonard, p. 18]

4 September - Thursday
"Traveled about 15 miles crossed the Platte and camped just before a ferious and cold rain which continued all night. I went out at 8 in the evening to build for the guard a large fire to keep the wolves off the cattle as they had killed an animal each night for 5 successive nights not but a few miles from our camp; at noon we obliged to leave one of the best cows we had as she was sick with the flux or Murrain, we gave her some [?] but to no use she was in fine order and large. Bro Mcantire and Chester Snider were appointed to return with us with two poor teams and 1400 lbs. of flour." [Leonard, p. 18]

"Crossed Muddy Creek and travelled 20 miles and late in the evening forded the Platte again for the last time. For five days we were not in camp for an hour after night and we were always up at daybreak preparing to start at 5. We met the wagons at Deer Creek which were sent with flour from the Valley to meet us. There were 5 wagons, one for each Company and each wagon had 1000 lbs. of flour in them. Two started for the Valley with our Company. German boys father died." [Wakefield, "Birmingham Dairy," & Hafen, *Handcarts*, p. 74]

5 September - Friday
"Very cold and rainy all day laid in camp, much snow near us on the Mountains, kept our Cattle together with some trouble." [Leonard, p. 19]

"Very wet today. Could not start it rained so much. Snow four feet deep on the mountains all around us." [Birmingham dairy, Hafen, <u>Handcarts</u>, p. 74]

6 September - Saturday
"Traveled 15 miles and camped at the last point of the river killed a beef creature and repaired some carts; the roads were very heavy indeed" [Leonard, p. 19]

7 September - Sunday
"Traveled 20 miles, lost a German boy at noon, camped at 4 O Clock on horse creek near greese wood and among a lot of Indians Capt Dan and Bro. McAntire were out all night but found not the young

First Handcart Company Log

was good for the first fourteen miles. Camped to have dinner beside a most beautiful creek of water. For the next eight miles the road is very sandy and heavy. Camped at thirty past six p.m. by side of Sweetwater, two miles from the crossing. A good camping ground. Good feed for the cattle. GEORGE NEAPPRIS died this evening. Age 24. Emigrated from Cardiff in Dan Jones' company."

8 September - Monday

"11 miles. Had dinner at Devil's Gate." [Walters]

"This morning GEORGE NEAPPRIS was buried on a sand ridge directly east of three rocky mounds. Two and a half miles from the crossing on the bend of the north side of the river, Crossed Sweetwater by a good bridge. The roads were in many parts rather rough. Had dinner beside an old trading post close by the Devil's Gate. Camped beside Sweetwater at thirty past five p.m. not far from a company of apostates." [Ellsworth, p. 108]

9 September - Tuesday

"The camp rolled at thirty past seven a.m. and traveled sixteen miles. The roads continued rather rough with a heavy headwind. Camped at five p.m. beside Sweetwater. An excellent camping ground. Killed a cow." [Ellsworth, p. 108]

10 September - Wednesday

"10, 11, 12 September, Sarah very poorly. Harriet quite well." [Walters]

"The camp rolled out at forty past seven a.m. and traveled eighteen miles. The roads tolerably good to Sweetwater crossing. After that it was sandy for seven miles. Camped at six p.m. on Sweetwater. A very indifferent camping ground. Poor feed." [Ellsworth, p. 108]

11 September - Thursday

"The camp rolled out at forty past seven a.m. and traveled nineteen miles. The first part of the journey the roads pretty good. No water for twelve miles. You will then come to a good stream of water and good feed. Take the left hand road. Traveled eight miles to a creek. A poor camping ground. Middling feed. Camped at six p.m. Brother McARTHUR'S company came up. They had traveled nearly night and day to overtake us."[[Ellsworth, p. 118]

Second Handcart Company Log

man. Came to where Capt Elsworth had camped the night before, as he had [?] to let the snow get out of the way before him as there had been considerable; roads quite heavy at the Willow Spring and [?] up those heavy hills, no wood but sage brush where we camped." [Leonard, p. 19]

8 September - Monday

"Traveled about 20 miles and camped near Independence Rock passed the Solaraties beds about 4 O Clock, but the rain had nearly spoiled it, lived on greece wood creek feed good Capt. Dan came up near night without the lost man, and the conclusion is that he was taken back by some men on their return from the Vallie of the Merchant train, they tried to get a boy to go back with them." [Leonard, p. 19]

9 September - Tuesday

"Again went 18 or 20 miles, but a about 4 O Clock Mariott drove into a chuck hole and broke a hind wheel all to pieces, Crandel concluded that we had to have the wagon but I fixed up the wheel temporarily and loaded it, so as to get it into camp a little after dark, we had an Indian with us when we made to sleep in our tent, to preserve him as we supposed from stealing a horse. The mail passed us a dark saying that Capt Elsworth is only 4 miles ahead." [Leonard, p. 19]

10 September - Wednesday

"Cold night heavy frost, up early repaired the wheel that was broken, 5 new spokes and done some other repairs and traveled 18 or 20 miles, over some dreadful sand road, at night camped near Rev. Brackenbury from the Vallie who gave me some news about the Vallie and the road camped at the 2nd crossing on Independence Rock good feed and feed. callers the 3 crossings. night cold and winds frost quite severe." [Leonard, p. 19]

11 September - Thursday

"Started at 7 traveled about 11 miles, made the 5th crossing at noon or a little before, here most of the people took dinner while we drove about 3 miles to good feed, started at half passed one, and after going 6 miles over heavy roads, struck the cut off a little after dark and then went about 12 miles over good road most of the, traveled till 11 O Clock at night and came upon Capt, Elsworths company, under a heavy hill, the moon shone beautifully, and

First Handcart Company Log

12 September - Friday
"The camp rolled out at forty-five past seven a.m. and traveled twelve miles. The greatest part of the road very hilly and rough. A good spring of water about six miles from where we started this morning. Camped at forty-five past one p.m. Good camping ground. Feed pretty fair. Plenty of good spring water, about two hundred yards from the road, right side." [Ellsworth, p. 108]

13 September - Saturday
"Travelled 28 miles. Camped at Pacific Springs. Trucked a blanked with a brother from the Valley who came from Gotherham, named Goldsmith, part of Bro. Bankses Wagon Co." [Walters]

"The camp rolled out at forty past seven a.m. and traveled twenty-eight miles. The road was very good. We took the cutoff six miles from where we started. There is a good creek of water and pleanty good feed two hundred years from where the road crosses the creek. Nine miles farther on there is another good creek and feed. It is not far from the head of Sweetwater. Camped at nine p.m. at the Pacific Springs. Here we came up with the main body of Captain BANK'S company. They had ten days clear start of us from Florence, MARY MAYO died of diarrhea. Age 65. Buried close to the big mountain left hand side of the road." [Ellsworth, p. 108-09]

14 September - Sunday
"Travelled 3 miles. Camped to mend hand carts and women to wash. Sister Mayer died." [Walters]

"The camp rolled out at nine a.m. and traveled three miles where there was plenty of feed for the cattle." [Ellsworth, p. 109]

Second Handcart Company Log

we unobserved poueraded our company and gave them 3 loud cheers which was returned by a tune or two from their band; we were soon among the saints who mingled together in happy groups till near mid night Capt Edd rather hated our coming upon him, but we had it to do in order to obtain feed for our cattle." [Leonard, p. 19-20]

12 September - Friday
"Started late and traveled not more than 14 miles, and again camped with Elsworth who in company with several others came to our tent where we had a jolly good time." [Leonard, p. 20]

13 September - Saturday
"A late start in consequence of waiting for Capt Edd. Started drive over the balance of the cut off, & camped on or near sweet water, killed a beef, Chambers son also came from the Vallie to meet and take his parent with their hand cart to the Vallie Capt Edd on 12 miles" [Leonard, p. 20]

14 September - Sunday
"drove about 15 miles and camped at Pacific creek 3 miles from the Springs, here we came up with Capt. Elswoth again we also had the pleasure of seeing Patriarch John Smith, Wm Smith who gave me news from my family Hinderson, Peter Vanorden was also with him we held meeting in the evening where Capt Dan put it upon me to take charge of the same; Bro. John gave us some good advise, exhorted the saints to faithfulness, secret prayer etc, several from Edds camp were at our meeting especially the girls." [Leonard, p. 21]

"On the [September] 14th we camped at Pacific Spring Creek, and there I took in 1000 lbs. of more flour, so as to be sure to have enough to do me until we got into the Valley, for I was told that that would

First Handcart Company Log

15 September - Monday
"The camp rolled out at seven a.m. and traveled twenty-six miles. A creek of water twelve miles from where we started. Also feed. Here we rested two hours. Sixteen miles we camped at Little Sandy. We got plenty of water by digging for it. Plenty of wood and pretty good feed. Camped at nine p.m. Very good roads." [Ellsworth, p. 109]

16 September - Tuesday
"The camp rolled out at thirty past eight a.m. and traveled twenty-three miles. Good roads. Crossed a splended creek of water five miles from Little Sandy. Camped on the banks of Big Sandy at seven p.m. Plenty of wood on the opposite side of the river. Poor feed for cattle." [Ellsworth, p. 109]

17 September - Wednesday
"JAMES BIRCH, age 28, died this morning of diarrhea. Buried on the top of sand ridge east of Sandy. The camp rolled at eight and traveled eleven miles. Rested four hours by the side of Green River. Forded the river about four p.m. and camped about six p.m. Good feed and camping ground." [Ellsworth, p. 109]

18 September - Thursday
"At eight a.m. the camp rolled out and traveled twenty-two miles. Good roads. Camped on Ham's Fork at seven p.m. Good feed for cattle; and wood." [Ellsworth, p. 109]

"An impressionistic picture of the handcarts in action, is given by Thomas Bullock who, with sixteen other missionaries bound for Britain and several en route to fields elsewhere, met the two first handcart caravans on September 18.

He sent his report to the *Millenial Star*, from Florence on October 28.

"We were very agreeably surprised by suddenly coming upon the advance train of handcarts, composed of about 300 persons, travelling gently up the hill west of Green River, led by Elder Edmund Ellsworth. As the two companies approached each other, the camp of missionaries formed a line, and gave three loud Hosannahs with the waving of hats, which was heartily led by Elder P. P. Pratt, responded to by loud greetings from the Saints of the handcart train, who unitedly made the hills and valleys resound with shouts of gladness; the memory of this

Second Handcart Company Log

be the last opportunity to get it." [McArthur Report & Hafen, *Handcarts*, p. 214-17]

15 September - Monday
"Traveled 27 miles after a severe rain and hail storm, shod the mule etc. Camped at 10 in the evening on little Sandy to the anoyance of Capt. Elsworth, [?] but [?]" [Leonard, p. 21]

16 September - Tuesday
"On account of confusion with Elsworth we laid by all day drove our cattle up the stream 4 miles as his were they good good feed, in the evening Capt. Bank came up with the Band who gave several lively tunes for the benefit of our company." [Leonard, p. 21]

17 September - Wednesday
"Traveled 23 miles and camped on big Sandy. Saw the grave of James Birch of Elsworths company, road gravelly and hard on our cattles feet [some?] feed at noon for our animals." [Leonard, p. 21]

18 September - Thursday
"Traveled about 18 miles crossed Green river at noon and went about 6 miles and camped at the trading post on [?] on the hill I had an ox; also passed or missed Parly as he took the cut of to big sandy." [Leonard, p. 20]

APPENDIX I: HANDCART Logbook for 17 July to September, 1856   237

FIRST HANDCART COMPANY LOG

scene will never be forgotten by any person present... They were very cheerful and happy, and we blessed them in the name of the Lord, and they went on their way rejoicing. The same day we met a company of hand-carts, led by Elder D. McArthur." [Birmingham dairy, Hafen, Handcarts, p. 75-6]

19 September - Friday

"The camp rolled at thirty past nine a.m. and traveled twenty-three miles. The roads good. A poor place for feed. Camped at nine p.m." [Ellsworth, p. 109]

20 September - Saturday

"The camp rolled out at forty-five past six a.m. and traveled nine miles to Bridger. The road rather rough and rocky. Camped at Bridger for the day. At fifteen past ten a.m. Killed a first rate fat ox. Shod several of the oxen." [Ellsworth, p. 109]

21 September - Sunday

"At seven a.m. the camp rolled and traveled twenty-two miles. The roads were good. Crossed several creeks. Passed a sulphur and soda spring. Camped at six p.m. Plenty of wood and fee, but no water." [Ellsworth, p. 109]

SECOND HANDCART COMPANY LOG

19 September - Friday

"Traveled to hamsfork. met on the way Asakel Z Tolcott and two other brethren with flour to meet the last hand cart train, a good many riding McCleve very sick as also the old German." [Leonard, p. 20]

20 September - Saturday

"This morning Honrick Elaker 56 years of age I took the charge of his burial a solemn scene took place as he was the 3rd who had died beside one that had been lost since leaving Winters Quarters. Traveled upwards of 30 miles arriving of Fort Bridger where we over took Capt Elsworth, in a great stun to be sure. Two of our cattle are rather tired and we have concluded to leave them with Square Robinson to recruit and save them" [Leonard, p. 20]

"On the 20th [September] we reached Fort Bridger..." [McArthur Report & Hafen, Handcarts, p. 214-17]

21 September - Sunday

"Rested a half day killed a fat cow that Robin turned out as church property he also let Elsworth have an ox. Obtained a few pair of mocasins for the lame, traveled 10 miles and camped on Rocky run, picked up two of Edds com who had been left." [Leonard, p. 20]

"From the 5th to the 21st, nothing particular occurred save the meeting of some wagons of flour from the valley for which we will have to pay at the rate of 18¢ per lb. when we get to the city... Passed Independence Rock. Crossed Green River which we had to ford with many smaller ones. Met some other wagons and people coming to meet their friends in the Company. Travelled at the rate of about 25 miles per day. Two days we travelled 32 miles each. Camped last night at Fort Bridger where we remained until 10 o'clock today. We are not 113 miles from the city. Henry Bouning fell down and fainted yesterday under the hand cart from fatigue. Had to be carried into camp which we did not reach until 10 o'clock at night." (No further diary entries.) [Wakefield, "Birmingham Dairy," & Hafen, Handcarts, p. 74-75]

First Handcart Company Log

22 September - Monday
"The camp rolled out at thirty past five a.m. and traveled twenty-three miles. Had breakfast six miles from where we started. About three p.m. met with BRIGHAM'S AND HEBER'S sons. They were glad to see us. About half past five we were taken in a thunder storm and traveled an hour and a half in it. Camped at six p.m. Plenty of water and feed. Wood rather scarce. The wagons with the tents did not arrive till twelve midnight. We were cold and wet. Still we felt all right." [Ellsworth, p. 109-10]

23 September - Tuesday
"The camp rolled out at twelve p.m. and traveled eighteen miles. The roads were pretty good. We forded the Weber about one p.m. and had dinner on the Weber banks. Camped about thirty past six p.m. Wood, water, feed plenty. We were visited by a few Indians." [Ellsworth, p. 110]

24 September - Wednesday
"The camp rolled out at seven a.m. and traveled twenty miles. The roads were rather rough and rugged. Camped about thirty past six p.m. Wood, water, feed, plenty." [Ellsworth, p. 110]

25 September - Thursday
"The camp rolled out at seven a.m. and traveled twenty miles. Crossed canyon eleven times. The roads a little rough. Had dinner at the bottom of Big Mountain. Crossed Big Mountain in two hours and fifty-five minutes. Camped at the foot of the Little Mountain at six p.m." [Ellsworth, p. 110]

26 September - Friday
"The brethren from the city sent us a wagon with provisions as we were rather short. At thirty past ten a.m. the camp rolled and traveled thirteen miles. About eight miles from the city we were met with Governor YOUNG and his counselors the Nauvoo brass band, the Lancers, and a great many others. We were first rate received in the city. Provisions of all kinds came rolling in to us in camp. The brethren of the city manifested great interest towards us as a company, which caused our hearts to rejoice and be glad." [Ellsworth, p. 110]

"The first two handcart companies reached Salt Lake Valley together on September 26th.... Wilford Woodruff, one of the Counsellors of President Young, describes the reception: 'One of the most interesting scenes that was ever witnessed in our Territory, was

Second Handcart Company Log

22 September - Monday
"This morning Sister Muir was delivered of a son and done well; drove to Bear River heavy clowdy weather, long drive" [Leonard, p. 20]

23 September - Tuesday
"Traveled to the mouth of Echo Kanion late when we arrived and a very cool night was near a camp who thretened Capt Edd as he had left some persons out all night who had suffered much as it rained very hard and they were wet so as to be obliged to lay in camp till near noon" [Leonard, p. 21]

24 September - Wednesday
"Made a heavy days drive and camped on the Weber, during the day broke 2 hand carts in Echo Kanion I also shod 2 lame oxen at noon" [Leonard, p. 21]

25 September - Thursday
"Traveled about 25 miles and camped after dark near the top of the big Mt done more shoeing of cattle as also picked up one of Capt Edds company who was left on East Kanion creek Sanders by name nearly dead we let him sleep in our tent Pat. Linch came and staid all night and told us that Capt Edd were at or between the mountains 10 miles ahead." [Leonard, p. 21]

26 September - Friday
"Started early although our cattle were much scattered I found a number of them on the top of the big Mountain. got them together and started without breakfast. came near the foot of the little Mountain where we overtook Capt. Elsworth company turned our cattle our to feed got breakfast receiving some beef from the city, we also gave the people a chance to clean up before going into the city, at 11 O'Clock started and came over the little Mt without doubling teams. Capt. Elsworth had started before us and it was reported that he intended to rush into the city before us' but Brigham heard that we were near and gave instructions that we all should come in together, so we were escorted in by Brigham Heber and many of our leading men and the Brass Band with hundreds of people all filled with the great joy to see literally

FIRST HANDCART COMPANY LOG

the arrival of two of the handcart companies on the 26th inst. Having heard the night previous that they were camped between the two mountains, President Young and Kimball, and many citizens, with a detachment of the Lancers, and the brass bands, went out to meet and escort them into the city. They met the companies at the foot of the Little Mountain. Elder E. Ellsworth led the first company, and Elder Daniel D. McArthur the second.

"After the meeting and salutations were over, amid feelings which no one can describe, the escort was formed, a party of Lancers leading the advance, followed by the bands, the Presidency, the Marshal, and citizens; then came the companies of handcarts, another party of Lancers bringing up the rear... I must say my feelings were inexpressible to behold a company of men, women, and children, many of them aged and inform, enter the city of the Great Salt Lake, drawing 100 handcarts, (led by Brother Ellsworth, who assisted in drawing the first handcart) with which they had travelled some 1,400 miles in nine weeks, and to see them dance with joy as they travelled through the streets... This sight filled our hearts with joy and thanksgiving to God... As I gazed upon the scene, meditating upon the future result, it looked to me like the first hoisting of the floodgate of deliverance to the oppressed millions. We can no say to the poor and honest in heart, come home to Zion, for the way is prepared...'" [Hafen, Handcarts, p. 76-7]

"The *Deseret News* reported the reception of the honored companies by the welcoming party: 'Ere long the anxious expected train came in sight, led by Captain Ellsworth on foot, and with two aged veterans pulling the front cart, followed by a long line of carts attended by the old, middle aged and young of both sexes.

"When opposite the escorting party, a halt was called, and their Captain introduced the new comers to President Young and Kimball, which was followed by the joyous greeting of relatives and friends, and an unexpected treat of melons. While thus regaling, Captain D. D. McArthur came up with his handcart company, they having traveled from the east base of the Big Mountain...

"The procession reached the Public Square about sunset, where the Lancers, Bands and carriages were formed in a line facing the line of handcarts; and after a few remarks by President Young, accompanied by his blessing, the spectators and escort retired and the companies pitched their tents, at the end of a walk

SECOND HANDCART COMPANY LOG

their anticipation realized. This was a day never to be forgotten joy by the hand cart people and sorrow and tears from many to see the worn out saints covered with dust and raggs truly apperantly pitiful objects yet had attained an honor above the riches of this life. Arrived at Union Square at sun down and mad comfortable for food through the exertions of the Bishops. And after I was clear of charge I [?] a warm windstorm to stay with S. A. W—" [Leonard, p. 21-22]

"...on the 26th of September, we arrived in this Valley, with only the loss of 8 souls. 7 died, and one, a young man, age 20 years, we never could tell what did become of him." [McArthur Report & Hafen, *Handcarts*, p. 214-17]

First Handcart Company Log

and pull upwards of 1300 miles. This journey has been performed with less than the average amount of mortality usually attending ox trains; and all, though somewhat fatigued, stepped out with alacrity to the last, and appeared buoyant and cheerful.

"And thus has been successfully accomplished a plan, devised by the wisdom and forethought of our President, for rapidly gathering the poor, almost entirely independent of the wealth so closely hoarded beyond their reach.'" [Hafen, *Handcarts*, p. 77-78]

"As they came down the bench you could scarcely see them for the dust. When they entered the City the folks came running from every quarter to get a glimpse of the long looked-for hand carts. I shall never forget the feeling that ran through my whole system as I caught the first sight of them. The first Hand Cart was drawn by a man and his wife. They had a little flag on it, on which were the words, 'Our President, may the unity of the Saints ever show the wisdom of his counsels.' The next Hand Cart was drawn by three young women...The tears ran down the cheeks of many a man who you would have thought would not, could not, shed a tear." [Larson, p. 203]

Second Handcart Company Log

27 September - Saturday

"Great Salt Lake City With the company most of the day in setling up matters and advising the poor and administering to the sick I was requested by the order of Brigham to baptize two individuals one a Dane sick and crazy and a Bro. Ellise a good but worn down sick man, took the Dane in a hand cart had him hauled to City Creek where I Baptised the two and confirmed them in connection with Bro Maxwell, who assisted me. Bro. Lorenzo Young sent some toast and tea which the poor fellows refished exceedingly well The Dane walked a goodly distance back, even further than he had done at any one time from the Upper Crossing of the Platte, at one time, the point where he had been taken crazy. Towards night my Wife came to meet me in a carriage drive by one Shepherd. We went to Levi Riters and staid all night" [Leonard, p. 22]

28 September - Sunday

"Went to meeting and was called to the Stand in connection with Brother Elsworth McArthur and Oakley. The two former spoke in the forenoon and we the latter in the afternoon mostly upon the hand cart system amid the anxious listening's of a vast congregation. After meeting rode home 16 miles taking with me Bro. Marrott one of our drivers.

First Handcart Company Log	Second Handcart Company Log
	When I came into the house my Wife had built I felt contented & happy
	"During the week remained at home most of the time receiving friends etc; the latter part however I rode down with Horton Height & went out to escort Brother Bunkers Company into the City on the 4th of Oct. they having made the trip across the plains in 2 months and 4 days being a little longer than we were coming. I also went to the Desert Fair and also to a Plowing Match. all exhibited great satisfaction" [Leonard, p. 22]

END NOTES

CHAPTER I

1. Day, Robert O., *And The Ways of God And The Ways of Man.*
2. 2 Thessalonians 2:1-4.
3. McConkie, *Mormon Doctrine*, p. 609.
4. Acts 3:19-21.
5. Ephesians 1:10.
6. McConkie, *Mormon Doctrine*, p. 634.
7. Acts 3: 19-21.
8. *History of the Church*, Volume 1, Ch. 22, p. 315; & Burton, *Discourses of J.S.* p.319.
9. D&C 27: 13-14 & Moses 7:62-64.
10. *Encyclopedia of Mormonism*, p. 536
11. D&C 45: 66-71.
12. D&C 84:4.
13. D&C 101:22.
14. Roberts, *Comprehensive History of the Church*, Vol.3, Ch.88, pp. 383-384.
15. Ibid., pp. 407-408.
16. Ibid, pp. 408.
17. Ibid, pp. 409-410.
18. Roberts, *Comprehensive History of the Church*, Vol.3, Ch.88, pp. 408-409.
19. General Epistle of the First Presidency, *Deseret News*, October 31st, 1855; & Roberts, *Comprehensive History of the Church*, Vol.4, Ch.98, pp. 83-84.
20. Ibid, p. 85.
21. Ibid, pp. 84-85.
22. Ibid, p. 85.
23. *Millennial Star*, vol. xviii, p. 377; & Roberts, *Comprehensive History of the Church*, Vol.4, Ch.98, pp. 85-86.
24. Roberts, *Comprehensive History of the Church*, Vol.3, Ch.88, pp. 403, 404-405.
25. Ibid, pp. 409-410.
26. *Encyclopedia of Mormonism*, p.1075.
27. Isaiah 2:2-3.

CHAPTER II

1. Bashore, Sonne, *Mormons On The High Seas.*
2. *Millennial Star*, 12 Jan 1856, p. 26, (See pp. 9-12 for details on the PEF.)
3. McAllister, *Excerpts From Journals*, p. 103.
4. Ibid., p. 104.
5. Sonne, *Saints...*, p. 54, & Sonne, *Ensign*, pp. 8-10.
6. Ibid.
7. Ibid.
8. Sonne, *Ensign*, pp. 8-10.
9. Sonne, *Saints...*, p. 53.
10. McAllister, *Excerpts From Journals*, p. 104.
11. Sabin, *Autobiography*.
12. McAllister, *Excerpts From Journals*, p. 105.
13. Ibid., p. 106-107.
14. Ibid.
15. McAllister, *Excerpts From Journals*, & Walters, *Journal*.
16. McAllister, *Excerpts From Journals*, p. 107.
17. Walters, *Journal*.
18. *Millennial Star*, p. 354.
19. Walters, *Journal*.
20. *Millennial Star*, p. 354.
21. McAllister, *Excerpts From Journals*, p. 108.
22. Ibid.
23. Walters, *Journal*.
24. *Millennial Star*, p. 354.
25. Ibid.
26. McAllister, *Excerpts From Journals*.
27. *Millennial Star*, p. 354
28. Walters, *Journal*.
29. Ibid.
30. Ibid.
31. McAllister, *Excerpts From Journals*.
32. Walters, *Journal*.
33. Ibid.
34. *Millenial Star*, p. 354.
35. Walters, *Journal*.
36. Ibid.
37. McAllister, *Excerpts From Journals*, p. 113.
38. Walters, *Journal*.
39. McAllister, *Excerpts From Journals*.
40. Ibid.
41. Walters, *Journal*.
42. McAllister, *Excerpts From Journals*, p. 111.
43. Walters, *Journal*.
44. McAllister, *Excerpts From Journals*.
45. Walters, *Journal*.
46. McAllister, *Excerpts From Journals*.
47. Ibid., p. 115.
48. Walters, *Journal*.
49. Ibid.
50. *Millenial Star*, 12 January 1856.
51. McAllister, *Excerpts From Journals*.
52. Walters, *Journal*.
53. Ibid.
54. *Millennial Star*, p. 354.
55. Walters, *Journal*.

[56] McAllister, *Excerpts From Journals,* p. 118.
[57] Walters, *Journal.*
[58] McAllister, *Excerpts From Journals.*
[59] Ibid.
[60] Ibid.
[61] *Millenial Star,* pp. 354-55.
[62] McAllister, *Excerpts From Journals.*
[63] Ibid.
[64] Ibid.
[65] *Millenial Star, Excerpts From Journals,* p. 355.
[66] Ibid.
[67] Walters, *Journal.*
[68] McAllister, *Excerpts From Journals,* p. 123.
[69] Ibid.
[70] Walters, *Journal.*

CHAPTER III
[1] Walters, *Diary.*
[2] McAllister, *Journals,* p. 124.
[3] McAllister, *Journals,* p. 124; & Sabin, *Autobiography;* & Walters, *Diary.*
[4] Stuart, James, *Three Years in North America* , p. 392.
[5] Charles MacKay, *Life and Liberty in America*, p. 122.
[6] *Millennial Star,* pp. 355-56 & McAllister, *Journals..* p. 124.
[7] Sabin, *Autobiography.*
[8] Kimball, *Rail/Trail,* pp. 11-12.
[9] Ibid., p. 12.
[10] Bell, *Life & Writings of John Jaques.*, pp. 107-108.
[11] Sabin, *Autobiography.*
[12] Knecht, *BYU Studies,* p. 55.
[13] Brown *Journal,* pp. 12-13.
[14] Knecht, *BYU Studies*, p. 56.
[15] Walters, *Diary.*
[16] Walters, *Diary* & McAllister, *Journals.*
[17] Kimball, *Rail/Trail Pioneers,* p. 12.
[18] Walters, *Diary* & McAllister, *Journals.*
[19] Hafen, *Handcarts to Zion,* p. 47.
[20] Sabin, *Autobiography.*
[21] McAllister, *Journals.*
[22] Ibid.

CHAPTER IV
[1] McAllister, *Journals..*
[2] Ibid.
[3] Hafen, *Handcarts to Zion,* p. 59.
[4] Walters, *Diary &/or Journal.*
[5] Ibid.
[6] Ibid.
[7] Hafen, *Handcarts to Zion,* p. 56.
[8] Walters, *Diary &/or Journal.*
[9] Ibid.
[10] Ibid.
[11] Wakefield, *The Handcart Trail.*
[12] *Illustrated Stories,* pp. 86-7.
[13] Hafen, *Handcarts to Zion,* pp. 54-55.
[14] Ibid., p. 59.
[15] McAllister, *Journals..*
[16] Ibid.
[17] Walters, *Diary &/or Journal*
[18] McAllister, *Journals..*
[19] Walters, *Diary &/or Journal*
[20] McAllister, *Journals..*
[21] Walters, *Diary &/or Journal*
[22] McAllister, *Journals..*
[23] Bashore & Haslam, *Mormon Pioneer Companies.*
[24] McAllister, *Journals..*
[25] Ibid.
[26] Ibid.
[27] Ibid.
[28] Ibid.
[29] Walters, *Diary &/or Journal.*
[30] McAllister, *...Journals..*
[31] Walters, *Diary &/or Journal.*
[32] Ibid.
[33] Ibid.
[34] Ibid.
[35] McAllister, *...Journals..*
[36] Walters, *Diary &/or Journal..*
[37] McAllister, *...Journals...*
[38] Crandal, *An Enduring Legacy,* p. 145.
[39] Bashore & Haslam, *Mormons on the High Seas,* item 94.
[40] Crandal, *An Enduring Legacy,* p. 145.
[41] McAllister, *Journals..*
[42] Crandal, *An Enduring Legacy,* p. 145.
[43] McAllister, *Journals..*
[44] Ibid.
[45] Walters, *Diary &/or Journal.*
[46] McArthur, *Report to Wilford Woodruff.*
[47] Larson, pp. 201-202.
[48] Bashore & Halsam, *Mormon Pioneer Companies.*
[49] McAllister, *Journals..*
[50] Walters, *Diary &/or Journal.*

CHAPTER V
[1] *Millennial Star,* 2 Aug 1856
[2] Walters, *Diary &/or Journal.*
[3] Galloway, *Annals of Iowa,* p. 444.
[4] Ibid.
[5] *Emigrant's Guide,* Please see the Appendix.

6 Walters, *Diary &/or Journal*.
7 Ellsworth, *Our Ellsworth Ancestors*, p. 96.
8 Leonard, *Handcart Journal*, p. 1.
9 *Millennial Star*, 2 Aug 1856.
10 Crandal, *An Enduring Legacy*, p. 145.
11 Ellsworth, *Our Ellsworth Ancestors*, p. 96.
12 Leonard, *Handcart Journal*, p. 1.
13 Galloway, *Annals of Iowa*, p. 445.
14 Ellsworth, *Our Ellsworth Ancestors*, p. 96.
15 Leonard, *Handcart Journal*, pp. 1-2.
16 Ellsworth, *Our Ellsworth Ancestors*, p. 96 & Galloway, *Annals of Iowa*, p. 445.
17 Leonard, *Handcart Journal*, p. 2.
18 Walters, *Diary &/or Journal*.
19 Ellsworth, *Our Ellsworth Ancestors*, p. 97.
20 Walters, *Diary &/or Journal*.
21 Ellsworth, *Our Ellsworth Ancestors*, p. 97.
22 Walters, *Diary &/or Journal*.
23 Leonard, *Handcart Journal*, p. 2.
24 Ibid.
25 Ellsworth, *Our Ellsworth Ancestors*, p. 97.
26 Leonard, *Handcart Journal*, p. 3.
27 Walters, *Diary &/or Journal*.
28 Galloway, *Annals of Iowa*, p. 445.
29 Leonard, *Handcart Journal*, p. 3.
30 Galloway, *Annals of Iowa*, & Ellsworth, *Our Ellsworth Ancestors*.
31 Galloway, *Annals of Iowa*, p. 445.
32 Leonard, *Handcart Journal*, p. 3.
33 Galloway, *Annals of Iowa*, pp. 445-446.
34 Walters, *Diary &/or Journal*.
35 Ellsworth, *Our Ellsworth Ancestors*, pp. 97-98.
36 Leonard, *Handcart Journal*, pp. 3-4.
37 Ibid.
38 Clayton, *Emigrants Guide...*
39 Walters, *Diary &/or Journal*.
40 Galloway, *Annals of Iowa*, p. 446.
41 Leonard, *Handcart Journal*, p. 4.
42 Walters, *Diary &/or Journal*.
43 Galloway, *Annals of Iowa*, p. 446.
44 Leonard, *Handcart Journal*, p. 4.
45 Walters, *Diary &/or Journal*.
46 Galloway, *Annals of Iowa*, p. 446.
47 Leonard, *Handcart Journal*, pp. 4-5.
48 Walters, *Diary &/or Journal*.
49 Galloway, *Annals of Iowa*, p. 446.
50 Leonard, *Handcart Journal*, p. 5.
51 Ellsworth, *Our Ellsworth Ancestors*, p. 98.
52 Leonard, *Handcart Journal*, p. 5.
53 Walters, *Diary &/or Journal*.
54 Galloway, *Annals of Iowa*, p. 446.
55 Leonard, *Handcart Journal*, p. 5.
56 Galloway, *Annals of Iowa*, pp. 446-47 & Ellsworth, *Our Ellsworth Ancestors*, p. 99.
57 Walters, *Diary &/or Journal*.
58 Leonard, *Handcart Journal*, p. 5.
59 Walters, *Diary &/or Journal* & Galloway, *Annals of Iowa*, p. 447 & Ellsworth, *Our Ellsworth Ancestors*, p. 99
60 Leonard, *Handcart Journal*, pp. 5-6.
61 Walters, *Diary &/or Journal*.
62 Ellsworth, *Our Ellsworth Ancestors*, p. 99.
63 Leonard, *Handcart Journal*, p. 6.
64 Walters, *Diary &/or Journal*.
65 Ellsworth, *Our Ellsworth Ancestors*, p. 99.
66 Leonard, *Handcart Journal*, p.6.
67 Walters, *Diary &/or Journal*.
68 Leonard, *Handcart Journal*, p. 6.
68 Ellsworth, *Our Ellsworth Ancestors*, p. 99.
70 Walters, *Diary &/or Journal*.
71 Ibid.
72 Galloway, *Annals of Iowa*, p. 447.
73 Leonard, *Handcart Journal*, pp. 6-7.
74 Walters, *Diary &/or Journal*.
75 Ellsworth, *Our Ellsworth Ancestors*, p. 100.
76 Leonard, *Handcart Journal*, p. 7.
77 Walters, *Diary &/or Journal*.
78 Ellsworth, *Our Ellsworth Ancestors*, p. 100.
79 Leonard, *Handcart Journal*, p. 7.
80 Walters, *Diary &/or Journal*.
81 Galloway, *Annals of Iowa*, p. 448.
82 Leonard, *Handcart Journal*, p. 7.
83 Walters, *Diary &/or Journal*.
84 Galloway, *Annals of Iowa*, p. 448.
85 Ellsworth, *Our Ellsworth Ancestors*, p. 100.
86 Leonard, *Handcart Journal*, pp. 7-8.
87 Walters, *Diary &/or Journal*.
88 Ellsworth, *Our Ellsworth Ancestors*, p. 100.
89 Leonard, *Handcart Journal*, p. 8.
90 Walters, *Diary &/or Journal*.
91 Galloway, *Annals of Iowa*, p. 448.
92 Leonard, *Handcart Journal*, p. 8.
93 Walters, *Diary &/or Journal*.
94 Ellsworth, *Our Ellsworth Ancestors*, pp. 100-101.
95 Leonard, *Handcart Journal*, p.8.

CHAPTER VI
1 Galloway, *Annals of Iowa*, p. 448 & Leonard, *Handcart Journal*, p. 8.
2 Sabin, *Autobiography*.
3 Walters, *Diary &/or Journal*.

[4] Ellsworth, *Our Ellsworth Ancestors*, p. 101.
[5] Leonard, *Handcart Journal*, p. 8.
[6] Walters, *Diary &/or Journal*.
[7] Leonard, *Handcart Journal*, p. 8.
[8] Ellsworth, p. 101
[9] Hafen, *Handcarts*, p. 67
[10] Larson, *Prelude to the Kingdom*, pp. 201-202.
[11] Sabin, *Autobiography*.
[12] Leonard, *Handcart Journal*, p. 9 & Walters, *Diary &/or Journal*.
[13] Walters, *Diary &/or Journal* & Ellsworth, *Our Ellsworth Ancestors*, p. 101 & Leonard, *Handcart Journal*, p. 9.
[14] Leonard, *Handcart Journal*, page 9.
[15] Ibid., pp. 9-10.
[16] Walters, *Diary &/or Journal*.
[17] Ellsworth, *Our Ellsworth Ancestors*, p. 101.
[18] Leonard, *Handcart Journal*, p. 10.
[19] Walters, *Diary &/or Journal*.
[20] Ellsworth, *Our Ellsworth Ancestors*, p. 101.
[21] Leonard, *Handcart Journal*, p. 10.
[22] Ibid.
[23] Walters, *Diary &/or Journal* & Ellsworth, *Our Ellsworth Ancestors*, p. 101.
[24] Hafen, *Handcarts to Zion..*, p. 67
[25] Walters, *Diary &/or Journal*.
[26] Ellsworth, *Our Ellsworth Ancestors*, p. 101.
[27] Leonard, *Handcart Journal*, p. 10.
[28] Sabin, *Autobiography*.
[29] Walters, *Diary &/or Journal*.
[30] Ellsworth, *Our Ellsworth Ancestors*, p. 101.
[31] Leonard, *Handcart Journal*, p. 10.
[32] Walters, *Diary &/or Journal*.
[33] Ellsworth, *Our Ellsworth Ancestors*, p. 101.
[34] Leonard, *Handcart Journal*, pp. 10-11.
[35] McArthur Report & Hafen, *Handcarts to Zion*, pp. 214-217.
[36] Walters, *Diary &/or Journal*.
[37] Ellsworth, *Our Ellsworth Ancestors*, p. 101.
[38] Leonard, *Handcart Journal*, p. 11.
[39] Wakefield, "Birmingham Dairy," & Hafen, *Handcarts*, pp. 71-72
[40] Sabin, *Autobiography*.
[41] Walters, *Diary &/or Journal* & Ellsworth, *Our Ellsworth Ancestors*, pp. 101-102.
[42] Ibid.
[43] William Clayton, *Come, Come, Ye Saints*, no. 30, L.D.S. Hymnal.
[44] Walters, *Diary &/or Journal* & Ellsworth, *Our Ellsworth Ancestors*, pp. 101-102.
[45] Ellsworth, *Our Ellsworth Ancestors*, pp. 101-102.
[46] Leonard, *Handcart Journal*, p. 11.
[47] Wakefield, "Birmingham Dairy," & Hafen, *Handcarts to Zion*, p. 72.
[48] Walters, *Diary &/or Journal*.
[49] Ellsworth, *Our Ellsworth Ancestors*, p. 102.
[50] Leonard, *Handcart Journal*, pp. 11-12.
[51] Wakefield, "Birmingham Dairy," & Hafen, *Handcarts to Zion*, p. 72.
[52] Ibid.
[53] Ibid.
[54] Walters, *Diary &/or Journal*.
[55] Ellsworth, *Our Ellsworth Ancestors*, p. 102.
[56] Leonard, *Handcart Journal*, p. 12.
[57] Walters, *Diary &/or Journal*.
[58] Ellsworth, *Our Ellsworth Ancestors*, p. 102.
[59] Leonard, *Handcart Journal*, p. 12.
[60] Walters, *Diary &/or Journal*.
[61] Ellsworth, *Our Ellsworth Ancestors*, p. 102.
[62] Leonard, *Handcart Journal*, p. 12.
[63] Wakefield, *Birmingham Diary*.
[64] Leonard, *Handcart Journal*, p. 12.
[65] Walters, *Diary &/or Journal*.
[66] Ellsworth, *Our Ellsworth Ancestors*, p. 102.
[67] Leonard, *Handcart Journal*, p. 12.
[68] Ellsworth, pp. 102-103.
[69] Leonard, *Handcart Journal*, p. 13.
[70] Wakefield, "Birmingham Dairy".
[71] Walters, *Diary &/or Journal*.
[72] Leonard, *Handcart Journal*, p. 13.
[73] Wakefield, "Birmingham Dairy".
[74] Ellsworth, *Our Ellsworth Ancestors*, p. 103.
[75] Walters, *Diary &/or Journal*.
[76] Leonard, *Handcart Journal*, p. 13.
[77] Ibid.
[78] Ellsworth, *Our Ellsworth Ancestors*, p. 103.
[79] Leonard, *Handcart Journal*, p. 13.
[80] Ibid., pp. 13-14
[81] Hafen, *Handcarts to Zion*, pp. 272-273.
[82] Leonard, *Handcart Journal*, p. 14.
[83] Ibid.
[84] Walters, *Diary &/or Journal*.
[85] Ellsworth, *Our Ellsworth Ancestors*, p. 103.
[86] Mary Ann Ellsworth, *Our Ellsworth Ancestors*.
[87] Sabin, *Autobiography*.
[88] Clayton, *Emigrant's Guidebook*.
[89] Walters, *Diary &/or Journal*.
[90] Ellsworth, *Our Ellsworth Ancestors*, p. 103.
[91] Sabin, *Autobiography*.
[92] Mary Ann Ellsworth, *Our Ellsworth Ancestors*.
[93] Walters, *Diary &/or Journal*.
[94] Ellsworth, *Our Ellsworth Ancestors*, p. 103.

[95] Leonard, *Handcart Journal*, p. 14.
[96] Walters, *Diary &/or Journal*.
[97] Ellsworth, *Our Ellsworth Ancestors*, p. 103.
[98] Leonard, *Handcart Journal*, pp. 14-15.
[99] Ellsworth, *Our Ellsworth Ancestors*, pp. 103-104.
[100] Walters, *Diary &/or Journal*.
[101] Leonard, *Handcart Journal*, p. 15.
[102] Walters, *Diary &/or Journal*.
[103] McArthur Report & Hafen, *Handcarts*, pp. 214-17.
[104] Ellsworth, *Our Ellsworth Ancestors*, p. 104 & Walters, *Diary &/or Journal* & Leonard, *Handcart Journal*, p. 15 & Wakefield, *Birmingham Diary*
[105] McArthur Report & Hafen, *Handcarts to Zion*, pp. 214-217.
[106] Crandal, *An Enduring Legacy*, p. 145.
[107] McArthur Report & Hafen, *Handcarts to Zion*, pp. 214-217.
[108] Ibid.
[109] Wakefield, "Birmingham Dairy," & Hafen, *Handcarts to Zion*, p. 73.
[110] McArthur Report & Hafen, *Handcarts to Zion*, pp. 214-217.
[111] Ibid.
[112] Ibid.
[113] Ibid.
[114] Walters, *Diary &/or Journal*.
[115] Ellsworth, *Our Ellsworth Ancestors*, p. 104.
[116] Leonard, *Handcart Journal*, p. 16.
[117] Walters, *Diary &/or Journal*.
[118] Ellsworth, *Our Ellsworth Ancestors*, p. 105
[119] Leonard, *Handcart Journal*, p. 16.
[120] Leonard, *Handcart Journal*, p. 16 & Wakefield, "Birmingham Dairy," & Hafen, *Handcarts to Zion*, p. 73.
[121] Ellsworth, *Our Ellsworth Ancestors*, pp. 105-106 & Walters, *Diary &/or Journal*.
[122] Leonard, *Handcart Journal*, pp. 16-17 & Wakefield, "Birmingham Dairy".
[123] Ellsworth, *Our Ellsworth Ancestors*, pp. 105-106; Leonard, *Handcart Journal*, p. 17.
[124] Walters, *Diary &/or Journal*.
[125] Wakefield, "Birmingham Dairy," & Hafen, *Handcarts to Zion*, p. 74.
[126] Leonard, *Handcart Journal*, p. 17.
[127] Ellsworth, *Our Ellsworth Ancestors*, p. 106.
[128] Walters, *Diary &/or Journal*.
[129] Sabin, *Autobiography*.
[130] Walters, *Diary &/or Journal*.
[131] Ellsworth, *Our Ellsworth Ancestors*, p. 106.
[132] Clayton, *Emigrant's Guide*, p. 12
[133] Walters, *Diary &/or Journal* & Ellsworth, *Our Ellsworth Ancestors*, p. 106.
[134] Wakefield, "Birmingham Dairy," & Hafen, *Handcarts to Zion*, pp. 74, 214-217.
[135] Leonard, *Handcart Journal*, p. 17.
[136] Walters, *Diary &/or Journal*.
[137] Ellsworth, *Our Ellsworth Ancestors*, p. 106.
[138] Leonard, *Handcart Journal*, p. 18.
[138] Clayton, *Emigrant's Guide*, p. 12.
[139] Walters, *Diary &/or Journal*
[140] Ellsworth, *Our Ellsworth Ancestors*, p. 106.
[141] Wakefield, "Birmingham Dairy".
[142] Leonard, *Handcart Journal*, p. 18.
[143] Walters, *Diary &/or Journal* & *Our Ellsworth Ancestors*, pp. 106-107.
[144] Leonard, *Handcart Journal*, p. 18.
[145] Ibid.
[146] Ellsworth, *Our Ellsworth Ancestors*, p. 107.
[147] Wakefield, "Birmingham Dairy".
[148] Leonard, *Handcart Journal*, p. 18.
[149] McArthur Report & Hafen, *Handcarts to Zion*, pp. 214-217.
[150] Walters, *Diary &/or Journal*.
[151] Ellsworth, *Our Ellsworth Ancestors*, p. 107.
[152] Leonard, *Handcart Journal*, p. 18.
[153] Ellsworth, *Our Ellsworth Ancestors*, p. 107.
[154] Leonard, *Handcart Journal*, p. 18.
[155] Ellsworth, *Our Ellsworth Ancestors*, p. 107.
[156] Wakefield, "Birmingham Dairy" & Hafen, *Handcarts to Zion*, p. 74.
[157] Ellsworth, *Our Ellsworth Ancestors*, p. 107.
[158] Leonard, *Handcart Journal*, p. 19.
[159] Wakefield, "Birmingham Dairy" & Hafen, *Handcarts to Zion*, p. 74.
[160] Ellsworth, *Our Ellsworth Ancestors*, p. 107.
[161] Ibid.
[162] Leonard, *Handcart Journal*, p. 19.
[163] Ibid.
[164] Ellsworth, *Our Ellsworth Ancestors*, p. 107.
[165] Leonard, *Handcart Journal*, p. 19.
[166] Ellsworth, *Our Ellsworth Ancestors*, p. 108.
[167] Leonard, *Handcart Journal*, p. 19.
[168] Walters, *Diary &/or Journal*.
[169] Ellsworth, *Our Ellsworth Ancestors*, p. 108.
[170] Ibid.
[171] Leonard, *Handcart Journal*, p. 19.
[172] Ibid.
[173] Ellsworth, *Our Ellsworth Ancestors*, p. 108.
[174] Leonard, *Handcart Journal*, p. 19.
[175] Ellsworth, *Our Ellsworth Ancestors*, p. 118.
[176] Leonard, *Handcart Journal*, pp. 19-20.
[177] Ibid.
[178] Ellsworth, *Our Ellsworth Ancestors*, p. 108.
[179] Leonard, *Handcart Journal*, p. 20.

[180] Clayton, *Emigrant's Guide*.
[181] Ellsworth, *Our Ellsworth Ancestors*, pp. 108-109.
[182] Leonard, *Handcart Journal*, p. 20.
[183] Ibid.
[184] Walters, *Diary &/or Journal*.
[185] Ellsworth, *Our Ellsworth Ancestors*, p. 109.
[186] Leonard, *Handcart Journal*, p. 21.
[187] McArthur Report & Hafen, *Handcarts to Zion*, pp. 214-217.
[188] Ellsworth, *Our Ellsworth Ancestors*, p. 109.
[189] Leonard, *Handcart Journal*, p. 21.
[190] Ellsworth, *Our Ellsworth Ancestors*, p. 109.
[191] Leonard, *Handcart Journal*, p. 21.
[192] Ellsworth, *Our Ellsworth Ancestors*, p. 109.
[193] Leonard, *Handcart Journal*, p. 21.
[194] *Millenial Star*.
[195] Wakefield, "Birmingham Dairy," & Hafen, *Handcarts to Zion*, pp.75-76.
[196] Ellsworth, *Our Ellsworth Ancestors*, p. 109.
[197] Leonard, *Handcart Journal*, p. 20.
[198] Ellsworth, *Our Ellsworth Ancestors*, p. 109.
[199] Leonard, *Handcart Journal*, p. 20.
[200] Ellsworth, *Our Ellsworth Ancestors* p. 109.
[201] Leonard, *Handcart Journal*, p. 20.
[202] Wakefield, "Birmingham Dairy," & Hafen, *Handcarts to Zion*, pp. 74-75.
[203] Ellsworth, *Our Ellsworth Ancestors*, pp.109-110.
[204] Leonard, *Handcart Journal*, p. 20.
[205] Ellsworth, *Our Ellsworth Ancestors*, p. 110.
[206] Leonard, *Handcart Journal*, p. 21.
[207] Clayton, *Emigrant's Guide*, pp.19-20.
[208] Ellsworth, *Our Ellsworth Ancestors*, p. 110.
[209] Leonard, *Handcart Journal*, p. 21.
[210] Ellsworth, *Our Ellsworth Ancestors*, p. 110.
[211] Leonard, *Handcart Journal*, p. 21.
[212] Ellsworth, *Our Ellsworth Ancestors*, p. 110.
[213] Leonard, *Handcart Journal*, pp. 21-22.
[214] Hafen, *Handcarts to Zion*, pp. 76-77.
[215] Ibid.
[216] Larson, *Prelude To The Kingdom*, p. 203.
[217] Woodruff.
[218] Hanson, [Booth] *Family History*, p. 5.
[219] Ellsworth, *Our Ellsworth Ancestors*, pp.110-112.
[220] Leonard, *Handcart Journal*, p. 22.
[221] Day, *Zion Gathered To This Place*.

BIBLIOGRAPHY

THE ENOCH TRAIN PIONEERS

2 Thessalonians 2:1-4. *Holy Bible*. King James Version.

Acts 3:19-21. *Holy Bible*. King James Version.

Annals of Iowa, "First Mormon Handcart Trip Across Iowa", October 1936

Argyle, Joseph 1818-1905, *Excerpts from Reminiscences and Journal May 1870-October 1894*. Church Archives Manuscript Record MS 340, p. 63.

Bashore, Melvin L. & Haslam, Linda L., *Mormon Pioneer Companies Crossing The Plains (1847-1868) Narratives, Guide to Sources in Utah Libraries and Archives*. Historical Department, The Church of Jesus Christ of Latter-day Saints, 1989, Revised Edition. pp. 138-92.

Bashore, Melvin L. & Haslam, Linda L., *Mormons On The High Seas, Ocean Voyage Narratives to America (1840-1890)*. Guide to Sources in the Historical Department of The Church of Jesus Christ of Latter-day Saints and Other Utah Repositories, Church Historical Department, 1984.

Bell, Stella Jaques, *Life and Writings of John Jaques, Including a Diary of the Martin Handcart Company*. Ricks College Press, pp. 95-117.

Bond, John, *Handcarts West in '56*. Second Publication, 1970, pp. 5-18.

Brown, Lorenzo *Journal*. Typescript, Brigham Young University-S, pp. 12-13.

Burton, Alma P., *Discourses of Joseph Smith*. Salt Lake City, Utah: Deseret Book Company, 1956.

Carter, Kate M., "Journal of William Holmes Walker," *Treasures of Pioneer History, Vol VI*. p. 254.

Clayton, W., *The Latter-day Saints' Emigrant's Guide: Being a Table of Distances, Showing All the Springs, Creeks, Rivers, Hills, Mountains...From Council Bluffs, to the Valley of the Great Salt Lake...* St. Louis: Missouri Republican Steam Power Press-Chambers & Knapp, 1848.

Clayton, William, *Come, Come, Ye Saints*, no. 30, *Hymns of The Church of Jesus Christ of Latter-day Saints*, 1985.

Crandal, Mary B., "Autobiography of a Noble Woman," *The Young Woman's Journal, Vol. VI*. Salt Lake City: George Q. Cannon & Sons Co., 1895, pp. 259-67, 318-23, 387-88, 427-28, 463-65, 506-09, 551-55.

Crandal, Mary Brannigan, *An Enduring Legacy, Vol 10*. Daughters of the Utah Pioneers, Salt Lake City, Utah 1987, p. 144-46.

Daughters of Utah Pioneers, *Our Pioneer Heritage*, Vol. 7. Salt Lake City, Utah, 1964, pp. 424-427

Daughters of Utah Pioneers, *Stories of the Handcart Pioneers*, Historical Pamphlet, January 1945. Compiled by Kate B. Carter, 1944, pp. 353-60.

Day, Robert O., "And the Ways of God and the Ways of Man." *The Enoch Train Pioneers, Trek of the First Two Handcart Companies*. Oviedo, Florida, Day to DayEnterprises, 2001.

Day, Robert O., "Oh God, Who Made These Seas to Roll." *The Enoch Train Pioneers, Trek of the First Two Handcart Companies*. Oviedo, Florida, Day to DayEnterprises, 2001.

Day, Robert O., "But Not Much Rest." *The Enoch Train Pioneers, Trek of the First Two Handcart Companies*. Oviedo, Florida, Day to DayEnterprises, 2001.

Day, Robert O., "Ever On To Zion." *The Enoch Train Pioneers, Trek of the First Two Handcart Companies*. Oviedo, Florida, Day to DayEnterprises, 2001.

Day, Robert O., Poem, "Zion Gathered To This Place" from the play, *The Enoch Train: Gathering To Zion*. Salt Lake City, Utah, 1994.

Deseret News, Vol. 6. "Emigrants for Utah, Ship S. Curling, For Boston, April 19, 1856.", p. 160, US/CAN Film 0026587.

Deseret News, Vol. 6. "Ship Enoch Train, For Boston, March 23, 1856.", p. 160, US/CAN Film 0026587.

Didriksson, *Our Pioneer Heritage, Vol. 7.* Daughters of the Utah Pioneers, Salt Lake City, Utah, 1964, pp. 486-87.

Doctrine & Covenants 17:13-14; 45:66-71; 84:4; 101:22.

Ellsworth, German E. & Ellsworth, Mary Smith, *Our Ellsworth Ancestors.* pp. 95-113.

Encyclopedia of Mormonism, pp. 536-37, 571-73, 1075-076.

"Enoch Train Adult Passenger List", from Jenny Lund, Museum of Church History and Art, 1994.

Ephesians 1:10. *Holy Bible.* King James Version.

Ferguson, James, "Foreign Correspondence", *The Latter-day Saints' Millennial Star.* No. 26, Vol. XVIII, Saturday, June 28, 1856.

Ferguson, James, "Report from the 'Enoch Train,'" *The Latter-day Saints' Millennial Star.* No. 23, Vol. XVIII, Saturday, June 7, 1856, pp. 353-56.

Galloway, Andrew, "Mormon Handcart Trip Across Iowa," *Annals of Iowa.* October 1936, pp. 444-49.

"General Epistle of the First Presidency," *Deseret News.* Salt Lake City, Utah, 31 October 1855.

Hafen, LeRoy R. & Hafen, Ann W., *Handcarts To Zion, the Story of a Unique Western Migration 1856-1860...* Glendale, California: The Arthur H. Clark Co., 1960.

Hafen, Leroy R., *Trans-Mississippi West, Hand Cart Migration Across the Plains.* Glendale, California: The Arthur H. Clark Company, pp. 103-21.

Hanson, Frances Hiley Booth, [Booth] *Family History.* In possession of Florence C. Youngberg, 3253 E. Marie Avenue, Salt Lake City, Utah 84109.

Hartley, William G., *Kindred Saints, The Mormon Immigrant Heritage of Alvin and Kathryne Christenson.* Salt Lake City: Eden Hill, p. 131-135.

Havighurst, Walter, *The Heartland Ohio, Indiana, Illinois.* Harper & Row.

Hinkley, Gordon B., "The Faith of the Pioneers," *Ensign*, July 1984, pp. 1-6.

Illustrated Stories From Church History, Vol. 14. Provo, Utah: Promised Land Publications, 1977, pp. 84-95.

Infobases Collectors Library 1997. Reference Softwared for Latter-day Saints, CD-ROM.

Isaiah 2:2-3, *Holy Bible.* King James Version.

Kimball, Stanley B., *Historic Resource Study Mormon Pioneer National Trail.* U.S. Department of Interior/National Park Service, May 1991.

Kimball, Stanley B., "Rail Routes", *Historical Atlas of Mormonism*, p. 62. L.D.S. Collectors Library, 1995.

Kimball, Stanley B., *Rail/Trail Pioneers To Zion: 1855-69: A Preliminary Study.* Unpublished paper prepared for delivery at MHA in May 1992. Southern Illinois University at Edwardsville, School of Social Sciences, Department of Historical Studies, 26 February 1992.

Knecht, William L., Brigham Young University Studies, Volume 17, No. 1. Provo, Utah.

Larson, Gustive O., *Prelude to the Kingdom, Mormon Desert Conquest, A Chapter in American Cooperative Experience.* Francestown: Marshall Jones Company, Publishers, pp. 194-205.

Leonard, Truman, *Handcart Journal.* 11 June 1856–26 September 1856.

Loomis, Leander V., *A Journal of the Birmingham Emigrating Company, The record of a trip from Birmingham, Iowa, to Sacramento, California, in 1850.* Salt Lake City: Legal Printing Co., Exchange Place., 1928, pp. 140-176.

Lowder, Emily Hodgetts, *Our Pioneer Heritage, Vol. 7.* Daughters of the Utah Pioneers, Salt Lake City, Utah, 1964, pp. 425-26.

MacKay, Charles, *Life and Liberty in America; or Sketches of a Tour in the United States and Canada.*

McAllister, John Daniel T., *Excerpts from Journals 1851-1906.* Church Archives, MS 1257, Manuscript Record, Reel 1, Vol. 2, pp. 103-124.

McArthur, Daniel D., *Report to Wilford Woodruff.*

McConkie, Bruce R., *Mormon Doctrine.* Salt Lake City, Utah, Bookcraft, Inc., 1958.

Millennial Star, 13 January 1856, pp. 26, 9-13.

Millenial Star, The Latter-day Saints, 28 June 1856, pp. 412-415.

Millennial Star, Volume xviii, p. 354, 377, 2 Aug 1856.

Moses 7:62-64, *The Pearl of Great Price.*

Richards, Franklin D., Spencer, Daniel, Wheelock, C. H., "General Instructions Perpetual Emigration Fund", *The Latter-day Saints' Millennial Star.* No. 2, Vol. XVIII, Saturday, January 12, 1856.

Roberts, B. H., *A Comprehensive History of the Church*, Volumes 3-4. Salt Lake City, Utah: Bookcraft, 1968.

Roberts, B. H., *History of The Church of Jesus Christ of Latter-day Saints* Volume 1. Salt Lake City, Utah: Deseret Book Company, 1978.

Sabin, Mary Powell, Excerpts From Her *Autobiography, 1926.* Church Archives, MS 3203, Manuscript Record, Access # 93760-ARCH-88, p. 6- .

Sonne, Conway B., *Saints On The Seas, A Maritime History of Mormon Migration, 1830-1890.* Salt Lake City: University of Utah Press, 1983.

Sonne, Conway B., *Ships, Saints, and Mariners, A Maritime Encyclopedia of Mormon Migration 1830-1890.* Salt Lake City, University of Utah Press, 1987.

Sonne, Conway B., "Under Sail To Zion," *Ensign.* Salt Lake City, Utah, July 1991, pp. 6-14.

Stegner, Wallace, *The Gathering of Zion, The Story of the Mormon Trail.* New York: McGraw-Hill Book Company.

Stewart, Elizabeth White, "Autobiography of..." *Ancestors of Isaac Mitton Stewart & Elizabeth White.* Compiled by Mary Ellen Workman, 1978.

Stewart, James, *Three Years in North America.* Edinburg, 1833.

Wakefield, Eliza M., *The Handcart Trail.*

Wakefield, Eliza, "Birmingham Diary."

Walters, Archer, *Diary.* Salt Lake City, Utah: Church Archives.

Walters, Archer, "Journal," *Utah Pioneer Biographies*," Volume 1. Salt Lake City, Utah: Family History Library, The Church of Jesus Christ of Latter-day Saints, pp. 113-118.

Walters, Archer, *Life Aboard The Enoch Train From The Journal of Archer Walters* and the *Millenial Star.*

Wilson, Thomas P., Pueblo, Colorado, "Hand Cart Experiences (Original)," *Historical Bulletin.* Pueblo, CO.: Spring, 1938, p. 10-11.

Index

A

Aaronic Priesthood 115
absolute knowledge of God 116
activities 17
Adam 2, 115
administered 68
administration of the priesthood 53
Agents of the Church 10
Ague 53
Allen , Charles 76
America is Zion 117
American Fever 53
American flag 39
amunition 82
animals 61
anointings 119
anti-Mormon hecklers 66
antiques 50
APPENDIX
   A : A Brief Account of the Apostacy, Restoration and Gathering of Modern Day Israel & the Perpetual Emigration Fund 113
   B: The Millenial Star on The Perpetual Emigration Fund 123
   C: Composite Passenger List of the Enoch Train 129
   D: Composite Passenger List of the Samuel S. Curling 143
   E: Births and Deaths - Alphabetical & by Date 158
   F: Days and Dates of Journey Breakdown by Travel Segments 160
   G: Clayton's, The Latter-day Saints Emigrant's Guide 164
   H: Handcart Logbook for 20 March – 6 June 1856 185
   I: Handcart Logbook for 9 June - 8 July 1856 198
   J: Handcart Logbook 17 July - 28 September 1856 214
apostasize 70
apostasy 1, 2, 113, 115
apostates 116
apostles 113, 114, 116
apples 81, 90
application for Passage. 8
Argyle, Joseph, Jr. 48, 75

Articles of Confederation 2, 114
Atlantic 13, 16
Atlantic Ocean 15
axeltree 68, 70, 86
   broke 2 axeltrees 68
axles with copper 80

B

Babylon 117
bacon 70, 72
Bailey, town of 70
band 14, 15, 20, 22, 28, 29, 52, 65, 104, 106, 110
bandannas 62
baggage, extra 64
baptised 81
baptism for the dead 119
baptismal font 119
baptized for their health 66
Barque *Architect of Windsor* 22
Barque *Emily Flyn* 16
bathe in the Platte 86
baths 51
batten down the hatches 18
Bear Creek 65, 66
Bear Creek Station 71
becalmed 17, 22, 28
BED
   bedding 50
   began to swim 53
   ticking 49
beef was killed 86
below decks 12
Bermingham, Patrick 83, 87
Bermingham, Patrick & Eliza 63
berry bushes 89
between decks for Meeting 29
Big Bear Creek 65
Big Pappy 82
Bill of Rights 2, 114
Birch the Ferryman 88
Birmingham Band 17, 21, 39, 52, 58, 104
BIRTHS: 13
   birth of a baby 11
   birth of the Savior 20
   child born 53
Black Hawk War 43, 70
blankets 83
body of a man float past 22
boils 53, 87
Book of Mormon 115, 117, 119
books 50

books for children 29
Boston 28, 29, 53
Boston Constitution Wharf 29
Boston Station 39
Bower, Joseph died 68
Bowering , Brother 82
bowering was down 83
Bowers, James died 68
Bowing, George & Ellen 52
boxcars 44
Brandy 89
bread 44
breakdowns 69, 80
breaking an ox yoke 62
breeze 70
bridge 42, 43
British Isles 13
British Mission 121
BUFFALO: 41, 89, 90
   buffalo beef 81
   buffalo chips 89
   buffalo country 80
   buffalo herd 89
   wounded two 89
bugle sounded 66
bullets 86
bunker 52, 81
bunks 12
bunks for passenger 7
Burdett 52
BURIED: 53, 68
   burial at sea 19, 21
   buried them by moonlight 65
   buried without a coffin 86
Burmingham band 17, 39
Burmingham Conference 68
Burminhams 64
butcher boys 41
Butler, William 54. 74, 90
buying cattle and wagons 79

C

California Emigrants return 89
California Gold diggers 89
calves 81
CAMP: 12, 53
   at Loop Fork 82
   general 64
   ground 45, 71
   Israel 76
   meeting 51
   of Indians 83
   remained in 65, 72, 76, 90

setting up 69
canoe 88
Captain of the Guard 14
Card, Brother 88
cargo 7
carry water with us 90
cart grease 69
Carthage Jail 116
carts mended 65
caskets 68, 70
castor oil 86
Catholicism 1, 115
CATTLE: 81
   cattle cars 41
   cattle for beef and milk 80
   cattle to be purchased 82
   cattle wandered off 61
   cattle were gone 90
   cattle, swam our 86, 89
   cattle, yokes 66
   wild cattle 64
celestial glory 117
celestial judgement 65
celestial law 42
challenge 21
chamber pots 12, 19
channel pilot 16
channels 43
cheers 64
chest-o-drawers 50
Chicago 41, 42, 44, 49
Chicago and Rock Island
   Railroad 42
CHILD, CHILDREN 17, 21, 26,
   50, 71
   books for 29
   born 88
   oranges for 29
   try to walk 62
china 50
church 51
church burnt 49
Church of Jesus Christ is
   officially organized 116
church services 71
city of Zion 117
Clark, John Cooper 53
cleaning 21
cleaning the ship 27
cleanliness 12, 17, 29
cleanliness, committee of 20
Cleveland 41

clothing 50, 51
Clotworthy, Hugh & Jane 27
clouds 84
COFFIN 53, 64, 68, 71, 80
   building 64
   child's 53
   for Bro. Card 74
Come, Come Ye Saints 52, 85
commesary 52, 80
company captain 48
compassion 65
complaints 21
conference departure office 11
Conference House 11
Conhauwers, Peter 74
Constitution 2, 115
consumption 17, 53, 64
contagious disorders 8
continents shall become one land
   again 118
contract 121
contributions 121
COOK:
   dinner 76
   little food to 83
   over an open campfire 50
   too tired to 83
COOKING 13, 20, 21
   articles for 9
   assignments 12
   facilities 12
   out of doors 54
   utensils 50
cookfires 62
Coon River 70
Cooper, Elder John 52
Council Bluffs 75
councils of heaven 118
counsel meeting 79
counterpane 49
covered 50
covered cart 50
covered wagons 50
Cowdrey, Oliver 116
cows 81
Crandal, Mary Brannigan 54, 63
Crandall, Spencer 12, 76, 81
Crandel, Dan 63, 81, 82, 86, 90
Crandle, Spicer W. 14, 21, 62, 72
crawling on hands and knees 88
crowding 41
cry with hunger 72
Cunningham, Bro. 70

Curling's Company 63
cut wood 50
cute companion 51
Cutters Park 81

D

daily issue 70-71
daily routine 83
Dalmanuta 71
damp clothes 51
dance 51
dancing 17, 20, 21, 22, 52
Davenport, Iowa 43, 44
Davis 52
DEATH:
   and burial 64
   body wrapped in sheets 91
   dead 53, 85
   deaths 80
   died 53, 91
decks were cleaned 14
demonstrations 62
departure from the ship 29
desolation and destruction 120
Devereux, Brother 20
Devereux, Hesther 17
Devereux, Sister 19, 20
Dickman 81
dim lights 17
discipline 12
discontent 66
discontented 80
disease 11, 12, 17
disloyal to your country 67
Dispensation of the Fullness of
   Times 1, 113
dissatisfaction 21, 63
doctor and Government officers
   14
doctor passed us 29
Doctrine and Covenants 37, 42,
   107, 116
doctrines of a religion 76
Dogett[?], John 52
Doney, Sister 88
double boxing of tin 63
doubling teams 88, 90
draw-pier 43
dreadful storm 73
driving the carts teams 63
drop hankerchiefs 22
dropped out 80, 89
drunks 41

DRY 51
   in the sun 51
   slew 90
Dunbar, 14-15
Dunbar, Wm. C 11, 12
dusty day 62
dusty roads 63
dwindling supplies 89

E

earth 117
ease 62
East 62, 63, 68, 76
East India Missions 13
Eatkin, Brother 83
Edmond, Capt 89
Elias 116
Elijah 116
Elk Horn 81
Elkhorn 86
Elkhorn River 83
Ellsworth, Captain Edmund 14, 28, 51, 52, 62, 64, 69, 72, 76, 80, 86, 89, 90
Ellsworth Company 62, 64, 69, 74, 81
Ellsworth, Bro. 21, 54, 72, 74
Ellsworth, Elder 21
Ellsworth's First Company 92
embarkation 9
emergencies 68
emigrant ships 29
emigrants 9, 11, 12, 75
Emigrants Guide 108, 164
emigrate 121
Emigration Department 8
endowment 2, 115, 116, 119
enduring to the end 87
England 49, 54, 116
Enoch 118
Enoch Train 7, 12,13, 15, 28, 29, 39, 42, 49, 54
Enoch Train pioneers 45
Enoch Train Saints 53
Enoch, Christina, 11
equality of women 63
equipment 68, 76
eternal blessing 65
eternal families 116
eternal life 117
Europe 120
exaltation 2, 115, 118, 119
excess weight 50

exiled 120
exploring parties 116
expulsion of the Saints from Zion 116
extermination order 116

F

facilities 42
fainted on the road 90
faith 53
falling away 113
family cart 49, 50
fancies 50
Far West 116, 118
favorable wind 17
Felt, Elder N. H. 29
Ferguson, Elder 21, 28, 29, 64, 65
Ferguson, James 12, 14, 21, 48, 51-53, 62, 64
Ferguson, President 29
FERRY: 40, 86, 88
   at Elk Horn 82
   at Luke Fort. 84
   bridge at Fort Demoin 69
   crossed the River 76
   ferry boat 54, 81
final preparations 11
find any game 89
finding fault 72
fine spring of water 90
fish, caught some 68
First Company 48, 61, 66, 71, 72, 80, 81, 84, 89, 90
First Company's camp 70
first light 64
First Presidency 120
flames 50
flat cart 49
flat terrain 66
Florence, hill out of 82
Florence, NB 54, 62, 76, 79, 80, 81
flour 50, 69, 70, 72, 80, 90
flour and saw mills 80
FOOD: 53
   available 41
   and general supplies 13
   and supplies 12
   biscuit 12, 21
   bread or biscuit 64
   daily issue of 50, 71
   little to cook 83
   potatoes 13, 20
   rations 72

   rotten 11
   staples 80
   stewed apples 83
   stored meat 13
   supply, supplement 80
   to supplement 89
   scanty breakfast of dough cakes 83
   sugar 70, 72, 81, 90
forded, 2 creeks 90
formal worship 68
Forres, Sister Hannah 70
FORT 41
   Fort Armstrong 43
   Fort Des Moines 68, 69
Four Mile Creek 69
four quarters of the earth 118, 119
France 86
France, Elder Joseph 65
Franklin, Bro. 12
French 53
frequent stops 41
front bar 49
Frost, John Edward 44, 52, 65
Fruge[?], Jane 53
fullness of the Gospel 119
Fullness of Times 2, 115
Fulmer, John S. 120
funeral. 19, 81

G

Galloway 66
Galloway, Elder A. 14, 76
gamblers 41
gang plank 14
Gardner, Gideon 66
GATHER(ed): 2, 7, 115, 118, 119
   to Zion 64, 118
   to "the Ohio 116
GATHERING: 1, 51, 113, 117, 118, 119
   firewood 71
   in the last days 2, 117
   Israel 89
   of Zion 2, 45, 116, 119
   place 7
   the poor to Zion 120
general agent 120
General Conference observed 20
Genoa 81
Gentiles 68, 70, 115, 119
glory of the Lord 118

glow of the campfire 52
goals of Zion 12
Godsall, Bro. 49, 52
gold fields of California 89
gold plates 115
good camping ground 90
good neighbors 50
Good news in the Vallie 89
good roads 63
Good Shepherd 117
Gospel plan 115, 117
Government Medical Inspector 8
grandfather clocks 50
Granger, Catherine 53
Granger, Walter 62
Grant, Bro George 81
Grant, David 54
Grant, George 81
grass bridge 88
graves, dedication of the 81
graves, digging 68
graveside service 81
graveyard 53
great commandments 42
green wood 50
Greenbush, New York 39, 40
grumbling 22
guards were asleep 90
guidebook 68
gullies 51
guns 82

H

Haliker, Eliza 80
hammer 68
HANDCART: 22, 45, 48-50, 53, 62, 63, 70-72, 76, 82
   boxed 66
   broke down 76
   companies 21, 52
   effectively packing 62
   flat handcarts 50
   Handcart Song 52, 91
   mended 90
   new 61
   open 49
   pushing/pulling a loaded 80
   repair 79, 91
   Saints 79
   strung out across the prairie 84
   to Zion 54
   upgrade the 80
   unloading and wagons 84
HANCART LOGBOOK
   20 March – 6 June 1856 185
   9 June - 8 July 1856 198
   17 July - 28 September 1856 214
hanging pot over a fire 50
Hardie 52, 53
Hardie, Janet 11, 15, 21
Hardy, Mathew 68
Hardy, Sister 90
Hargraves, Agnes 15
Hargraves, Enoch Train 21
Hargreave, Samuel 72
harassment 66
harvesting rye 89
hat, broad brimmed 84
hatched down 12
hatches battened down 17
Haven, Jesse 11
Haven, Jim 12
head and foot board 71
healings 53
health 28
healthy passengers 11
Heaton, Elder 50, 65
heavy rain 91
heavy sand 88, 90
heavy sand hill 90
heavy walking sticks 80
Heffing 81
help ourselves to a wagon 80
herbs 53
Hetherington 76
hilly & rough environment 66
hilly country 69, 76
Hodgess 53
Hodgett 14, 52
hole in the deck 26
Holihue, Father 76
Holly, Elder James 52
Holy City 118
Holy Ghost 114, 115
horses 50
Hosannah 28
House of the Lord 118
Hudson River 40
Hunt, (J) 50
Hunt, A. 12
Hunt, John A. 14, 52
Hunter, Edward 121
hunting 50
hygiene 13

I

Illinois 42
illness 48
immigrant cars 41
Independence 116, 118
independent wagon company 52
INDIANS: 67, 83
   been shot 83
   chief took my cart 83
   got drunk 83
   Indian Creek 68
   Indian meal 76
   Indian Town 74
instructed the Twelve 116
interest 120
interest 'if required.' 121
Iowa City 29, 39, 41, 44, 45, 48, 49, 51, 54
Iowa City campground 49, 51, 52
Irish channel 15
iron axle 50
iron hoops 80

J

Jerusalem 117
Johnston, William & Elizabeth 15
Jones, Brother pull away 81
Jones, Captain Daniel 53
Jordan Creek 76
journey of faith 7
Judah 117

K

Kay, John 11
Kennsington 68
KEYS 119
   and powers 119
   of the gathering 116
   of the gathering of Israel 119
   of the gospel of Abraham 116
   of my kingdom 118
killed a beef 90
Kimball, Heber C. 121
Kimball, Wm 79
kindling 50
Kirtland 116, 118
Kirtland Temple 116, 119

L

lack of privacy 11
lake 51
landscape 41
last days 113, 115, 119
Latter-day Saints' Emigrants' Guide 62
law is received by revelation 116
leadership organized 45
Leasly, Sister 20
Lee, Bro. 49
Lee, John 64, 65
Lee, John D. 120
Lee, William 65
Leonard, Truman 11, 14, 50, 62, 63, 65- 67, 69, 72-74, 79, 91
Liberty Pole camping ground 82
lies and slander 67
lightning 75, 84
limited space 50
Linley's 52
liquor 63
listened attentively 64
LISTS:
   Emigrant's Guide 108
   Enoch Train Passenger List 31
   Enoch Train Passengers Not Listed 59
   First Handcart Company 55
   Second Handcart Company 57
Lister, James and Ann 63
Little Bear Creek 65
little Papoose 82
Little, Samuel A. 11
Liverpool 11, 16, 53, 54
Liverpool dock 7
Lloyd, Elizabeth 53
Lloyd, John 66
loaded 44
Lockwood 72
Lord appears to Joseph Smith and Oliver Cowdery 116
Lord's day 51
lost ten tribes 1, 113
loud thunder 84
Loup fork 89-90
Loup-fork ferry 89
Lourermore, Mother 81
Ludert 81
Ludert Sister 70
luggage 9, 39-41, 44, 45, 48
Luke Fort Ferry 86
Luther, Martin 1, 114
lye soap 51
Lyon, Sister Mary and Elder Thomas 11

M

MacCarter, Bro. 68
MacKay, Charles 40
mail 19
mail and trading station 74
make some money 79
malnutrition 11
MAPS:
   Enoch Train Pioneer Railroad Route From Boston to Iowa City 42
   From Florence, Nebraska to Fort Laramie, Wyoming 82
   Handcart Trail – Fort Laramie To Jeffrey City, Wyoming 99
   Handcart Trail – Jeffery Wyoming To Salt Lake City, Utah 104
   Iowa City, Iowa to Florence (Winter Quarters), Nebraska 61
   Route From Liverpool to Boston 14
man killed 89
MARRIAGE:
   celestial 116
   principle of 20
marked the cattle 63
markers 70
Martin, Edward 11
martyred 2, 116
Maxwell, Arthur 14, 29, 52, 63, 73, 74
McAllison 20
McAllison, Mrs. 27
McAllister, John D. 11, 21,45, 51, 62
McArthur, Daniel D. 11, 12, 20, 52, 62, 69, 72, 76, 80, 82, 90-92
McArthur's Company 73, 74, 92
McArtland, Elizabeth 52
McConkie 113
McGow 76, 81
McGowe 82
McGraw, Elder 80
McHodgett, Mrs. 15
McNaughton 88
McNaughton family 89
mean spirited 68
medical comforts 9
medicine 14
MEETING: 22, 52, 53, 63, 66, 76, 80, 86
   below deck 29
   between decks 29
Melchizedek Priesthood 115
men who were dictating 72
meridian of time 1, 113, 114, 115
Met a Company coming from California 88
Middle River 71
Midwife, Janett Hardie 11
mildewed 51
milk, pint of 87
milked a cow 50
millennial era 117
Millennial Star 8, 10
Millennial Star instructions 11
Millennium 1, 114
Mishenebotany 75
mishap with mules 90
missing cattle 61
missionaries 54, 116, 119
Mississippi River 42, 44
Missouri 116
MISSOURI RIVER:
   crossed the 76
   trade and purchase 80
mob 116
mob violence 116
money digger 67
moonlight night 21
MORMON 115
   missionaries 7
MORMONISM 52, 62, 68, 72
   practical 20
   preached 63
Moses 116, 119
Mosketoe Creek 76
mountain of the Lord 117
mountains 45, 51
mule shod 82
mule teams 74
mules 50
mules ran off with a heavy ox yoke attached 82
muley 90
murmurers disobeyers of counsel 72
music 17

N

Nauvoo 116, 118
New Jerusalem 117, 118
New Testament 29
Nine Mile Creek 70
Nishnabotna River 74
North bend of the Platte 88
North Skunk 66
Norton, Iowa 66
not Christians 67
note of thanks 29
nursing techniques 53

O

Oakley, Brother John 86, 90
Oakley, Elder John 66, 76
obedient 42
October conference 120
OLD:
   apostate 80
   mobocrat 70
   Mormons 76
   Nauvoo Mormons 76
   sailor 25
   shawl 73
   Winter Quarters 76
Omaha 82
Omahas 83
omnibuses 39
Only Begotten 118
open cargo hatch 18
open-air fire 50
operation 17
oranges for the children 29
ordinances 119, 120
organized search 73
out-fit for the Plains 9
outhouses 50
oven 50
overcast sky 84
overcrowded 11, 12
owners of the Ship 29
OX, OXEN: 50, 81
   Beaux 81
   broke yoke & false tongue 62
   dead 82
   team 50
   three yoke strayed 61
   yoke timber 81
   yokes 80

P

P.E. Fund Emigrants 9
pace themselves 68
PAINTINGS:
   A Coffin For Little Emma 71
   A Tall Tale At Sea 24
   At the Docks 10
   Emigrant Camp at Iowa City 46
   Funeral at Sea 27
   Handcart Pioneers Heading To A Home In Zion 87
   Indian Chief Pulling A "Little Wagon" 83
   Life Below Decks 18
   Little Arthur Parker Returned to His Mother 75
   Pioneer Passenger Train 40
   Mother Bathgate leads pioneers towards Devil's Gate 78
   *Sailing Ship **Enoch Train*** 6
   Steam Ferry "Nebraska" 77
   Steamer Ferry on the Mississippi 45
   Struck by Lightening on the Trail 84
   Taking an Omnibus to the Train Station 38
   Two Types of Handcarts 51
   Waiting at the Train Station 43
Palace' Cars 41
paradisiacal glory 117
parents 50
Parker, Robert and Ann 73
Parker, Arthur was missing 73
passage to Boston 29
passed the doctor 28
PASSENGERS:
   Passenger Acts 8, 9
   cars 40, 44
   population 13
   sleeping area 14
patience 13, 17
pay 7
peacemakers 42
Perks, Bro. P.M. 11. 12
Perpetual Emigrating Fund 49, 119, 120
Perpetual Emigration Fund 7, 12, 41, 50, 120, 121
personal items 50
Peter 2, 116
physical exertion 80

Pigeon Creek 76
pilot 29
pilot Boat *"Jane"* 29
PIONEER(s): 45, 50, 80
   Pioneer passenger class 40
   pioneer tombstone 70
Plan of Salvation 28
Platte River 82, 86, 88
POEMS:
   And The Ways Of God And The Ways Of Man 1
   But Not Much Rest 71
   Ever On To Zion 72
   Zion Gathered to This Place 112
pollution 115
polygamy 51
poor 2, 115, 119, 120
porpoises 20
Porter, Elder N. L. 14
Posty[?], N.T. 12
pot 45
potatoes 13, 20
Powell, John 80
Powell, Mary 13
Powell, Mother 13
prairie 50, 51, 68
Prairie Creek 74, 89, 90, 91
Prator, Sister child 65
Pratter, Lora 64, 65
Pratter, Richard 64, 65
prayers 16, 21, 72, 83
PREACH: 52
   Mormonism 64, 69, 70
   the Gospel 67, 70
precaution 80
preparations for a successful journey 11
Presidents of each 20 63
priesthood 116, 118, 119
primeval and perfect state 117
printing press 1, 114
privacy 50
Protestant revolution 1, 2, 114
provisions 8, 9, 22, 48, 63, 73
price of passage. 8
public ministry 116
puke buckets 17
purchasing livestock 49
pure in heart 2, 115, 119

Q

quarantine 28, 29
quarter deck 14
quiet games 71
quick consumption 68
quilts 83

R

Raccoon River 70, 71
railroad, 40
rails 68
rails end 44
railway station 39
RAIN: 48, 53, 88
   blowed our tent down 71
   rain clouds 84
   rain deck 12
Ramsey , Bro. 81
Ramsey, John 71
Ramseys, Bro child 70
Ransay, John 71
read 51
rebaptised 52, 81
Reed, James 82
Reed, Sister 70
Reformation 1, 114
religious awakening 2, 114
renascence 114
REPAIR 50, 76, 79, 80
   bridge 42
   handcarts 68-70, 72, 79, 91
   repairing 71
rest periods 68
rested 83, 86
restitution of all things 2, 116
restocking point 79
RESTORATION 1, 2, 114, 115, 117, 119
   of the Church 1, 113
   of the Gospel 115
   of all things 119
revelation 116, 119
revolutionary struggle 2, 114
Rich, Capt. Henry S. 15, 28
Rich, Captain Henry P. 13
Richards, Franklin D. 14, 20, 121
Richardson, Peter and Eliza 80
rifles 50, 80, 89
roared out like a lion 52
Robinson's 62
rock cut out of the mountain 2, 115

Rock Island 42
rope 50
rotten food 11
rough Emigrant 9
rough road 73, 76
rowdies and apostates 80
Rudd, D. 12
rush to get on the boat 89
rusty iron barrels, 12

S

Sabbath 21, 22, 51, 64, 76, 90
Sabbath day 71
Sabin, Mary Powell 80
sacrament 65, 68
safety 85
sailor, old bumped into 22
sailors 12
saints so cheerful 63
Salt Lake City 118
Samuel S. Curling, sailing ship 49, 54
sanctified 119
sanctuary 116
Sanhedrin 1, 113
sanitary facilities 12
sanitation 11
saw mill 71
scale of provisions 9
scattering of Israel 1, 113
Schinn's, Sydney 69
school 51
Schooner Flag of Truce 29
Schroder 52
scripture reading 71
scriptures 19
scurvy 13
sea rough 21
sea shall give up her dead 19
sealing powers 116
search 73
seasick 16
season 50
Second Coming 1, 2, 113, 116, 117, 119
Second Company 62, 66, 73, 81, 82, 89-91
secret combinations 115
seeking work 49
select cows and cattle 81
servants 11
Seventy 116
sewing 54

Sfrien[?] , Martin 12
shafts 49
shake down 61
Shell creek 88
shell fish out of the creek 90
Shinn, Maria 53
Shinn, Robert and Eliza 70
ship's masts 18
shoes 50, 79, 81
shoot game along the trail 80
shot by some scoundrel 82
Sickness 53
side pieces 49
silhouettes 51
Silver Creek 75, 76
sing(ing) 20, 52, 65, 76, 91
singletree 49
Six mile Creek 69, 70
Skunk Creek 66
SLEEP, SLEEPING 52, 83
   area 7, 12
   in wet clothes 74
   quarters 12
   space 17
slop buckets 17
small-pox 8
Smith , Brother Aniki 91
Smith, Joe 67
Smith, Joseph, Jr. 2, 115-119
Snow, Lorenzo 120
Snow, Willard 120
soap 51
socialize 52
soldiers 41
son 68, 69
songs of everlasting joy 118
sorrow 65
soured 51
South Africa 13
South Coon 71
South Fork 90
South Skunk bridge 68
Spencer 52, 53
Spencer, Brother 62, 79
Spencer, President Daniel 51, 52
spinning a yarn 52
Spirit 51
Spirit of Christ 114
spirit of the Camp 63
St. Louis 49, 80
stand in holy places 118
STEAM/ FERRYBOAT/TUG:
   Independence 7, 14

Nebraska 76
Plymouth 41
steamboat 44, 82
steam ferry-boat 76
steep stairs 12
steers, saw pair of 68
Stevenson, Isabella 80
stewardship 61, 79
stored water 68
storehouse 42-44
storm 12, 53, 72, 73
storm at sea 18
storytellers 42
stowaways 15
strangers 52, 63, 65, 68, 72, 76
stream 51
stroll in the moonlight, 52
Stuart, James 40
Studard, James 85
stumpy 25
sugar 70, 72, 81, 90
Summer Quarters 81
Sunday 65, 68, 72, 76, 80, 88
supperless, go to bed 90
supplies 50, 70, 76
sustain the general authorities 20
swaping 50
Switzerland 13

T

tabernacle 118
tall tale 26
Taylor, John 41, 53, 120
tea 90
team of horses 50
temple 116, 118, 119
temporal 119
ten tribes 119
TENT: 9, 14, 17, 21, 22, 27, 48- 51, 54, 62-65, 68, 70, 75, 76
  captain 48
  damaged 72
  issued 48
  of water 68
  pitched 54, 63, 69, 72
  pitching tents in the rain 88
  poles 88
  repaired 80
  settlement 45
  splitting and blowing over 75
  tenting 9
  the wrong way 74
  twenty-one persons in father's big round 83
  was riven to tatters 73
testimony 62, 64, 72, 119
thieves 41
thimbleless axle 49
Third Handcart Company 81
THUNDER 75
  heavy thunder storm 89
  loud 84
  storm 71, 73, 75, 81, 82, 88
  thunderbolt 85
time for departure 13
tin and iron 66
tobacco smoking 22
Toledo 41
tolerance 13
tools 50, 64, 71
Toronto 116
town 69
toys 50
trail 89
TRAIN: 41, 42, 44, 45, 47, 54
  cars 41
  sparks from the engines 41
  stops 41
  trip 53
travel across Iowa 80
trek to Zion 76
trial of faith 87
troublesome 67
tubs 51
Turkey Creek 72
Turkey Grove 88
Two good springs 88
Tyler, Daniel 52
Typhoon 27

U

Utah 9, 45, 118
Utah Valley 7

V

Valley of the Great Salt Lake 45
Van Cott 51
victuals 21
visitors 51, 70

W

wages 79
WAGON: 45, 50, 63, 68, 71, 76, 80, 88
  bought 82
  cover material 9
  difficulty in getting the wagons over 90
  equipment 79
  heavily loaded 82
  riding in 72
  top of 22
  train 76, 80
  wait for supplies 82
  wheels buried 88
Walker, Henry 85
Walker, Joseph 76
walking very fast 72
Walters, Archer 48, 79, 85, 90
Walters, Harriet 43
Wanless, Sister 82
wash 81
washboard 50
washing 13, 41, 51, 71, 76, 119
washing clothes 66, 76
washings 120
WATER: 11, 17, 20, 21, 50, 64, 66, 68-72, 74, 76, 83, 88
  and potatoes 21
  drinking 12, 41
  no water 88
  only what we carried 90
  ration 13
  scarce 82
  served 21
  source 68
  stops 64
  up to our knees in   88
Webb, E. G. . 51-52
Webb, Johnson T. 52
weighed 50
weighed anchor 14
weighing the handcart luggage 50
well 89
Welling, Job little son interred 66
wet clothes 88
wet clothing and bedding 53
wet to the skin 75
whales 20, 21
wheat and the tares 117
Wheelock, Bro 14
wheels and axels 62
White. Elias and Elizabeth 52
whisky, drinking 66
whooping cough 65, 70

wicked 118
wide track 49
William, Betsy, Taylor 85
Williams, Roger 115
Willson's 67
Wilson 66, 67
Winkle, Rip Van 84
Winter Quarters 79
Winter Quarters cemetery 81
without murmuring 63
women to wash 91
WOOD 11, 12, 17, 64, 66, 68-72, 74, 76
   no wood 88, 89
     frame houses 40

Wood River 90
wooden barrels 12
Wooley, F. 76
work for the dead 117
worship 51
worship meeting 90
worthy mother 65
wounded 83

Y

Yankee Doodle 28, 29
Year of Jubilee 120
yoke 50, 64
Young, Brigham 41, 119
Young, Brigham prophecy 49
Young, Brigham's challenge 47
Young, Brigham Jr 41
Young, Joseph A. 11

Z

ZION: 1, 2, 49, 50, 52, 79, 113, 115- 119
   could wait 80
   fellow citizens of 65
   for safety 118
   gather to 45, 64
   of America 117

About the Author

Robert O. Day (1935 - 2002) was a Professor of Communication and Theatre Arts from East Tennessee State University, in Johnson City Tennessee. During his 30+ year in education, he taught at Brigham Young University, Southern Illinois University and East Tennessee State University. At the latter he served as director of high school and college forensics/debate, and in that capacity he directed numerous tournaments, being twice called on to serve as state director of the Tennessee High School Speech and Drama League.

A master storyteller and specialist in Elementary Oral Language Arts, for many years he conducted seminars and workshops throughout the Southeast. A notable public speaker and presenter, he wrote, directed and starred in a thirty part television series in Oral Language Arts for educational television.

Author of The Mormon Battalion, The Lord's Faithful and two dozen other books, he also has to his credit twenty-five children's stories, six dozen plays and readers theatre scripts, and numerous poems and choral speaking arrangements. After his retirement, with his wife he served four missions, one of which was at the Museum of Church History and Art, where he wrote, directed and presented two new Church historical chamber theatres, "Nine Blasts of the Cannon" and "The Enoch Train Pioneers, Gathering to Zion."

The inspiration for most of his writing came from his eight children, eighteen grandchildren and one great-grandchild. But his involvement in genealogy and family, history lies at the foundation of his interest in historical works, with the discovery that many of his ancestors were a part of the historical events of the pioneers and the growth of the Church.

www.ingramcontent.com/pod-product-compliance
Lightning Source LLC
Chambersburg PA
CBHW082113230426
43671CB00015B/2689